PRINCIPLES AND METHODS OF LAW AND ECONOMICS

This is an introductory book that targets the reader who aspires to apply economic analysis but seeks a technical introduction to its mathematical techniques or a structured elaboration of its philosophical principles. It juxtaposes economic analysis with moral philosophy, political theory, egalitarianism, and other methodological principles. It then presents the details of methods, such as model building, derivatives, differential equations, statistical tests, and the use of computer programs.

Nicholas Georgakopoulos is Professor of Law at Indiana University School of Law. He received his master's degree and doctorate from Harvard Law School, where he specialized in finance and the regulation of financial markets. His publications are cited prominently, including citations by the U.S. Supreme Court and the Securities Exchange Commission.

Principles and Methods of
Law and Economics

Basic Tools for Normative Reasoning

NICHOLAS L. GEORGAKOPOULOS

Indiana University

CAMBRIDGE UNIVERSITY PRESS
Cambridge, New York, Melbourne, Madrid, Cape Town, Singapore, São Paulo

Cambridge University Press
40 West 20th Street, New York, NY 10011-4211, USA

www.cambridge.org
Information on this title: www.cambridge.org/9780521826815

First published 2005

Printed in the United States of America

A catalog record for this publication is available from the British Library.

Library of Congress Cataloging in Publication Data
Georgakopoulos, Nicholas Leonidas.
Principles and methods of law and economics : basic tools
for normative reasoning / Nicholas L. Georgakopoulos.
p. cm.
Includes bibliographical references and index.
ISBN 0-521-82681-0 (hardcover) – ISBN 0-521-53411-9 (pbk.)
1. Law and economics. 2. Law–Methodology.
3. Economics–Mathematical models. I. Title.
K487.E3G46 2005
340′.11–dc22   2004029141

ISBN-13 978-0-521-82681-5 hardback
ISBN-10 0-521-82681-0 hardback

ISBN-13 978-0-521-53411-6 paperback
ISBN-10 0-521-53411-9 paperback

In memory of my mother.

May justice and welfare end random violence.

Contents

Preface

This book breaks with several traditions of legal scholarship. Rather than focus on one topic, it seeks to show how broad the application of economic analysis of law can be. Rather than explain existing knowledge, it seeks to show how new methodologies develop. Rather than convey the safety of stability, it seeks comfort in the reality of change. My hope is that it will serve as an adequate introduction for ambitious readers who are eager to follow the bright tradition of innovative legal scholarship.

I hope that this book, which is to a significant extent the result of this approach, helps to orient new jurists in an increasingly complex field. Several voices within the legal academy readily use new methods, expressing with deed their belief that the law of diminishing returns must apply to methodological efforts as well. This book owes much to those pioneers, too numerous to count. The breadth of this book cannot help but force a brevity that is unfair to every one of its topics.

The overall shape of this book, however, is due to the extraordinary editor of Cambridge University Press, Finola O'Sullivan. She provided significant guidance toward an exciting target. Also very significant was the help of her colleagues at Cambridge University Press, John Berger and Scott Parris. Unusually deep is my gratitude to my dear colleague Daniel Cole at Indiana University Law School–Indianapolis. Also voluminous was the help of Andrew Klein and Stephen Utz. I have received great benefit from comments of John Armour, Judge Guido Calebresi, John Donohue, Peg Brinig, Judge Richard Posner, Mark Ramseyer, Eric Rasmusen, Steve Shavell, Peter Siegelman, Jay Weiser, and George Wright.

I stress my gratitude to my numerous teachers, in temporal order: my parents and schoolteachers, my professors at the Athens University

Law School, Greece; my professors at Harvard Law School, and particularly my doctorfather, Reinier Kraakman; my professors at Harvard Business School; my colleagues at the University of Connecticut and Indiana University, both in Indianapolis and in Bloomington; my co-authors of the second edition of Blumberg on Corporate Groups (Aspen, 2004); and, finally, the numerous presenters at the seminars that I have had the luck to attend in several schools, the law and economics seminar of Harvard Law School, the finance seminar of Harvard Business School, the faculty seminar of the University of Connecticut School of Law, the law and economics seminar at Yale Law School, which received me with unmatched hospitality; and the law and economics seminar at the Law School of the University of Chicago, as well as the presenters at the annual meetings of the American, Canadian, and European associations of law and economics. To all my professors and almost all the presenters I subjected to questioning and for the occasions that it may have crossed any boundaries, I apologize.

Deep thanks to Liz and Vicki. No bounds have my thanks to my children, Lee and Dimitri. They taught me more than they think. They lost more of my time than I would have liked. Their forbearance is admirable. Their support is precious. They make magic daily and every day magical.

Introduction: Innovation in Legal Thinking

This book introduces principles and methods of economic analysis of law, also known as "law and economics." Principles are the fundamental conceptions, assumptions, or beliefs that are common to those who employ economic analysis of law. Methods are the tools, techniques, or tricks they use. The aggregate of all legal thinkers could be imagined as a massive workshop. All human knowledge and events are the inputs that the workshop of jurists uses. The outputs include judicial decisions, statutes, proposals for changes of rules, and interpretations. To a novice, this workshop seems cavernous and daunting. This book is a guide to that area of the workshop where economic analysis of law occurs and introduces the use of its tools. The principles section shows the common understandings, assumptions, and goals, what problems economic analysis of law engages. The methods section explains its main tools.

For students who are uncomfortable trying to learn the universe of legal thinking, understanding the direction of this book may be daunting. Let us start our travel through economic analysis of law with a simplifying metaphor. Rather than jurists, let us act as managers of an apartment building. How should we act in our managerial capacity? If this question is too abstract, suppose we have reached a concrete problem. Our building's heating system has failed. What should we do?

A. Proposals, Consequences, and Ideals

The building manager must react to the problem. Study the manager's decision by separating three components: proposals, consequences, and ideals. Proposals are the alternative plans for immediate action. The manager proceeds to predict the consequences to which each

1

choice will lead. Finally, the manager compares the consequences with his long-term, relatively constant ideals. This reveals which choice promotes best the manager's ideals. A novice manager may consider two proposals, fixing the heating system or replacing it with an identical unit. A seasoned manager may develop a third alternative proposal and consider replacing the unit with one that uses a different source of energy.

The adoption of each proposal produces specific consequences. The building manager's alternative proposals may produce different immediate expenditures, different maintenance costs, different resulting levels of humidity, different ranges of temperature fluctuation, and a different sense of fulfilling civic obligations about energy conservation or avoidance of pollution. Consequences include fines for violating fire regulations and the depletion of the building's funds that would preclude future repairs.

Finally, the manager compares the consequences of each proposal with his ideals. The manager's ideals may be to satisfy the residents, to attract residents who would pay greater rents, or to minimize expenses at the cost of some dissatisfaction. Ideals tend to be independent of the context in which the problem arose; they tend to be the constant, long-term targets that guide action. The manager can finally choose the proposal that promotes his ideals best.

In the sphere of legal thinking, proposals are the alternative interpretations or rules. Each proposal will lead to different consequences. The legal system will choose the best for its ideals. The analogy to the building manager tries to make this juxtaposition more concrete.

This book approaches legal thinking on the basis of separating proposals, consequences, and ideals. Individual jurists choose proposals based on their consequences to promote the ideals of the legal system. The proposals may be different statutory provisions or different interpretations. The consequences are the resulting actions and reactions of individuals, the outcomes to which each proposal would lead. The proposal that leads to a consequence that furthers most the ideals is the preferred proposal.

Economic analysis of law helps develop alternative legal proposals, helps ascertain their consequences, and assesses which consequences best advance the established ideals. From one perspective, economic analysis of law does not establish ideals. Ideals are selected by social mechanisms outside economic analysis of law. A simplistic explanation may state that ideals are set through the political system and, in democratic systems, that ideals are the product of majority vote. Economic analysis of law applies and develops principles, approaches, methods, or tools that seek to make each task as objective and scientific as possible. Those that have reached a sufficient level of technique comprise the second part of this book, which seeks to explain how to use those tools, Chapters 7–12. The first part of the book, Chapters 1–6, discusses the principles that drive the application of economic analysis of law.

B. Toward Scientific Analysis of Law

To its users, economic analysis of law is the greatest innovation in legal thinking at least since the code of Hammurabi – since the very idea of having laws. With modern "law and economics" the law becomes a formal, scientific, often quantifiable field of study. The importance of this development cannot be understated. For thousands of years, fundamental questions about how to organize society were imponderables. Is democracy the best political system? Does the death penalty deter? Should abortion be banned? May potentially addictive drugs be taken for entertainment? Economic analysis of law may not answer all such questions. Nevertheless, law and economics does offer hope of producing a method for answering them. Economic analysis has already answered numerous others. For example, economic analysis persuasively shows that the tort system is desirable, or that the prohibition of insider trading is desirable.

Law and economics presents a methodology that its users believe overcomes the limitations of less quantitative approaches to law, mainly those associated with moral philosophy or political theory. The scientific justification and optimization of rules removes those rules from the set of contested rules that do not have a known optimal shape.

Some claim that economic analysis of law is itself a moral philosophy and that it resembles "rule utilitarianism" or "preference utilitarianism." This categorization, however, is partly misleading. The deployment of the methods used by economic analysis of law does not depend on acceptance of a utilitarian moral philosophy. Moreover, economic analysis of law is not a methodological slave to any form of utilitarianism. Some economically minded jurists feel they can restate moral philosophies in economic terms and apply the tools of economic analysis of law to fulfill the ideals of each moral philosophy. From this perspective, the tools of economic analysis of law are agnostic. They can be used by communists, capitalists, or stoics. Each user of its tools may have a different conception of the ideal toward which the tools of economic analysis of law are used.

The first few chapters discuss the principles of economic analysis of law. This book starts with the juxtaposition of what many consider the goal of economic analysis of law, social welfare, and moral philosophy.

The chapters that discuss more technical matters, from mathematical modeling to statistics, make heavy use of graphics. Law students routinely seek to avoid algebra. This book uses graphics as visual aides to present the technical knowledge without relying on algebra.

General books on law and economics are not rare, but the emphasis on economic methods rather than legal subjects and the heavy use of examples and illustrations may set this one apart. Several other authors follow the example of the leaders, the classic textbook of the renowned scholars Robert Cooter and Thomas Ulen. Their book introduces economic analysis of law by rigorously establishing the economic analysis that supports the principal areas of private law. An easier economic approach is followed with a highly approachable style by Peter Grossman and Daniel Cole. The indefatigable and prolific Richard Posner reduces the coverage of technical economics and covers a broader spectrum of law. Barnes and Stout produce a casebook version of economic analysis. Seidenfeld follows the rigorous economic method while reducing the span of law, as does Miceli.

All these books and likely several omitted ones belong in every scholar's library. They may give some of their readers, an appearance of a fixed pairing of a method of economic analysis with some area of law. That correspondence is artificial and limiting. Legal subjects change. New economic methods are born. Economic analysis of law is evolving. The appearance that a single method of economic analysis applies best to specific areas of law gives a false impression of solidity that may stifle creative argumentation. As teachers, most law professors try to encourage novel arguments and try to elicit creative legal thinking even against some student reluctance. This book tries to apply each economic method to several legal areas.

Books on law and economics also seem very difficult. Even law professors who specialize in law and economics have trouble decoding passages in those books. Yet, the difficulty does not lie in incomprehensible mathematics or dense text. Much of the difficulty is in the latent assumptions that underlie the economic approach to law and in false impressions about it. In response, this book starts from those fundamental assumptions, the principles of law and economics. Those chapters are intended for readers who find that law and economics has a partly alien character in legal discourse. Chapter 1 seems to engage formal logic but it is crucial for adapting the scientific method to law. The discussion of normative reasoning may be quite important for readers who approach law from the sciences as well as for readers who are apprehensive about the quantification of law. The former need to realize that normative reasoning is very different from the positive reasoning of science. The latter need to take comfort that normative reasoning is an inseparable component of legal thought.

Those who find moral reasoning intuitive cannot approach economic analysis without the juxtaposition of moral philosophy and economic analysis of law, as discussed in Chapter 2. Many may approach law from political science. Chapter 3 connects law to the political process. Chapter 4 engages redistribution because law is intimately related to the distribution of wealth. The related positions of law and economics are confusing because of genuine disagreement among scholars. The chapter stresses the shared common ground, which makes the disagreements seem marginal.

The leading and most radical methodological innovation of economic analysis of law is the "Coase theorem," or, more properly, the presumption of irrelevance of legal change that Coase's analysis implies, also known as the invariance principle. The theorem is very intuitive, almost self-evident, to those who can build the abstract world it assumes. Chapters 5 and 6 engage Coase's idea as the formidable structure that it is. The remaining chapters are about methods.

Economic analysis of law receives additional power from the continuity, volume, and rigor of economic research. Yet, many lawyers find the settings analyzed to be simplistic and the articles of economics journals to be incomprehensible, full of jargon and obscure conventions. Chapter 7 introduces the language of economic journals with the hope of increasing access to that research. It also includes a discussion of the method of optimization by using derivatives and the method of differential equations.

Chapters 8 and 9 bring a neglected topic into focus by exploring how probability theory informs legal analysis. Although the topic dates from the Renaissance, it is underutilized in law.

Most of lawyers' activity is related to business, even outside the specialties that are explicitly about business and finance. Chapter 10 introduces some financial innovations related to valuation and Chapter 11 discusses option pricing and derivatives. The consequences for policy are legion.

No method of analysis that seeks practical application can avoid statistics as the scientific method of observation. Chapter 13 introduces statistical methods after Chapter 12 provides guidance on using spreadsheet programs for simple applications.

Chapter 14 concludes the book with a look at methodologies that are still nascent in law, such as fractals, evolutionary theory, and cellular automata. These new methods hold some promise but have not found as much application in law as they might. In light of the continuous search for methodological improvements, they may be instructive examples of qualified success.

Too many topics seem to pass in a rush. That is the glory of the topic. Law and economics is a young method. The scholar who understands it does not simply obtain a tool. The method also transports the scholar to the edge of vast unexplored territory that beckons.

For the reader who seeks more guidance on how the topics of this book correspond to those of scientific and economic analysis more broadly, Table 0.1 tracks the correspondence of major historical scientific ideas to chapters and subchapters of this book. From the set of recent innovations, Table 0.1 reports only those rewarded with Nobel prizes. This set is certainly too small, but the result should reveal how vast the undertaking of bringing legal thinking closer to science is.

A note about style may help. Although this book aspires to the international market, it uses the spelling conventions of legal publications in the United States. The spelling differences are minor and can be summarized in the phrase "labor to favor colorful neighbors" (rather than "labour to favour colourful neighbours"). Because this book is likely to be used outside the U.S. legal academy, its citation format is that of general science. The principal differences regard the location of the number of volumes, the year of publication, and the page. This book uses a pattern where the title of the book or journal appears italicized, followed by the number of the volume – not the page – then the year and, after a colon, the pages. For example, a reference to page 55 of a journal article starting on page 44 with the title "Title" authored by "Author" and published in volume 99 (year 2000) of the publication "Obscure Law Journal" would appear as Author, "Title," *Obscure Law Journal* 99 (2000):55. The pattern of legal publications in the US would tend to be *Author, Title*, 99 OBSCURE L.J. 44, 55 (2000).

Table 0.1. *The correspondence of chapters to major scientific contributions*

Contribution	Contributor	Chapter
Optimization by solving the derivative	Newton, Leibnitz	"Modeling Negligence Law: Optimization" in Chapter 7
Differential equations	Newton, Leibnitz	"Modeling the End of Affirmative Action: Differential Equations" in Chapter 7
Probability theory	Pascal, Fermat	Chapters 8 and 9
Normal distribution	Gauss et al.	"The Normal Distribution" in Chapter 9
Least-squares regression	Gauss, Legendre	Chapter 13
Vote cycling (Nobel 1972)	Arrow	Segment on voting in Chapter 3
Public choice (Nobel 1986)	Tullock, Buchanan	Segments on voting in and public choice in Chapter 3
Capital asset pricing model (Nobel 1990)	Sharpe, Miller, Markowitz, et al.	Chapter 10
Coasean irrelevance (Nobel 1991)	Coase, Calabresi	Chapters 5 and 6
Ubiquity of incentives (Nobel 1992)	Becker	Fundamental assumption throughout, discussed in "Ubiquitous Importance of Incentives" of Chapter 2
Game theory (Nobel 1994)	Harsanyi, Selten, Nash et al.	Chapter 3
Optimal tax (Nobel 1996)	Mirrlees, Vickrey	Discussion of redistribution exclusively by taxation in Chapter 4
Call option valuation (Nobel 1997)	Black, Merton, Scholes	Chapter 11
Welfare economics (Nobel 1998)	Sen	Discussions of social welfare in Chapter 2 and distribution of wealth in Chapter 4
Two-step regression with selection (Nobel 2000)	Heckman	"Observations That Are Filtered by a Threshold" in Chapter 13
Bounded rationality (Nobel 2002)	Kahneman, Smith	"Bounded Rationality" in Chapter 3

C. BIBLIOGRAPHICAL NOTE

Every chapter ends with a bibliographical note that identifies further reading. An introductory chapter like this one can point out an omission. This book does not cover microeconomic theory and microeconomic equilibrium because their normative use is specialized, arising mostly in antitrust law. Readers who are convinced that market forces tend to be desirable and who may be frustrated over the absence of a chapter on microeconomic equilibrium might be comforted by the identification of destructive economic dynamics by Jack Hirshleifer, *The Dark Side of the Force: Economic Foundations of Conflict Theory* (New York: Cambridge University Press, 2001).

Part 1: Principles

1. From Formal Logic to Normative Reasoning

This book is about normative reasoning. If the science of logic could perform legal normative reasoning, then this book would be about the principles and methods of logic, and it might have contained a chapter akin to this one showing how economic analysis could help normative reasoning but in a way different than syllogistic logic. This chapter shows why logic cannot perform legal reasoning. The juxtaposition of logic and normative reasoning also clarifies what normative reasoning is.

To provide a consistent example illustrating each chapter's goal, every chapter has an introductory example based on the same legal opinion, *Meinhard v. Salmon*.[1] The facts that are relevant here are simple. Salmon received a lucrative offer from Gerry, a business acquaintance. The offer could have expanded Salmon's business. Unbeknownst to Gerry, Salmon's business, which was the reason for their acquaintance, had a secret partner, Meinhard. If Gerry knew that Salmon operated in two capacities, as an individual and as a member of a partnership, then Gerry may have specified which of the two he selected as the recipient of his offer. Meinhard, the invisible partner, claimed the offer should be treated as made to the partnership. The litigation that Meinhard started eventually reached the highest court of the jurisdiction and the famous American judge, Benjamin Cardozo, and his colleague Andrews, who is almost equally famous for his vocal dissenting opinions. Previously established law did not answer the question directly. The judges could not mechanically apply formal logic. Instead, they were forced to use informal normative reasoning to choose an interpretation and decide

---

[1]   249 N.Y. 458 (1928). The text of the opinion is reproduced in Appendix A.

the case. This chapter shows how formal logic fails and jurists must use informal normative reasoning.

One of the most fundamental hurdles faced by scholars who start exploring law and economics is the change in the mode of reasoning. Law and economics has a normative focus that leads to a change in the level of certainty and the burden of proof of the argumentation compared with that of the positive argumentation and reasoning that dominates most other physical and social sciences. The positive (i.e., descriptive) statements of science can be restated as syllogisms of formal logic. Solid syllogistic reasoning leads to each scientific conclusion, making it either true or false. Interpretation and lawmaking, however, are focused on what the law should be, that is, on normative conclusions. Normative conclusions cannot be treated as true or false. In the language of logic they are not *truth valued*. Scholars who are habituated to the reasoning process of science face a double frustration, the loss of the compass of truth and the adaptation to a mode of reasoning that produces something other than truth, which we can call desirability. Granted, law and economics scholarship makes descriptive statements that are truth valued. The component of law and economics that has practical value for the design and evolution of the legal system, however, uses reasoning that is not truth valued. The value of economic analysis of law is that it produces normative conclusions of vastly greater certainty than other methods. The methodological rigor of law and economics produces normative conclusions that approach the certainty of positive scientific conclusions.

This chapter discusses the attempts to fit legal reasoning into formal logic and distinguishes formal logic from the less structured normative reasoning that takes place in practice. Formal logic has studied the problems of the normative syllogism under a heading called deontic logic, from the Greek δέον (THAY-on), which means obligation. The differences of the normative syllogism of law from deontic logic are important, as are the limitations of deontic syllogisms that make them not just different but also inappropriate for legal normative syllogisms. Economic analysis narrows this gap, bringing normative reasoning much closer to reaching the compelling conclusions of formal logic.

A. FORMAL DEONTIC LOGIC

Formal logic is the analysis of syllogisms in general. One of the roles of logic is the development of closed sets of enumerated functions that produce a satisfactory system of logic. The usual examples regard categorization and assignment of attributes, such as "Pericles was an Athenian; all Athenians spoke Greek; therefore Pericles spoke Greek." The system of logic that would handle legal obligations is deontic logic.

Deontic logic is distinguished from logic systems of positivism, description, or categorization by including in the system of logic statements (or functions) of obligation and its corollaries, namely permission and prohibition. When categorization is the objective of a system of logic, it includes functions that handle the placement of objects in categories. For example, its functions recognize that if an object belongs to a sub-category, then it also belongs to the parent category. In other words, from "spaniels are dogs" and "Spot is a spaniel," such a system of logic would draw the conclusion "Spot is a dog." Simultaneously, such a logical system would recognize that having a common feature might not lead two items to belong in the same category. It should reject the conclusion "Spot is a cat" based on the premises "Spot has a tail" and "cats have tails."

Systems of deontic logic are designed to have the capacity to derive conclusions about obligation. Suppose we defined a system of logic that contained two functions, one signifying membership in a group and a second imposing obligation. The statement of obligation "kindergarten teachers must have fingerprints on file with the police" would combine with the membership statement "Jeri is a kindergarten teacher" to conclude with the obligation, "Jeri must have fingerprints on file with the police." This is a truth-valued conclusion. It is equivalent to the application of unambiguous law. It ignores the desirability of the rule. Law and economics seeks to determine the desirability of the rule, namely whether Jeri or teachers in general should have fingerprints on file.

B. Formal Logic's Failure in Normative Reasoning

Deontic logic, despite the promise it might hold, suffers inherent limitations that prevent it from being applicable to legal rules, at least in its current state. Deontic logic is unable to cope with the surprises that are unavoidable in any real legal system.

Formal logic consists of a closed set of known functions used to derive conclusions. Normative reasoning would need to use those known functions to derive new rules and interpret the existing ones. Although interpretation can be fairly easy using common sense, it may be impossible according to formal logic if the surprise was not foreseen at the time the system was designed.

Continuing the example of the kindergarten teachers' obligation to have fingerprints on file, consider Jeri's initial hiring to be a kindergarten teacher. As soon as the contract is formed, Jeri is a kindergarten teacher but does not have fingerprints on file. This violates strict formal logic. To avoid considering this a violation, the deontic system must be refined, perhaps by including a grace period of the time necessary to take the actions required to meet initial applications of deontic functions. Such a principle would allow newly hired kindergarten teachers without fingerprints on file to provide them.

The lack of a grace period is not the only imperfection of this system of deontic logic. Other surprises may reveal imperfections. A further imperfection appears by supposing that a fire destroys the files. A strict logician would conclude all teachers would be in violation and conclude that the proper response to a fire would be to leave all kindergartens unstaffed. Common sense would let a judge respond to the fire by violating strict logic and allowing teachers to enter their classrooms. Perhaps the judge would obligate those kindergarten teachers who would no longer have fingerprints on file to provide them within some time. Furthermore, if such an obligation were predicted to cause congestion, special delays would be tolerated.

A system of formal logic would also be frustrated by the complexity of the actual settings in which laws apply. Adjusting one rule may alter the incentives about activities that appear unrelated. Consider that Jeri is a judgment-proof kindergarten teacher. The knowledge of the system of logic informs Jeri that a fire that would destroy the fingerprint files would not interrupt Jeri's employment as a kindergarten teacher, which is Jeri's only possible employment. Jeri sees a fire that is spreading toward the files and which only Jeri can stop with no risk. The knowledge of uninterrupted employment may weaken Jeri's incentives to stop the fire. The impact of the fingerprint law on the effort to extinguish a fire may stretch the imagination. Nevertheless, the example does set in motion informal normative reasoning. An inquiry into the likelihood of the undesirable outcome (the expansion of the fire that a different rule would prevent) may be made and alternative rules may be explored and evaluated. Conceivably, the fingerprint obligation should only flex for unavoidable disasters, rather than any accidental destruction.

Formal logic does not appear to have the flexibility to address successfully the unexpected. The acceptance of new functions and unpredictability seems necessary for normative reasoning. In other words, normative reasoning may need to be imperfectly specified. It may need to be informal.

C. The Informal Normative Syllogism

A normative argument can be analogized to a formal syllogism. Consider the example of the premise "the function of tort law is to minimize the cost of accidents," the potentially false second premise "strict liability produces less accident costs than any other rule (i.e., minimizes the cost of accidents"), and the conclusion "strict liability should be part of tort law." This syllogism bears some kinship to a deontic syllogism concluding with an obligation but it is not truth valued. Unlike the example's kindergarten teacher who truly *must* have fingerprints on file, a judge may choose not to include strict liability in tort law because of other arguments. The informality of normative reasoning converts a syllogism into an argument. Formal logic draws inescapable conclusions from syllogisms. Normative reasoning weighs arguments and draws qualified conclusions.

Formal logic can draw seemingly qualified conclusions by using probabilistic statements. This type of qualification differs from that of the normative reasoning because its qualification is all the possibilities that this line of reasoning considered. The qualified conclusions of formal logic retain the nature of being truth valued, whereas normative reasoning does not become truth valued. For example, a qualified deontic premise is "most kindergarten teachers must have fingerprints on file." Keeping as the minor premise "Jeri is a kindergarten teacher," the conclusion becomes: "Jeri likely must have fingerprints on file." The conclusion is qualified but not false. As a probabilistic statement, it may be truth valued. Convert the previous tentative but normative premise to a probabilistic and positive one. The new major premise is "95% of kindergarten teachers have fingerprints on file." The conclusion becomes "Jeri has fingerprints on file with 95% probability." Probability theory handles positive probabilistic statements, a subject discussed further in Chapters 8 and 9.

The nonexclusive formulation of the general (major) premise ("most . . . have") has some affinity with the premises of normative legal analysis that correspond to general principles. Compare the statement "tort law mostly minimizes accident costs" to "tort law only minimizes accident costs." The latter is absolute and much more objectionable. The proof of the latter is a negative one, requiring that all other possible functions of tort law be rejected.

A major reason for the inability to assign exclusivity to premises of normative syllogisms is that they apply to the future. Future societies may find ways to increase social welfare that we cannot foresee. A future society could obtain social welfare from a tort system that performs a function in addition to minimizing accident costs.

This open-ended nature of the major premise reduces the precision of the syllogism but helps overcome the limitation of formal logic that it cannot adapt to unanticipated changes. A rule that was adopted for one reason may, with time, serve a different purpose. This new function of the rule can guide the rule's interpretation.

Proposals, Consequences, and Ideals in Normative Reasoning

The analogy of normative reasoning to a probabilistic syllogism is inapposite when we focus on the statement that identifies the proposed rule that best fulfills the rule's ideal. Recall the separation of proposals, consequences and ideals in the introduction. Normative reasoning corresponds to a syllogism with a premise about the law's ideals and a premise linking proposals to consequences and ideals. Consider the previous hypothetical rule that strict liability should be part of the law of torts because it minimizes accident costs. One premise establishes ideals (call it the "ideals' premise") and is "tort law [mostly] seeks to minimize accident costs." The next premise selects one proposal and states that its consequences fit the ideal best. This we can call consequences' premise and it is "strict liability minimizes accident costs." The normative conclusion seems inescapable, "strict liability should be part of the law of torts." The analysis above examined the lack of precision of the ideals' premise. Although the question of the appropriate ideal is important, much of normative reasoning involves the consequences' premise. The analysis of legal rules focuses on establishing consequences and determining which specific rule best promotes the goals.

The consequences' premise of the normative syllogism is very complex. The legal scholar must perform research to find existing alternative rules or interpretations and must use creativity in interpretation and drafting to construct plausible improvements. The resulting array of rules must be compared and evaluated with an eye to identifying the one that serves best the ideals established by the ideals' premise. This task combines research, creativity, and critical assessment. When the proposal that serves those goals best has been identified, the consequences' premise has been formed. Combined with the ideals' premise, it leads to the conclusion recommending the adoption of the proposal.

Formal logic reveals a tentative nature in this study of consequences. Rather than an absolute statement about the best possible proposal, the resulting statement is only the best proposal among the alternatives that were actually considered. This caveat is unavoidable. The alternative rules or interpretations are limited by the imagination of the scholar.

The difference between searching for the best proposal among all imaginable ones and searching among actual, finite alternatives must not be underestimated. Legal improvements are creations rather than discoveries.

In addition to involving innovation, the statement about consequences in the archetypal normative syllogism is complicated by the comparison of the consequences of the various rules. This comparison must be made through the prism of individuals' adjustments to the rules. The development of plausible alternative proposals (rules or interpretations) does not allow immediately a statement about consequences. Individuals react to rules and their reaction to each proposed rule must be estimated. Coase's thesis that rules would be irrelevant in a world without imperfections or frictions is also a breakthrough for the evaluation of the reactions to hypothetical rules. The first part of this book, on principles, builds up to Coasean analysis, which is reached in Chapters 5 and 6. Coasean irrelevance identifies the reactions to hypothetical rules. Because without frictions or obstacles, individuals would render the rules irrelevant; the idealized reactions of individuals would tend to be those that render the proposal irrelevant. The analysis then examines the setting to derive the actual reactions to the alternative proposals and select the proposal that has the consequences that promote the ideals most. Chapter 5 elaborates on the deployment of Coasean irrelevance as part of normative reasoning. Several additional hurdles hampering the use of law and economics lie in the way of reaching this methodological breakthrough.

D. Concluding Exercises

Exercise 1.1: Reduce a court opinion to two syllogisms. First, extract the deontic syllogism of formal logic that applies the law to the facts of the case. Second, extract the informal normative syllogism that the court used to choose this particular interpretation of the law. Notice how much easier the first step is. The second step is easier if the opinion contains a dissent and you try to extract the normative syllogism of the dissent. Let me offer as an example the famous *Meinhard v. Salmon* case (which is reproduced in Appendix A). Judge Cardozo, writing for the court, held that a managing partner who was offered a business opportunity while the other partner was undisclosed receives the opportunity for the partnership and must share it. Cardozo's opinion suggests that the ground for this conclusion is that morality dictates that fiduciary obligations should be broad. The dissent of Judge Andrews argues that this was merely a joint venture, and broad fiduciary obligations should not apply. From this, one could extract the deontic syllogism of formal logic:

> **Premise:** Offers to partners of undisclosed partnerships are offers to the partnership.
> **Premise:** Salmon received this offer while acting as a partner of an undisclosed partnership.
> **Conclusion:** This offer is received by the partnership.

Juxtapose this ostensibly compelling application of the law to the underlying informal normative syllogism:

> **Premise:** Morality dictates that the fiduciary obligations of partners should be broad.
> **Premise:** Offers made to partners of undisclosed partnerships might have been made to the partnership if it had been disclosed, that is, are ambiguous.
> **Conclusion:** Offers to partners of undisclosed partnerships should be considered offers to the partnership.

Rather than appearing as a compelling application of the law, the underlying normative syllogism highlights that the premise the fiduciary duties "should be broad" needs justification. Jurists who use economic analysis of law likely find Cardozo's opinion arbitrarily moralistic, as has Judge Posner, and search for arguments about why broad fiduciary obligations are beneficial, as I have.[2]

---

[2] Judge Posner categorizes *Meinhard* among Cardozo's unsatisfactory moralistic opinions in Richard A. Posner, *Cardozo: A Study in Reputation* (Chicago: University of Chicago Press, 1990):104–5. The broad fiduciary obligations of *Meinhard* are

Exercise 1.2: Try the same exercise on famous opinions, such as Cardozo's *Palsgraf* (a railroad is/is not liable to the victim of the explosion of a package) or *Sherwood v. Walker* (the sale of a cow that turns out to be pregnant is/is not voidable for mistake); repeat for infamous ones, such as *Dred Scott* (a master and a slave travel together voluntarily to a jurisdiction that does not recognize slavery; the master's property right in the slave is/is not recognized), or *Lochner* (laws limiting the hours that bakery employees may work is/is not a violation of their freedom of contract as constitutionally guaranteed by the "due process" clause).[3] What do you conclude?

E. BIBLIOGRAPHICAL NOTE

A classic introduction to formal logic is Morris R. Cohen and Ernest Nagel's, *An Introduction to Logic*, 2nd ed. (Indianapolis, IN: Hackett Publishing Co., 1993). Primers on deontic logic remain quite technical. See Lamber M. M. Royakkers, *Extending Deontic Logic for the Formalisation of Legal Rules* (Dordrecht: Kluwer Academic Publishers, 1998); James W. Forrester, *Being Good & Being Logical: Philosophical Groundwork for a New Deontic Logic* (Armonk, NY: M. E. Sharpe, 1996); Risto Hilpinen, *Deontic Logic: Introductory and Systematic Readings* (Dordrecht: Reidel, 1971).

---

argued to reduce costs of administration and financing by this author in Nicholas L. Georgakopoulos, "*Meinhard v. Salmon* and the Economics of Honor," *Columbia Business Law Review*. (1999):137.
[3] *Palsgraf v. Long Island R.R. Co.*, 248 N.Y. 339 (1928); *Sherwood v. Walker*, 66 Mich. 568, 33 N.W. 919 (1887); *Dred Scott v. Sandford*, 60 U.S. (19 How.) 393 (1857); *Lochner v. New York*, 198 U.S. 45 (1905).

2. Social Welfare versus Moral Philosophy

Many scholars object to economic analysis of law because of a belief in morality and moral philosophy. This chapter compares moral philosophy with law and economics as tools for interpreting and producing legal rules. This juxtaposition of moral philosophy and economics also reveals that economic analysis does take into account moral preferences.

The setting of *Meinhard v. Salmon* can illustrate the difference between economic and moral reasoning about law.[1] Salmon received a lucrative offer from Gerry, a business acquaintance. The offer could have expanded Salmon's business. Unbeknownst to Gerry, Salmon's business, which was the reason for their acquaintance, had a secret partner, Meinhard. If Gerry knew that Salmon operated in two capacities, as an individual and as a member of a partnership, then Gerry may have specified to which of the two he addressed his offer. Meinhard, the invisible partner, claimed the offer should be treated as made to the partnership. The litigation that Meinhard started eventually reached the highest court of the jurisdiction and the famous American judge, Benjamin Cardozo, and his colleague Andrews, who is almost equally famous for his vocal dissenting opinions. Previously established law did not answer the question directly. The study of moral philosophy would be of little assistance to Cardozo and his colleagues in deciding this novel question of law. The desirable interpretation is found by using economic analysis of law.[2]

---

[1] 249 N.Y. 458 (1928). The text of the opinion is reproduced in Appendix A.
[2] Some may be confused by the opinion's use of moral language. Moral rhetoric, like Cardozo's language about a punctillio of an honor most sensitive, is different from moral reasoning, which should explain why the partners' relation must be subject

20

The study of law is much more than learning the mechanical application of rules. Like most other objects of study, the ideal is improvement rather than replication of existing techniques. In the study of law, the ideal is the improvement of the legal system. Legal philosophies, however, disagree on what constitutes an improvement of the legal system. Economic analysis of law takes the position that the proper ideal of the legal system is the promotion of social welfare, that is, the maximization of the satisfaction of individuals' preferences. This description places economic analysis of law in a specific position in the taxonomy of philosophies.

The objective of this chapter, however, is not to explore the taxonomy of legal philosophies. Moral philosophy or moral instinct can be a hurdle on the path to economic analysis of law. One who believes in morality may reject the predictive aspect of economic analysis that individuals pursue their own self-interest. Belief in morality may also, independently, produce an objection to the normative message of law and economics that law should be designed to increase welfare. Paradoxically, economic analysis of law objects less to the former statement than to the latter. Essentially, for economic analysis, individuals act to satisfy their preferences, and preferences for complying with a code of ethics are included. Designing law according to morality is tantamount to forcing people to comply with a code of ethics that they may not have chosen. Forcing people to comply with an undesired ethic cannot be justified. Understanding the disagreement between moralists and law and economics requires us to return to the basics. How can moralists object to the idea that the law should promote social welfare?

This description of the economic analysis of law stresses the focus on rules and the satisfaction of preferences. These two features clearly distinguish economic analysis of law from hedonism or "act-utilitarian" theories and place it near those of "rule utilitarianism" and "preference

---

to high honor requirements. The opinion's economic wisdom, despite remaining unstated, but which is repeatedly displayed by numerous opinions of Cardozo, suggests that Cardozo had an extraordinary intuition about the economic consequences of law. Not only may he be a master of law and economics – silently and before the discipline even existed – but he also may have had the extraordinary rhetorical talent to hide economic reasoning that may have been too complex. The economic genius of the *Meinhard* opinion includes desirable allocation of risk, incentives for effort, and compensation of management; they are explained in Nicholas Georgakopoulos, "*Meinhard v. Salmon* and the Economics of Honor," *Columbia Business Law Review* (1999):137–164.

utilitarianism."[3] Act utilitarianism justifies actions, whereas rule utilitarianism justifies rules. Preference utilitarianism changes the focus from pleasure to the satisfaction of preferences. Economic analysis of law examines rules rather than actions and gauges social welfare in terms of the satisfaction of preferences. Economic analysis combines the two theses of "rule utilitarianism" and "preference utilitarianism."

This description also allows the placement of economic analysis in the broader categories of philosophical approaches. By evaluating rules based on their goals or consequences, economic analysis of law can be categorized as a consequentialist theory. Consequentialist theories are a subset of teleological ones. Teleological theories focus on purposes and functions; consequentialist theories focus on consequences.

This categorization distinguishes economic analysis from legal theories that are essentialist. Essentialist theories focus on fundamental attributes or properties.

To clarify these distinctions, allow me to use the example of a recurring phenomenon in my household that I treat as excessive – the watching of television by one of my children. The child is watching a television show and I make a statement intending to end that activity. The hypothetical statements that follow illustrate the categories used here to describe economic analysis and distinguish it from other approaches to legal thinking.

"Children are not supposed to watch such shows." This justification seems to assume some essential attributes of children and of this type of show that are incompatible. This argument seems essentialist.

"You told me yesterday that you would become a professional athlete. I do not think watching TV furthers that goal." This argument adopts a goal that the child has set, becoming a professional athlete, and uses it to evaluate the activity. Teleological is probably more apt a description of it than consequentialist. While the statement is closely related to consequences, it does not point out either the consequences of watching TV, nor does it identify the activity of which the consequence is becoming a professional athlete.

"You will not have time to do your homework." This seems to be a consequentialist argument because it focuses on the consequences of the activity. This argument is unlikely to be considered hedonistic, because the child would not enjoy doing homework.

---

[3] See, in general Daniel M. Hausman and Michael S. McPherson, "Taking Ethics Seriously: Economics and Contemporary Moral Philosophy," *Journal of Economic Literature* 31 (1993):671.

"You would have more fun playing outside." This is probably a hedonistic argument. It is also a consequentialist argument. The consequence of playing outside is fun.

"If you really want to play for your school's team, you should run instead of watching TV at this time of day." Although this argument is very similar to the teleological one, it goes a step further in suggesting a rule, to run at this time of day. Moreover, unlike the hedonist argument that rested on pleasure, this focuses of the satisfaction of a preference, the preference to play for the team. Thus, it resembles preference and rule utilitarianism.

Economic analysis of law focuses on social welfare, but social welfare is not an easy subject. Social welfare has practical difficulties – sometimes it is difficult to determine, sometimes the preferences of different individuals may be irreconcilable or contradictory, as discussed in Chapter 4 about voting systems. To those who practice law and economics, social welfare is a simple and accommodating ideal despite its problems. That the law seeks to maximize social welfare means that the law is the servant of society. That economic analysis subscribes to this view shows that it takes a non-interventionist view of the law. This fundamental tenet of economic analysis also makes it subordinate not only to society's interests but also to philosophical and methodological innovations and empirical findings that may show what the social interest is. Thus, economic analysis of law seeks to dominate neither society nor science. This deferential attitude of economic analysis is most clearly visible in the "pragmatism" of Richard Posner's recent work.[4] New social attitudes should lead to new law and new methods of determining social preferences should become part of economic analysis.

A. Ideals behind Law and Economics: Welfarism and Pragmatism

Moral philosophers pressure the economic analysis of law to define the moral ideal behind its focus on social welfare. The principal responses from within law and economics are by Louis Kaplow and Steven Shavell and by Richard A. Posner. Kaplow and Shavell are

---

[4] Richard A. Posner, *The Problems of Jurisprudence* (Cambridge, MA: Harvard University Press, 1990) (hereinafter *"The Problems of Jurisprudence"*); Richard A. Posner, *Cardozo: A Study in Reputation* (Chicago: University of Chicago Press, 1990) (hereinafter *"Cardozo"*); Richard A. Posner, *Overcoming Law* (Cambridge, MA: Harvard University Press, 1995) (hereinafter *"Overcoming Law"*).

professors at Harvard Law School. Richard Posner is the most prolific author in law and economics. After a career as Professor of Law at the University of Chicago, he served as Chief Judge of the U.S. Court of Appeals for the Seventh Circuit, where he has senior status.

Professors Kaplow and Shavell argue that social welfare includes moral preferences and call their proposal welfarism.[5] In their choice of terminology, they follow the welfarism of Amartya Sen, who sought to validate the premises of economic analysis. The welfarism of Kaplow and Shavell seems closer to utilitarianism than that of Sen, which seems to depend on the necessity of the tension between freedom and rational choice.[6] According to Kaplow and Shavell, moral philosophy is subsumed into individuals' preferences. Thus, the legal system can be satisfied in promoting the choices that individuals make in the marketplace.

Richard Posner has proposed that law and economics fits within the philosophical framework of pragmatism that flowered at the end of the nineteenth century.[7] Pragmatism concedes that some questions might be unanswerable, but it seeks to utilize all available evidence and scientific innovations in the best possible way. From the pragmatist perspective, economic analysis of law is welcome as a new technology, as a methodological innovation that improves legal analysis. From a pragmatist perspective, the inability to answer immediately metaphysical questions does not detract from the appeal of economic analysis of law, because pragmatism concedes that at least some metaphysical questions have no answers. Non-pragmatists will tend to view this concession as excessive. Any attacks by traditional legal philosophers claiming imperfection of pragmatism are hardly persuasive for scholars of the economic analysis of law because no superior alternative is proposed.

Social welfare is paramount in both of these approaches to the ideals or first principles of law and economics. The juxtaposition of social welfare with the goals of other approaches to law reveals economic analysis has an unusually flexible and non-interventionist attitude.

Moral philosophies set the ideals that the legal system should pursue. Instead of taking social preferences and examining ways to satisfy

---

[5] Louis Kaplow and Steven Shavell, *Fairness versus Welfare* (Cambridge, MA: Harvard University Press, 2002).

[6] Amartya Sen, *Rationality and Freedom* (Cambridge, MA: Harvard University Press, 2002) (hereinafter "*Rationality and Freedom*").

[7] Posner, *The Problems of Jurisprudence*; Posner, *Cardozo*; Posner, *Overcoming Law*.

them, moral philosophies determine goals that may contradict individual preferences. The ideal of stoicism, for example, is the bearing of adversity with equanimity. Consider a hypothetical individual, Peter Hurt, who, when in pain, relieves part of pain's discomfort by screaming. Abiding by stoicism and not screaming reduces the satisfaction of Hurt's preferences. A legal philosopher who derived ideals from stoicism might argue that the legal system should help Peter Hurt to bear pain with equanimity. Perhaps, such reasoning would lead to an expanded prohibition of breaching the peace, so that if Peter Hurt were to scream he would also be liable for breaching the peace. A law-and-economics approach asks what is better for Peter Hurt and all other victims and may excuse screaming by individuals in pain.

B. Juxtaposition with Other External Derivations of Ideals

Law and economics takes social preferences as an input and seeks to design the legal system to best satisfy them. Thus, the ideal that the legal system pursues is external, derived from outside the discipline of law and economics. Two other important schools of legal thought can be interpreted as proposing the derivation of an ideal from outside. The derivation of moral principles from the legal system may be associated with formalism. A more recent proposal by Rawls, often called contractarianism, captured much attention. Rawls sought to simulate the agreement that members of society would have reached "behind a veil of ignorance." Members of society should ignore the details of the position that each would have.

Both schools proceeded to derive conclusions from the application of their methods. Because the result is that they pursue an ideal, these philosophies do not have the flexible, non-interventionist nature of economic analysis of law. However, ignoring their conclusions, the proposals for deriving principles from outside the discipline itself bear a methodological affinity with economic analysis of law that is worth distinguishing.

i. Deriving Ideals from Existing Rules (Including Formalism)

If the ideals derive from the existing web of legal rules, then the study of those rules reveals the essential first principles. Law-and-economics scholars would counter that such derivation is elusive and prevents legal change. An example illustrates the types of objections that an economically minded jurist might raise to the idea of deriving principles from existing rules.

Suppose that the study of existing law revealed a principle in conflict with social welfare. Suppose that a new measure would clearly increase social welfare. For example, take a walled country that is defending itself against a hostile siege. Its philosophers have deduced from its laws that its ideal is the responsible expression of free will. Someone argues that all its citizens be allowed access to keys to the doors of the wall, to exercise responsibly their freedom to open the doors. Should that argument persuade? The philosophical approach would be open to debate even if it concluded against broad access to keys. A law-and-economics jurist would counterargue that social welfare avoids this argument because the safety of the many citizens ends the discussion.

If this example seems too contrived, take the setting in the mid-seventies when highways in the United States had no speed limits and suppose that a philosopher espoused that the legal system expressed the ideal of free will. Upon the arrival of the oil crises, the society decides that a speed limit would save gas and alleviate the shock of the crisis (and suppose that were true). Should philosophy persuade society not to enact the gas-preserving speed limits?

These examples do not attempt to rebut centuries of work by philosophers. The idea is to see the reaction of economic analysis to the proposal that the ideals that guide the design of rules be derived from the web of rules itself.

ii. Rawls' Contractarianism

John Rawls formulated a philosophical approach that contained a method of deriving its ideals.[8] Rawls proposed that the principles for the organization of society – the fundamental legal rules – should be selected by simulating an agreement reached behind "a veil of ignorance," by the members of society, without each knowing their position, skill, luck, or other attributes that would determine each individual's success or welfare. This "contractarian" process had significant appeal. A jurist who subscribes to economic analysis of law will tend to doubt that the "veil of ignorance" process can determine social preferences.

---

[8] John Rawls, *A Theory of Justice* (Cambridge, MA: Harvard University Press, 1971).

Part of Rawls' conclusions was to advocate a more equitable distribution of wealth than what would arise from market forces. Chapter 4, discusses how arguments for aggressive redistribution can be built on economic analysis, including egalitarian preferences. However, the derivation of the need for redistribution from "behind a veil of ignorance" rather than from egalitarian preferences, would seem dubious to an economically minded jurist. Individuals who might have agreed behind the veil to a certain distribution of wealth will have an incentive to deviate from this agreement *ex post*, as illustrated by Nozick.[9] The graphic example is that of a basketball game in a society that has agreed behind the veil on a distribution of wealth that precludes paying the players for the game. If everyone in the audience prefers to give up a small fraction of their wealth to see the game, one cannot argue that the game should not occur. It is hard to argue that the audience must not amend their contract and enjoy the game. Of course, the same analysis applies to every market transaction: the beneficiary provides a service that the other side values more than its price. Insisting on a previously agreed distribution reduces welfare by precluding market transactions. Nozick's argument indicates that contractarianism can slip into paternalistic attitudes, but economic analysis of law would tend to accommodate new preferences.

Whereas contractarianism may seem appealing because of the consensual agreement it assumes, the agreement assumed by contractarianism will likely fail to seem objective to economically minded jurists. Since it is impossible to ascertain objectively the content of the agreement reached behind the "veil," contractarianism fails to offer law-and-economics scholars the objectivity of economic analysis.

Again, the idea is not to rebut contractarianism as a methodology but to indicate the economically minded jurist's reactions. A contractarian approach could benefit from the methods of economic analysis of law, because those methods could reveal that the choices behind the veil of ignorance would have been different from the actual choices on the market.

iii. The Potential Equivalence of Derived Ideals and Preferences

These theories are *methods* for deriving moral principles or ideals. They were discussed, not as moral philosophies of law, but as tools that

---

[9]   Robert Nozick, *Anarchy, State, and Utopia* (New York: Basic Books, 1974).

derive ideals either from the web of the legal system or from a simulated agreement behind the veil of ignorance. That the ideals were not created by each philosophical school but were derived is an appealing component of those philosophical approaches. Because their principles are derived, they are better able to withstand attacks claiming they are arbitrary. Here lies a similarity with law and economics, because it also derives social welfare from observed actions.

A jurist who uses law and economics can try to derive the ideal from existing rules. Traditional approaches to law, such as Blackstone's and Langdell's, had a similar feature. Internal legal analysis has a long tradition: in the late nineteenth century, the teaching of Langdell and the new civil codes; and significantly earlier, the treatise of Blackstone and the Justinian codification.[10] All extracted principles from pre-existing decisions, be they laws or judicial opinions. Economic analysis explicitly adopts similar techniques when it uses quantitative methods to analyze caselaw and to determine its underlying function. A notable example of this approach exists in a notoriously vague area of corporate law known as veil piercing. Corporations limit the liability of their shareholders. A corporation provides a shield against loss, the "corporate veil," because liability imposed on the corporation does not burden its shareholders, even if the corporation's assets are exhausted. Veil piercing is an exceptional measure that makes shareholders liable. Quantitative studies of court opinions about veil piercing seek to establish the patterns that lead courts to ignore limited liability in contract and tort cases.[11]

Law and economics can also use methods reminiscent of Rawls' search for the agreement behind the veil of ignorance. A law-and-economics scholar would expect the contractarian derivation to match the promotion of social welfare. Because rational individuals behind the veil would seek to maximize their expected welfare, they would reach an agreement that would exactly reflect the social welfare. From this perspective, the contractarian process for deriving an ideal should lead to the same ideal that is included in law and economics. From the perspective of economic analysis of law, a different conclusion is false, likely a misspecification. The agreement behind the veil will neither deviate from maximizing expected welfare nor prohibit the

---

[10] Tony Honore, *Tribonian* (Ithaca, NY: Cornell Univ. Press, 1978); A. M. Honore, "The Background to Justinian's Codification," *Tulane Law Review* 48 (1974): 859.
[11] See Robert B. Thompson, "Piercing the Corporate Veil: an Empirical Study," *Cornell Law Review* 76 (1991):1036.

future adoption of rules that will maximize welfare. The response of economic analysis of law to someone arguing for a different choice, as does Rawls, is that it reveals a false specification of preferences. If individuals would chose an egalitarian regime, that choice corresponds to a shared preference for equality. Therefore, the egalitarian agreement and the agreement that most satisfies preferences, that is, maximizes welfare, are identical. For the difference between veil and maximization to remain, the Rawlsian must point to circumstances where maximization would indicate a choice that would have been precluded behind the veil. This, essentially, would be a counter to Nozick's example about the basketball player. Important also is the realization that societies can and do prevent future errors by adopting constitutions.[12]

Law and economics is open to all methods for determining social preferences. Both methods, trying to determine social preferences from the web of existing rules and the Rawlsian approach of trying to simulate an agreement behind a veil of ignorance, can be useful. Indeed, within the framework of Posner's pragmatism, every method that produces valid results is expressly acceptable. Once social preferences are determined, they guide legal design.

C. Distinguishing Features of Economic Analysis

This chapter does not intend to dwell on the moral philosophy of law and economics. Strict analysis may reveal some imperfections of its leading philosophical descriptions, welfarism and pragmatism. Scholars that use the methodologies of economic analysis of law would eventually resolve them. The juxtaposition of economic analysis with moral philosophy reveals some important foundations that economically minded jurists share.

---

[12] The analysis of the text suggests that the Rawlsian argumentation could become important in the consideration of any new rule. The basis for the Rawlsian argument must be that behind the veil, society would have chosen to prevent its adoption. The new rule must increase welfare and the Rawlsian analysis must argue against it. Furthermore, the setting must not allow the objection that the welfare analysis in favor of the amendment is false – akin to Ulysses' pleas to join the Sirens while under the influence of their spell. If the welfare analysis is false, no conflict exists between it and the agreement behind the veil. Rather, the rule is in conflict with both maximization and the Rawlsian analysis. From the perspective of designing a constitution, however, and, in particular, the process for its amendment, guarding against future errors should be a central concern.

i. Avoidance of Moral Relativity

Moral relativity is by no means a new concern of philosophy. Moral relativity means that the same moral precept, the same moral ideal, can produce different rules depending on the context in which it arises. As a result, the same moral principle is consistent with different and contradictory rules. Moral relativity may also imply that different individuals or groups reach different conclusions about morality. Moral relativity, therefore, means that principles fail to gauge and guide the legal system with objectivity.

Economic analysis of law seeks to develop rules that will apply in every case and promote welfare in the sense that they will satisfy our preferences as much as possible. The ambition of developing rules of general application is the antithesis of moral relativity.

ii. Preference for Applications over Refinement of Principles

It is important to notice that of the many scholars in economic analysis of law, only a handful devote significant effort to defining its fundamental principles and quickly move to other projects. The examples of Posner and of Kaplow and Shavell are indicative. Scholars in economic analysis of law feel that their efforts are more meaningful and productive when applying its methods rather than refining its principles.

This does not mean that the fundamental principles of economic analysis of law are not knowable or describable. Nor do the scholars who seek applications believe that the existing descriptions of the fundamental principles of economic analysis cannot be further refined. Rather, the choice to pursue applications likely stems from a belief that existing descriptions of welfare maximization are sufficient and that little social gain can stem from perfecting its definition. The effort that a scholar would expend refining welfarism or pragmatism would be much better spent in applying the tools of economic analysis to specific issues.

iii. Ubiquitous Importance of Incentives

Implicit in the belief that economic analysis of law can apply to any rule is the belief that individuals respond to incentives in all areas of activity. The resistance to this position may motivate some scholars to only consider arguments based on economic analysis of law in issues of economic relations. Many scholars, led by Gary Becker, have shown that economic analysis applies to every relation, even the most emotional, such as interactions within the family.[13] Accordingly, scholars have applied economic analysis of law in family issues.[14] Empirical evidence offers support.[15]

That incentives do have an effect on every activity should not be controversial for legal scholars. The study of law would be a paradoxical enterprise if individuals routinely ignored incentives. The very existence of law implies a belief that individuals do respond to incentives.

That incentives have an effect in every area of activity does not mean that individuals have complete knowledge and an infinite ability to process complex situations to ascertain with precision their incentives. Incentives have an effect regardless of rationality. The problems of bounded rationality are discussed further in Chapter 3 in the section "Bounded Rationality."

iv. Treatment of Preferences as Objective

Some scholars within economic analysis of law avoid moral philosophy because they see moral choices as expressions of tastes. In contrast to a subjective discussion about moral tastes, economic analysis seeks to maximize welfare by satisfying tastes. Although moral philosophers call this a moral choice, to the scholar of economic analysis it is an objective pursuit.

This objectivity of maximizing preferences also indicates that it is not truly a moral theory of justice. Moral rules are limiting and

---

[13] See, in general, Margaret F. Brinig, *From Contract to Covenant: Beyond the Law and Economics of the Family* (Cambridge, MA: Harvard University Press, 2000); *Marriage and Divorce: A Law and Economics Approach*, ed. Anthony W. Dnes and Robert Rowthorn (Cambridge: Cambridge University Press, 2002). Gary S. Becker, *Social Economics: Market Behavior in a Social Environment* (Cambridge, MA: Belknap Press of Harvard University Press, 2000); Gary S. Becker, *A Treatise on the Family* (Cambridge, MA: Harvard University Press, 1991); Gary S. Becker, *The Essence of Becker*, ed. (Ramón Febrero and Pedro S. Schwartz (Stanford, CA: Hoover Institution Press, 1995).

[14] Lloyd Cohen, "Marriage, Divorce and QuasiRents; Or, 'I Gave Him the Best Years of My Life'," *Journal of Legal Studies* 16 (1987): 267; Margaret F. Brinig and Steven M. Crafton, "Marriage and Opportunism," *Journal of Legal Studies* 23 (1994):869.

[15] See, for example, Allen M. Parkman, "Unilateral Divorce and Labor Force Participation Rate of Married Women, Revisited," *American Economic Review*, 82 (1992):671.

operative only if they contradict the raw calculus of welfare. From this perspective, welfare maximization is not a moral theory, despite being a normative theory. The scholar who accepts maximization as the self-evident goal of the legal system is puzzled by the treatment of utilitarianism as a moral theory by moral philosophers. Not every normative statement is a moral one. Otherwise, the result appears to be circular reasoning: utilitarianism is unacceptable because it is a moral theory that accepts preferences as superior to morality. The desirability of satisfying preferences is a tautology, not a contestable moral statement. The primacy of preferences may be an important hurdle for understanding economic analysis. An example illustrates the reasoning leading to the conclusion that the satisfaction of preferences is a tautological objective, rather than a contestable moral theory.

Take as an example of a moral theory, an absolute ban on killing – thou shalt not kill. Consider a killing that clearly increases social welfare, whether that is a killing in self-defense, or a killing which alters the course of history that prevents massive atrocities and countless deaths. By hypothesis, the welfare calculus is clear and supports the killing, making this a simple issue for law and economics. A society's choice to pursue the moral rule and prohibit the killing does not make the welfare analysis a moral one. The legal system may choose to reduce welfare in pursuit of a moral goal. The alternative is that the legal system chooses to maximize welfare with no compromises. Welfare maximization ranks these alternatives with respect to the welfare they produce, but this does not make the top alternative into a moral theory. In essence, welfare maximization is the logical consequence of the recognition of individuals' preferences. The statements that their satisfaction is good and, its normative corollary, that rules and their interpretation should maximize the satisfaction of preferences are logically compelled. A moral philosopher may interject a moral theory that argues for a different normative guide, but that will necessarily imply the repudiation, and subordination, of preference satisfaction to that moral ideal. From the perspective of law and economics, this subordination can only be acceptable if a stronger preference in favor of the moral principle exists.

Thus, when moral philosophers argue that the utilitarianism that underlies the economic analysis of law is just another moral theory of justice that makes welfare the gauge of justice, the same way that providing self-actualization or moral fulfillment may be the goals of different judicial philosophies, they are wrong. The foundation of economic analysis of law is factual, the satisfaction of preferences, rather than moral. Individuals have preferences. This is a fact from which we can determine what increases individuals' welfare, which is to satisfy those preferences. Naturally, the legal system should attempt to provide more satisfaction of preferences rather than less. Thus, the theory of justice of economic analysis of law flows from fact with no interjection of moralizing. The moral philosophers, of course, would object by stating that individuals *should* obtain self-actualization or moral fulfillment. To the law-and-economics scholar, those objections are preferences – either preferences of individuals or preferences of the moral philosophers. As preferences, they would be part of any welfarist approach, but their weight and importance would be dramatically smaller than if they were believed to be universal ideals.

Economic analysis of law is valid despite the influence of the environment on preferences. The notion that circumstances may influence preferences does not mean that preferences are subject to continuous large fluctuations or radical change. If preferences have characteristics that interfere with a conclusion of a specific piece of analysis, law-and-economics scholars would consider the analysis incomplete and seek to refine it accordingly.

Law-and-economics jurists do not ignore evidence that the environment shapes preferences. Rather, such evidence informs and refines the analysis. Education or art may enable individuals to fulfill better their preferences and may shift their preferences so that individuals derive greater enjoyment from satisfying their preferences. For example, music lovers may enjoy only folk music if they are uneducated, whereas if they are educated, the same individuals enjoy more musical genres in ways that are more fulfilling. Economic analysis includes the enhanced future welfare in its evaluation of policies about education or art.

Economic analysis rests on the satisfaction of preferences. This is its power; it does not depend on the characteristics of preferences, such as educability. The educability of preferences seems to weaken the foundations of economic analysis of law because the goal to satisfy them seems to become illusory. Educability does not imply constant and large changes of preferences. The better understanding of preferences and their formation strengthens the economic analysis of law because it allows the goal of maximizing human happiness to be achieved better.[16]

v. Lack Bias for Rule Proliferation

Economic analysis of law places a very high burden of proof on attempts to justify legal rules. A foundational tenet of economic analysis of law is the Coasean irrelevance theorem: that, in an ideal world, individuals would reach optimal arrangements regardless of the law.[17] A premise of law and economics, in other words, is that law may be irrelevant. Rather than starting with a regulatory premise, economic analysis of law starts with an objection to regulation that analysis must overcome.

When a legal scholar accepts this methodological approach of economic analysis of law, moral philosophical approaches to law appear to have a self-fulfilling prophesy in favor of creating more law. Because the starting point is the "aught," the outcome is too often a rule and the associated expansion of regulation. To the jurist of law and economics, rules need justification that is more stringent.

vi. Orientation Toward the Future

A fundamental predilection of economic analysis of law is that it is oriented toward the future. The environment, individuals, and activity change constantly. The evaluation of rules and their interpretation occur in a dynamic environment. This attitude stands in stark contrast to both original intent and formalism.

Original intent is inescapably static. Interpretation is static because the starting point defines the goal. If the morals expressed by the rules exclusively determine the moral goals and purposes of rules, then rules cannot react to changed socioeconomic circumstances. Moreover,

---

[16] This conclusion may seem undermined by an argument that is premised on the idea that withholding education leads to simpler preferences that are easier to satisfy. It is clear that the satisfaction of educated preferences produces greater welfare than the satisfaction of simple ones. Moreover, education likely produces some welfare directly. Therefore, accepting the educability of preferences cannot lead to a recommendation for less education.

[17] Ronald H. Coase, *The Firm, the Market, and the Law*, 2nd ed. (Chicago: University of Chicago Press, 1990); Ronald H. Coase, "The Problem of Social Cost," *Journal of Law and Economics* 3 (1960):1.

adherence to original intent defies its goal of improving society. Since the rules themselves define the goal, this method would never show the rules to be undesirable.

Formalism is similar. Formalism calls for adherence to the rule's text. It produces a similar result inasmuch as it objects to all arguments regarding interpretation other than linguistic. It precludes change and improvement.

The study of law is a heartless and fruitless exercise unless accompanied by the goal of improving society. In understanding and pursuing this improvement, economic analysis does not promote its own values, unlike other philosophical approaches to law. Economic analysis takes its objectives from society by trying to read social and individual preferences. The preceding discussion, however, did not engage the problem of aggregating the different preferences of individuals in a society. This issue is the intersection of economic analysis of law with political philosophy. It is a challenging subject and Chapter 3 explores it.

D. Concluding Exercises

Exercise 2.1: Choose one of the moral philosophies. Examples may be those of the epicureans, the stoics, or the cynics. Try to restate that philosophy's position as a description of an individual's preferences. For example instead of describing the epicurean school as the one believing that individuals should pursue their material desires, describe it as the one comprising the individuals whose strongest preference is the pursuit of material desires. How would this group fare as a minority in society? How would a different minority group fare if the majority had those preferences?

Exercise 2.2: Someone who accepts the utilitarian premises of law and economics would also accept that even the most altruistic people do maximize their welfare. Consider the example of Mother Teresa and accept that she truly derived joy from helping others. The good that she did was facilitated and increased by charitable donations to her organization. Suppose that some of her major donors would not give if they thought that Mother Teresa was maximizing her own welfare. Would this reaction be rational? If the spread of economic analysis of law reduced those donations, is it still desirable? Are the acts of reading this book or pursuing economic analysis of law evil?

E. BIBLIOGRAPHICAL NOTE

The perspective of seeing incentives in every aspect of human behavior is pioneered and discussed in the book by Gary S. Becker, *The Economic Approach to Human Behavior* (Chicago: University of Chicago Press, 1976).

Becker's columns in *Business Week* offer examples of economic applications to an extraordinarily wide variety of topics. Their collection is Gary Stanley Becker, Guity Nashat Becker, *The Economics of Life: From Baseball to Affirmative Action to Immigration, How Real-World Issues Affect Our Everyday Life* (New York: McGraw-Hill, 1997).

The leading theoretical foundations of law and economics, pragmatism, and welfarism are Richard A. Posner, *The Problems of Jurisprudence* (Cambridge, MA: Harvard University Press, 1990); Louis Kaplow and Steven Shavell, *Fairness versus Welfare* (Cambridge, MA: Harvard University Press, 2002).

The leading economist to connect with moral philosophy is Amartya Sen. His books are the leading applications of economic reasoning into philosophical problems. See Amartya Sen, *Development as Freedom* (New York: Anchor Books, 2000); Amartya Sen, *Rationality and Freedom*; Amartya Sen, *On Ethics and Economics* (Cambridge, MA: B. Blackwell, 1992).

Amartya Sen and Bernard Williams collect essays about the treatment of utilitarianism in contemporary philosophy in Amartya Sen and Bernard Williams (eds.), *Utilitarianism and Beyond* (Cambridge: Cambridge University Press, 1982).

3. From Political Philosophy to Game Theory

The acceptance of democratic traditions misleads some into objecting to economic analysis of law on the basis of a belief in majority rule. The essence of such an objection could be that a proposed interpretation is acceptable only if it follows the majority's will rather than an economic demonstration of its desirability. This chapter shows that majority rule may lead to undesirable outcomes. Thus, legal reasoning that defers to the majority's will may produce undesirable interpretations, whereas legal analysis that relies on economic methods, that is, law and economics, could lead to more desirable ones.

Again, *Meinhard v. Salmon* can illustrate the importance of the difference between political and economic analysis.[1] Salmon received a lucrative offer from Gerry, a business acquaintance. The offer could have expanded Salmon's business. Unbeknownst to Gerry, Salmon's business, which was the reason for their acquaintance, had a secret partner, Meinhard. If Gerry knew that Salmon operated in two capacities, as an individual and as a member of a partnership, then Gerry may have specified which of the two he selected as the recipient of his offer. Meinhard, the invisible partner, claimed the offer should be treated as made to the partnership. The litigation that Meinhard started eventually reached the highest court of the jurisdiction and the famous American judge, Benjamin Cardozo, and his colleague Andrews, who is almost equally famous for his vocal dissenting opinions. Previously established law did not answer the question directly. If the court over which Cardozo presided decided the case by trying to ascertain the majority's preferred rule, then they may have been led to select an

---

[1] 249 N.Y. 458 (1928). The text of the opinion is reproduced in Appendix A.

undesirable interpretation. The desirable interpretation was the product of law and economics.

This chapter also engages political theory as a hurdle impeding the understanding of law and economics. This chapter speaks to the scholar who believes that law and economics is pointless because the law is shaped by the majority. The resulting peek into mechanisms for social decisions, however, forces a closer look into the ideas of economic analysis. Therefore, after the discussion of some concepts of political theory, this chapter opens the analysis of collective decisions with voting.

Economists engaged the political scene by applying the model of self-interested actors on government and politics. The resulting analysis is categorized under the heading *public choice*. Because public choice uses game theory as its predominant quantitative method of analysis, the chapter also introduces *game theory*. Once within the realm of social decision making, this chapter also visits two more related methodological branches of economic analysis that use game theory, the analysis of *social norms* and the identification of patterns of systematic errors that economists label *behavioralism* or *bounded rationality*.

These are large topics, about which much more can be, and has been, written. This chapter gives minimal coverage, in particular, because it appears in the segment on principles. However, for scholars and jurists to accept the simplifications of economic analysis of law, it should be helpful to demonstrate that methods exist that engage the issues that may give economic analysis the appearance of lack of realism, such as the assumption of perfect knowledge, the infinite ability to analyze the circumstances, and the social pressure to which individuals succumb. Not only does economic analysis engage these issues, but law and economics builds useful arguments on that analysis.

A. POLITICAL THEORY

Economic analysis of law maintains the principle of adhering to the satisfaction of preferences. Whereas in the previous chapter the pursuit of preferences was juxtaposed with the pursuit of other goals established by moral philosophies, here the pursuit of preferences is treated as accepted. The issue is to see how political philosophies interact with the pursuit of the jurist who, using economic tools, seeks to satisfy social preferences. This issue touches political philosophy because social preferences are not expressed directly. The study of the systems by which societies make choices is, traditionally, the realm of political philosophy.

Contemporary political thought in the legal academy engages ideas such as *civic republicanism* on the value of participation, *perfectionism* on the value of culture, and *legal process* on the desirability of the administrative state. All those theories refine the details of political interaction. These theories do not propose major changes to the democratic ideal. Democracy and majority rule, however, are a puzzle for law and economics. The first step is to establish how economic reasoning understands democratic decision making.

i. Inefficiencies of Majority Rule

As soon as a jurist accepts the principle of economic analysis of law that the legal system should maximize social welfare, the rule by majority loses its appeal. Whereas individuals' comparisons among alternatives involve nuanced compromises between preferences that could influence complex choices, majority rule simply enacts the first choice of the majority without regard to such nuances as its cost to the minority or the majority's harm from a policy that satisfies the majority. It is obvious that the majority can take decisions that do not promote social welfare, because the majority could enact a policy that gives it a small gain at a large cost on the minority.

The pure majority rule cannot be reconciled with the idea of maximizing social welfare because it ignores the preferences of minorities. It is no accident that the long-lived democratic systems deviate from this unalloyed version of majority rule by having several layers of representation and by requiring in numerous settings supermajority or near consensus. Such deviations from majority rule may be argued to allow some democracies to approach social welfare more, at the expense of some inability to make decisions.

The jurist who seeks to determine social preferences obtains little information from a bare majority vote. This is a paradox that calls for analysis and the proposal of alternatives to majority rule. Indeed, political science embraces economic methods and adopts the goal of social welfare often under the title *rational choice*.

As if intending to complete the repudiation of the perfection of majority rule, economic analysis also points out the possibility of its indeterminacy. If no candidate receives an absolute majority in the first round of an election, all candidates can win the second round depending only on who is eliminated. This phenomenon is known as *cycling*. An example clarifies.

The election has three candidates, Yoda, Obi-Wan Kenobi, and Qui-Gon Jinn. Each candidate is supported by one third of the voters (fans of *Star Wars* who know these characters, among whom Yoda would command an overwhelming majority, would object to the tie but – borrowing Yoda's phrasing – necessary for the example, it is). Yoda's voters rank Obi-Wan second, preferring him to Qui-Gon. Obi-Wan's voters rank Qui-Gon second. Finally, Qui-Gon's voters rank Yoda second. Consider that Qui-Gon is eliminated from the second election. Yoda wins because he also receives the votes of the fans of Qui-Gon. Consider that Obi-Wan is eliminated. Qui-Gon wins because he also receives the votes of the fans of Obi-Wan. Finally, consider that Yoda is eliminated from the second election. Obi-Wan wins because he receives the votes of the fans of Yoda.

Cycling occurs in elections with more than two choices, but its cause is that majority vote ignores intensity of preferences and, therefore, also the ranking of the candidates by the voters. We will see two attempts to overcome this problem through the design of voting systems later in this chapter. With this background about the economist's reaction to majority rule, the next paragraphs visit the nonquantitative scholarship that seeks to refine the existing democratic system. The one that is uniquely associated with legal scholarship is the legal process school.

ii. Legal Process: Explaining the Administrative State

The late nineteenth century and the New Deal introduced a new tool of government, administrative agencies. Although the novelty of administrative agencies has faded, for legal scholars they involved a radical transformation of the conventional separation of powers. Administrative agencies exercise executive powers, make rules, and adjudicate them. In other words, they exercise authorities that conventionally belong to the executive, the legislature, and the judiciary. The leading reaction of legal scholarship became known as the *legal process* school. It remains an interesting attempt to address this major change of the political environment.

According to legal process, the different branches of government have different "competences" or skills, what economists would call comparative advantages. The legislature is understood to offer a venue for reaching agreement or compromise between groups with different interests and the courts to be adept at fact-finding and evolving the common law. The justification of administrative agencies rests on the development of specialized areas of knowledge that created a need for the administration of their regulation by specialists. Thus, legal process considers the administrative agencies as groups of specialists who are at the best position to administer an area of law that corresponds to new complex technological interactions.

Prime examples of administrative agencies that conform to this vision are the Securities and Exchange Commission's oversight of the issuance and the trading of securities or the Federal Communications Commission's supervision of the airwaves and allocation of the frequency spectrum. The trading of securities is very different from the trading of ordinary goods. The details of the trading arrangements are subject to technological improvements that do not influence other markets, such as the development of electronic trading or the switch from prices in eighths to prices in cents. The airwaves are similar. The development of FM radio, cellular and satellite telephony, wireless computing, and the administration of the corresponding broadcast licenses frequently raises new issues of a specialized nature. Requiring legislative action for addressing such issues would be doubly wasteful. The central legislature does not have the specialized knowledge necessary for such regulation. Moreover, legislating about these specialized areas would divert the legislature's finite time and attention from other legislative issues, where its attention would bring improvements.

The legal process analysis is founded on the idea that the process of making, enforcing, and adjudicating specialized rules can be improved by moving some powers from the branches to specialized administrative agencies. The improvement is not a monetary one but one of capacity. Restated in economic terms, the legal process school justifies agencies as more efficient makers, enforcers, and adjudicators of specialized rules than the traditional branches. If the legal process school had arisen more recently it could be part of economic analysis of law.

Because of this affinity, the evaluation of the legal process school from the perspective of economic analysis of law is anticlimactic. Economic analysis is ready to accept arguments for radical change, including change of the system of government and separation of powers that administrative agencies skirt. Upon proof that administrative agencies are desirable, economic analysis could even accept that the tripartite separation of powers should be explicitly increased to four to include administrative agencies.

iii. Civic Republicanism

Civil republicanism is as a refinement of the democratic system. The fundamental tenet of civic republicanism is the desirability of citizens' participation in the deliberative and democratic processes.[2] As a school of normative thought, civic republicanism argues that deliberation is an objective that should influence the design of the political system. From the perspective of civic republicanism, a political system that induces the deliberation and participation of more individuals is more desirable than a political system with less participation.

Civic republicanism is not obviously desirable from the perspective of law and economics. Granted, civic republicanism, by inducing more participation and better decision making, may produce better policies. That improvement, however, does not justify it. From the perspective of law and economics, citizens would recognize the improvement and choose to participate by the ideal amount. If individuals gauge accurately the potential gains from participating in the deliberation, they would participate the ideal amount. No inducement to participate in additional deliberations would be justified, because the additional participation would be undesirable. Forced participation is undesirable and paternalistic.

One way to support civic republicanism would be to show that the decision of citizens to participate is systematically biased. The proof that citizens participate in less than optimal numbers allows the conclusion that more participation is desirable, in accord with civic republicanism. A comparison of two types of arguments showing inadequate participation is instructive.

Consider the argument that citizens underestimate the value of the future improvements that their participation would bring. This is

---

[2] See, for example, Iseult Honohan, *Civic Republicanism* (New York: Routledge, 2002); Adrian Oldfield, *Citizenship and Community: Civic Republicanism and the Modern World* (New York: Routledge, 1990). Numerous contemporary leading scholars in the legal academy take positions near civic republicanism, see, for example, Bruce A. Ackerman, "Constitutional Politics, Constitutional Law," *Yale Law Journal* 99 (1989):453; Frank Michelman, "Bringing Law to Life: A Plea for Disenchantment," *Cornell Law Review* 74 (1989):256; Cass R. Sunstein, "Preferences and Politics," *Philosophy & Public Affairs* 20 (1991):3.

logically plausible insofar as demonstrating insufficient participation. However, an argument based on systematic errors entails an element of contradiction because it distrusts the reasoning of the citizens whose deliberation improves political decisions.

The second argument builds on the idea that political participation entails a collective action problem. The benefits of better government are shared. Each citizen who deliberates bears the full cost of the time the deliberation consumes. Each citizen would prefer to enjoy the benefits of good government while others bear the cost of deliberation. This gives each citizen an incentive to take a free ride on the effort of others. This functions as a tendency toward inadequate political participation, again justifying the incentive in favor of participation that civic republicanism advocates.

The first argument rested on systematic errors. The second started from the self-interested individual's reaction to the setting. Individuals do make errors, even systematic ones, but rarely does it seem appropriate to start with the assumption that decisions are false. When the premise is systematic error, the argument becomes stronger if evidence of the error exists. In the absence of evidence, a law-and-economics scholar would gravitate toward the second argument, because it is founded on correct decisions.

iv. Perfectionism

Perfectionism argues that the government should provide services that improve qualitatively the welfare of its citizens.[3] Examples of governmental activity that fit the thesis of perfectionism are public education and the subsidization of the arts. Perfectionism is similar to civic republicanism in advocating activity that individuals would not otherwise undertake. Therefore, the comparison of perfectionism with the goal of maximizing social welfare follows a similar dialectic. When the advocate of perfectionism recommends more schooling or museum subsidies, the sceptic responds by asking why individuals would not purchase the additional education or not buy museum tickets at non-subsidized prices. The advocate of perfectionism would fall back to arguing that individuals underestimate the gains from education and

---

[3] See, for example, George Sher, *Beyond Neutrality: Perfectionism and Politics* (Cambridge: Cambridge University Press, 1997); Thomas Hurka, *Perfectionism* (Oxford: Oxford University Press, 1993).

culture and that the ideal amount of education and culture would only be attainable with a governmental subsidy.

Perfectionism has the appeal of agreeing with the nearly universal practice of subsidized education. The nature of education seems to validate this. Students cannot know what benefits they would derive from the additional skills they would learn. A small adjustment adapts the same argument to cultural learning. The gain from the cultural experience is unknown to the potential museum patron or, generally, to the potential consumer of cultural activity.

This discussion was a brief juxtaposition of political theories with the analysis of law and economics based on social welfare. Both civic republicanism and perfectionism begin by identifying a desirable political arrangement, more participation, more education and culture. From the perspective of law and economics, the desirability of deliberation and education does not directly justify public policy because individuals have the capacity to pursue what they find desirable. To justify policy, an argument must persuade that individuals fail to take the desirable action.

B. VOTING SYSTEM DESIGN

The previous paragraphs looked at political theory from the perspective of the ideal of welfare maximization of economic analysis of law. Although political theories such as civic republicanism and perfectionism were found to have some differences but also to be reconcilable with welfare maximization, majority rule was clearly rejected as mechanism for making decisions. The rejection of the dominant method of political decision making begs the question of how the economic analysis of law can improve majority rule.

From the perspective of law and economics, the ideal toward which the design of voting systems strives is the emulation of the choices in markets. Because goods have prices, buyers' decisions are very nuanced. Prices allow the intensity of preferences to shape decisions. The price system can allocate finite product to the buyers with the most intense desire for the product, particularly if opportunities to create wealth are truly equal.[4] The reflection of intensity of demand in prices

---

[4] The price system also favors the rich. If everyone started life with identical resources, then the bias in favor of the rich would actually be a bias in favor of those who produce more. To the extent that society chooses not to eliminate wealth discrepancies to preserve incentives for work and entrepreneurial risk taking, the discriminatory effect of the price system is a reflection of those incentives for productivity.

stands in contrast to the defect of majority rule, the equal weight of each vote regardless of the intensity of each voter's preference.

The most notable improvement from majority rule was a proposal by Borda to the French Academy in 1770.[5] The Borda ballot requires voters to rank the candidates or proposals, assigning zero points to the least desirable candidate and proceeding all the way to the most strongly desired candidate who would receive a number equal to the number of candidates on the ballot minus one.[6] The count adds the points each ballot gave to each candidate and the winner is the candidate with the greatest score. Ties can be resolved by simulating a runoff between the tied candidates, with no need for a new round of voting.

An example of the Borda count: Suppose the electorate consists of 30 voters and the candidates are three, Yoda, Obi-Wan, and Qui-Gon. Each candidate is supported by a third of the voters. The second choice of Yoda's fans is Obi-Wan, and the second choice of Obi-Wan's fans is Qui-Gon, but Qui-Gon's fans divide in their second choice, with eight favoring Yoda and the rest favoring Obi-Wan. Therefore, the ballots take four forms. The ten fans of Yoda cast ballots of "Yoda: 2; Obi-Wan: 1; Qui-Gon: 0." Obi-Wan's ten fans vote "Obi-Wan: 2; Qui-Gon: 1; Yoda: 0." The eight fans of Qui-Gon whose alternative is Yoda vote "Qui-Gon: 2; Yoda: 1; Obi-Wan: 0" and the remaining two vote "Qui-Gon: 2; Obi-Wan: 1; Yoda: 0."

The candidates' Borda score is the aggregation of all the ballots' numbers. The Borda score for Yoda is calculated by adding the ten votes of two points from his fans, plus Obi-Wan's fans' ten votes of zero points, plus Qui-Gon's fans' votes, which are split into eight votes of one point, and two votes of zero points, which produces a score of 28 ($28 = 10 \times 2 + 10 \times 0 + 8 \times 1 + 2 \times 0$). The same process reveals

---

The law-and-economics approach to the very complex issues of egalitarianism, redistribution, and taxation is discussed in Chapter 4.

[5] See, Peyton Young, "Optimal Voting Rules," *Journal of Economic Perspectives* 9 (1995):55–6; see also, for example, Duncan Black, *The Theory of Committees and Elections* (Cambridge: Cambridge University Press, 1958):61–4, 156–9, 178–80; Peter C. Ordeshook, *Game Theory and Political Theory: An Introduction* (Cambridge: Cambridge University Press, 1986):68; see also Eric J. Gouvin, "Truth in Savings and the Failure of Legislative Methodology," *University of Cincinnati Law Review* 62 (1994):1346 n. 233.

[6] The number of points given to the least-preferred candidate is not important provided all ballots use the same numbers and the increments are equal. An election with three candidates would produce the same winner by using the Borda count even if the ballots gave 1–2–3 as points, same if 10–20–30 or 137–138–139.

Table 3.1. *An example of voting using Borda's method*

	Voters' ranking				
	Y>O>Q	O>Q>Y	Q>Y>O	Q>O>Y	
Per ballot for Y	2	0	1	0	
Per ballot for O	1	2	0	1	
Per ballot for Q	0	1	2	2	
Voters in group	10	10	8	2	**Borda scores**
Group for Y	20	0	8	0	28 for Y
Group for O	10	20	0	2	32 for O
Group for Q	0	10	16	4	30 for Q

Obi-Wan receives 32, and Qui-Gon receives 30. The winner is Obi-Wan. A tie would be very unlikely and would not require a runoff election. If the vote were different so that Obi-Wan and Qui-Gon were tied, a study of the ballots would reveal who would have prevailed in a simulated election between only the tied candidates.

The example may be seen more clearly in Table 3.1. The four columns correspond to the four types of ballots cast, that is, the four groups of voters. The ranking of the candidates by each group of voters is shown by their initials in the header row, so that Y > O > Q indicates Yoda's fans whose second choice is Obi-Wan and third choice is Qui-Gon. The first three rows indicate the score that each ballot assigns to each candidate. The next row has the number of voters in each group. The last three rows indicate the total score that the voters of each column contribute to each candidate. Each entry is the product of each ballot's points multiplied by the number of voters in the group. Adding those scores across all four groups produces each candidate's Borda score, which is displayed at the rightmost column.

The Borda method leads to a victory by Obi-Wan. Obi-Wan wins because he is the second choice of a plurality of the voters, ten of Yoda and two of Qui-Gon. Qui-Gon is the second choice of only Obi-Wan's ten voters, and Yoda is the second choice of only eight of Qui-Gon's voters. Despite that first choices are split equally, the Borda count reveals a preference for Obi-Wan. This partly overcomes the weakness of majority voting of ignoring the intensity of preferences. If the minority's first choice is also the second choice of the majority while the minority ranks low the majority's favorite, a minority candidate may win.

The Borda method also resolves the cycling problem that is part of Arrow's impossibility theorem. Recall that the above-mentioned ranking of voter preferences would exhibit cycling in a majority vote. After a first round of voting with no winner, every candidate could win a second round if the right candidate were eliminated.

Borda's method has two failings. It measures imperfectly the intensity of preferences and it is susceptible to manipulation by the addition of alternatives.

The Borda method accounts imperfectly for the intensity of preferences because it predetermines the weights that correspond to each ranking of candidates. Voters may evaluate the alternative outcomes in different ways. Some voters may be nearly indifferent between candidates, whereas others would be devastated by a loss of their favorite candidate. Nevertheless, the effect of their votes under the Borda count is the same. From this perspective, the Borda count creates an arbitrary weighting of preferences. Election outcomes would differ if these values were 10, 7, and 0, or 100, 99, and −1.

The Borda method is susceptible to manipulation by the addition of irrelevant alternatives on the ballot because that addition changes the number of candidates and the weighting of the votes. Add Mace Windu as a fourth candidate to the preceding example. Mace Windu is the least preferred candidate for all voters except three of the eight Qui-Gon fans who had Yoda as their second choice. For those three, Mace Windu is the third rather than the last choice. The new ballots give scores of 3, 2, 1, and 0 to the four candidates. Tallying the results reveals that Qui-Gon defeats Obi-Wan.[7] The addition of the irrelevant candidate did change the result.

---

[7] The scores are Yoda 58, Obi-Wan 59, Qui-Gon 60, and Mace Windu 3. The following table illustrates the same method as Table 3.1, omitting the first panel with the votes per ballot:

	Voters' ranking					
	Y>O>Q>M	O>Q>Y>M	Q>Y>O>M	Q>Y>M>O	Q>O>Y>M	
Voters in group	10	10	5	3	2	Borda scores
Group for Y	30	10	10	6	2	58 for Y
Group for O	20	30	5	0	4	59 for O
Group for Q	10	20	15	9	6	60 for Q
Group for M	0	0	0	3	0	3 for M

A recent proposal tries to improve voting by combining it with the payment of a price or tax. With the intention of simulating the price system, the proposal tries to obtain information akin to a bid from the voters. Voters must bid for their favorite alternative; ballots state how much the voter is willing to pay for this proposal to win. A leading version of voting by bids, known as the demand-revealing process or Clarke tax, was offered by Tideman and Tullock.[8] Its advantage is that the payment is conditional and may even be rare. This is a major administrative simplification compared with a strict Clarke tax that would be payable with every ballot.

The demand-revealing process compares the total valuation that the votes for each proposal indicate and selects the one that is valued most. Therefore, a proposal supported by large bids by a minority may win over a proposal that the majority supported with small bids.

A central test for understanding the demand-revealing process is whether a vote changes the winner of the election. A vote changes the winner if without that vote the winner would be different. Proposals that win by a large margin and are supported by a large majority of small bids would typically not have outcome-changing votes, because no single vote would make a difference. If no single vote changes the winner, then no voter makes a payment. If a vote does change the winner, then that voter makes a payment. The payment may be smaller than the bid of the ballot. The payment is only the amount that is necessary for changing the winner. An example might help and it brings back the setting of *Star Wars*.

The planet Tatooine is a famous stop in the pod-racing circuit but its existing pod-racing course is worn and outdated. A new pod-racing arena is proposed and the residents will decide by a vote. The alternative is an improved shield-power grid. Interplanetary tensions are rising and the defence of Tatooine requires it. Let us focus on the vote cast by the aggressive pod racer Sebulba. Sebulba's vote indicates a preference for the pod-racing arena by thirty intergalactic credits ($). Tallying the other ballots' bids shows a sum of $540 in favor of the arena and $560 in favor of the shield. Without Sebulba's vote, the shield would have won. Because Sebulba's vote changes the winner, Sebulba must make a payment. The valuation by other voters of the

---

[8] Nicolaus Tideman and Gordon Tullock, "A New and Superior Process for Making Social Choices," *Journal of Political Economy* 84 (1976):1145.

arena at ₡540 implies that it needs ₡20 to defeat the shield's valuation by its voters. Therefore, Sebulba's payment is ₡20.

Sebulba's rival on the pod-racing circuit, Anakin Skywalker, also votes in favor of the arena. Anakin indicates a willingness to pay up to ₡9 for the pod-racing arena. From Anakin's perspective, the sum of others's bids for the arena, including Sebulba's vote, is ₡561 (the ₡540 that were others' votes from Sebulba's perspective include Anakin's nine; ₡540 − 9 + 30 = 561, which is more than the ₡560 for the shield). Anakin's vote does not change the outcome and Anakin does not make a payment.

If Anakin were to increase his bid to ₡32, then Sebulba would not have to make a payment either, because Sebulba's vote is not necessary for the victory. Anakin's increased bid means that votes for the arena other than Sebulba's increase. Now, other votes for the arena are ₡563 (540 − 9 + 32 = 563). Sebulba's vote does not change the winner.

The demand-revealing process appears to overcome the problems of majority rule. The intensity of minority preferences is taken into account. This also eliminates cycling. The demand-revealing process also avoids the problems of the Borda voting that weights are not related to intensity of preferences and that irrelevant alternatives may alter the outcome. The advantage of this proposal is that it simulates the choices under the price system, because those who favor one outcome may be called to pay up to the amount that corresponds to their preference.

The demand-revealing process has different weaknesses. It is manipulable, it may not accurately reflect preferences, and it may be biased against less wealthy voters in an unacceptable way.

The demand-revealing process can be manipulated by coalitions of only two voters. Two voters can avoid the tax by ensuring that the vote of each does not change the outcome. They need only agree to vote in favor of the same proposal and indicate exorbitant preferences. Suppose Sebulba agrees with Anakin to cast ballots that indicate a ₡1,000,000 preference for the station. The valuation of each conspirator's vote swamps the difference between the projects according to the other voters. Either conspirator's vote can be removed without changing the outcome. Because neither vote changes the outcome, neither one pays the tax. This, of course, eliminates the credibility of the valuations.

The similarity of the demand-revealing process to the price system also makes it susceptible to wealth differences. Although the Clarke tax does not expressly disenfranchise the poor, it does diminish their voting power to only a fraction of the voting power of the wealthy. The wealthy may be willing to risk sizable amounts even on a weak preference, whereas the poor may only assign a small amount to their strongest preferences. This converts the Clarke tax proposal from a system that favors strong preferences to a system that favors strong wallets. Economists may not be very concerned about this because they accept the analogous power that the price system grants to the wealthy as a consequence of an inducement of productivity (see note 4). The application of this reasoning to political elections is likely disconcerting to legal and political scholars. The allocation of legislative and executive authority is quite different than the allocation of goods. When the industrious and the lucky individuals obtain legislative power, they have the ability to influence the rules of the game. Economic reasoning suggests that they will ensure that they keep winning.

The experience with the design of voting systems validates the name of Arrow's impossibility theorem. The design of a perfect voting system does appear impossible. Indeed, the more recent research implicitly concedes that the ideal system is unattainable by having its contribution be the frequency with which a system produces the correct results.[9] In other words, Arrow's impossibility still holds and no voting system can overcome it and be perfect. A voting system's superiority lies in that it minimizes the instances where it fails.

The application of economic principles to political issues has developed into a discipline called *public choice*. The demand-revealing process is an example of the contemporary scholarship categorized under that heading. To a significant extent, the problems that public choice examines are caused by the difficulty of group activity, or collective action. A breakthrough for the analysis of collective action has been the development of game theory.

C. GAME THEORY

Collective-action problems tend to be analyzed by using the methods of game theory. The principal idea of game theory is that a single player can often predict the choice of the other side, which simplifies

---

[9]   See, for example, Partha Dasgupta and Eric S. Maskin, Efficient Auctions, *Quarterly Journal of Economics* 115 (2000):341. They also offer a lay version of their analysis, Partha Dasgupta and Eric Maskin, "The Fairest Vote of All," *Scientific American*, March 2004, 92.

the player's choice. The player makes the best choice given that the opponent makes the best choice. It is possible that this pair of choices (which in the language of game theory are *strategies*) gives neither party an incentive to switch to a different one. If so, the pair of strategies is stable and forms a *Nash equilibrium*. In the language of game theory, the determined strategies are called "pure" so the stable result of the game is also a "pure strategy equilibrium."

If either party has an incentive to deviate, then it appears that the game does not have a predictable or stable outcome. If the same parties played the game repeatedly, they would change strategies. Game theory overcomes this indeterminacy by letting the players choose probabilistic strategies that define the distribution of choices. A player may have a strategy of playing "cooperate" with 75 percent probability and playing "defect" with 25 percent probability. The result is that the opponent's expected results are blends of the nominal results, weighed by probabilities. Because this probabilistic approach produces a mixed result, the language of game theory calls it a "mixed strategy." If a mixed strategy induces a constant response, pure or mixed, and neither side prefers a change, the result is a "mixed-strategy equilibrium."

Game theory studies the result of stylized games where two individuals – occasionally more – choose their actions while recognizing the importance of the other players' choices. The available actions tend to come from a narrow set of only a handful of actions. The recognition of the importance of other players' actions makes information about those actions a crucial component of the specification of the game.

Game theory uses numerous variations of games. Two types of games have found legal applications. Those two principal types of games are called "pure-motive" games, because each player has a single motive. The two pure-motive games are named according to the challenge they pose to the players. One is the "cooperation" game, and the second is the "coordination" game.

i. Cooperation Games: Prisoner's Dilemma

The game that has found most application in legal analysis is the cooperation game. The leading example is the prisoner's dilemma (Table 3.2). The prosecutor gives two isolated prisoners a bargain. If one confesses, that one will receive a reward, but if both confess, they receive mere leniency. The result is that each prisoner also knows the consequences of both confessing, both not confessing, only the other confessing, and

Table 3.2. *The prisoner's dilemma, in standard form*

		Column prisoner	
		Confession	No confession
Row prisoner	Confession	lenient, lenient −100, −100	reward, heavy 50, −500
	No confession	heavy, reward −500, 50	no conviction, no conviction 0, 0

only the other not confessing. If they both confess, then both receive lenient sentences. If both do not confess, then the prosecution will (or may) be unable to convict either. If only the other confesses, then the other receives the reward and our prisoner receives the heavy sentence. Vice versa, if only our prisoner confesses, then the other receives the heavy sentence and our prisoner receives the reward.

Obviously, the description of the game is overly complex. Game theory illustrates such simple games in a table that shows player choices and consequences. One player's choice is the row and the other player's choice is the column. In this setting where each player has two possible actions, confess or not, the resulting table is a two-by-two matrix of four cells. Each cell contains two numbers, the outcome or payoff for each player. This representation is called the "standard form" of the game.

Thus, the standard form of the prisoner's dilemma has cells composed of the four possible outcomes: reward, no conviction, lenient punishment, and heavy sentence. It becomes more vivid if we assign values to the outcomes. For example, the reward is $50, lenient punishment is a fine of $100, and heavy punishment is a fine of $500.

The best outcome for the players jointly is for neither to confess. Yet, the self-interest of each prisoner suggests a different action. If the other is silent, our prisoner can do better by confessing to receive the reward. Yet, if each follows his self-interest they both confess and receive punishment, albeit lenient. They fare worse by following their self-interest.

This paradox of the prisoner's dilemma is overcome if they credibly commit not to confess. The prisoner's self-interest argues against believing a statement by the other because of the other's incentive to deviate. Therefore, an external mechanism that creates a credible commitment is necessary. Consider the creation of an authority that imposes large penalties for breaking promises. As soon as one player promises not to confess, then the other no longer has any reason to fear that the first may deviate on the basis of self-interest. Scholars consider that contract law serves as a mechanism that produces credible commitment.

Environmental problems are also attributed to collective action. Each potential polluter bears in full the cost of proper disposal or of cleaning emissions, but the benefit of a clean environment accrues to all members of society.

Collective-action problems abound and attempts to overcome them explain several legal arrangements. Controlled oil extraction and fishing are such examples. The common pool of oil or fish is preserved by the efforts of those who comply, whereas violators seek to take advantage of the preserved pool. The system of the Federal Deposit Insurance Corporation that insures deposits at banks seeks to stave off a collective-action problem known as a "run on the bank." Depositors, worried about the solvency of the bank that holds their savings, run to withdraw them before the bank's funds are exhausted. The ensuing self-fulfilling prophesy is captured in a scene of the film "It's a Wonderful World." Jimmy Stewart, playing the nice local banker, explains to depositors that the money of each is secured by the property of other depositors. More withdrawals by depositors would lead to foreclosure sales, which would lead to a reduced valuation of the collateral and would further worsen the appearance of insolvency. Much of bankruptcy law is explained as an effort to prevent the same problem that is created when lenders fear that a borrower may fail and each lender races to get liquid assets, eliminating the borrower's ability to overcome the financial difficulty.[10]

An acute collective-action problem appears when the acquisition of the information that is necessary to make a decision is costly. The correct decision will produce a benefit, but a shared one. This raises the possibility that no single voter's share of the benefit exceeds the cost of becoming informed, with the result that no voter is informed

---

[10] The authors that trumpeted collective-action problems as the leading justification of bankruptcy law are Thomas Jackson and Douglas Baird. Jackson, *The Logic and Limits of Bankruptcy Law* (Cambridge, MA: Harvard University Press, 1986) (hereinafter *Logic and Limits of Bankruptcy*); Douglas G. Baird, *The Elements of Bankruptcy* (Westbury, NY: Foundation Press, 1992) (hereinafter *Elements of Bankruptcy*). A more recent position sees this collective-action problem as just one of numerous threats that insolvency and its fear place on productivity. See Nicholas Georgakopoulos, "Bankruptcy for Productivity," *Wake Forest Law Review* 37 (2002):51.

and the correct decision cannot be made. Again, several institutional and legal arrangements are explained as trying to avoid this collective-action problem. The creation of groups for obtaining costly information may be part of the function of rating agencies, labor unions, and corporate disclosure obligations.[11] Rating agencies assess the risk that corporations will default on their obligations to investors and assign a rating that conveys their assessment of that risk. The disclosure that securities laws impose on corporations transmits information to their shareholders to enable them to choose how to vote.[12] When labor unions negotiate wages with the employer, their demands and negotiating position depend on their perception of the employer's profitability. Neither individual investors nor individual employees could afford to look closely into the finances of vastly complex organizations.

Markets can also provide solutions to collective-action problems, weakening the argument for a legal response. Examples are the sale of information, such as that offered by the magazine *Consumer Reports* or by travel guidebooks. The publisher buys the many competing products or services, subjects them to tests, and communicates the results to the subscribers to its magazines or the buyers of its reports. Travel guidebooks test the lodging and eating accommodations of competing establishments and compare them for travelers. No individual consumer or traveler could afford to obtain this information.

ii. Coordination Games: Driving Side

The leading application of coordination games in legal scholarship is the role of legal institutions in establishing norms for coordination. The main example from game theory is the stag hunt, but the leading illustration in legal scholarship is on which side of the road to drive. Drivers do not care about the choice and are equally happy driving on the left (as in the United Kingdom and Japan, for example) as on the right (as in the Americas and continental Europe, for example). Drivers care

---

[11] Disclosure obligations also induce the provision of extra information, favoring frequent traders and fostering liquidity, see Nicholas L. Georgakopoulos, "Why Should Disclosure Rules Subsidize Informed Traders?" *International Review of Law & Economics* 16 (1996):417 (hereinafter "Disclosure Rules").

[12] See, for example, William Carney, "Fundamental Corporate Changes, Minority Shareholders, and Business Purposes," *American Bar Foundation Research Journal* (1980):69.

Table 3.3. *The choice of driving side, in standard form*

		Coming driver	
		Left side	**Right side**
Going driver	**Left side**	safe, safe 100, 100	collide, collide −100, −100
	Right side	collide, collide −100, −100	safe, safe 100, 100

strongly, however, about coordinating with drivers coming from the opposite direction. To avoid frontal collisions, drivers of both directions must drive on their left side or both on their right. The outcome of coordination is safe arrival. The outcome of driving on opposite sides is frontal collision. The standard form of the game, displayed in Table 3.3, uses a gain of 100 for safe arrival and a loss of 100 for frontal collision. The drivers of the two directions are "Coming Driver" and "Going Driver."

The best outcome is to coordinate. The paradox is that both drivers are indifferent about their choice and care only about coordination. Thus, coordination games only pose a problem if the drivers do not know the side on which the other will drive and cannot communicate. Unlike cooperation games, like the prisoners' dilemma, the two players do not need a commitment mechanism, because neither has an incentive to deviate from the announced conduct. The players need only a pre-announcement mechanism.

The need for a pre-announcement mechanism is surprisingly interesting. Social, economic, and technological evolution lead to new settings where coordination is the problem. A rule or agreement about any specific coordination problem is useless for the future coordination problems. For example, the rule about driving sides did not help the choice of computer communications protocol. Rather, a systematic solution to coordination problems must have the dynamic nature of being able to solve future coordination problems.

iii. Game Theory in Legal Scholarship

The main challenges of applying game theory in legal scholarship tend to be two. The first challenge is to fit the complexities of actual interactions to the simplified games that game theory handles. The second is to propose the rules or interpretations that prevent the undesirable outcomes. Neither one is unique to game theory.

Most applications use the prisoner's dilemma and cooperation games. One of the concluding exercises asks for justifications of contract law, bankruptcy law, and international restrictions about fishing on the basis of game theory.

A more surprising application of game theory is in norms and bounded rationality, which are the subject of more extensive discussions later in this chapter. A recent interesting application serves as a brief diversion. The expressive functions of the law have been supported by analysis using cooperation games.

The application of coordination games to law begins with the identification of a real-life setting and the demonstation that it is analogous to a coordination game. Richard McAdams examines litigation versus mediation and analogizes it with hawk-dove, a game that has a feature of coordination games. Going through trial is a very costly proposition for the litigants. Nevertheless, neither litigant is willing to appear conciliatory. That would be similar to playing "dove" opposite "hawk" and handing the gains from the agreement to the opponent. Game theory does not offer a way out of this setting, where the litigants' unwillingness to compromise makes them unable to avoid the litigation expenses.

Previous research that sought to evaluate mediation found it wasteful. The premise of that analysis was the absence of a common ground for settlement. If the parties agreed about the probabilities of trial outcomes, then they would settle at the expected outcome. Adding risk aversion would suggest a range of possible settlements. Because they have not settled, the premise is absent; both litigants estimate the expected trial outcome in their favor. Against those inferred beliefs, when the mediator proposes a settlement, one party views it as inferior to trial and rejects the settlement. Therefore, the non-binding nature of the mediation makes it a futile step.

The analysis of Prof. McAdams proposes to evaluate mediation against the background of game theory. The litigants' resistance to a settlement pushes them to action that would hurt both, that is, places them in a setting analogous to a prisoner's dilemma. The mediator's role is to signal strongly what the trial outcome would be and make the litigants realize that insisting on trial is nothing but a waste of litigation expenses. Effectively, the mediator converts the game back to hawk-dove and prevents the outcome of hawk-against-dove.

D. Social Norms

Related is the recent exploration in the field of social norms, although part of it belongs with bounded rationality in the next sub-section. Social norms are informal rules of conduct that are sufficiently strong as to be binding or nearly so. Law and economics is concerned about norms for many reasons, including that social norms may be the environment in which legal rules operate, that they may interfere with the incentives that the legal system seeks to create, and that the legal environment may have the capacity to influence them, opening a new avenue for, hopefully, beneficial consequences of law design. Studying norm creation and ways to change norms to improve social welfare is part of the realization that the world is more complex than the black box of perfect markets. Not only are markets complex and imperfect, but the web of rules to which individuals are subject is also more complex than older law and economics assumed, because of social norms.

An example from the effort against school gangs will illustrate the interaction of economic analysis of law and social norms. Innercity schools plagued by students' gang participation were seeking ways to combat it. Gang members would bring guns to school and brandish them at other students, thus gaining status and machismo for themselves. The gang would also benefit from this, because membership in it confirmed status which, in turn, not only attracted membership, but also provoked similar or escalating displays of machismo from rival gangs.

Conventional law and economics analysis would approach the gun-display problem as one of intensity, concluding that the prohibitions against firearms did not work because the incentives for compliance that they created on their subjects, the gang members, were not strong enough. The way to increase the intensity of a prohibition would be to increase penalties and enforcement, producing a greater expected penalty. Escalating penalties and enforcement may also increase the machismo involved in brandishing a gun and the associated benefit from the offence.

A slight twist, however, made a great difference. In the schools of Charleston, South Carolina, the enactment of a reward for turning in a gun-carrying student was surprisingly effective.[13] The reward breaks

---

[13] Dan M. Kahan, "Social Influence, Social Meaning, and Deterrence," *Virginia Law Review* 83 (1997):364 and n. 62, 63.

the vicious cycle of displays of gang machismo. Instead of the display showing bravado, it was likely to lead to apprehension. With the display gone, also gone are the machismo and the attractiveness of the gang.

The success of the norm-breaking rule is striking. Understanding its function is valuable because its success can be extended to other similar problems. One can think of gang activity outside schools, but also other problems that stem from youth machismo. Such problems may include speeding or aversion to condom use. Variations of this analysis may be effective in such settings. Perhaps the success of this measure suggests experimentation with measures such as rewarding passengers who turn in speeders or the development of a norm rewarding condom users in high-risk communities.

This example, however, also illustrates the limitations of norm analysis. The fortuitous solution to the gang-bravado problem was not the result of theoretical inquiry into norms but of the local authorities' practical ingenuity that was likely ignorant of norms. The legal analysis of norms only provides an explanation for the measure's success, and an explanation that is speculative and unproven, and which may not operate in other settings. The level of surrounding wealth may interfere with the potency of the threat of being turned in, and norms against ratting or against cooperating with or even trusting the police may also change the rule's effect. An environment may exist where the rule might have the opposite of the intended effects, where bystanders fear turning the offender in to the authorities and the display of bravado, thus, gains further in machismo. The complexity of norms means that norm-based explanations have a post hoc character and that the normative value of their applications is still rudimentary.

Despite all these shortcomings, the analysis of norms might yet bear fruit. Eric Posner, continuing the family tradition of faith in individual rationality set by his father Richard, studies norms as products of a rational society and explains them by using game theoretical analysis of signals. His analysis explains how patriotic rituals may function, rituals that range from saluting the flag to not questioning government propaganda to the escalation of McCarthyism and ethnic warfare against minorities, such as Jews in Nazi Germany or Serbs in Bosnia.

Eric Posner sets up a game where individuals of two types, trustworthy about their devotion to the nation and not trustworthy, seek to signal their trustworthiness and obtain the corresponding benefits. Under some circumstances, such as a national fear of, or aversion to, an outside entity, the result is strong signals and polarization. Using

McCarthyism as the example, Eric Posner suggests that fear of the Soviet Union and evidence of its spying led people to choose to signal their national pride by ostracizing Communists.

The signaling model for social norms is appealing because it restores faith in rationality that the preoccupation with norms might have eroded. Those mass hysterias may be explainable in rational terms. As Posner indicates, however, the sociopolitical environment is too complex for normative recommendations with predictable consequences. The main normative proposal is a general support for constitutional protections that help individuals who might try to break such escalating signaling games. Concrete proposals are only a hoped-for fruit from future advances of this methodology.

E. BOUNDED RATIONALITY

One more branch of law and economics that uses methods of game theory is the analysis of bounded rationality. Traditional economic analysis assumed the parties had complete information and could determine the optimal action. Voluminous psychological evidence suggests that individuals make systematic errors and do not take into account all available information.[14] Given the phenomenon of bounded rationality, legal scholars study how the legal system should react. Perhaps the law could attempt to help individuals overcome such errors. Otherwise, the law could shield and protect individuals from their errors. These two vastly different approaches are worth illustrating.

The example of a proposal designed to help overcome imperfect reasoning comes from my work on the disclosure obligations that the securities laws impose.[15] Disclosure obligations were a paradox because under assumptions of perfect rationality no need arises for disclosure obligations. Firms disclose voluntarily all information that the securities markets find valuable. The conventional explanation for this universal voluntary disclosure is that traders penalize silent firms by assuming they face average prospects and news. In such a pricing environment, however, firms with expectations that are above average will state this to investors to reap the benefit of higher prices. When all

---

[14] See, in general, Daniel Kahneman, Paul Slovic, and Amos Tversky, *Judgment under Uncertainty: Heuristics and Biases* (Cambridge: Cambridge University Press, 1982) (hereinafter *Judgment under Uncertainty*).
[15] Georgakopoulos, "Disclosure Rules" 417.

(or even only many) of the firms with above-average news do disclose, the averaging unravels. Investors adjust their expectations of news to the new below-average aggregation. A new layer of firms is led to disclose their information, until only the very worst are left silent. That no empirical evidence supported this proposition was problematic, but its supporters could argue that because disclosure was mandated, the setting for voluntary disclosure did not arise.

This peculiar paradox of voluntary disclosure unravels when the assumption of perfectly rational investors is abandoned. From various directions in the finance literature, it became clear that erring traders could survive, some prices could be false, and some firms might not feel any pressure to disclose.[16] Erroneous prices, however, are not enough to justify mandated disclosure. After all, market professionals may be able to obtain the same information themselves. Then, disclosure rules appear as a subsidy to those traders, as they no longer need to search for their information. This subsidy seems even more puzzling.

The puzzle's answer lies in erring investors. Investors are often wrong about valuations of corporations. Having a few better-informed professionals is insufficient because an uncompetitive group of informed traders will let prices fluctuate away from accurate valuation to extract profits. The role of disclosure rules is to disillusion erring traders and to increase the ranks and competitiveness of the informed

---

[16] J. Bradford De Long, Andrei Shleifer, Lawrence H. Summers, and Robert J. Waldman, "The Survival of Noise Traders in Financial Markets," *Journal of Business* 64 (1991):1 *et seq.*; J. Bradford De Long, Andrei Shleifer, Lawrence H. Summers, and Robert J. Waldman, "Positive Feedback Investment Strategies and Destabilizing Rational Speculation," *Journal of Finance* 45 (1990):379 *et seq.*; J. Bradford De Long, Andrei Shleifer, Lawrence H. Summers, and Robert J. Waldman, "Speculative Dynamics and the Role of Feedback Traders," *American Economic Review* 80 (1990):63 *et seq.*; J. Bradford De Long, Andrei Shleifer, Lawrence H. Summers, and Robert J. Waldman, "Noise trader risk in financial markets," *Journal of Political Economy* 98 (1990):703 *et seq.*; Andrei Shleifer, *Inefficient Markets: An Introduction to Behavioral Finance* (Oxford, New York: Oxford University Press, 2000); Andrei Shleifer and Robert W. Vishny, "The Limits of Arbitrage," *Journal of Finance* 52, no. 1 (1997):35; Kenneth A. Froot and Maurice Obstfeld, "Intrinsic bubbles: The Case of Stock Prices," *American Economic Review* 81, no. 5 (1991):1189; Rappaport and White, "Was There a Bubble in the 1929 Stock Market?," *The Journal of Economic History* 53, no. 3 (1993):549; Andrei Shleifer and Robert W. Vishny, "Equilibrium Short Horizons of Investors and Firms," *American Economic Review* 80 (1990):148; Fisher Black, "An Equilibrium Model of the Crash," *NBER Macroeconomics Annual* 3 (1988):269; John Haltiwanger and Michael Waldman, "Rational Expectations and the Limits of Rationality: An Analysis of Heterogeneity," *American Economic Review* 75 (1985):327; Christopher P. Chamley, *Rational Herds* (Cambridge: Cambridge University Press, 2004): 315–57.

traders whose trading can prevent false prices. Thus, disclosure rules are a subsidy to informed traders, but a subsidy that is desirable because it improves the accuracy of market prices and protects uninformed investors from trading at false prices.

The rules on the labeling of food products and nutritional supplements can be justified on similar grounds. Consumers can establish the composition of the foods and can make correct nutritional decisions. Labels facilitate this process, subsidizing correct nutrition. Labeling also makes the information that different producers provide comparable, thus producing an external benefit (one that also drives uniform rules on corporate accounting) that individual producers would not provide, even if they were induced by the market to provide nutritional information.

These approaches, rather than protecting individuals from the consequences of their errors of cognition, seek to help individuals (or the markets) overcome the errors. A different approach is for the legal system to attempt to prevent the harm due to irrationalities from occurring. The legal system can also answer the problems of bounded rationality with benign paternalism.

An example of a provision possibly designed to prevent harm from systematic errors is the limitation of the ability to incur gambling debts. Gambling debts are invalid in several legal systems, usually because they are considered immoral, but they are also under express prohibitions.[17] The discomfort toward gambling debts or their immorality may be related to a defect of reasoning or, to use economic jargon, to bounded rationality. From the perspective of a scientific approach to law, however, the term "immorality" is vacuous. If individuals enjoy gambling, the rules that restrict that enjoyment need concrete justification.

The limitation of the ability to incur gambling debts can be considered to address the systematic error of over-optimism. Individuals borrow to gamble, falsely overestimating their probability of success. Over-optimism drives a destructive vicious cycle of losing, borrowing, and losing.

---

[17] In the United States courts have refused to enforce wagers with the belief that gambling was "thought to encourage shiftlessness, poverty, and immorality."

See E. Allan Farnsworth, *Contracts*, 2nd ed. (Boston: Little Brown, 1990): §5.2 n. 4. For an express prohibition see, for example, § 844 A.K. (Civil Code of Greece; "No obligation is incurred from game or gamble.")

From a perspective of perfect rationality, of course, the prohibition against gambling debts – and gambling – makes no sense. Because it is a voluntary exchange, both sides must experience gain. The gain of the casino or the superior gambler is obvious, it is a probabilistic gain. Although a particular gamble may result in a loss, over the long term, performance is determined by averages and the probabilistic gain will become a real gain.

The rational gain for the disadvantaged side may be less tangible but can be equally real. Many rational people visit casinos and bet in games of pure luck, that is, games with no strategic input allowing the player to improve the odds. The value of such gambling is that it provides entertainment. Because running casinos does not provide any other side benefit to society, the entertainment that gambling produces is the sum of its contribution to social welfare.

Thus, from a *laissez-faire* perspective, impeding contracting about gambling impedes the creation of social welfare in the form of entertainment. Moreover, from the perspective of the able gambler in a game with some skill, the same impediment prevents the full exploitation of this skill. Because most other skills are exploitable, the impediments against gambling that the legal system erects appear to create an expropriation of this skill. Systematic errors answer both these points.

First, the entertainment value that gambling produces is real, but due to over-optimism, some consumers underestimate its price. Thus, they are led to pay more in the form of gambling losses than the value of the entertainment they receive, making gambling a welfare-reducing arrangement. An example should make this point obvious. Suppose the casino has a probability of 55 percent of winning each game, whereas the player due to over-optimism calculates that as being only 51 percent. Betting 10 each time and playing 100 games in an hour, the player expects to lose 51 and win 49 for a net loss of 2 games or 20 per hour. The reality, however, is one where the casino wins 55 and the player 45, for a net loss of 10 games or 100 per hour. A consumer who would not pay 50 for the enjoyment from each hour of gambling, influenced by over-optimism, will reach the false conclusion and spend time gambling.

The expropriation of gambling skill is not relevant from an economic perspective because it does not focus on the consumer and the surplus that the product (gambling) generates. The possibility for over-optimism plays only a secondary role in rebutting this argument.

Over-optimism implies that the gambling skill will be erroneously demanded and the impediment that the law creates against the able gambler is just a form, extreme perhaps, of consumer protection. From this perspective, gambling skill becomes equivalent to confidence art. That exploiting it is impeded is natural. Moreover, that some skills are rendered unexploitable by the legal system is a perfectly sound policy if we remember that equal distribution of wealth maximizes welfare and deviations from equality – the ability to exploit ones' abilities – are justified for the purpose of providing incentives for the creation of social welfare. Because gambling may actually reduce social welfare, gambling skill is justifiably not exploitable.

Modern financial markets have given rise to a phenomenon that underlines this point. This has arisen in the markets for options for individual stocks or indices. Options markets appear to be populated by ex-gamblers, top players of bridge, backgammon, and other games that stress skill in handling probabilities. Satisfying investor demand for options requires complex probability calculations. Investor demand is spread across options of different strike prices and different maturity dates. Options traders make the market – satisfy demand – by determining the probabilistic link of the various offers, strike prices and maturities. This is a skill very closely related to gambling, but it produces a benefit – satisfaction of investor demand – with little danger of false demand. When able gamblers are diverted from the casino tables to the option markets, not only do investors get the benefit of a more liquid options' market, but casual gamblers may also face better odds at the gambling tables and get their entertainment at a smaller cost.

These two approaches that the legal system may take with regard to systematic errors have a small but important difference. The first illustrates how the law may attempt to help individuals overcome their cognitive limitations, as it does by imposing corporate disclosure obligations. The second illustrates how the legal system may attempt to prevent individuals from committing errors, as it does with the various impediments to gambling. These two choices, however, are vastly different in the consequences that they have and the environment they create.

Insulating individuals from their errors stops the flow of information between the legal system and its subjects and removes the incentives that individuals would otherwise have to overcome their errors. In combination, these two consequences may create a third. No mechanism may exist to determine whether individuals can overcome the systematic error. Without such a mechanism, it may be impossible to conclude that the insulating rules are unnecessary. Finally, rules insulating from cognitive limitations may have an undesirable consequence in that the activities they induce in individuals who seek to circumvent the rule are more pernicious than the alternatives.

The flow of information from the application of the law to the decision of how to design the law is crucial. Law design must be informed about its consequences so that its effectiveness and desirability can be assessed. Indeed, much of the attraction of economic analysis of law lies in its allowing some quantification and empiricism. A significant fraction of law-and-economics scholarship is about the "efficiency of the common law." This controversial claim rests directly on the premise that the disputes that reach common law courts carry information about the quality of the law so that the exercise of judicial discretion has the consequence of improving the legal system.[18]

The importance of informing legal decision makers about the performance of the legal system is self-evident and does not depend on the correctness of the theory of the efficiency of the common law or of any other theory of how the legal decision makers use information to improve the legal system. The attractiveness of the efficiency of the common law is that it produces a hypothesis of legal improvement despite that judges may not try to improve the law. Unless legal decision makers are indifferent to the quality of the legal system, such a theory is not necessary. Hopefully, legal decision makers do try to improve the legal system and information about its performance is beneficial.

Rules that prevent the consequences of errors of cognition stop the production of information about this activity and its regulation. The elimination of the error prevents the legal decision makers from finding out whether the rule's benefits outweigh its costs. Compare the performance of a prohibition on gambling with a tax. Suppose that the tax counters individuals' over-optimism. If players think themselves 20 percent more likely to win than they really are, then a 20 percent

---

[18] See, for example, Eric A. Posner, "Law, Economics and Inefficient Norms," *University of Pennsylvania Law Review* 144 (1996): 1697; Gillian K. Hadfield, "Bias in the Evolution of Legal Rules," *Georgetown Law Journal* 80 (1992): 583; Todd J. Zywicki, "The Rise and Fall of Efficiency in Common Law: A Supply-Side Analysis," *Northwestern University Law Review* 97 (2003):1551; Richard A. Posner, *Economic Analysis of Law* 5th ed. (Cambridge, MA: Aspen Publishers, 1998).

tax would lead them to accurately value the cost of their gambling entertainment. The result would be that the consumption of gambling would be correct because its cost would not be underestimated.

Suppose now that the tax was set at a wrong level or that individuals' risk calculus either improved or deteriorated. The result would be a change in the demand for gambling that would not be satisfactory. If the tax were larger than consumers' underestimation of their expected losses, consumers would find the tax excessive, preventing accurately calculated gambling. If the tax were smaller than consumers' underestimation of their losses, consumers would find themselves gambling too much. In either case, a sensitive legal system can recognize its error, but this may not be possible with an outright prohibition. If the legal system eliminated borrowing for gambling, some gambling would be prevented. Setting aside the valid point that the gambling that is prevented may not be the gambling that should be prevented, let us focus on the information flow. How would the excess demand for gambling loans be noticed? It would not be noticed, because gamblers would simply use other borrowing to gamble. Consumer feedback in the form of demand for legislation is also less likely to appear if the prohibition is too weak. As no lending already occurs, a convenient proposal for a further restriction is not forthcoming.

The elimination of learning may be a more important defect than the lack of feedback to the lawmaker. Provisions that prevent individuals from their systematic errors produce an environment where overcoming these errors is irrelevant. As a result, individuals do not learn to cure their errors. Compare a disclosure regulation of gambling with the lending prevention. Those who are prevented from gambling because of the lending limitations have no incentives to overcome their cognitive errors. Those who are told that on average individuals underestimate their hourly losses by 20 percent are induced to improve both their play and the monitoring of their losses. An example using a gambling tax produces the same conclusion. Someone who manages to increase gambling ability will have a bigger reduction of losses under the tax than without the tax. An improvement of monitoring losses retains its beneficial effect. Those who realize that per hour of gambling they are losing 100 before tax, 120 after tax, may not need the protection of the tax, but they can use this information to make better decisions about their entertainment. The paternalistic elimination of the harm results in the predictable elimination of the incentive to overcome the error.

The combination of these two effects, the stop of the flow of information and the elimination of the incentive to learn, may produce a third consequence. The legal system does not discover the effect of the rule, individuals do not overcome their cognitive limitations, and the result may be immobilization of legal evolution. Even if the legal rule that protects from the consequences of cognitive errors is optimal at the time of its adoption, the dynamics of no feedback and no learning lead to no evolution.

Of course, the difficulty of evolution of paternalistic rules is not absolute. A good example of a paternalistic rule seeking to protect individuals from errors may be the prohibition era in U.S. history. The prohibition of all alcoholic drinks may be considered to address cognitive errors if we think that individuals lose their self-control as they drink, so that they over-consume a substance to harmful degrees. The prohibition removes the opportunity for individuals to commit this type of error.

The prohibition of alcoholic beverages was a characteristically paternalistic rule. The prohibition meant that individuals' changing attitudes toward drink would not be visible so as to inform the desirability of the prohibition. Moreover, if individuals could not drink, they would not be able to develop self-control. The result should be a static prohibition, one that would preclude society from questioning its desirability after changes in tastes, education, or self-control. From this perspective, the prohibition of alcohol may seem very similar to other paternalistic rules, such as the prohibition of the less addictive narcotics like marihuana or ecstasy, or the imposition of excessive speed limits.

F. Concluding Exercises

Exercise 3.1: Think of one of the myriads of details of the political system that makes it deviate from a pure system of majority rule. The representative rather than direct nature of the democratic system is one example. Others are the division of several legislatures in two bodies (bi-cameralism) the process for a veto and for its over-ride, or the existence of a constitution and its amendment process. The list of such anti-majoritarian features continues. How does the anti-majoritarian feature you selected change the rule by majority? Does that feature make the political system approach one that would aim for the maximization of social welfare or is this departure from majority rule contrary to social welfare? How do individuals and politicians react to the anti-majoritarian feature you selected, and what are the consequences of this reaction? Contrast your analysis with the traditional justification of this feature in political philosophy.

Discussion: Most of the anti-majoritarian provisions prevent the majority's choice from taking effect. If the majority persists, its choice will eventually dominate. A presidential veto may lead to the defeat of this president at the next elections. In a system of bi-cameralism, if the body that is elected for the longer term resists an innovation, its majority may be replaced by election. One conclusion may be to consider that the function of counter-majoritarian features is postponement. If they influence outcomes, however, then their consequence must involve more than simple delay. The layered decision makers who have different terms may function as a safeguard against legislating on temporary preferences. The majority cannot satisfy its new preferences by a single vote. Several votes are necessary to replace several layers of decision makers. When preferences cannot influence law fast, individual citizens can also adjust their demands. Instead of seeking that the government satisfy the preferences of the citizenry, citizens may seek to produce a system that allows or helps individuals to satisfy their preferences independently. The result, then, may lead individuals to favor limited government, liberal regimes, and expansive freedoms.

Exercise 3.2: Create two arguments in favor of mandatory voting by citizens, one based on systematic errors and one based on structural bias (compare the arguments about civic republicanism with public choice's rational apathy). What evidence would support each argument?

Corporations use a single system for quantifying their results, the rules of accounting. Part of the benefit of accounting is standardization that facilitates the comparison of the numbers from different corporations. Sociologists could produce (and have) indices that measure political attitudes. Should a similar standardization be imposed on political candidates and parties? Should political parties and candidates announce the index that quantifies their positions?

Discussion: This exercise expands on the idea that law-and-economics scholars tend to expect individuals to be able to act in their self-interest. This creates a bias in favor of arguments that rest on structural bias rather than systematic errors. However, the next step is to examine what evidence supports each argument's premise. The common experience in large democracies is that a sizable fraction of the population does not vote. The economic analysis of public choice does not find that phenomenon paradoxical and calls it rational apathy. It is not clear what evidence can distinguish rational apathy from erroneous apathy. Even accepting that individuals do routinely err, what evidence supports the premise that they will err in the direction of insufficient participation rather than excessive participation?

The ideas about standardizing or quantifying political positions is analogous to the discussion that compares policies that prevent the harm from systematic errors to policies that help overcome the error, such as labeling and disclosure. Mandated voting would be analogous to a policy that prevents the harm from inadequate participation. Standardization and announcement of the political index would help voters determine which candidate or party is the best match for them. Those are analogous to policies that help overcome errors. Civic republicanism's desire to increase political participation should favor standardization and index announcement over mandated voting. After all, the mandated votes could remain uninformed and false. Standardization and index announcement are less paternalistic and less intrusive than mandated voting and they do not preclude the citizens who want to explore in greater detail the candidates' position from doing so.

Exercise 3.3: Use game theory to justify fishing limitations contract law, and the provisions of bankruptcy law that prevent individual creditors from obtaining satisfaction and impose a court-supervised process of selling assets.

Discussion: The regulated subjects contain great complexity, but one aspect of all corresponds to a prisoner's dilemma. Limitations of fishing that prevent over-fishing allow the population of fish to reproduce. Presumably this preserves a perpetual supply of fish that has greater value than consuming the current population of fish. Despite each individual fishing enterprise's recognizing this gain, each fears that others may violate the law and prevent reproduction. Hence, the prisoner's dilemma; self-interest may be self-destructive.

Contract law, if it is effectively enforced, allows parties to bind themselves to a specific course of action. This lets them overcome prisoner's dilemmas.

The collective procedures of bankruptcy law have been famously seen as a resolution to a similar collective-action problem. Each creditor may recognize that the debtor's chances at surviving a crisis are good if creditors show lenience. However, if other creditors of this debtor do exercise their rights and obtain satisfaction, no value may be left for others. Acting individually, creditors may destroy value that they would preserve if they were acting collectively as one creditor. See Jackson, *Logic and Limits of Bankruptcy*, and Baird, *Elements of Bankruptcy*.

Exercise 3.4: A type of voting that is rarely covered in discussions of political voting is cumulative voting. Several jurisdictions allow cumulative voting for the election of members of the board of directors by shareholders of corporations. Each share casts a number of votes equal to the number of positions, that is, directors being elected. All those votes, however, may be cast for the same candidate. The positions are filled by the candidates in the order of votes received.

Suppose a corporation has a board with nine members. Shareholders holding 1,000 shares vote, that is, 9,000 votes are cast. The shareholders split into two groups. If the dominant group wants to elect all nine directors, how many shares must the minority group control to foil, by electing one director, the dominant group's plan? Two directors? Three directors? Can you state the general formula for the number m of minority shares necessary to elect a number d of directors when a number s shares vote for p positions?

Discussion: The solution lies in comparing the votes per candidate that the two groups can produce. If the majority attempts to elect nine directors, it splits its votes nine ways and each candidate receives one ninth. The number of majority shares is the total number of shares s minus the minority's shares m, namely $s - m$. They cast a number of votes p per share, or in total $p \times (s - m)$. Splitting them over nine candidates produces $p(s - m)/9$ per candidate. The minority group votes all its shares for one candidate. The minority group's total votes are the product of the number of shares by the number of positions, namely $m \times p$. If those are more than a ninth of the votes, the minority candidate receives a position on the board. A tie would occur if $m\,p = p(s - m)/9$. Solving for the number of minority shares shows the number necessary for a tie. If the minority has more shares, then its candidate wins.

Repeating for the case where the minority tries to elect two candidates changes this setting in only two ways. The minority's votes are
divided by two. The majority needs to only elect eight directors to prevent the minority's plan. The resulting equation is $m\,p/2 = p(s - m)/8$.
In the three-director case, the equation would become $m\,p/3 = p(s - m)/7$.

This reveals a pattern. When the minority tries to elect d directors,
the equation is $m\,p/d = p(s - m)/(p - d + 1)$. Solving this for d shows
the number of directors that a given number of minority shares can
elect. Chapter 7 shows how to use *Mathematica* to solve equations
such as these.[19]

G. BIBLIOGRAPHICAL NOTE

An extraordinarily thorough survey of how economists have engaged
problems of politics is Gary J. Miller, "The Impact of Economics on
Contemporary Political Science," *Journal of Economic Literature* 35,
no. 3 (1997):1173–1204.

A very readable and ambitious introduction to game theory is Eric
Rasmusen, *Games and Information: An Introduction to Game Theory*,
2nd ed. (Cambridge, MA: Blackwell Publishers, 1994). A technical
but thorough introduction to game theory is D. Funderberg and J.
Tirole, *Game Theory* (Cambridge, MA: MIT Press, 1991). See also,
Prajit K. Dutta, *Strategies and Games* (Cambridge, MA: MIT Press,
1999). The quantitative analysis of politics is exemplified in a classic
book by Kenneth J. Arrow, *Social Choice and Individual Values*, 2nd ed.
(New Haven, CT: Yale University Press, 1970). One more Nobel Prize-
winning author analyzes political institutions in the book by Douglass
C. North, *Institutions, Institutional Change and Economic Performance*
(Cambridge: Cambridge University Press, 1990).

Public choice is epitomized in the book by James M. Buchanan and
Gordon Tullock, *The Calculus of Consent* (Indianapolis, IN: Liberty
Fund, 1999). An economic analysis of constitutional law on its way
to becoming a classic is Robert D. Cooter, *The Strategic Constitution*

---

[19] Hint: In *Mathematica*, the command for solving equations is `Solve` [ ]. Its syntax has
two elements, the equation and the variable. The equation must use two equal signs
instead of one to enable comparison rather than assignment. For example y=a+b x
would assign to the variable y the value "a+b x." Not having the comparison function
means the *Mathematica* has no equation to solve. The proper form of the command
Solve is `Solve` [*lhs*==*rhs, variable*].

(Princeton, NJ: Princeton University Press, 2000). Insights from attention to constitutional details emerge in the book by George Tse-
belis, *Veto Players: How Political Institutions Work* (New York: Russell
Sage Foundation; Princeton, NJ: Princeton University, 2002). The classic application of game-theory problems in social settings is the book
by Robert Axelrod, *The Evolution of Cooperation* (New York: Basic Books, 1984). Equally a classic is the book by Mancur Olson, *The
Logic of Collective Action: Public Goods and the Theory of Groups*
(Cambridge, MA: Harvard University Press, 1971). The legal perspective on game theory is offered by Douglas G. Baird, Robert H. Gertner,
and Randal C. Picker, *Game Theory and the Law* (Cambridge, MA:
Harvard University Press, 1984).

Bounded rationality is captured in the book by Kahneman et al.,
Judgment Under Uncertainty (cited in note 14).

Numerous applications of analysis using norms are discussed by
Eric A. Posner, *Law and Social Norms* (Cambridge, MA: Harvard
University Press, 2000). Essays on bounded rationality are collected
by Cass R. Sunstein in *Behavioral Law and Economics* (Cambridge:
Cambridge University Press, 2000).

Uniquely prominent among alternatives to law and economics is the
critical legal studies school. It is politically motivated in a loose sense
because it sees law as a reflection of the existing political structure and
advocates a more egalitarian one. See, in general, Roberto M. Unger,
The Critical Legal Studies Movement (Cambridge, MA: Harvard University Press, 1986).

4. The Importance of Distribution of Wealth

An egalitarian intuition is an almost universal human trait. The desire of some jurists to promote equality leads them to reject law and economics because it appears to ignore egalitarian concerns. This chapter explains how scholars using law and economics tend to treat equal distribution of wealth, why they appear to ignore the value of redistribution, and that scholars using law and economics may actually share their critics' desire for redistribution. The teachings of law and economics, however, indicate that redistribution is often best performed by the tax system. Unless this presumption is rejected, legal interpretation should not sacrifice gains in exchange for redistribution.

The tension between redistribution and economic analysis of law can be illustrated with *Meinhard v. Salmon*.[1] Salmon received a lucrative offer from Gerry, a business acquaintance. The offer could have expanded Salmon's business. Unbeknownst to Gerry, Salmon's business, which was the reason for their acquaintance, had a secret partner, Meinhard. If Gerry knew that Salmon operated in two capacities, as an individual and as a member of a partnership, then Gerry may have specified which of the two he selected as the recipient of his offer. Meinhard, the invisible partner, claimed the offer should be treated as made to the partnership. The litigation that Meinhard started eventually reached the highest court of the jurisdiction and the famous American judge, Benjamin Cardozo, and his colleague Andrews, who is almost equally famous for his vocal dissenting opinions. Previously established law did not answer the question directly. If Cardozo and his court decided the case by choosing the interpretation that would tend

---

[1] 249 N.Y. 458 (1928). The text of the opinion is reproduced in Appendix A.

72

to favor in such disputes the poorer party, they might have produced an undesirable interpretation (see also exercise 4.1).

Social welfare cannot be separated from questions of distribution. This correct position functions as a hurdle that impedes accepting much of the analysis of law and economics. This chapter seeks to help the reader approach the analysis without dropping intuitions in favor of re-distribution. Scholars in law and economics are sensitive to distribution as an issue, but their argumentation does not start with redistribution. Because the preference for redistribution varies, it is too subjective to serve as a foundation for argument. Scholars in law and economics, therefore, find merit in not starting with redistributive concerns. After the analytical foundation is laid, then distribution may enter to qualify the conclusions. In many instances, however, the conclusion is reached without addressing questions of distribution. Readers who treat dis-tribution as the major concern that it is have difficulty assessing the conclusions of such arguments. Not surprisingly, a law-and-economics argument that ignores redistribution is suspicious to jurists unfamiliar with the treatment of redistributive concerns by law and economics. Many object to law and economics because of this.[2]

This chapter seeks to allay such suspicions and objections by show-ing how law and economics deals with redistributive concerns. This justifies the postponement of dealing with redistribution until after the foundations of the analysis are laid. This postponement is a principle of law and economics that the reader must accept to approach the anal-ysis. To justify the postponement, this chapter explains the treatment of redistributive concerns by law and economics, which involves a rig-orous methodology. The result is that this chapter too straddles the separation of principles and methods, as did Chapter 3 that addressed political philosophy next to game theory. To justify the postponement of distributional concerns, this chapter is forced into the territory of optimal tax theory. Scholars within law and economics who accept an extreme version of the optimality of optimal tax theory argue that

---

[2] A discussion of the use of the theories of Coase to avoid concerns with the distribution of wealth, along with an attempt to reclaim Coase for the Left, is in Pierre Schlag, "An Appreciative Comment On Coase's The Problem of Social Cost: A View from the Left," *Wisconsin Law Review* 1986:919. The point that law and economics ignores distributional concerns is widely observed, *id*. (collecting citations). See also Jules L. Coleman, "Efficiency, Utility, and Wealth Maximization," *Hofstra Law Review* 8 (1980): 509. The explanation for why economic analysis of law ignores the distributive effects relies on the power of the state to redistribute wealth. *See* A. Mitchell Polinsky, *An Introduction to Law and Economics*, 2nd ed. (Boston: Little, Brown, 1989): 7–10.

redistributive concerns must not influence the analysis.[3] Others within law and economics, including this author, find exceptions.[4]

Common sense indicates that equal increases of wealth have greater impact when added to small, rather than large wealth. This observation forms an argument for strong redistribution. Redistribution, however, distorts productivity incentives. Thus, we have an insoluble conflict stemming from different time horizons. Redistribution will cause an immediate boost but may hamper subsequent economic productivity. Because, from a long-term perspective, productivity is paramount, the case for redistribution becomes weak. The first two sections of this chapter introduce this contradiction while taking us a little deeper into theories of utility.

The third section explores the aversion to redistribution by rules and the main responses to it within economic analysis of law.

---

[3] Two of the leading figures in law and economics, Professors Louis Kaplow and Steven Shavell of Harvard Law School, explicitly defend the position that distributional concerns should be delegated to tax analysis. See Steven Shavell, "A Note on Efficiency vs. Distributional Equity in Legal Rulemaking: Should Distributional Equity Matter Given Optimal Income Taxation?," *American Economic Review* 71, no. 2 (1981):414 (hereinafter *Efficiency vs Distributional Equity*) and Louis Kaplow and Steven Shavell, "Why the Legal System is Less Efficient than the Income Tax in Redistributing Income," *Journal of Legal Studies* 23 (1994):667 (hereinafter *Redistributing*); and Louis Kaplow and Steven Shavell, "Should Legal Rules Favor the Poor? Clarifying the Role of Legal Rules and the Income Tax in Redistributing Income," *Journal of Legal Studies* 29 (2000): 821 (hereinafter *Clarifying*). They also argue that the law should not pursue goals other than increasing welfare. Louis Kaplow and Steven Shavell, "Fairness Versus Welfare," *Harvard Law Review* 114 (2001):961; Louis Kaplow and Steven Shavell, "Notions of Fairness Versus the Pareto Principle: On the Role of Logical Consistency," *Yale Law Journal* 110 (2000):237. Their thesis, however, allows (and requires) the pursuit of redistribution if, and only if, it increases aggregate welfare, which is consistent with the analysis of this article.

[4] This chapter shares ground with Nicholas L. Georgakopoulos, "Solutions to the Intractability of Distributional Concerns," *Rutgers Law Review* 33 (2002):279 (hereinafter Georgakopoulos, *Distributional*). Several members of the younger generation of law-and-economics scholars – who entered legal academia since about 1990 – have explicitly taken the opposite position and have defended the pursuit of redistributive goals with non-tax rules. See, for example, Mathew D. Adler and Eric A. Posner, "Rethinking Cost-Benefit Analysis," *Yale Law Journal* 109 (1999):204–9 (hereinafter *Cost-Benefit*) (arguing that utility can be compared between persons, which leads to a validity of distributional concerns); Christine Jolls, "Behavioral Economic Analysis of Redistributive Legal Rules," *Vanderbilt Law Review* 51 (1998):1656 (hereinafter, Behavioral Analysis of Redistrib.) (arguing that cognitive errors may indicate that distributional goals can be pursued more effectively with non-tax legal rules rather than with tax rules). Some in the law-and-economics community also argue that redistribution beyond that which maximizes aggregate welfare is desirable, *see* Chris W. Sanchirico, "Deconstructing the New Efficiency Rationale," *Cornell Law Review* 86 (2001):1003 (hereinafter Deconstructing).

A. Redistribute!

The importance of the distribution of wealth is neither self-evident nor contradictory to economic analysis. On the contrary, economic analysis has shown its importance, which springs from the phenomenon of diminishing marginal utility of wealth. This "diminishing marginal utility" is a feature of the law of diminishing returns and the utility functions that reflect the reaction of each individual's welfare to changes in the world, in this case to changes of wealth. Economic analysis proceeds to justify freedom of contract and the freedom for individuals to alienate their wealth and to benefit from exchanging the products or services they provide. This justification of property and freedom of contract does reject a forced equal distribution of wealth. This *laissez-faire*-ist rejection of complete redistribution does not also show that any redistribution is undesirable.

Utility functions are artificial constructions, designed to reflect individual preferences and tastes. The usefulness of constructing utility functions is that they allow a more precise analysis of choices. Although they have the defects of any attempt to simplify a complex process, they are of profound use. They are, by design, the constant but also unobservable guides of individual decisions. The utility functions that are of interest when analyzing distribution of wealth take a single input, wealth, and produce a single output, utility. All else being equal, more wealth is better than less. The way in which utility increases in response to increases of wealth has a notable feature that is captured by the notion of the diminishing marginal utility of wealth.

Diminishing marginal utility of wealth means that equal incremental increases of wealth produce different and diminishing increments of welfare, which is an accurate description of attitudes toward wealth.[5]

---

[5] Risk aversion defines the shape of the function of utility of wealth. The coefficient of risk aversion determines the curvature of the function, which is a solution to a differential equation of the given type of risk aversion, most realistically, constant relative risk aversion. See also exercise 7.3 which derives utility-of-wealth functions reflecting different types of risk aversion. Coefficients of risk aversion much above four are not considered realistic. See, for example, Rajnish Mehra and Edward C. Prescott, "The Equity Premium: A Puzzle," *Journal of Monetary Economics* 15 (1985):145. For some applications in legal issues and further citations *see*, for example, Lawrence Blume and Daniel Rubinfeld, "Compensation for Takings: an Economic Analysis," *California Law Review* 72 (1984):587–8 (collecting citations in n. 99); Nicholas L. Georgakopoulos, "Frauds, Markets and Fraud-on-the-Market: The Tortured Transition of Justifiable Reliance from Deceit to Securities Fraud," *Miami Law Review* 49 (1995):671 (showing that risk aversion influences traders' capacity to correct prices); Nicholas L. Georgakopoulos, "Meinhard v. Salmon and the Economics of Honor,"

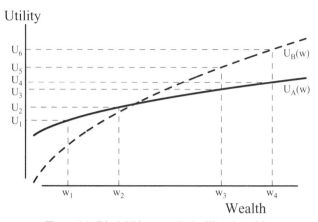

Figure 4.1. Diminishing marginal utility of wealth.

This leads to a strong argument that redistribution of wealth would increase total welfare.[6] Giving to the poor tends to increase their welfare (or utility) more than the reduction caused by withdrawing the same increment of wealth from the rich. The strength of the argument about diminishing marginal utility of wealth is visible in its graphical representation. Figure 4.1 depicts wealth along the horizontal axis, or x axis, while the vertical or y axis represents utility, welfare, or happiness. (Focus on the solid line U_A, ignoring the dashed U_B that will make a point later.) The first few incremental increases of wealth, such as the one from point W_1 to W_2, produce large increases of welfare, such as the one from U_1 to U_2. Equal increases of wealth being added to larger wealth, such as the one from point W_3 to W_4, lead to smaller increases of welfare, from U_3 to U_4. This pattern continues, and further incremental increases of wealth have an ever-smaller effect on welfare.

Some have objected that the argument for redistribution that is based on the diminishing marginal utility of wealth is inaccurate because the increments of utility of different people cannot be compared.[7] Because different individuals' utilities are unknown,

Columbia Business Law Review 1 (1999):161 (showing that risk aversion implies that broad fiduciary obligations are desirable).

[6] This is not a novel proposition, dating from more than 100 years ago. *See* F. Y. Edgeworth, "The Pure Theory of Progressive Taxation," in E. Phelps (ed.), *Economic Justice* (1973):373–4.

[7] See, for example, Bernard Williams, "A Critique of Utilitarianism," in J. J. C. Smart and Bernard Williams, *Utilitarianism: For and Against* (Cambridge: Cambridge University Press, 1973), (hereinafter *Utilitarianism*) 75; Mark Geistfeld, "Reconciling Cost-Benefit Analysis with the Principle that Safety Matters more than Money,"

diminishing marginal utility of wealth only argues that aggregate welfare would increase if wealth were redistributed among individuals whose utilities respond to wealth in identical ways. Because individuals' happiness is strongly idiosyncratic, redistribution may take from wealthy individuals amounts that contribute more to their happiness than to that of the recipients of the redistribution. This refusal to compare utilities when taken to the extreme is clearly wrong.

Figure 4.1 shows a second utility function with a dashed line, $U_B(w)$, which is more sensitive to changes of wealth. If redistribution reduces this individual's wealth from W_4 to a wealth of W_3 to produce an increase from wealth W_1 to wealth W_2 in someone whose utility follows $U_A(w)$, it is conceivable that this redistribution may not increase aggregate welfare. It takes from someone who is very sensitive to wealth and gives to one who is nearly indifferent to wealth. The utility of the former would be reduced from U_6 to U_5, which may be more than the utility of the latter is increased, namely from U_1 to U_2.

Although this objection is valid in theory, the pragmatism of its practical application circumvents it easily.[8] First, this objection is extremely unlikely to be true, in general, because general redistribution takes from many wealthy to give to many poor. Avaricious wealthy scrooges who place a very high value on their last few coins are mostly constructs of fiction. It is virtually inconceivable that the last few units of wealth are on average enjoyed more by all wealthy than the same amount would be enjoyed, on average, by the poor recipients of redistribution.

New York University Law Review 76 (2001):135–6; Amartya Sen, "Utilitarianism and Welfarism," *Journal of Philosophy* 76 (1979):463; see also Amartya Sen and Bernard Williams (eds.), *Utilitarianism and Beyond* (Cambridge: Cambridge University Press, 1982) (collection of essays by leading proponents of differing views). A return to the notion that utility can be aggregated, however, has at least one prominent supporter among economists. *See* John C. Harsanyi, "Cardinal Utility in Welfare Economics and in the Theory of Risk-Taking," *Journal of Political Economy* 61 (1953):434; John C. Harsanyi, "Cardinal Welfare, Individualistic Ethics, and Interpersonal Comparisons of Utility," *Journal of Political Economy* 63 (1955):317–20; John C. Harsanyi, "Nonlinear Social Welfare Functions: Do Welfare Economists Have a Special Exemption from Bayesian Rationality?," *Theory and Decision* 6 (1975):311. Some contemporary philosophers also seem to agree. See, for example, R. M. Hare, *Moral Thinking: Its Levels, Method and Point* (Oxford: Clarendon Press, 1981); J. J. C. Smart, "An Outline of a System of Utilitarian Ethics," in Smart and Williams, *Utilitarianism* 1.

[8] The impossibility of comparing interpersonal utilities is also rebutted by Mathew D. Adler and Eric A. Posner, "Rethinking Cost-Benefit Analysis," *Yale Law Journal* 109 (1999): 165, 204–9, hereafter Adler and Posner, "Cost-Benefit."

Moreover, although the objection that the wealthy are such because they like wealth would reject *complete* redistribution, it is not valid when leveled against the partial redistribution that is desirable. To clarify this objection to redistribution, suppose that enough redistribution has taken place that the rich half of the population is richer than the poor half by two coins. Taking one coin from the wealthier half and giving it to the other half would achieve complete redistribution.

This last piece of redistribution may well not increase aggregate welfare, because this coin is hardly certain to be more enjoyable to the poorer half. When the two levels of wealth are so close it is likely somewhat easy to move from one to the other. The composition of the groups is largely a matter of choice of effort rather than a matter of skill or chance. The choice to belong to the richer group is made by those who derive the most utility from that additional margin of wealth; therefore, taking from this group is taking from individuals whose utility is more sensitive to wealth, and giving to the other group is giving to the group that is less sensitive to wealth. Thus, the potential for different enjoyment of wealth among individuals does rebut an attempt to use diminishing marginal utility of wealth as an argument for complete redistribution. Complete redistribution is undesirable on several other grounds, however, as shown below.

The same argument (that the wealthy may on average be so much more sensitive to wealth that redistribution reduces aggregate welfare) is not persuasive when leveled against partial redistribution. Some of the poor may be very sensitive to wealth but unlucky or unskilled, and some of the wealthy may not be particularly sensitive to wealth but may be very skilled or lucky. Accordingly, the membership in the two groups is mixed. When taking all members of each group into account, although the wealthy group may have some extra individuals of high sensitivity to wealth, it also contains some who are relatively insensitive to wealth.

Similarly, although the poor group may have some extra individuals who are relatively insensitive to wealth, it must also contain some who are quite sensitive to wealth. Even if the two groups have somewhat different composition, the membership is likely not dominated by sensitivity to wealth. Therefore, although some redistribution would be taking from those who are sensitive to wealth and giving to the relatively less sensitive, reducing aggregate welfare, much redistribution takes from those who have been lucky or skilled and gives to those who have not had luck and skill. Partial redistribution is still justified

because it takes increments from those of deep wealth, reducing utility relatively little on average, and gives increments to those of small
wealth, increasing utility much, on average. Therefore, the inconclusive
nature of close comparisons of utility does not argue against redistribution that stops well short of complete redistribution.

B. Do Not Redistribute!

With the same breath, however, economic analysis rushes to counter
these arguments. Although redistributing wealth may increase total
welfare, much greater increases of welfare can be achieved by increasing productivity. The evolution of human well-being during the past
few hundred years shows the inescapable truth of this. Human welfare
has increased much less from redistribution efforts, such as the French
or Communist revolutions, than by increases in productivity, such as
the industrial revolution, mass transportation and communication, or
the information revolution. The effect of redistributing revolutions can
even be argued to be negative. The economic explanation would be that
they eroded productivity incentives. The revolutions destroyed the existing productivity incentives of the previous system. The revolution
also undermined the confidence that the next legal system would endure and in both countries it failed to endure. Lack of confidence in
the legal system's ability to protect property rights erodes the incentive
for productivity embedded in the institution of private property. Redistributing existing wealth may produce a one-time increase in welfare
due to equality, but an erosion of productivity incentives is a permanent
handicap, the cumulative effect of which, over decades, is massive.

   The failure of the redistributing revolutions underscores the point
that the well-being of humanity depends on production rather than
capital. In the most elementary terms, survival depends on the production of food, but even in sophisticated societies, welfare depends
on the production of goods and services. Because humanity's immediate need is for products, rather than the means that produce them,
wealth as capital is a derivative of its product. Capital has value only
because of the product it generates; idle capital has value only because
of its potential to generate product if it becomes active. Thus, the first
problem with redistribution is that to the extent it redistributes capital or potential capital it may influence productivity. The other much
more important and widely recognized problem is that redistribution
schemes interfere with the incentives for productivity.

Redistribution influences productivity incentives because it breaks the connection between individuals' productive efforts and their welfare. A complete redistribution would require the absence of private property and equal distribution of all social products. We must compare the incentives under these circumstances to incentives under systems where individuals appropriate their own product or benefit from their productivity.[9] Obviously, individuals whose product will be shared have incentives that differ vastly from those of individuals who will enjoy exclusively the fruit of their labor and whose enjoyment, therefore, is tied to their productivity.

Enjoying the fruit of one's labor makes the private welfare of each individual depend on the value that each produces. Sharing the redistributed product makes the private welfare of each individual depend on avoiding personal effort and relying on the efforts of the other members of the society. Thus, redistribution produces an incentive for every member of society not to be productive. Even if some or many members do not succumb to this incentive, others will and social product will be lost. The legal system must address the incentives not of the noble-minded but of those with comparatively more base motives, which echoes vividly in the views of the early law-and-economics scholar Justice Oliver Wendell Holmes regarding the "bad man's" law. Holmes considered that the law must be written and interpreted from the perspective of the "bad man" because the law had to thwart his efforts to circumvent the law.[10] Similarly, the economic incentives that the law gives must be viewed from the perspective of the "bad" or, rather, self-interested and irresponsible persons, who would not voluntarily perform their share of society's work. According to the

---

[9] My effort to avoid terms that refer to property concepts is as obvious as it is futile. The difficulty of stating the idea of "benefit from effort" without using terms referring to ownership and property is apparent and not at all coincidental. The acquisition of a property right in the product of one's labor is a simple and nearly perfect incentive to produce. Many societies, however, develop norms of sharing the appropriable product of an individual's labor, for example, the hunter's kill. The existence of such norms might be offered as a counter example, but it is not. The individuals who share the appropriable fruit of their labor are usually compensated with various tangible and intangible benefits. Evolutionary anthropology delights in finding examples of such apparently altruistic conduct that gets very tangible rewards. For an entertaining narrative of such "trades" see Jared M. Diamond, *Why is Sex Fun? The Evolution of Human Sexuality* (New York: HarperCollins, 1997).

[10] Oliver Wendell Holmes, "The Path of the Law," *Harvard Law Review* 10 (1897):459 ("If you want to know the law and nothing else, you must look at it as a bad man, who cares only for the material consequences . . . ").

law-and-economics view, Holmes' warning can be written: The law must be designed for the "irresponsible man."

In addition to distorting the productivity incentives of individuals, redistribution may interfere with the productivity of capital. This problem is a result of the redistribution of capital, rather than the redistribution of product that caused the distortion of productivity incentives that was analyzed above. Thus, it only arises when the social planner, persuaded that redistribution of income is undesirable because it erodes incentives, inquires into why the wealth that has already been accumulated should not be redistributed, leaving future income to produce its incentives without distortions. The simple objection can be that without a commitment that such a redistribution will not happen often, individuals will react to the possibility of occasional redistributions of wealth the same way as to frequent and anticipated redistribution of income. Even if wealth redistribution is rare enough – for example, if it is only acceptable in the form of an estate tax – it has negative consequences. It indirectly biases individuals toward consumption as opposed to investment, and it directly distorts the allocation of resources away from capital formation and toward consumption.

Individuals react to an anticipated redistribution of wealth by devaluing income that capital assets will produce after the redistribution. Thus, capital assets are less valuable to individuals than is the value of the capital asset to society. When individuals decide whether to save by investing in a capital asset or to consume, consumption will appear more appealing to an individual than it is from the perspective of society. Society, of course, will exist after the redistribution and value the income that invested capital would have produced after that date. Sophisticated markets for capital assets will mitigate this problem, because they may allow the sale of the assets before the redistribution and the consumption of the proceeds. Nevertheless, the problem will persist for any assets that are not trading in a nearly perfect market. Even in our environment of advanced markets, this exception clearly includes family businesses. An example illustrates this distortion on investment and the potential salutary effect of capital markets.

Imagine that society as a whole has determined that it would give up consumption of ten loaves this year to obtain eleven next year. Thus, society considers 10 percent an adequate compensation to forego immediate consumption and interest rates are at 10 percent. An entrepreneur has a business that can be made more productive by an investment. The increase in productivity is 11 percent of the invested amount. Thus, an entrepreneur with no concern about enjoying any part of the future value of the business would make the investment. Not only is foregoing consumption justified by the future gains, but our entrepreneur would also borrow at 10 percent, invest, and the 11 percent product would cover the interest and leave a profit. The investment, of course, is also socially desirable.

Fear of wealth redistribution will prevent this socially desirable investment. Suppose the entrepreneur will die this year and knows that his heirs will pay a 10 percent tax on the value of the business. Now the investment is no longer sensible for the entrepreneur's family. By foregoing consumption of, say, 100 loaves, they would be able to make 11 more loaves every year, which corresponds to an increase in the value of the business by 110 loaves (the 11 loaves annually, capitalized at the 10 percent rate). They will not enjoy this increase in value, however. After the 10 percent tax on the increased value, they will only net a value of 99. Thus, redistribution distorts investment incentives and socially desirable investments will not be made.

A market would induce the correct decision by the entrepreneur only if full value could be had for the business. But if the buyers are to be induced to buy, selling entrepreneurs will have to accept a discount. Full value in this case would be 110 loaves, that is, the value of the future production of 11 loaves annually, discounted at 10 percent. If the discounts and transaction costs of the market imply that the entrepreneur will receive 10 percent less than full value, the investment is still unattractive, because it requires an investment of 100 and can be sold, net of costs and discounts, for 99 (i.e., 90% of 110).

Wealth redistribution also directly distorts the allocation of resources away from capital into consumption. To the extent that it means taking from the rich and giving to the poor, redistribution of wealth likely takes funds that would become capital and gives them where they will become consumption. This is true because the wealthy who are being taxed do not put their first but their last units of wealth into capital investment, whereas the poor, who receive the redistributed funds, have a strong bias to consume rather than invest.

A different description of this effect is that the state takes funds from users with low discount rates – from the rich for whom additional consumption today is of little interest – and gives them to users with high discount rates – to the poor who would improve their lot immediately rather than take a chance on the future. This is not to say that saving is inherently better than consumption; the socially optimal compromise between saving and consuming must be made. The point is that the hypothetical redistribution creates a bias in favor of consuming, which arguably wastes socially desirable investment opportunities. This is not a complete evaluation of the estate tax, which has several advantages (compare exercise 4.2).

One might counter that redistribution does not influence incentives because the acquisition of wealth is random. If the acquisition of wealth were a truly random lottery, redistribution would simply reverse the results of the lottery with no effect on incentives. Wealth creation, of course, is not truly random because it also depends on many other factors such as effort, ambition, and skill.[11] Under the lottery scheme, the tax rate should be inversely related to the deterministic contributors to wealth creation such as effort, and skill, so that the one who exerted greater effort and skill of two equally wealthy individuals should be taxed less.[12] Nevertheless, a socially undesirable bias would still exist. Some activities involve highly risky and uncertain rewards and such a policy would deter them. Take oil exploration or filmmaking. The rewards from the activity are so unpredictable that it can be analogized to a lottery in which winning is weakly related to skill or ambition. Entrepreneurs search for oil only because they could benefit from "winning the lottery." A redistribution scheme that takes the gains away for not being the product of skill ignores that entrepreneurship and the creation of value is also a matter of taking chances. If society does not let the winner keep chance's reward, society will be missing chances for gains.[13]

---

[11] A comprehensive survey of the theories that produce unequal wealth also discusses the possibility of randomness (called the "Stochastic Model" of wealth) and finds that they are refuted by the evidence. *See* Gian Singh Sahota, "Theories of Personal Income Distribution: A Survey," *Journal of Economic Literature* 16 (1978):8 ("In one of the most comprehensive tests of stochastic theories . . . finds significant evidence against practically all the major assumptions of these models").

[12] This concept would also preclude actual lotteries, betting, and games of chance. Note that the determinants of wealth creation in the sentence of the text do not include ambition, which has an ambivalent reception in the tax literature, which seems to suggest that wealth created by ambition but without effort and skill should also be taxed more heavily. Unless ambition is considered an affirmatively undesirable motive, the analysis of the taxation of wealth accumulations due to luck that follows in the text, will also apply to the taxation of wealth accumulations due to ambition.

[13] Entrepreneurial risk taking and wealth accumulation as a consequence of chance are identical concepts. For example, one cannot argue that entrepreneurial risk taking should not be taxed more because every individual who was exposed to the same risk would enjoy the same reward. As a matter of probability, out of the numerous risk takers, only the lucky ones enjoy the rewards. If the reward occurs with 10 percent probability, for example, this implies that only one of every ten risk takers

The conflict between the idea that redistribution increases welfare and the realization that it also destroys productivity is stark. It may be an inescapable conflict of organized society. Nevertheless, economic analysis of law does address the problem. The conventional approach has been to delegate redistributive concerns to tax policy. Recently, some exceptions from this position have been identified.

C. DELEGATING REDISTRIBUTION TO TAX POLICY

Once redistribution is accepted, be it as little or as much as each jurisdiction chooses to provide when compromising between future and current welfare, the question becomes how the legal system should provide it. Law-and-economics scholars with a *laissez-faire*-ist streak have argued that taxation should be the exclusive means for redistributing wealth.[14] The foundation of the thesis is that using non-tax law to redistribute wealth distorts the operation of the markets. Therefore, redistribution by means of non-tax law reduces welfare. The conclusion is that redistribution, barring exceptional circumstances, should occur through taxation. This reasoning, despite being technically correct, is substantively false in at least two ways. First, actual taxation has large distortionary effects, making the premise false. Second, even the distortionary effects of an optimal tax outweigh the distortions of several kinds of non-tax redistribution.

The model that is offered as proof of the superiority of redistributing through the tax system is very simple. Suppose that an optimal substantive (non-tax) rule exists, but an inferior one may provide some additional redistribution. Compare the adoption of the redistributing rule to maintaining the optimal rule while using the tax system to achieve the same redistribution while producing the least possible distortions on incentives. We are told that the latter alternative is superior.

---

will enjoy the reward. Neither does the issue change by conditioning the answer on a choice to accept the risk. Answering that the entrepreneurs who chose to take the risk should still be entitled to the reward does not negate probability theory, for not every uncertainty is consciously accepted. For example, if accidental good luck, such as the discovery of penicillin while conducting other chemical experiments, were taxed, then conducting chemical experiments would be deterred. If conducting chemical experiments tends to induce uncertainty – bad burns, for example, as well as valuable discoveries – such a tax would deter chemical experiments and the associated but remote gains. Conversely, compensating the burns would overly encourage an activity that may be undesirable from an expected value perspective.

[14] *See* Kaplow and Shavell, "Clarifying, " 821; Kaplow and Shavell, "Redistributing," 667; Shavell, "Efficiency vs. Distributional Equity," 414.

Because of the efficient rule and the minimized distortive tax, society is better off than under a suboptimal rule and non-minimized distortions of taxation.

It should be obvious that this thesis is a truism. Tax is assumed to produce distortions equal to those of the redistributive effect of the non-tax rule. A more accurate model should acknowledge that the additional tax might cause greater distortions than the non-tax rule, in particular, as long as taxation takes the wasteful shape of increasing marginal tax rates. An increase of an inefficiently designed tax burden may induce a greater distortion than any distortion caused by the redistributive rule. Then, the comparison is of two different compromises between wealth and redistribution. Using the optimal non-tax rule with a more distortionary tax regime to redistribute wealth must be compared to using a less distortionary, but redistributive rule, with a less distortionary tax system. The conclusion is that either compromise may be superior.

A graphical representation of this dispute helps resolve the different claims. The graph has two dimensions, redistribution and the substantive performance of the non-tax rule at issue. In the example of torts, the metric may be the total cost of accidents, namely the cost of care to avoid accidents plus the cost of injuries from accidents that do occur. The optimal tort rule minimizes total accident costs, and the dispute is whether a tort rule that redistributes more is preferable to a combination of the optimal tort rule and more taxation to produce the same amount of additional redistribution.

Proponents of redistribution by non-tax rules (the opponents of the Shavell position) envision a third dimension in the same graph. The third dimension is not visible in Figure 4.2. The dimension that is not visible is the social welfare that the rule produces, and we can think of it as the "altitude" of a "mountainous" surface. The two visible dimensions are accident costs and redistribution. Accident costs reach a minimum at the optimal tort rule, which is also associated with some amount of redistribution. This is represented by the point marked "Best rule (most gain)."

The curve of the figure is the frontier of redistribution and accident cost avoidance that variations in the tort regime provide. The outcomes that can be attained by varying the rule correspond to the shaded area marked "Possibilities by variation of the rule."

Suppose that someone would propose a slightly more redistributive tort rule, which would be suboptimal in terms of accident costs.

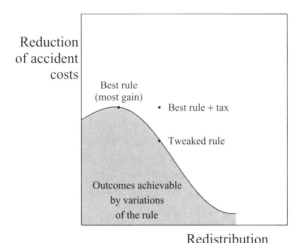

Figure 4.2. Redistribution by substantive rules and by taxation.

This tweaked rule, although it produces more accident costs, appears superior because of the additional redistribution it provides. In the graph, the proposal corresponds to the point "Tweaked rule." It seems to provide society with more welfare because it corresponds to more redistribution.

The opponents of redistributive rules respond that the tweaked rule is dominated, for two reasons. If total accident costs are greater, society's total welfare is reduced. No matter how this welfare is distributed, it cannot produce more welfare than redistributing the maximum wealth, which exists when accident costs are minimized. In other words, redistribution from the best rule always produces more welfare than redistribution with greater accident costs.

When redistribution is performed by tax while using the optimal non-tax rule, then a third outcome is feasible. On the graph this would correspond to the point marked "Best rule + tax." That point necessarily produces more total welfare than the tweaked rule. Because it corresponds to the same lowest possible accident costs as the best rule, it has the same coordinate along the accident-cost axis. Because it entails more redistribution, it has a greater coordinate on the redistribution axis. In other words, it is necessarily better than the tweaked rule.

This is correct if the tax system is the least costly mechanism of redistribution. However, a recent estimate of the cost of the distortion due to the income tax in the United States is \$2.65 per dollar raised.[15] The idea that the costs of taxation must be taken into account when deciding its level is part of the conventional understanding of the economics of taxation, the seminal work being that of Pigou and having a long pedigree.[16] Just as different taxes produce different consequences in terms of distortions, different means of redistribution do too.

The side opposing redistributive rules explains that the distortion of the tax system is a distortion due to redistribution and any redistributive scheme will have the same distortion. In other words, a tweaked rule involves the same distortion due to redistribution as the tax and starts from a lower (suboptimal) level, here from a greater cost of accidents.[17] This is known as the *double-distortion* argument.[18] An optimal rule would cause no distortions, but a tax, even if optimal, distorts incentives for work. A suboptimal redistributive rule causes one distortion because it is not optimal, and a second distortion because of the reaction to the rule's function as a tax.

For example, consider that a society consists of two individuals, a productive one (the skilled) who has high income and a less productive one (the klutz) with less income. Suppose the skilled makes twenty loaves each week and the klutz only makes five loaves. An income tax reduces productivity by inducing the more productive one to work less.

An income tax rule can redistribute without interfering with the baking process, but it will deter work. Impose an income tax of 60 percent on the number of loaves over ten. If the skilled still produces twenty loaves, the income tax will take six and give them to the klutz. The klutz adds the six loaves to the five he makes and enjoys eleven, while the skilled enjoys fourteen. We need to treat the skilled as a self-interested person, however. Without the tax, the skilled enjoyed the

---

15 *See* Martin Feldstein, "How Big Should Government Be?," *National Tax Journal* 50 (1997):197.
16 Arthur C. Pigou, *A Study in Public Finance* (London: Macmillan, 1928).
17 See Kaplow and Shavell, "Redistributing ," 667.
18 See, for example, Sanchirico, "Deconstructing," 1014. Sanchirico argues that redistribution based on features or manifestations of skill and well-being other than income will not produce the double distortion. If non-clumsiness is such a feature, adjusting tort damages downward, is argued, would not induce avoidance of work and income. Indeed it would not, but the skilled and well-off would have an incentive to distort their image toward clumsiness – take more risks and engage in more activity not just to take advantage of the lower cost of accidents, but also to appear clumsy. Hence, the proposal produces a new double distortion. It distorts not only the activity, such as care, but also the manifestation on which redistribution is based, such as the appearance of clumsiness.

last one of the twenty loaves barely enough to keep working. When the tax is imposed, the skilled knows he will not enjoy that entire loaf, and he prefers to rest or play. Whether the skilled will quit two, four, or six loaves before he would without the tax, we cannot know. Suppose that the skilled chooses to make fifteen loaves, paying three to the tax (60% × 5 = 3) but still enjoying twelve. The skilled has twelve loaves and additional relaxation, while the klutz has eight. The two together have fewer loaves than without the tax but the distribution of loaves is more egalitarian, because the skilled has only four loaves more than the klutz has. Despite that the reaction of the skilled to the tax is so petty and wasteful, this result is better than a wasteful redistributive rule.

Consider, first, a desirable rule. Suppose both bakers sleepwalk once every week, entering the other's bakery and, unwittingly, enjoying an early morning snack at the other's expense. The cost of this event is that the victim, weak without breakfast, makes two loaves less. This makes the unregulated weekly production sixteen loaves. The rule entitles victims to get the breakfast that the other was baking. When the rule is imposed, the total loaves go up from sixteen back to twenty. Instead of a tax, now, tweak this optimal rule to get some redistribution out of it while reducing its efficiency. In addition to getting the other's breakfast, have the victim use the other's bakery for a day. The bakery of the klutz is a mess, the skilled does not benefit from the new rule, stays in his bakery, so the new rule costs nothing to the klutz. The bakery of the skilled is in perfect order each morning, ready to make four loaves. The klutz makes four loaves and keeps them, leaving the bakery a mess, and is not capable of producing four loaves the next day.

The tweaked rule has some waste. The skilled, being petty, responds to the potential daily loss in the same way as to an income tax. The skilled leaves work earlier and leaves the bakery slightly messy, making only three loaves each day instead of four. The weekly production of the skilled is not quite fifteen, because the mess the klutz leaves prevents the skilled from making three loaves. Suppose he only makes one loaf instead of three. The skilled makes thirteen loaves each week, five lost to the redistributive effect of the rule, and two lost to the inefficiency that the rule imposes. When the desirable rule is tweaked to provide redistribution, the skilled ends each week with ten loaves: thirteen that he made minus three that he paid for sleepwalking. The klutz ends up with eight loaves, five that he made and three that he got from the skilled.

The result looks appealing from a redistributional perspective, per-haps superior to the tax, as the klutz has only three less than the skilled. Nevertheless, a tax would do better, argues the side opposing redis-tributive rules. A tax would not produce the inefficiency of the loss of two loaves. Returning to the optimal sleepwalking rule and increas-ing the tax to 75 percent would further induce the skilled to cut back, and make, say, fourteen loaves. After giving three to the klutz, they have eleven and eight. The klutz has the same number of loaves, and the skilled has one more. Although the tax chills the incentives of the skilled to work, it does not impose the inefficiency of the tweaked rule. The tax imposes one distortion whereas the tweaked rule imposes two. The tweaked rule is not superior to the optimal rule coupled with an ad-ditional increment of income tax that produces the same redistribution.

Based on this reasoning, the side opposing redistributive rules ar-gues that tweaked rules are not superior to optimal rules coupled with an additional increment of optimal income tax, although they allow that in exceptional cases they may be. Economic analysis has produced several counterarguments. The principal ones are that the assumption of optimal taxation is likely false, that rules can be designed to take advantage of systematic errors, that rules can be designed that induce the most productive individuals to work more, and that rules may re-distribute welfare without the chilling effect of a tax.[19]

This chapter does not propose the thesis that all law-and-economics arguments must ignore redistribution. The optimality of optimal tax exists relative to other taxes, not every possible legal and organizational innovation. Rather, the thesis is that law and economics can and should devise structural redistributive proposals. The exercises try to move in that direction.

D. CONCLUDING EXERCISES

Exercise 4.1: This exercise completes the example that opened the chapter. Suppose that Cardozo and his court had selected the

---

[19] The point that rules can be designed to take advantage of systematic errors is de-veloped by Jolls, "Behavioral Analysis of Redistrib.," 1656 (arguing that cognitive errors may indicate that distributional goals can be pursued more effectively with non-tax legal rules rather than with tax rules). The other points were made by this author in Nicholas L. Georgakopoulos, "Solutions to the Intractability of Distri-butional Concerns," *Rutgers Law Review* 33 (2002):279 (hereinafter *Distributional Concerns*).

interpretation that the court would adopt on the basis of its redistributive appeal rather than its economic superiority. Thus, the court might have concluded that financiers were likely to be wealthier than managers and, to promote redistribution, concluded that offers with ambiguous recipients, such as the one received by Salmon or the partnership, were to be construed as offers to the individual rather than the business. With respect to *Meinhard v. Salmon*, this construction would have defeated Meinhard's claim. What would be the consequences of such a choice for future partnerships between financiers and entrepreneurs and for the economy of the jurisdiction (the state of New York)?

Discussion: A first step in analyzing this question is to recognize that partnerships established after the opinion would take the law that the opinion would establish into account. Consequently, financiers should recognize the reduced appeal of investments into partnerships as (silent) partners. If other jurisdictions did not pursue similar redistributive interpretations, then *ceteris paribus*, financiers would prefer to finance enterprises in the other jurisdictions. To the extent they would invest in the redistributing jurisdiction, entrepreneurs would compare investments in new ways, disfavoring passive investments and favoring, for example, investments in their own businesses and making loans. The consequences of the redistributive interpretation could have been terrible. The formation of new businesses could have been impeded. The economic growth and the new jobs that follow new business would be hurt. The paucity of jobs would reduce wages. The redistributive interpretation, according to this reasoning, would hurt the poor rather than help them. The class of financiers may have enjoyed undiminished income by investing in other jurisdictions.

Exercise 4.2: Think about the systematic errors that may be involved in the burden one feels from the estate tax compared with the burden from an income tax. Which do you think has a greater chilling effect on work?

Discussion: The comparison of income and estate tax can be approached in various ways. One approach would posit that the expected payment be kept the same from the perspective of the individual. Thus, the substitute for a given payment for income tax would be a larger future payment for estate tax. If the two were truly equivalent, what would the effect on effort be? If an individual sought to minimize their estate tax, how could they reduce the amount that they would eventually owe? How would effort spent in consumption compare with effort spent in production as strategies?

If the payment for the estate tax were to be made equal to that of the income tax from the perspective of the individual, how would the amounts differ to account for the passage of time? If an interest rate is applied, should it be the rate at which individuals lend to the government, or the rate at which individuals borrow?

A different adjustment would seek to prevent the adoption of the substitute tax from having an impact on the revenue of the government (making the adoption "revenue-neutral"). Of course, that is easier said than done, particularly if the choice of the tax influences the amount of work.

Consider also the impact of uncertainty. An entrepreneur in a risky business may experience great variation of income from year to year. How does that influence the choice between the two taxes?

Exercise 4.3: Airlines, when faced with an overbooked flight, offer passengers a reward in money and free travel for giving up their seats. What are the effects of these arrangements on redistribution?

Discussion: An approach to the effects on distribution of the airline rewards for seats is that an individual who has flexible time receives some value for giving a seat to an individual who has pressure to arrive on time at the destination. Arguably, pressure to arrive on time correlates with being busy and having greater income whereas flexibility correlates with less income. Then, the airline's buyout is redistributive; it charges a higher price to the pressed (and, therefore, productive) passenger and gives a discount to the flexible (and perhaps less productive) traveler.

Exercise 4.4: Turn to a much smaller tax. "Bottle laws" require a payment at the purchase of every bottle or can of drink for environmental reasons. The payment is nominally a refundable deposit. Consumers get the refund when they return the bottle for recycling. In practice, many consumers do not collect the refund. Instead, they dispose their bottles or cans and others take them for recycling and earn the refund. Effectively, consumers who do not recycle treat the payment as a tax that produces recycling and cleanliness. What is the distributional effect of bottle laws? Does the cleanliness that bottle laws induce accrue evenly within rich and poor neighborhoods? What are the distortions of incentives caused by bottle laws? Would an income tax that would fund additional street cleaning be superior?

Discussion: Bottle laws appear to transfer the deposits from those who do not recycle to those who actually pick up the cans. To observe the re-distribution in a more remarkable scale, employ Coasean irrelevance. For irrelevance to exist, those who do not recycle should fund addi-tional street-cleaning crews. Would all neighborhoods equally provide the additional cleaning? Compare a poor urban neighborhood with a secluded luxurious suburb. If the urban area would provide less clean-ing, then the bottle laws produce cleanliness at the poor areas where it would not have existed otherwise. The cost is the distortion on demand of drinks caused by the deposit. By comparison, an incremental income tax that produces the same cleanliness has the inescapable distortion of effort that any income tax has. Even without considering additional advantages of bottle laws (such as the mobilization of bottlers' logis-tical expertise and competition toward recycling) they are substantive rules that are likely superior to an income tax. Income tax is far too blunt an instrument to provide a solution that is so fundamental and creative.

Exercise 4.5: Suppose that a jurisdiction has excessive tort liability burdening traffic accidents. Commuters in this jurisdiction divide into wealthy and poor. The jurisdiction requires drivers to have insurance but only toward the payment of the compensatory amount of liability, leaving the excessive component uninsured. Also, this jurisdiction's bankruptcy law allows individuals to make a bankruptcy filing and avoid the payment of all existing debts provided they exhaust their existing assets in paying existing creditors. Accordingly, all victims of accidents have oversized tort claims. If their claim is against a wealthy individual, it gets paid. A bankruptcy filing by the wealthy would be pointless because their assets exceed their liabilities. However, if the claim is against a poor individual, it is often not paid because the poor individual is insolvent, and files for bankruptcy.

Review the distortions caused by the excessive tort liability and any redistributive gain it may have. Does the double-distortion argument remain in full force?

Discussion: This exercise studies the assertion of the double-distortion theory that a redistributive rule will have the impact of a tax on the activity that is burdened by the redistributive rule. In the exercise, the activity is driving and if it were burdened by a special tax, the result would be less driving and a tendency to substitute driving with a different means of transportation. The burden of excessive liability in this example, however, may not have this effect because it seems not to have any effect on the poor drivers and only impose a burden of wealthy drivers. Granted, wealthy drivers consider driving as an activity burdened with a special tax. Because this rule does not have the effect of a tax on the poor, it is superior to an incremental optimal tax, which would distort driving decisions generally. The double-distortion argument does not disappear insofar as poor individuals have a reduced incentive to become rich because they will bear the risk of the excessive tort liability. However, because their conduct matters, the excessive liability only functions as an incentive to take excessive care when driving after becoming rich rather than an incentive not to become rich. To the extent that this reduces the liability of the wealthy, it may seem to reduce the redistributive impact of the excessive liability; fewer dollars than expected will change hands because of the extra care. The extra care by the wealthy does have a non-monetary redistributive effect in favor of the poor because they need to expend less effort on precaution.[20] They might have other possible gains, such as not experiencing demeaning driving by the wealthy.

Exercise 4.6: Compare public housing with equivalent monetary subsidies. A subsidy would help those making less than a threshold income. Public housing would provide the same assistance to the same individuals but would be visible because individuals would live in addresses recognized as public housing projects. Gifted individuals who in the past earned the high income or who will earn it in the future are eligible for support during a time that their income is artificially low (e.g., during training). Suppose that employers would like to recognize the gifted individuals and would offer them a high wage. Employers face the problem that all individuals pretend to be gifted and the employer only determines who is gifted after a long period on the job. How does the housing subsidy distort incentives compared with the monetary subsidy?

Discussion: This example builds on a complex model where one side, here the employers, cannot believe the other side's statements ("I am gifted") but where a costly conduct exists that separates the groups,

---

[20] This point is also discussed in Georgakopoulos, *Distributional Concerns*, 304–7.

here refusing the housing subsidy. That conduct only exists if it is visible. In the example, the visibility of the employee's address allows employers to recognize the skilled. Once this pattern establishes itself, then gifted candidates decline the subsidy and are hired. Ungifted candidates cannot afford to decline the subsidy because, even though they would be hired, they would also soon be fired.

E. BIBLIOGRAPHICAL NOTE

The importance of equitable distribution of wealth has been stressed by Amartya Sen, *Inequality Reexamined* (New York: Russell Sage Foundation; Cambridge, MA: Harvard University Press, 1995). This theme also appears in several of his books that were discussed in the bibliographical note to Chapter 2.

Optimal taxation may be a crucially important subject, but it does not make gripping reading. Joel Slemrod and Jon Bakija break that stereotype with *Taxing Ourselves: A Citizen's Guide to the Debate over Taxes*, 3rd ed. (Cambridge, MA: Massachusetts Institute of Technology, 2004). Several essays are collected in Joel Slemrod (ed.), *Tax Policy in the Real World* (Cambridge: Cambridge University Press, 1999). Introductory texts include Richard Abel Musgrave and Peggy B. Musgrave, *Public Finance in Theory and Practice*, 5th ed. (New York: McGraw-Hill Book Co., 1989). The optimal tax discussion appears mostly in journals. See, for example, Helmuth Cremer and Firouz Gahvari, "Uncertainty, Optimal Taxation and the Direct Versus Indirect Tax Controversy," *Economic Journal* 105 (1995):1165; Joel Slemrod, "Optimal Taxation and Optimal Tax Systems," *Journal of Economic Perspectives* 4, no. 1 (1190): 157. The field's winner of the Nobel Prize presents his work in James Mirrlees, *Welfare, Incentives, and Taxation* (Oxford: Oxford University Press, 2000).

Legal scholarship reflects a similar lack of engagement with this important topic. The few exceptions include Stephen G. Utz, *Tax Policy: An Introduction and Survey of the Principal Debate* (St. Paul, MN: West Publishing Co., 1993); Georgakopoulos, "Distributional Concerns"; Lawrence Zelenak and Kemper Moreland, "Can the Graduated Income Tax Survive Optimal Tax Analysis?" *Tax Law Review* 53 (1999): 51; Joseph Bankman and Thomas Griffith, "Social Welfare and the Rate Structure: A New Look at Progressive Taxation," *California Law Review* 75 (1987): 1905.

5. Coase and Law's Irrelevance

The late Professor Ronald Coase stated a counterfactual hypothesis that led to a revolution in legal thinking. This hypothesis, despite being against fact, produces an extraordinary hurdle for legal analysis, but it is an enormously powerful tool. The counterfactual hypothesis is that in an ideal world, all activity would be the optimal one. Changing the law would lead only to the adjustments that would return all activity to the optimal. Therefore, in such an ideal world, legal change and, by extension, law would be irrelevant. After explaining this counterfactual construct of *Coasean irrelevance*, this chapter shows how jurists in law and economics can use it to show that legal change is desirable. If a jurist can show that a new rule would lead to activity nearer the optimal than the current rule, this constitutes proof that at least that legal change must occur.

The facts of *Meinhard v. Salmon* help illustrate the importance of the potential irrelevance of law.[1] Salmon received a lucrative offer from Gerry, a business acquaintance. The offer could have expanded Salmon's business. Unbeknownst to Gerry, Salmon's business, which was the reason for their acquaintance, had a secret partner, Meinhard. If Gerry knew that Salmon operated in two capacities, as an individual and as a member of a partnership, then Gerry may have specified which of the two he selected as the recipient of his offer. Meinhard, the invisible partner, claimed the offer should be treated as made to the partnership. The litigation that Meinhard started eventually reached the highest court of the jurisdiction and the famous American judge, Benjamin Cardozo, and his colleague Andrews, who is almost equally famous for his vocal dissenting opinions. Previously established law

---

[1] 249 N.Y. 458 (1928). The text of the opinion is reproduced in Appendix A.

did not answer the question directly. Cardozo and his court would or should have been aware that future partnerships like that of Salmon with Meinhard would adjust their terms in reaction to the law that the court would set. If the reaction would cancel the effect of the opinion, then the change of the law would be pointless. If, however, Cardozo and his court could predict that future activity of partners would improve (approach the optimal) even after adjusting to the change, then the court's efforts would be truly justified. Then, the court's analysis would have overcome Coasean irrelevance and would provide a new rule that would increase welfare.

Coase realized that, as individuals attempt to circumvent rules, they press toward economic optimality. Although this realization may seem to resist regulatory impulses, it will also justify rules that remove obstacles that prevent individuals from reaching optimal arrangements.

Ronald Coase's Nobel Prize rewarded more than his pointing out that individuals counteract changes of the rules. Coase identified the direction and the destination of individuals' efforts, finding that in an ideal world, individuals' bargaining would restore the optimal allocation or setting. Coase probably embarked on this inquiry as an extension of exploring firm size, the optimal location of the boundaries separating firms from markets. He changed that question into the "make or buy" decision. If a firm decides to make an item, then the firm will have a larger size than if it decides to buy the item from the market. Transforming the question of firm size into "make or buy" is ingenious and reveals that Coase recognized enormous flexibility in people's affairs and organizations. When firms realize that the cost of buying an item is less than the cost of making it, they cease its production. The firm's productive activity changes depending on relative costs. The sensitivity that Coase saw in firms' activities seems related to the sensitivity that he saw in individuals' activities.

A. Coasean Irrelevance

Economic theory posits that activity is arranged to minimize costs and maximize benefits. Coase recognized that when the law moves an entitlement away from its optimal holders, they would be in the best position to re-acquire it. Because the new holders are not the optimal ones, they do not derive as much benefit from it and prefer to sell it back to its optimal holder. This bargain restores the optimal allocation. This phenomenon is also called the invariance principle. The allocation that the law imposes is irrelevant if this bargaining can occur unimpeded, and, vice versa, if bargaining is obstructed then a legal measure may be necessary to reach the optimal allocation.

The breakthrough for legal reasoning lies in the opposite of this statement. If bargaining is obstructed and the existing allocation is sub-optimal, then a legal intervention is necessary to approach the optimal allocation. This is a corollary that makes law necessary. It overcomes the inadequacy of normative reasoning and offers a truth-valued normative conclusion. After Coase, some laws are truly necessary. Before focusing on this, it is important to understand Coasean irrelevance and how the costs of transacting impede the parties' bargain. An example illustrates.

The classic example involves ranchers and farmers bargaining about fences in the shadow of laws about fencing. Fences protect farmers' crops from trampling but they impede ranching. Before starting the explanation of irrelevance, it is important to see that fencing depends on costs and benefits. If a single person engaged in both farming and ranching, he or she would decide to fence his or her farm only if this increased the total production. Coasean irrelevance means that in an ideal world, despite different owners of the farm and the ranch, the outcome (fences or not) depends on total costs and benefits rather than law. Fencing depends on total costs and benefits because each side can pay the other to waive its legal rights. The two sides can agree only if their arrangement brings them closer to the optimal.

Suppose, first, that farmers gain from fences more than the presence of fences harms ranchers. Fencing harms ranchers by 50 and helps farmers by 100. Coasean irrelevance means that fencing occurs regardless of the law. If the law allows fences, clearly farmers erect fences. Coasean irrelevance becomes salient if the law gives ranchers a right to "open range." Despite the open-range law, fencing occurs by agreement. The law entitles ranchers to the absence of fences, but the two sides can reach a deal to restore fences. Farmers are willing to pay up to 100 to have fences. Ranchers are fully compensated against their harm from fencing if they receive 50. This leaves ample room for an agreement. In exchange for a payment between 50 and 100, ranchers allow fencing. Thus, if fencing is superior, it occurs in theory regardless of the law's allocation of the choice between ranchers and farmers.

Coasean irrelevance also holds in the opposite situation where no fencing is superior. Suppose that the absence of fences helps ranchers more than it hurts farmers. Removing fencing costs farmers 50 but benefits ranchers by 100. Coasean irrelevance becomes salient if the law gives farmers the right to have fences. Despite the law, an agreement prevents fences. Ranchers are willing to pay up to 100 for the fences' removal. Farmers are fully compensated if they receive 50 or more, leaving ample room for an agreement. In exchange for a payment between 50 and 100, farmers will waive their right to fences. Thus, if the absence of fences is superior, it occurs in theory regardless of the law's allocation of the choice between ranchers and farmers.

B. NORMATIVE USE

Coasean irrelevance has the beauty of elementary simplicity, but it is also disturbing. It goes against the intuition that law is relevant. Rather than being frustrated by this contradiction, jurists in law and economics use Coasean irrelevance as a tool. Coasean irrelevance reveals how the actual interactions of individuals differ from those that would take place in an ideal world. This difference may justify rules to overcome it.

i. Revealing Imperfections

The conventional application of Coasean irrelevance uses it to reveal the ways in which reality differs from the ideal world where law is irrelevant. The process starts with the identification of the ideal outcome, that is, the set of conducts or interactions that are desirable. Because they are desirable, in the ideal world of Coasean irrelevance they would occur without regulation. The question becomes what are the impediments that prevent the desired reactions, that is, the hurdles that prevent Coasean irrelevance from materializing. This process identifies why private initiative fails and justifies a normative response. The law-and-economics jurist who has identified the impediment to ideal conducts has also identified a need for a legal response. The jurist can proceed to recommend how to overcome the impediment.

This use of Coasean irrelevance can also reveal gaps or imperfections in the edifice of economics as a theory that explains human behavior. After an example of the use of Coasean irrelevance to identify targets for regulation, the discussion turns to the typical causes of failures. This chapter discusses the usual cause, transaction costs that prevent bargains. Other causes that prevent Coasean irrelevance are discussed in the next chapter.

ii. An Example

For our example, replace ranchers with polluting manufacturers and consider environmental rules. Coasean irrelevance indicates that in a perfect world environmental regulation would be irrelevant because polluters and individuals would reach the optimal agreement for reducing pollution. Nevertheless, pollution regulation seems eminently justified. Jurisdictions without pollution regulation have experienced unacceptable pollution as the examples of the liberalized eastern European states reveal.[2] Why do manufacturers and farmers fail to reach the optimal bargain?

Numerous reasons impede the bargain with polluters. Millions of individuals in a region would have to expend a lot of effort and money to communicate their concerns, to reach a coherent, single negotiating stance, to engage all polluters and persuade them to accept the individuals' suggestion. The monetary and non-monetary costs involved with reaching a decision such as to install filters in smokestacks, persuading manufacturers, and implementing the installation are massive. Regulation of pollution is justified because the Coasean bargain is so costly that it will not be reached.

This example illustrates the main reason for the failure of Coasean irrelevance, transaction costs. Coasean irrelevance fails – and regulation is justified – for other reasons. Agreements may not be reached because of negotiating tactics (holdouts), errors, or asymmetric risk preferences. Finally, Coasean irrelevance does not apply to effects on wealth and its distribution. Accordingly, distributional consequences may also justify rules. As we saw in Chapter 4, redistribution rarely does motivate substantive rules, because taxes usually redistribute better. The next paragraphs discuss transaction costs. The other failures are the subject of the next chapter.

C. Transaction Costs: The Usual Suspect

Transaction costs are seen as the main reason for failures of Coasean irrelevance. Transaction costs are the costs of reaching an agreement as opposed to the costs of fulfilling it. Irrelevance does not arise because the cost of reaching the bargain outweighs its benefits.

---

[2] See Daniel H. Cole, *Instituting Environmental Protection: From Red to Green in Poland* (London: Palgrave Macmillan, 1997).

Some confusion surrounds the precise definition of transaction costs and their distinction from the costs that parties incur after the contract. Whereas transaction costs are borne in the process of reaching an agreement, fulfillment costs are borne after the agreement in the course of its performance and fulfillment. Fulfilment costs may include costs of performance, monitoring, or enforcement. The cost of performance is the principal obligation of the party. Monitoring and enforcement ensure obtaining the benefits from the other side's performance.

Transaction costs can be difficult to discern because they are extraordinarily common; they truly exist at every interaction. We are so used to incurring these costs that they become virtually unnoticeable. What, for example, are the transaction costs of going to the theater? Consider first the effort spent learning the available shows and selecting one. Other costs are queuing for tickets, the travel to the theater, and perhaps parking.[3] These are transaction costs because they are part of reaching the deal, rather than enjoying and fulfilling it. The main transaction involves an exchange of money (the price of the ticket) for admittance to a performance. Two theater patrons who expect to enjoy a play equally may reach different conclusions because they live at different distances from the theater. Suppose that the first lives in an apartment within a short walk, while the second must drive a long distance to reach the theater. Their two exchanges are identical because they obtain the same enjoyment from the play and pay the same ticket price. Whereas that exchange is appealing to the neighbor, the hassle of driving and parking may dissuade the distant patron from a transaction the substance of which is appealing. That hassle prevents an otherwise desirable exchange.

Reaching a binding, long-term contract involves much more significant costs. The mere negotiation of a complex contract is a major effort that likely requires legal expertise and perhaps other specialized skills and knowledge, such as of valuation and deal structure. The monetary nature of legal and brokerage fees makes clear that they are transaction costs. Even without any monetary transaction costs, the parties likely expend significant non-monetary costs in reaching an agreement.

---

[3] Some might object that some of these items are not costs because they do not involve monetary expenditures. Decisions are influenced by non-monetary concerns. Therefore, non-monetary burdens must be included in the calculus of decision making. Because economic analysis studies decisions on the basis of comparisons of costs and benefits, all items that sway decisions by functioning as costs or benefits must be included, including non-monetary ones.

When trying to define transaction costs, their juxtaposition with fulfillment costs is particularly revealing. Again, the setting is confusing because no consensus exists for the term for non-transaction costs. The term "fulfillment" costs corresponds to the substance of incurring costs in the course of, and with the purpose of, fulfilling the contract. Transaction costs, by contrast, are incurred in the course of, and with the purpose of, entering into the contract. It is important to know that both transaction costs and fulfillment costs can be monetary or non-monetary and both include opportunity costs as well as actual expenditures.

Some examples help sort these various types of costs. Pink tomatoes are a hypothetical product that is extremely perishable: they spoil if they are not constantly refrigerated. Suppose that John enjoys eating fresh pink tomatoes and one of the few places where he can obtain them is his local farmers' market, where area farmers sell their produce every Monday evening from 4 P.M. to 6 P.M.

1. John usually buys enough pink tomatoes for the entire week. Yesterday, his refrigerator broke. A local restaurant would let John store the tomatoes in the restaurant's refrigerator at some expense. The cost of refrigeration is not a transaction cost. Despite the increased cost of refrigeration, going to the market and entering into the transaction of buying the tomatoes has not become less appealing. The tomatoes themselves are less appealing. If John decides not to rent refrigerator space from the restaurant, he will not buy tomatoes. The cost of enjoying them is too high. He would not buy tomatoes even if the seller delivered them. Refrigeration is a monetary cost that is not a transaction cost.

2. John's refrigerator is repaired, but the bus drivers go on strike. To get to the farmers market, John must hire a taxi at some expense greater than the bus fare. The taxi fare is a transaction cost for tomato purchasing. If the seller appeared with the tomatoes at John's door, John would buy them. The cost of getting to the transaction prevents the consummation of it. It is a monetary transaction cost.

3. As 4 P.M. approaches on a Monday with no bus strikes or refrigerator failures, John finds out that his favorite band will hold their only show for the year at 4 P.M. John chooses whether to buy the tomatoes or attend the show. Going to the farmers' market

precludes attending the show. Going to the show is the opportunity cost of going to the market. If the opportunity cost is too
high, John will attend the show. John's enjoyment of the show
creates a time conflict that seems to be a transaction cost that
takes the form of a non-monetary opportunity cost. The tomatoes are still appealing to John but he is forced to give them up
to obtain the greater gain of attending the show. If the seller
were available at a different time, then John would also buy the
tomatoes.

4. John receives an invitation to visit for a week a dear friend
who lives in a different city, where pink tomatoes are not sold.
John cannot transport his tomatoes with him. John chooses
whether to buy the tomatoes or to visit his friend. Visiting his
friend precludes enjoying the tomatoes but the cost of going to
the market is unchanged. Visiting his friend is an opportunity
cost of having the tomatoes. If the opportunity cost is too
high, John will not buy the tomatoes. Visiting his friend is the
opportunity cost of enjoying the tomatoes. John would not buy
the tomatoes even if the seller appeared at his door. The visit is
an opportunity cost, but it is not a transaction cost.

No easy test exists that would identify transaction costs without
ambiguity. One test examines the consequences of enlarging the cost.
Enlarging transaction costs does not influence the desirability of the
agreement but frustrates it by making the agreement not worth entering. By contrast, enlarging costs of fulfillment makes the contract
undesirable by eliminating the gains from trade. Moreover, costs of
fulfillment can be surprises that render the contract unattractive after
the agreement. By contrast, transaction costs tend not to cause losses
because they tend to stand in the way of reaching the agreement. If
transaction costs turn out to be surprisingly high, the usual consequence
is that the agreement is not reached, rather than one side regretting its
decision to agree. In other words, transaction costs should have the effect of impeding the parties from capturing gains, rather than the effect
of reducing those gains. Let us try this imprecise tool for distinguishing
transaction from fulfillment costs in a few examples.

Return to the example of ranchers and farmers. Consider the following variations.

Ranching used to be more productive but now farming is. The
old agreement of ranchers and farmers was to grant to ranchers an

easement to graze. Suppose that, for the elimination of an easement, some specific clauses must be included in a document (a deed or a contract), and that it must be notarized and recorded. Consider the various costs involved in this contract: costs of grazing, fencing, trampling, and drafting the document, notarizing, and recording it. Which are transaction costs? Grazing, fencing, and trampling are the substantive reasons that motivate the contract. As costs, they are substantive and they cannot be considered transaction costs. The costs of drafting and recordation fall at the opposite extreme. Neither party sees drafting or recordation as part of its principal contractual duties or benefits. A twist that shows their nature as transaction costs is to suppose that the gains from trade are very small so that the contract is barely desirable. In other words, alter the setting so that the contract is at the limit of not being worthwhile. Any increase, from that setting, of the drafting or recordation costs would preclude the agreement despite that its substance remains desirable. Any increase of the cost of the performance of a substantive part makes the agreement itself undesirable.

Hypothesizing some values makes the example more concrete. Farming produces gains of 80 without trampling but 60 with trampling. Ranching produces gains of 110 if the cattle can cross (and trample) the farm but 91 if not. Since trampling costs 20 to farmers and 19 to ranchers, they should agree to do away with it. If drafting and recordation cost 0.40, then 0.60 of gains remain for the parties from a deal. One possible agreement is that the farmer pays 19.30 to the rancher and incurs the drafting and recordation expense of 0.40. The rancher receives an amount that justifies foregoing trampling. The farmer spends less than the gains from no trampling. If the cost of drafting and recordation were 1.01, then they would leave no room for an agreement. Despite that a ban on trampling is advantageous in substance, the agreement is unappealing. A reduction of the costs of drafting and recordation would restore its appeal.

i. Vantage Point Makes Transaction Costs

The conclusion of the example that drafting and recordation are transaction costs must not be generalized to be an inviolable principle. A twist of the example illustrates that drafting costs can also function as fulfillment costs.

As ranchers and farmers negotiate and draft their agreement, they consider the ease of its amendment. With some additional drafting expense, the parties can make the contract easier to adapt to new circumstances, more flexible. Is the additional expense on flexibility a transaction cost?

Although drafting costs are usually transaction costs, this setting allows one to argue that this particular incremental cost of drafting is not a transaction cost. The decision to pursue flexibility comes from the parties. In exchange for the costlier drafting, the parties obtain an increment of flexibility, such as an option to unilaterally terminate their contract. Rather than block the gains, this increment of drafting cost seems to create substantive gains, arguing against categorizing it as a transaction cost and for treating it akin to consideration, that is, the premium paid for an option. Thus, the example shows that a single type of costs may have components that take the opposite character from usual.

Granted, some enforcement costs, including some legal fees, are transaction costs. The preceding analysis does not also argue that all enforcement costs (and legal fees) are transaction costs. The possibility for innovations in the design of enforcement indicates that at least part of enforcement costs is not a transaction cost because it is discretionary. One must also realize that the vantage point influences the characterization of a cost as a transaction cost. Enforcement costs that seem to be transaction costs from the parties' perspective are not transaction costs from society's perspective. The legal fees that parties seek to avoid are instrumental for the improvement of the legal system (and the reduction of future legal fees).

ii. Innovations Transform Transaction Costs

Any change in the law that imposes a cost as a condition for enforcement limits the benefits parties obtain from contracts. A comparison of contracts with informal understandings suggests that enforceability is a distinguishing feature of contracts. The parties, however, can influence the cost of enforcement. They can include in the contract clauses or rights that make enforcement less costly. The influence of contract design on the cost of enforcement brings enforcement costs closer to fulfillment costs. The inadequacy of the contract induces innovation. A better contract clause that produces less costly enforcement would allow a greater number of mutually advantageous contracts. Parties who knew the pointlessness of contracts without the new clause refrained from using contracts in some settings. In the same settings after the new clause appears, parties can use contracts and capture gains.

If a contract with a less costly enforcement scheme was truly impossible, then those costs of enforcement would seem closer to transaction costs. They could be analogized to artificial barriers that preclude the contract (and that prevent the gains it would bring) rather than attributes of the setting that reduce the gains that a contract can produce.

iii. Litigation Costs: Transaction Cost or Not?

A problem with assuming enforcement costs are transaction costs is that context matters. Despite that the cost of litigation may prevent some parties from collecting, litigation provides a service to society by advancing legal interpretation by filling the gaps in the law. Despite that it is a transaction cost for the parties, litigation produces a benefit for society. Society would incur a cost to obtain the refinement of interpretation, the coverage of gaps, the resolution of contradictions between rules and their adaptation to the evolving socioeconomic circumstances. Therefore, litigation can be interpreted as producing a service that society obtains. In exchange for it, society spends resources on the legal system. The litigants also expend resources which, from their perspective, likely are transaction costs.

Two interesting implications arise from this analysis. First, jurisdictions may differ in extracting services from litigation. Second, the design of the legal system may be able to prevent litigation costs from being experienced as transaction costs by the parties. International comparisons inform both.

iv. Example: Increasing Social Gain from Private Litigation

Litigation is a zero-sum game from the parties' perspective. Its byproducts, however, have value for society. The clarification of ambiguous laws, the interpretive coverage of omissions, and the resolution of contradictions between laws are undeniably desirable. Jurisdictions have differences in how they extract these benefits from litigation.

Because every law leaves openings for interpretation, one of the services that litigation provides is interpretation. Laws can be interpreted consistently so that similar disputes obtain the same outcome. Otherwise, laws can be interpreted arbitrarily and similar disputes lead to dissimilar outcomes. Naturally, consistency is preferable but for consistency to exist, the legal system must provide some means for interpretations not to change, that is, for interpretations to solidify.

Several details of the legal system facilitate the solidification of interpretation. A leading one is the use of written opinions. Without written opinions, consistency of interpretation may be impossible. Consistency also requires repetition of prior interpretations. Of further assistance is a habit, norm, or preference for adhering to prior interpretations. A system of appeals to a higher court that monitors interpretations would similarly enhance consistency. These seem to be universal features of legal systems. All liberal democracies use written court opinions, have norms for consistent interpretation, and employ review by appellate courts. Thinking back a few centuries or about systems besides liberal democracies should remind us that these features are neither necessary nor obvious. They are legal technology that is enormously important.

Despite these basic similarities, the legal systems of liberal democracies do have great differences. A particularly profound difference may be the division in "common law" and "civil law" systems. Many think that the primary difference between the two jurisdictions is whether court opinions are "primary" sources of law, that is, have a binding effect on subsequent decisions. The strong discussion about the propriety of judicial activism suggests that judges do deviate from narrow adherence to precedent. No similar debate seems to arise in civil law jurisdictions. Rather, those jurisdictions seem to have mechanisms that prevent judicial activism, perhaps unwittingly.[4] Common law presents the opposite setting, producing an environment that induces activism, again likely unwittingly. These arguments suggest that common law jurisdictions that elevate judicial decisions to primary sources of law actually place part of the responsibility of legal evolution on courts. The lawmaking function of the courts is not limited to establishing rules; it also reflects the updating of rules by courts. The endpoint of this argument is that common law systems place part of the burden of updating the law on courts rather than the alternative source of legal rules, legislatures.

These statements are limited. Courts in civil law jurisdictions may also occasionally update rules. Moreover, jurisdictions within each

---

[4] Nicholas L. Georgakopoulos, "Independence in the Career and Recognition Judiciary," *Chicago Roundtable* 7 (2000):205.

group do differ. This sequence of hypotheses does not argue that every common law jurisdiction assigns the entire task of updating rules exclusively to courts and that all civil law jurisdictions preclude their courts from ever performing any updating. A nuanced view is certainly more accurate. Common law jurisdictions tend to have courts perform more of the task of updating than civil ones. This analysis also has limited breadth. Judicial activism may have other consequences in addition to updating rules, perhaps negative ones. Although the limited breadth of the analysis precludes a conclusion about the desirability of judicial activism, the conclusion that common law courts do more updating is secure.

The inquiry into updating started as an inquiry into jurisdictions' gains from courts. Because updating the law is a desirable service, the conclusion that common law courts update more than civil courts do means that common law jurisdictions tend to obtain that service from their courts more than civil law jurisdictions do.

One more caveat – this difference will influence other functions of the legal system. For example, as common law jurisdictions assign more of the updating task to courts, they reduce the corresponding demand on legislatures. This indicates one may find repercussions for legislatures.

The exploration of the services that legal systems obtain from litigation was undertaken for the purpose of recognizing the changing nature of transaction costs. The litigation expense that is a transaction cost for the parties provides desirable services to society. This is an important observation. The economist dislikes transaction costs but the observation above precludes economists from jumping to the normative conclusion "first, kill all litigation." This contradiction can be the basis for normative analysis.

v. Normative Implications for Litigation of the Analysis of Transaction Costs

Because Coasean irrelevance is a normative tool, the study of it and of transaction costs should include a normative extension. Moreover, the analysis above contains a major tension that requires resolution. The tension is that litigation has value for society while being a transaction cost for the parties, yet society defines the rules and institutions of litigation. If litigation were solely a transaction cost, society's legal system should eliminate it. Its value for society indicates some amount of litigation is desirable. When a contradiction contains choices of the legal system, improvement must be possible. This must be fertile ground for normative analysis.

Facile proposals are easy. They would involve reducing the cost of litigation while compromising the benefits society receives from litigation. Consider, for example, a proposal to replace courts with summary tribunals that do not publish their opinions. This type of dispute resolution might reduce the cost of litigation to the parties. Because opinions would not be published, this scheme would eliminate the gains to society from consistency of interpretation. The tribunals would resolve disputes, but other tribunals would not know their interpretations.

The challenge is to design a litigation system that reduces parties' litigation expenses and, ideally, eliminates them, while maintaining or increasing the benefits that society obtains from litigation. Because the current state of research cannot specify accurately the benefits of litigation for society, it is unlikely that a proposal can be identified as optimal. Nevertheless, some proposals would be recognized as improvements compared with the status quo.

A British experiment with criminal defense funding offers a framework for thinking about alternative regimes. Likely concern that the expenditure of criminal defence was beyond individuals' budgets, the British government established a fund for criminal defence. Unlike nationalized medicine, this is not nationalized criminal defence. (After all, because criminal defence is litigation against the government, nationalized criminal defence would nearly be an oxymoron.) Rather, the British system supervises the reimbursement of law firms, which receive normal fees and the selection of which is made by the client and defendant.[5] A defining feature of this system is that the defendant retains the powers of the client, despite the government funding. Thus, this can be called a government-funded, litigant-directed system.

The experience with the British system is brief and conclusions are necessarily tentative. Nevertheless, it may be an extraordinary solution to a major problem. Litigation becomes costless for the client. By comparison, a system that lets defendants pay for their criminal defence causes wealth to influence the quality of defence. In the United States, the legal system tries to avoid injustice by funding the defence of the indigent. The result is underfunded representation that becomes inadequate representation and leads to biased justice.

---

[5] Norman Lefstein, "In Search of Gideon's Promise: Lessons from England and the Need for Federal Help," *Hastings Law Journal* 55 (2004):835 *et seq.*

Part of the appeal of the government-funded, litigant-directed scheme is that litigation only appears to be costless. The appearance is due to the absence of any cost for the client. Compared with a system where some litigation does not occur or occurs under inadequate conditions, its cost is likely increased. The focus should be on quality. The additional litigation of the British criminal system is not its central feature. Many defendants receive better representation than they could afford. Courts obtain the benefit of better advocacy. The judicial system approaches the ideal of treating all defendants equally with respect to wealth.

The result seems ideal: no cost and improved quality. The next chapter explores other failures of Coasean irrelevance.

D. Concluding Exercises

The changing nature of costs is very important. The first two exercises explore the change in perspective that changes transaction costs into fulfillment costs and vice versa.

Exercise 5.1: Recall daily activities of a character from literature or of yourself during the past few days. Which efforts or actions are akin to transaction costs and which are akin to fulfillment costs? Consider the efforts that seem to be a transaction cost. From which perspective are they a fulfillment cost?

Exercise 5.2: The table is a list of activities. Each activity entails effort, which in the language of economics is a cost. That effort is exerted in the context of a contract or informal arrangement. The effort is a transaction cost from the perspective of one actor and a fulfillment cost from the perspective of another. The first row is the table is completed as a guide. The activity is getting the newspaper to the reader's home (or office). In the arrangement between the newspaper and the reader, its delivery is not necessary because the reader can purchase the paper in person and carry it home. The typical reader does not derive enjoyment from getting the newspaper and that effort corresponds to a transaction cost. For the delivery clerk whom the newspaper hires to deliver the paper, however, the effort to deliver the paper is a principal component of the job. Accordingly, the delivery is a fulfillment cost from the perspective of the clerk.

Complete the table. For each activity, find two parties, subjects or roles. One from whose perspective the activity is a transaction cost and one from whose perspective the activity is a fulfillment cost. Place the party that bears it as a transaction cost in the column "T-Cost for . . . " and the party that bears it as a fulfillment cost in the column "F-Cost for . . . "

Activity	T-cost for . . .	F-cost for . . .
Getting home the newspaper	reader	delivery clerk
Reading the newspaper		reader
Glancing at advertisements in the newspaper		ad agency
Booking travel reservations		
Travel to holiday location		
Purchase of gas or ticket for commute to work	employee	
Effort spent at work		
Effort spent selecting a school		publisher of school selection guide
Effort spent learning at school		
Effort spent improving law		
Effort spent informing citizens about new law		
Effort spent adjusting conduct on account of new law		

Exercise 5.3: This sequence of questions tries to demonstrate the use of Coasean irrelevance in the context of normative argumentation. To avoid the heat of feeling about the issue, it takes us back to a Star Wars setting. In a small, poor planet at the outskirts of the galaxy lives Watto, a shopkeeper. He has Anakin Skywalker as a slave. Watto's ownership of Anakin is advantageous to him because Anakin is gifted in building and repairing pod racers. Slavery is widely accepted there.

The exercise requires this setting to be a steady state from a normative perspective, that is, to not already produce pressure for the abolition of slavery. This requires some heroic assumptions that make slavery irrelevant for Anakin.

If slavery were to be abolished, Anakin would choose to be employed by Watto in pod-race repair. Also, the competitive wages for pod-race repairers would be such that Anakin's lifestyle would not change at all and Anakin would be equally happy despite the abolition of slavery. Unrealistic as these assumptions may appear, they produce Coasean irrelevance. That is a necessary background condition because the exercise focuses on the following event.

Someone discovers that Anakin possesses a mental power (the Force) that makes him one of the few individuals suitable for becoming a Jedi Knight. A representative of the Jedi order offers to buy Anakin's freedom from Watto at a high price, but Watto refuses. If Anakin were not Watto's slave, he would have accepted an offer to join the Jedi. On these facts, the law-and-economics normative argument about the desirability of slavery on this planet follows the reasoning "slavery is undesirable because it prevents Anakin from joining the Jedi." How does this argument depend on Coasean irrelevance?

Discussion: It should be apparent that Coasean irrelevance fails because slavery produces a different outcome than its absence. Because the change of a rule makes a difference, its impact on at least the welfare of Watto, Anakin, and the Jedi order is revealed. From the example's statement, we know that Anakin and the Jedi order prefer the outcome that slavery prevents. We also know that Watto dislikes this outcome. His refusal to release Anakin is what prevents Coasean irrelevance. The complete line of reasoning might take a shape similar to the following:

* Coasean irrelevance requires that slave owners accept all reasonable offers that would reallocate their slaves' labor where those would prefer.
* Watto's behavior indicates that slave owners do not always do so.
* Therefore, slavery is undesirable.

Needless to say, this is a minimal justification of the undesirability of slavery. The argument against slavery can be strengthened by considering the impossibility of the slaves borrowing to buy their freedom. Furthermore, suppose Watto receives several offers for his slaves each year. He seeks to extract the most profit from each trade. Therefore, he needs to insist on a price very close to the buyer's reservation price. If Watto reduces what he asks, more trades will occur but Watto will not obtain new information about possible changes in buyers' reservation values. This last problem is a negotiation holdout and is one of the topics discussed in the next chapter.

E. Bibliographical Note

Because of the overlap with the next chapter, please refer to the next chapter's bibliographical note.

6. More Failures of Coasean Irrelevance

The previous chapter introduced the normative use of Coasean irrelevance and the main obstacle to irrelevance, transaction costs. This chapter continues by exploring the less conventional reasons that prevent irrelevance.

A. NEGOTIATION HOLDOUTS

The standard analysis of Coasean irrelevance presumes that the parties reach an agreement in every instance where it is advantageous for them, that is, whenever the total gains exceed the total costs, including transaction costs. In an ideal world of perfect and symmetric information, each side knows the other side's valuation and, when room for it exists, an agreement seems inescapable. In a world of imperfect information, however, occasional bluffs and ruses are plausible negotiating tactics. The side that seeks the advantage by the "holdout" negotiating tactic does risk losing the agreement. This means that Coasean irrelevance may occasionally fail despite that an attractive bargain is available. The bargain is not reached because of bargaining tactics that prevent it.

This failure seems highly artificial without an example that shows the potential appeal of "holdout" tactics. Suppose that the gain from each agreement between a rancher and a farmer about fencing is 20 and they would normally split it equally. Ranchers know, however, that 20 percent of the farmers succumb to hard negotiating tactics and accept 3, leaving 17 for the rancher. A 5 percent fraction of farmers dislikes hard negotiation and refuses to deal after experiencing it. If a rancher expects 100 negotiations with farmers, cooperative negotiation produces 10 for the rancher in all 100 instances. Hard negotiation

112

results in a loss of five agreements and extra gains in ten (the rest remain unchanged). The five lost agreements cost 50 (five times the gain that would have been obtained by avoiding the holdout, which is 10) but that cost is less than the gains. The rancher receives 17 instead of 10 in ten agreements for a gain of 70. After accounting for the lost deals, the hard negotiating tactics produce a net gain of 20 and appear to be an appealing strategy for the rancher. Society's assessment differs. The holdout strategy did not increase the gains. Each agreement still produces gains of 20 in sum for both sides. The hard negotiation does no more than change their division, sending more toward the rancher. From society's perspective, the only consequence of hard negotiation is the loss of five bargains that would each create a 20 gain. That loss comes with no mitigating features.

When hard negotiating tactics are appealing to the participants, some bargains may fail to occur. Because Coasean irrelevance depends on bargains materializing, it does not occur in such settings.

The potential for holdouts qualifies Coasean irrelevance. An unqualified Coasean irrelevance obtains only if all advantageous bargains occur, whereas holdouts indicate that some bargains might not be reached. The qualifications that holdouts impose on Coasean irrelevance depend on the frequency and nature of the holdouts, that is, on their quantitative and qualitative implications. Of further interest is the question of symmetry. In some settings, holdout tactics may operate with equal force against buyers and sellers. The implications for Coasean irrelevance of this setting would be quite different from one where one side endures the most of holdout tactics.

Holdouts have only quantitative consequences if they only distort price or the number of bargains. The example had some farmers capitulate to holdouts. Their bargains were more advantageous for ranchers than the baseline of equal division. Compare the alternative that all bargains occur and the division of the gain is even, which leads to Coasean irrelevance. The other terms of the agreement are the same in holdouts and not. The effect of holdouts is limited to price and the non-occurrence of some bargains. Because holdouts in that setting only influence the price and number of bargains, their effect can be considered only quantitative.

Holdouts could also influence the bargains' terms, their nature, the conduct of parties, or the background in ways that are unrelated to price. Those changes might not influence the number of bargains. Nevertheless, holdouts with qualitative effects likely produce outcomes that differ from Coasean irrelevance. That difference likely has a qualitative component, next to the quantitative nature of the number of lost bargains.

The example also displayed a lack of symmetry because only ranchers used holdout tactics and only farmers succumbed to them. In a symmetrical setting, the effect would be the same on both sides.

Whether they are symmetrical, quantitative or qualitative, holdouts may cause a deviation from Coasean irrelevance. Without holdouts, in an otherwise ideal environment where individuals are trusting and divide gains evenly, individuals' bargains and conduct would produce Coasean irrelevance. Because the threat of holdouts changes bargains and conduct, it can prevent Coasean irrelevance. Therefore, a law that reduces this cost of holdouts and lets conducts approach the optimal would be preferable.

This conclusion does not imply assigning a right to the group that would most often buy the right. It may be more important to avoid holdouts than to reduce the number of bargains. One group may use holdout tactics when buying rights but not when selling them. Then, assigning the right to that group would avoid holdouts and could be preferable to assigning the right to the group that is more likely to place the highest value on the right. Assigning the right to the latter group would reduce the number of bargains (and transaction costs) but would also produce a social loss due to bargains sacrificed to holdouts.

Thus, the appropriate legal response to holdouts may be the opposite of the appropriate response to transaction costs. Because transaction costs are considered the primary cause for failures of the Coase theorem, this difference could have practical importance. When Coasean irrelevance fails because of transaction costs, the desirable response of the legal system is to reduce transactions or their costs. This, for example, guides the default terms of contract law or the allocation of property rights.

An example underscores this difference, that although transaction costs argue for reducing transactions, holdouts may argue for increasing them. Returning to the farmer-rancher example, assume that if an agreement is desired, each would enter it with a specific member of the other group. The number of such pairings is 100. Suppose that if the law entitled ranchers to no fences, in 70 of the rancher-farmer pairings, the farmer would acquire the right to fences. If transaction costs prevent 10 percent of the agreements from materializing, they indicate that farmers should have the right to fences. This allocation leads to 30 of the rancher-farmer pairings needing an agreement rather than 70.

The loss of 10 percent due to transaction costs means that of all the pairings, only three (rather than seven) fail to reach the optimal outcome. If instead the problem is holdouts and only ranchers use tactics that prevent 10 percent of agreements only when they buy rights, then assigning the right to ranchers is preferable. Because farmers do not use holdouts, despite that agreements occur in 70 of the pairings, all 100 pairings do reach the optimal.

Despite that holdouts appear to have significant policy implications, they have drawn little attention. The problem of holdouts fails to produce generalizable conclusions, echoing a drawback that appears to a lesser degree in the problem of systematic errors.

B. Systematic Errors

Psychological inroads into economic analysis have revealed weaknesses in the assumption of rationality. Evidence indicates individuals make systematic errors. The relevant implication for Coasean irrelevance is that some advantageous bargains may appear undesirable due to errors and, therefore, may not materialize. Errors are an objection, not only to Coasean irrelevance but also to economic analysis in general. They were discussed under "Bounded Rationality" in Chapter 3.

C. Risk Aversion

Individuals are averse to risk. The intensity of risk aversion varies by individual and by setting. Uncertain gains are discounted and each side may discount the other's offer by different amounts. Appealing Coasean bargains may appear unappealing after the sides adjust for risk.

Society may also be averse to some risks that influence all of society, such as depressions or wars. Those sources of risk tend to be rare. A more usual setting involves uncertainties that do not involve global harm. Uncertainty that involves local or specialized harm joins a multitude of other such uncertainties when it is considered at a social level.

Society is not risk averse when each source of uncertainty is one of numerous and unrelated sources of risk. In those cases, society is diversified and, therefore, risk neutral. Society would accept to add one more advantageous wager to the numerous wagers it effectively takes. Society would not discount the gains from each for uncertainty because their aggregation produces a diversified stake. Akin to an investor who is risk neutral when holding a diversified portfolio, society is risk neutral about the many independent uncertainties. When society is risk neutral and expects gain from a bargain but individuals' risk aversion makes them not pursue that gain, the result is a failure of Coasean irrelevance. The socially superior arrangement does not occur.

To construct an example that would illustrate the effect of aversion to risk, it is necessary to quantify it. Suppose that farmers who allow the passage of cattle suffer probabilistic harm. Instead of losing a specified amount, they lose one of two amounts depending on the conditions. Suppose that if worms create their tunnels near the surface, the cattle cause greater harm. The farmers' harm is 55 if the tunnels are high and 25 if not. The tunnels are equally likely to be high or low, suggesting an expected loss of 40. The uncertainty, however, is distasteful to farmers.

For practical purposes, it is important to clarify that the tunnels' location cannot be determined. Otherwise, the parties could address the uncertainty in their agreement. For example, the agreement could specify that low tunnels are a condition for cattle's passage or that the farmer's compensation depends on the tunnels' location. Private contracting is remarkably resourceful and routinely outwits stylized hypotheticals. Nevertheless, for the purpose of the example, the farmers must be unable to avoid this uncertainty.

Suppose that the farmers' distaste for the risk is equivalent to a loss of 12.[1] Despite that they, on average, lose 40, they treat that uncertainty as a cost of 52. The farmers are averse to risk and require this additional 12 to become indifferent to bearing it. The farmers would need a comparable inducement to suffer other displeasures of the same size. This compensation is necessary for them to bear the risk, to sit on the proverbial pins and needles.

The farmers' aversion to risk influences the capacity to reach an agreement with the ranchers. If the ranchers benefit from their cattle crossing the farmers' land by 50, risk aversion precludes the possibility for an agreement. The farmers do not accept less than 52 and the ranchers do not offer more than 50.

Because risk is distasteful, one might think that avoiding it may be appropriate. The conflict with what is socially ideal becomes clear if we

---

[1]   A technical note explains the provenance of this figure. This is approximately the discount that farmers with wealth of 30.375 would place on a 50 percent chance to lose 30 and have 0.375 if they exhibit constant relative risk aversion with a coefficient of 1. See discussion and references in Chapter 4, note 5 and accompanying text. See also exercise 7.3 which derives utility-of-wealth functions reflecting different types of risk aversion and exercise 8.4 which corresponds to this footnote.

aggregate all farmers. Make all farmers form a single corporation and contribute their land in exchange for shares. All farms are identical and all farmers receive the same number of shares. The corporation only engages in the negotiation with the ranchers and the farms are its only assets. Each farm's harm is not related to that of other farms. Because the corporation holds many farms, about half will have high tunnels and half will have low ones. Although half the farms suffer harm of 55 and half of 25, the corporation suffers harm of about 40 per farm. As a result, no farmer is exposed to the uncertainty. Each farmer loses 40 due to the passage of cattle. The result is that the farmers would want their corporation to accept any payment over 40 from each rancher. Society's attitude toward local risks is analogous to the corporation example. Society contains all farmers and loses about 40 per farm.

The uncertainty that individual farmers dislike does not exist for society. When agreements that would create value from society's perspective do not occur because of risk aversion, this phenomenon is a failure of private contracting to achieve the socially optimal outcome. A rule that gives ranchers the right to cross farms is preferable in the example. Because the farmers' risk aversion has not been cured, however, the impetus still exists for them to reach a bargain with the ranchers against trampling.

Because the cattle induce harm of 52, farmers offer up to that amount for the ranchers to stop crossing, that is, for the ranchers not to exercise their right. Ranchers accept offers over 50. A deal seems feasible at about 51 where ranchers would promise not to cross farmers' land. The attempt to avoid the waste of risk aversion by assigning the right to ranchers appears to fail.

Because of this incentive to reinstate the wasteful arrangement, the new allocation of rights is not stable. For the solution that the legal system imposes to be stable, it must either contain a mechanism that prevents agreements to return to the suboptimal outcome or provide a substantive solution that cancels farmers' aversion to risk. Naturally, the latter is a vastly superior arrangement. A substantive solution is stable and allows further improvements. It is stable because the farmers will not want to avoid the risk and it is flexible because it can adjust to future changes of the relative values of ranching and farming and allows further improvements of the risk-sharing mechanism. The farmer-rancher example can show this.

Suppose that the law did assign the right to cross through farmers' land to ranchers. Because farmers suffer a loss that, due to their aversion to risk, they value at 52, they seek to induce ranchers not to exercise their right. Ranchers, in turn, are ready to accept not to cross the farmers' land if they receive compensation over 50. Numerous farmer-rancher deals are imminent. Because these would cancel the attempt to avoid the waste due to risk aversion, a response seems desirable.

i. Imposing a Transaction Cost

Consider, first, the response of requiring a fee of 20 before enforcing any agreements about crossing land. This would eliminate the impending agreements. Because farmers would need to pay 20 to have an enforceable agreement to avoid harm of 52, they would only offer up to 32. The ranchers would decline that offer because they find only offers that exceed 50 appealing. The fee prevents the agreements as any transaction cost would. The parties continue to find the agreement desirable in substance.

This imposition of a transaction cost seems to achieve the goal of preventing the agreements that would re-create the waste of risk aversion. However, transaction costs have undesirable consequences for the long term. Suppose that farming became more profitable so that avoiding trampling is worth 51 instead of 40. Even if farmers lost their aversion to risk, the fee of 20 would not allow them to reach an agreement with the ranchers that would prevent cattle from crossing into their land. The point, of course, is that this is undesirable. Under the new conditions, society is better off without the cattle crossing the farms. Private contracting would prevent cattle crossings but the fee stands in the way.

The transaction cost solidifies the allocation of rights to ranchers and prevents innovative contracting. Replacing the fee with a substantive solution of the problem of risk aversion yields a sharply different outcome.

ii. Substantive Solutions of Risk Aversion

A solution of the problem of risk aversion is substantive if it aligns preferences with those of society as opposed to preventing an agreement that the sides consider desirable. If either law or contract produces a substantive solution, then the drive toward an undesirable contract (and a suboptimal allocation of rights) disappears. Moreover, a substantive solution need not impede contracting and, therefore, the incentive for innovations remains. Thus, a substantive solution maintains the optimal setting in the short term and preserves the optimal path in the long term.

Continuing the rancher-farmer example, suppose that an insurance scheme is created to address farmers' risk. The risk for the farmers is that the crossing cattle may reduce the farm's product by either 25 or 55, each outcome occurring with 50 percent probability. The terms of the insurance are that each farmer may purchase a policy for 14 and will receive 26 when this farmer's property suffers the high damage. Restated with conventional insurance terms, the policy has a premium of 14 and a deductible of 29. In probabilistic terms, farmers who buy a policy reduce their risk. If the good outcome materializes, they suffer damage of 25 and have paid the premium of 14, for a net loss of 39. If the bad outcome materializes, they suffer damage of 55, receive an insurance payment of 26, and have paid the premium of 14, for a net loss of 43.[2] Thus, the uncertainty is between losing 39 and 43. Compared with the risk of either losing 25 or 55, the insurance has vastly reduced the farmers' risk.

Again, we can assign a value to the burden of bearing this risk. Suppose that farmers consider bearing this risk equivalent to a loss of 1. Their new calculation is that cattle harm them either 39 or 43, on average 41. Adding the suffering from the risk brings the total harm to 42. The ranchers still demand 50 to forego crossings.

The high aversion to risk that farmers exhibited (without insurance) produced an inferior arrangement. Even regulation granting ranchers the right to cross farms would be countered by the farmers because they would induce ranchers not to cross their farms. The insurance contract that allows farmers to reduce risk also prevents the suboptimal arrangement. The insurance that reduces farmers' risk gives stability to the allocation of the right to ranchers. More importantly, the insurance scheme avoids the need for allocating the right to trample to ranchers.

The superiority of substantive solutions is that they preserve the incentives to innovate. That becomes clear by considering any improvement of the insurance scheme or that the crossing of farms by cattle became inferior. In the former case, the new insurance scheme would attract business. In the latter case, farmers and ranchers could reach a new agreement.

---

[2] The astute reader might notice that this insurance scheme produces a surplus. Because all insured farmers pay 14 and half the farmers receive 26, the surplus is 2 for every two farmers. The surplus covers the cost of administering the insurance scheme.

D. Distribution

The strong, routine, and unavoidable distributional effects of law lead to one of the main sources of frustration with Coasean irrelevance. Whereas law and economics focuses on the allocation that occurs after the parties adjust to the law, lawyers tend to focus on the net consequences for the parties. This difference in focus can be restated as between the economy and its individuals. The economist focuses on the economy and its total product. The lawyer focuses on individuals and their position. Coasean irrelevance only exists from the economist's viewpoint. Law is relevant for individuals even if it is irrelevant for the economy and its total product. Naturally, if Coasean irrelevance does not materialize, then the rules matter for both total product and individuals. Therefore, the analysis applies only if Coasean irrelevance does materialize. Coasean irrelevance becomes a necessary background assumption.

If the law established a suboptimal allocation, the parties' bargain would restore the optimal allocation. That bargain establishes a payment, usually from one party to the other. This payment places the parties in different positions than they would have under the optimal rule. The total product is the same but one party enjoys more of that product.

Revisiting the farmer-rancher bargain illustrates this concern. Suppose the *status quo* is a rule that allows the farmers to erect fences against trampling by cattle. Suppose that ranching is more profitable and ranchers do bargain with farmers and pay farmers not to erect fences. The bargain restores the optimal allocation. The farmers enjoy the benefits of the ranchers' payment. A change of the law that prohibits fences will eliminate this payment. The label "irrelevant" fits the change of the regime only for those who ignore individuals and focus on total product.

The payments violate Coasean irrelevance from individuals' perspectives and their direction matters for individuals. From a policy perspective, the direction of the payments can have distributional consequences. The direction of the payments may not matter if the payments cancel out or are unrelated to wealth. If the payments tend to occur from the poor to the wealthy, they aggravate concerns about the distribution of wealth. If the payments tend to occur from the wealthy to the poor, they may mitigate distributional concerns. Therefore, distributional policy seems likely to argue in favor of rules that induce a payment from the wealthy to the poor.

Nevertheless, the conventional analysis argues against that position. In part, this argument was discussed in Chapter 4, which explained redistribution. The discussion in Chapter 4 compared redistributive rules with taxation as redistributive schemes and pointed out that taxation, particularly if it follows the schedules that bring it close to optimal tax, tends to be preferable according to the double-distortion argument. Chapter 4 discussed how any income tax causes a distortion because it reduces individuals' drive to produce, the *chilling effect* of the tax. Equal redistribution, through either a tax or a redistributive rule, produces an equal chilling effect. Because the redistributive rule is different from the optimal rule, it produces an additional distortion. Because the rule has two distortions, the tax is preferable.

When we revisit that argument here, our attention is on Coasean irrelevance, not taxes and their chilling effect. If Coasean irrelevance holds, however, then the double-distortion argument disappears. Coasean irrelevance means that a bargain restores the optimal, with no loss in productivity. Therefore, if a particular redistributive rule is consistently circumvented by a bargain, it does not produce the second distortion. Naturally, because Coasean irrelevance depends on stringent assumptions, such as lack of transaction costs and complete knowledge, redistributive rules may be circumvented by bargains but never consistently. Double distortion is unavoidable. Nevertheless, the administration of the tax system is costly. In some exceptional instances, redistribution through Coasean bargains could involve a smaller cost.

In closing, it is important to realize that the failure of Coasean irrelevance does not have a closed listing of reasons. The failures of irrelevance correspond to imperfections of market interactions in an economic sense. Research that will reveal new imperfections will also identify new reasons for the failure of Coasean irrelevance and provide new guidance for better regulation.

E. Concluding Exercises

Coasean irrelevance brought a radical change and a scientific standard to legal analysis. Surprisingly, the use of Coasean irrelevance does not require any quantitative tool. The analysis can proceed in the textual mode that is traditional in law, with only the additional realization that in an ideal world individuals would reach the optimal conducts. This realization, however, is utterly radical and imposes a new rigor on arguments. Before the advent of Coasean irrelevance, the abstract conception of a better arrangement of conducts could form the basis of an acceptable legal argument. After the advent of Coasean irrelevance, such an argument is incomplete. It is missing the demonstration that private bargaining does not make legal change pointless.

Exercise 6.1: Return to the farmer-rancher example and assume that ranchers have the right to trample farmers' land. Suppose that ranchers and farmers, by agreeing to override the existing allocation of trampling rights, can create additional value of 50. That is the net amount produced from 160 of gain from the increased production of farms and 110 in costs burdening ranchers. This society has two norms that establish the parameters of bargaining. A norm of self-sacrifice does not let a party take its costs into account. A norm of fairness requires equal division of gain. Accordingly, when both sides to a transaction abide by these norms, they divide equally the gains of 160 to farmers and ignore the costs of 110 for ranchers. This means that ranchers receive 80 and suffer costs of 110, meaning that they lose 30 in such agreements. The ranchers who do not share these norms decline these terms and ask for about 135. Farmers who feel strong the norm of equal division consider this demand excessive and refuse. Farmers who do not abide by the norms agree. Accordingly, whenever a norm-abiding party must reach an agreement with a self-interested party, no agreement is possible. Does the allocation by the law of the right to trample matter in this society?

Discussion: It should be obvious that law does matter in this society. The purpose of the question is to review the assumption of the self-interested decision making of economics, juxtaposing it to an assumption of "moral" action. A large body of research, mostly using experiments, has found that players do deviate from self-interested action in favor of "fairness."

Exercise 6.2: Suppose that research reveals that individuals do not act pursuant to their self-interest. Rather, a stronger predictor of individual action is "fairness," as an intuition or social norm. How is such a finding a failure of Coasean irrelevance? How should this inform legal argument and interpretation?

Discussion: This question takes no easy answer. Norms or intuitions of fairness can destroy productive capacity. (See exercise 6.1.) Yet, norms or intuitions of fairness are very important tools for cooperation. Fairness, equality, and self-sacrifice may even be imprinted onto our decision-making mechanism by evolution that favored the groups that had these guidelines for conduct. In primitive society, survival of a group may have depended on its members being willing to distract attacks by offering themselves as bait. Considering that such influences have no use in modern society may be simplistic and pointless. Society may have no choice but sacrifice some productivity (or some optimality) to non-self-interested decision making. Moreover, it may be desirable to preserve such methods of decision making to overcome a future unexpected challenge.

Exercise 6.3: Suppose that a society has no property concept and makes decisions by majority vote. The society has two groups, ranchers and farmers. Farmers are about 75 percent of this society and the remaining 25 percent are ranchers. The total product of this society is 10,000 per year but the two groups do not contribute proportionately. All the farmers' product is 4,000 (in aggregate) and the ranchers' product is 6,000 (in aggregate), which means that ranchers are more than twice as productive as farmers. The existing arrangement prohibits ranchers from crossing (and trampling) the land devoted to farming. The ranchers suggest that they should be allowed to cross farmland. A vote is taken and the proposal fails to garner a majority. Is this the correct decision?

Discussion: This question reviews the point of the chapter on political theory. The majority vote may fail to account for the size of the gain for ranching. It is possible that letting cattle cross farmlands produces greater gain than the harm suffered by farming. In a majority vote, however, the vote of the many farmers outweighs that of the fewer ranchers. In other words, the decision does not take into account intensity of preferences.

The problem in constructing this hypothetical is that it turns into an endorsement of property rights, whereas it is intended as an illustration of a drawback of deciding by majority. Granted, property rights prevent the problem from arising. If the ranchers and the farmers had property rights in their product, then they would reach a decision by bargaining. Again, someone might counter that the ranchers should be able to buy the farmers' votes. Political voting systems, however, are designed to prevent the enforceability of vote-buying agreements. In this, they differ from corporate voting where votes follow shares and are traded routinely. Professor Carney offers an analysis of corporate voting and the required majority for mergers on the basis of different preferences.[3]

If the item at the focal point of the dispute is not subject to property rights, then the optimal outcome may be unknown. The evaluation of decision-making processes may be impossible. Describing this setting as a failure of Coasean irrelevance may seem inappropriate although it is correct in the sense that a different voting system or political system would produce a different outcome. Calling it a failure of Coasean irrelevance seems misleading if it suggests that the parties (farmers and ranchers) did not act to reach a bargain. In this hypothetical, a bargain seems impossible regardless of either party's actions. Rather than a failure of private initiative, this example is closer to a failure of the law to provide the tools and incentives for the parties to bargain, such as property rights and contract law.

In a different sense, however, the legal system is in the hands of the parties. This is particularly true in this example where society is comprised exclusively by farmers and ranchers. This restores some truth in the notion that the parties failed to act. They failed to produce a legal system that would enable their bargain. Indeed, property law scholars identify a correspondence between scarcity and the development of property rights but this process is neither fast nor inescapable.[4] Moreover, the development of a legal system is a collective action of the society. A vicious cycle appears. To overcome the collective action problem, society must overcome a collective action problem.

Exercise 6.4: Evaluate the development of corporate law. A precursor of corporations is considered the East India Company, which allowed members to partially outfit a ship with *joint stock*. The concept of joint stock would allow merchants who could outfit at most a few ships individually, to divide their stock-in-trade over several ships. The trip to the East Indies and back was perilous and many ships were lost.

---

[3] See William Carney, "Fundamental Corporate Changes, Minority Shareholders, and Business Purposes," *American Bar Foundation Research Journal* 1980:69.

[4] See, for example, Edmund Kitch, "The Nature and Function of the Patent System," *Journal of Law & Economics* 20 (1977):275–80 ("[T]he property rights literature has viewed the central problem as one as scarcity").

Why would a merchant prefer to outfit several ships using joint stock rather than outfit few exclusively at the same cost?

Bring the analysis to contemporary corporations. An entrepreneur who creates a corporation has the option of selling a fraction of his stock to investors in the stock market. The entrepreneur can invest the proceeds in several different investments, including the stocks of other corporations. Several reasons support this action. Can you state an explanation related to risk aversion?

Discussion: Medieval merchants and modern entrepreneurs have the same motivation. They avoid exposing much of their wealth to a single risk. If one in ten ships sink, the merchant would rather have that occur to one tenth of the capital. Similarly, if one in ten corporations fail, the entrepreneur would rather see that happen to one tenth of the portfolio. If they left all their funds in a single project (ship or corporation) then bad luck would be devastating.

Exercise 6.5: Consider the question of the fiduciary obligations of corporate managers about business opportunities they identify. In the course of managing the corporation, managers learn of opportunities. Opportunities vary in nature, with some having a subject close to that of the corporation and some far. Investments in those opportunities have hope for superior profit compared with other investments.

Consider two alternative rules. Under one rule, the manager may take advantage of the opportunity. The second rule allocates the opportunity to the business. Does the manager's risk aversion suggest one as superior?

Discussion: The analysis must start by acknowledging that, if Coasean irrelevance materializes, the manager and the owners of the business receive the same rewards under either rule. If the rule gives opportunities to the manager, the owners will have the business pay to the manager a smaller salary and bonus leaving more profit for the business. If the rule gives opportunities to the business, then the business will pay the manager a larger salary and bonus. A well-functioning market induces the equivalence between the two rules. If the rule gives the opportunities to the manager, businesses that produce most of their return in opportunities will not attract investors unless the manager takes a reduced salary. Thus, the total returns that each side enjoys remain constant but their composition changes. The returns can be composed either entirely of contractual salary plus bonus or of a mix of opportunities and salary plus bonus.

Between owners and managers, however, risk aversion burdens only one of the two sides. The business cannot eliminate risk. Owners can diversify by owning small parts of many businesses and, therefore, tend to be neutral toward risk. Managers, however, cannot avoid bearing the risk of failure of their business.

Therefore, when the manager retains opportunities as compensation, that is risky compensation. Opportunities materialize occasionally. When the composition of the returns a party enjoys change, the risk that the party bears also changes. If the mix includes the opportunities, it involves more risk than if the mix was composed entirely of contractual payments. The party who has the aversion to risk, that is, the manager, finds the risky package less appealing. Thus, despite the nominal equivalence, the enjoyment of the total returns does depend on who receives the opportunities. The party that is neutral toward risk should receive the riskier package that includes the opportunities.

The allocation of the opportunities between the business and the manager involves many more considerations. The incentives that the manager has may influence the creation of opportunities and the allocation of managerial effort. My analysis of those arguments, including the one above about risk, concludes that the implication of broad fiduciary obligations that the business gets the opportunities is desirable, see N. Georgakopoulos, "*Meinhard v. Salmon* and the Economics of Honor," *Columbia Business Law Review* 1999:137 *et seq*.

F. Bibliographical Note

The related works of Ronald H. Coase are collected in Ronald H. Coase, *The Firm, the Market, and the Law* (Chicago: University of Chicago Press, 1990). An excellent exposition of the Coase theorem exists in David Freedman, *Law's Order: What Economics Has to Do with Law and Why It Matters* (Princeton, N.J.: Princeton University Press, 2000). Readers in law schools that have access to CALI's electronic lessons (at www.cali.org) may find useful the electronic lesson Nicholas Georgakopoulos, "Coasean Irrelevance" (2000).

Part 2: Methods

7. Mathematical Modeling

Modeling requires the restatement of the issue using symbols or numbers built into equations. If the analysis can restate an issue using equations, then it does not simply employ one new tool but unlocks the vast and expanding toolset of mathematical methods. However, this leading tool of law and economics may be a skill or mindset that seems inaccessible to a neophyte. Some of the mathematical tools that take advantage of modeling form the subject of later chapters. This chapter introduces the language and methodology of modeling and two powerful mathematical methods, the optimization by solving derivatives and the prediction of the path of gradual change by differential equations.

Even modeling can be introduced with *Meinhard v. Salmon*.[1] Salmon received a lucrative offer from Gerry, a business acquaintance. The offer could have expanded Salmon's business. Unbeknownst to Gerry, Salmon's business, which was the reason for their acquaintance, had a secret partner, Meinhard. If Gerry knew that Salmon operated in two capacities, as an individual and as a member of a partnership, then Gerry may have specified which of the two he selected as the recipient of his offer. Meinhard, the invisible partner, claimed the offer should be treated as made to the partnership. The litigation that Meinhard started eventually reached the highest court of the jurisdiction and the famous American judge, Benjamin Cardozo, and his colleague Andrews, who is almost equally famous for his vocal dissenting opinions. Previously established law did not answer the question directly. Suppose that Cardozo and Andrews each produce a different model that supports and explains their different opinions. If both models rest on the same foundational assumptions, then one would likely contain

---

[1] 249 N.Y. 458 (1928). The text of the opinion is reproduced in Appendix A.

an error that the precision of mathematics would reveal. If both models receive mathematically correct solutions then their concrete nature should reveal the source of their differences. Perhaps, this would allow for an interpretation that would address both concerns. For example, Cardozo might prefer broad duties to place the risk about opportunities on the shoulders of the financiers who are likely to be diversified; Andrews might prefer narrow duties to avoid the uncertainty about the status of transactions. Recognizing this difference, they may have agreed on an interpretation that would satisfy both interests.

The experience of the legal system has been one of recognizing ever more complexity in social and economic arrangements. This stands in sharp contrast with the simplification that is necessary for mathematical modeling. Thus, from the side of legal analysis comes scepticism toward the simplifying assumptions that are necessary to allow the modeling of any setting or interaction using mathematical tools.

Economic analysis may be motivated only partly by a desire to be all encompassing, and a drive toward precision competes and may dominate. Contributions to economic thought are often incremental improvements of explaining human interaction in quantifiable terms. Each such contribution to economic thought is a small brick in a big building that aspires to understand human motivation. The components of economic thought are parts of a larger theory to which inconsistencies may be delegated. For example, the theory of the formation of prices by supply and demand may be considered to fail to explain the pricing of securities, public goods, or monopolistic goods. In response, the economics discipline does not reject as too simple the model of supply and demand. The contribution of the simplification is that it explains some conduct with great force of persuasion and prediction. That gaps remain is of little concern; the gaps are regrettable, but they should be covered by subsequent research.

Legal thought, by contrast, cannot postpone resolution with such ease. Silence is a choice with normative consequences. When simplifying assumptions render the analysis inapplicable to a segment of interactions, the legal thinker cannot let those await future resolution. Either the rule suggested for the rest of the situations – those that fit the simplifications necessary for the mathematical model – should apply to those that do not fit the analysis, or those should continue being subjected to the previous regime.

Despite these methodological drawbacks or conflicts with the expectations of conventional legal analysis, the drive toward mathematical methods has overtaken law and economics. This chapter discusses the principal obstacles that a general reader encounters when attempting to comprehend articles written using the conventions of economists. After a description of mathematical symbols and idioms, this chapter discusses modeling methodology, optimization by solving derivatives and differential equations.

A. Symbols, Functions, and Idioms

Economic models may seem unapproachable to the legal reader. The typical jurist has little recollection of mathematics and equations and is used to text that is very explicit and that follows a strict logical order. Economic text too often seems to be a jumble of equations accompanied by idiosyncratic, dense text that makes a vast multitude of assumptions. Naturally, economists would disagree. Although economic writing is very different from legal writing, both follow strict logic. Legal readers can certainly understand the logic, if they can tackle the format in which it is presented. The following paragraphs seek to overcome three hurdles: the use of symbols, functions, and idioms.

A model uses letter symbols to represent the sizes, quantities, or intensities of activities, prices, or fines. By convention, each symbol is a single letter, and a subscript or a superscript may further identify it. For example, a model may use t as the symbol for the travel time and, if the model examines two individuals, it may use t_1 and t_2 for the travel times of each. An even more abstract version may examine an unknown number of individuals, often symbolized as N, and the travel times will take subscripts from 1 through N. When the model discusses the travel time of any one of those individuals, as opposed to a specific one, it will use a "counter" subscript, often i or j. Second subscripts or superscripts may be used to represent more information, for example, a model comparing travel by air with travel by car may use $t_{i,a}$ and $t_{i,c}$ to refer to the times that individual i spends in airplanes and in cars.

Notation may be quite confusing to the reader. Many authors make a conscious effort to produce a readable model. A first step is intuitive symbols. Cost is often c, time is often t, probability is often p, and the number of items or individuals is often N. Equally conventional, although less intuitive, is the use of i and j for the various "counters."

Related is the problem of the use of undefined functions, often $f(.)$ or $g(.)$, which include their array of parameters, so that a function that uses time t and cost c to obtain its (unspecified) outcome, would take the form $f(t, c)$. The economist would read this as "function f of t and c," meaning that it is an undefined equation that produces a value by using as inputs the values of t and of c.

Some confusion of the lay reader is caused by idiosyncrasies of notation, such as the omission of the multiplication operator or the use of unusual signs, such as the signs for summation ($\sum \ldots$), product ($\prod \ldots$), and integration ($\int \ldots$). Some of these usages do not agree with the recollections that nonquantitative readers have from their high school education. All these signs, of course, can take several terms inside the summation, product, or integral and can be used in equations that contain other terms. Each deserves an explanation.

The multiplication operator is omitted in scientific writing. Although a high school student would use a symbol, perhaps a dot or star, as the sign of multiplication, scientific writing omits it. The omission might be traced to speech, where "three miles" rather than "a mile, multiplied by three" is the normal usage. The confusion, however, can be severe when several symbols are multiplied, as in std. If s indicates speed, t indicates hours, and d indicates the number of days per week that travel takes place, std is a multiplication that might be clearer to the nonquantitative reader if it were expressed as speed*time*dspw.

The summation sign ($\sum \ldots$) sums a repetitive formula that involves one or more symbols that change with a counter. Continuing the example of travel time, suppose that the model wants to add the travel times of all individuals. Travel time is symbolized by t and each individual's time is identified by a subscript, denoted by the counter i. This addition is likely written $\sum_i t_i$, which is read "the sum of all tee-sub-eye, over all eyes." A more explicit notation would state that society is composed of N individuals and write total time as $\sum_{i=1}^{N} t_i$, which is read "the sum of all tee-sub-eye with eye from one to en." A more conventional way to write the same would be $\sum_{i=1}^{N} t_i = t_1 + t_2 + \cdots + t_{N-1} + T_N$.

The same process can be used with the product sign. Accordingly, $\prod_{i=1}^{N} x_i$ is read "the product of ex-sub-eye, with eye from 1 to en." The more conventional equivalent equation would take the form $\prod_{i=1}^{N} x_i = x_1 \times x_2 \times \cdots \times x_{N-1} \times x_N$.

The integral sign performs a function analogous to summation but applies to a continuous variable that does not refer to a countable item. It usually finds applications in probability theory, where if a probability density function is $g(x)$, the probability of obtaining a realization between x_1 and x_2 is $\int_{x_1}^{x_2} g(x) \mathrm{d}x$. Note that, unlike summation and product, the integral sign is bracketed on the right with the dx. This identifies

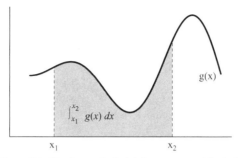

Figure 7.1. The integral of $g(x)$ from x_1 to x_2 (shaded).

the symbol that varies with the integration, in this case x. Summation and product identify the symbol that changes by placing it under the summation or product sign, as the symbol i was placed above. The integration example above would be read "the integral of gee-of-ex with ex running from ex-one to ex-two." It does not have a more conventional representation because it does not contain discrete items that are being added. Integration corresponds to the area under the curve defined by its equation, in this case, $g(x)$ between the specified values. Figure 7.1 shows the visual representation of the integral, which is the shaded region between x_1 and x_2 under the curve defined by the function.

The difficulty in understanding economic writing is not limited to the use of unfamiliar signs in equations. The textual exposition is often obscure to anyone who has not developed the skill for reading economics journals, which present extraordinarily complex concepts in articles that are only a few pages long. For the reader who is used to legal text, the result is obscure. Legal argumentation is by design approachable to the reader who understands some basic concepts of law. Because its purpose is to persuade, legal text reaches for the reader, explaining each step in the reasoning. Economic argument is drafted with an eye to publication in refereed journals. The refereeing process acts as a quality filter. The existence of the filter, rightly or not,[2] lightens the burden of proof that the reader demands and allows the author not only to use dense language, but also to skip the logical steps that the author considers easily understood. To the legal reader, economic writing

---

[2] The capricious and biased nature of refereeing is illustrated vividly by George Shepherd's collection of rejections of famous articles, including Nobel Prize-winning ones, *Rejected: Leading Economists Ponder the Publication Process*, ed. George B. Shepherd (Sun Lakes, AZ: Thomas Horton and Daughters, 1995).

often appears conclusory and unsupported. Despite the disagreeable appearance, economic argumentation has great value for legal analysis. Its inapproachability to the lay reader, however, is not exhausted at the style of argument. Economists are writing for economists. Not-surprisingly, specialized writers writing for a specialized audience drift into habits of usage that are far from conventional.

The unconventional usage has developed to such an extent that it is difficult to identify its particulars. Some striking ones are the elliptical definition of symbols, the use of parentheses to illustrate the opposite case, the words *endogenous*, *exogenous*, and *stochastic*, the use of clauses such as "increasing in," "normalizing to 1 without loss of generality," or "the second order condition holds."

When an economics essay describes its model, the author needs to define many symbols in little space. The convention is to treat the symbols of the variables akin to nouns and place them after the nouns that they represent. For example, the phrase "individuals $i = 1, 2, \ldots, N$ travel by car or rail using vehicles $v = c, r$ in time $t_{i,v}$ to reach their destination. The aggregate time a is $a = \sum_{i=1}^{N} \sum_v t_{i,v}$," states the premise of the analysis, defines the symbols for numerous variables, and presents one of the foundational formulas of the model. A more readable exposition would be noticeably longer:

> The aggregate travel time, represented by a, is calculated by summing over individuals and vehicles. The number of individuals that populate society is represented by N. Each individual's travel time is represented by $t_{i,v}$. The subscript i identifies the individual and takes values from 1 to N, inclusive. The subscript v refers to the vehicle. The symbol v takes either the value c or r, corresponding to travel by car or rail. The aggregate time is a result of a double summation. A summation of the travel times of the same individual in different vehicles produces the total travel time for each individual. This is $\sum_v t_{i,v}$. The second summation takes these totals of each individual's time and adds them across individuals to obtain the aggregate travel time: $a = \sum_{i=1}^{N} \sum_v t_{i,v}$.

The difference between the economists' summary statement and the explicit description and buildup of the equation is such that the short version may appear as a caricature or as a result of intentional obfuscation. Neither is true. The condensed prose is routine practice.

Whereas the second, slower exposition is much easier to follow, for the legal reader it is still inadequate because it does not defend its method. The resulting equation that is a starting point for economic analysis is an undefended conclusion for the legal reader, who is likely to wonder whether travel times are justifiably added without adjusting for differences, such as the difference of the traveler's effort or comfort, of time of day, of the scenery, or of the company. What the economist considers a premise that requires no support appears to the legal reader as a conclusory statement.

That a legal reader finds the economist's premise to be conclusory reflects a fundamental difference between their approaches. Legal reasoning starts from the specific, such as the individual commuter's attributes, which form a unique combination. Legal reasoning proceeds to the general by examining the application of a general rule, as for example by asking whether this commuter qualifies for a subsidy. Economic reasoning looks past the details that separate individuals because the details prevent the formation of a general understanding. Economic reasoning produces a general explanation of conduct. In the commuting example, the general understanding may be that commuting patterns correlate with wealth because less wealthy commuters tend to travel by bus. The general explanation of conduct that the economic analysis produces will not match every detail of every setting, but it may be a very good approximation. Obviously, not every person who can afford a car avoids the bus, and some individuals who cannot afford a car may still use one, perhaps by carpooling.

The importance for the legal scholar of understanding the economic model is that the model may inform policy. The patterns of bus ridership can become arguments about law. Legal scholars who seek to reduce the emission of pollutants or who seek to increase camaraderie and social cohesion, may desire to induce more travel by bus. Each goal uses the economic conclusion differently. Bus subsidies would be structured differently if the goal were to reduce pollution than if the goal were to increase social cohesion. Scholars who seek to increase self-reliance or to enlarge the sphere of privacy may desire more private car ownership. Again, they would likely advocate different policies to reach each goal.

When jurists consider using economic models, the model's validity becomes important, particularly because every model's premises can be attacked as conclusory. The validity of the general model is not defended at the stage when the model's foundational assumptions are laid; its validity rests largely and primarily on an overall intuition whether the deviations are details that likely cancel out as opposed to being major discrepancies that may lead to a different overall model.

The epistemological comparison of the economic with the legal method of reasoning is a vast undertaking that does not fit here. One can reasonably conclude that the economic method has a greater risk of error but offers the prospect of a greater reward. The error is due to the possibility of the development of a model that is inaccurate or false. An insistence, like that of legal reasoning, that each step be proven might have prevented the development of false models. The greater reward is that the model may constitute a major improvement of the understanding of our interactions that can lead to improved law and improved technologies or institutions.

In addition to the fast and elliptical construction of a model's premise, economic texts also tend to follow idiosyncratic usage or jargon in several aspects. Confusing to the legal reader is the use of parentheses to refer to opposites, as opposed to using them for definitions or explanations, as is the habit in legal texts. The economists' motivation for this practice is the brevity. Thus, economic text will often describe its effects only once and include the opposite in the exposition by using parentheses. Take the example of an article about travel times, where the author seeks to communicate to the reader that the model uses average travel times and adds to the average a random variable that corresponds to the effect of congestion. Unusually low congestion makes the realized travel time less than the average, whereas unusually great congestion makes it greater than average. The economic text may communicate this juxtaposition by using parentheses in a single clause, such as "average travel time is increased (decreased) when traffic congestion is unusually great (little)."

As if intending to confuse the legal reader, economic models refer to individuals as "agents." Economic agents make independent decisions and are not part of an agency relationship.

The words *endogenous, exogenous,* and *stochastic* are standard fare in economic modeling but are distant to the legal reader. In setting up the model, the author will choose variables that take values before the analysis of the model takes place, whereas other variables take values as a consequence of the reactions and interactions of the model. The former are exogenous, so called from the Greek etymology of the word, which indicates they have their genesis outside, whereas the latter are endogenous, generated in the model. In a model of commuting times that depend on the spread and number of existing subway stations, those would be exogenous, whereas individuals' choices of commuting vehicles and the taxing authority's allocation of a maintenance and improvement budget between rail and road would be endogenous. The distinction of endogenous and exogenous variables is important for the design and the evaluation of the model. If a model treats as exogenous a variable that can be argued to be influenced by the reactions of individuals or institutions that the model studies, then the model would be more realistic if it treated it as endogenous and derived it. If the consequence of such a change is major, the plausibility of the model is undermined.

The word *stochastic* only applies to an exogenous variable and regards its generation. Exogenous variables that are not stochastic are likely treated as constants by the model. This means that the decision makers of the model know the value of nonstochastic variables or at least know they are constant. By contrast, stochastic variables are random. The decision makers may eventually be faced with realizations of the random variable, but the model at most grants them knowledge of its distribution function, so that they can optimize their conduct according to probability theory. The chapter on probability distributions, Chapter 9, discusses the treatment of randomness more extensively.

Notably disorienting to legal readers is the practice of using "increasing" or "decreasing" to express relationship between variables. A variable is said to be increasing in or with a second variable, if the first takes larger values when the second variable takes larger values: "weight is increasing in height" means that the tall are heavier than the short.

Further frustrating the legal reader, the economic text may use the notation of derivatives to express relations, perhaps even omitting any textual description. The economic article may posit that "weight w is a function of height h, where $w'(h) > 0$." This means that the derivative of weight with respect to height is positive, indicating a positive slope for the function $w(h)$, which means that more height leads to more weight. The legal reader may still be trying to suppress the objection that weight may depend on numerous other variables that are ignored.

The model may further specify the relation of weight and height by using the second derivative, for example, mentioning that $w''(h) < 0$. The first derivative specifies whether the function is increasing or decreasing. The second derivative specifies whether it does so increasingly or decreasingly. An increasingly increasing function, for example, may start almost horizontal at small values of its variable but becomes steeper as the variable increases. A decreasingly increasing function starts steep but grows flatter. Economic idiom calls the former *convex*

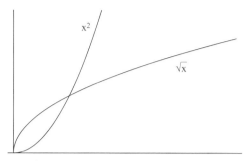

Figure 7.2. Concave and convex functions.

and the latter *concave*. The function $f(x) = x^2$ for $x > 0$ is convex and has $f' > 0$, $f'' > 0$, that is, is increasingly increasing. The function $f(x) = \sqrt{x}$ for $x > 0$ is concave and has $f' > 0$, $f'' < 0$, that is, is decreasingly increasing. Both functions are increasing in x, for $x > 0$. See Figure 7.2.

The clause "normalizing to 1 [without loss of generality]" is an analytical practice, rather than a linguistic idiom. Nevertheless, its discussion fits here because the frustration it causes readers appears related. When the analysis can properly be performed on fractions, models may normalize to 1 the aggregate quantity. Instead of counting instances, the model can then proceed by analyzing fractions. This practice is confusing to the reader who does not realize that "normalizing to 1" does not mean assuming that a large number *is* 1, but means that the analysis will be performed on fractions of the total. Thus, the economist may normalize to 1 the population in society and analyze the consequences of changes of policies, preferences, or conditions on the conduct of the population in terms of changes of the fraction of the population that follows one practice, say, commutes by rail. The clause "without loss of generality" means that this adjustment of the model does not prevent its general applicability. Despite that a quantity, such as population, is generalized to 1 instead of being left as a variable with an undefined value, the model still applies regardless of the actual figure, that is, regardless of actual population. The model applies because its analysis is based on fractions. Those fractions would be the same if the actual figure of the population had been used.

Equally cryptic to the above is a phrase, appearing usually in a footnote, that "the second order condition holds." The phrase accompanies the derivation of maximum or minimum solutions. The usual method of establishing a maximum is to take the derivative of the function with

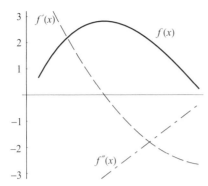

Figure 7.3. The maximum of a function $f(x)$ and its derivatives.

respect to the variable and to solve it for that variable after equating it to zero. This identifies the position where the function is flat, which is potentially where it reaches its maximum or minimum. The means to establish that the solution is a maximum or a minimum is to calculate the function's second derivative at that point. If it is negative, it indicates that the function's slope is decreasing at the point where it is flat, hence that this flat region is a maximum. The decreasing slope marks it as a maximum because it implies that the function's slope was increasing before it went flat and is decreasing after. Vice versa, a positive second derivative indicates a minimum. The sign, positive or negative, of the second derivative is the second-order condition. The sign of the second derivative indicates a maximum or minimum. Figure 7.3 illustrates a function $f(x)$, the solid line. The function has a maximum. Its derivative is $f'(x)$, the dashed line. It takes positive values while the function slopes up toward the maximum and negative values where the function slopes down away from the maximum. Because the derivative slopes down, it has a negative slope. That slope is the second derivative of $f(x)$, marked $f''(x)$, the dot-dashed line. Inescapably, at the maximum of $f(x)$ its derivative is zero and its second derivative is negative.

When the text identifies a solution as a maximum by indicating that the second-order condition holds, this implies the author's assertion that the second derivative is negative (or positive, if finding a minimum). Whereas the legal reader would have expected a demonstration of the second derivative's sign, the economic reader relies on the refereeing process to have verified that implicit assertion. The next section offers a model that illustrates this method.

With this new language established, pass to the construction and design of models. The next section discusses premises of models.

B. Simplification and the Model as a Premise

The model arranges symbols and functions in one or more equations that constitute the premises and the foundations of the model. The first equations of the model often are the arrangement of the symbols that represent the issues that the individuals of the model use to guide their decisions. In other words, the first equation is the formula that guides the individuals' decisions. If the model has been explained well, these first equations will not be controversial despite that they would not and could not capture every possible concern or parameter influencing conduct.

The omission of some of the concerns or parameters that influence conduct is very disconcerting to critics of economic analysis of law while hardly creating any concerns within the ranks of economic analysis. Critics see the omission of some concerns as invalidating the conclusions, whereas the users of the models recognize that excluded concerns may lead to different results. The objection that some concerns are not included in the model can even be considered spurious, because concerns and argumentation about the motivations of human conduct may not be finite; any method of reasoning will always omit some issues. At the stage when the model is founded, the conscious omission of some concerns is often phrased as a set of assumptions.

In modeling transportation choices, for example, an author may state an assumption that the enjoyment of each means of transportation is identical. This simplifying assumption allows the model to ignore preferences for different transportation means, but if a consistent preference for one mode of transportation exists, the assumption will likely lead to a false conclusion. If, for example, most commuters prefer trains to busses, a model that ignores this preference will have a bias for less commuting by train and more commuting by bus than would be optimal. A municipality that uses such a model to choose how much bus and rail transportation to offer would offer too few trains and too many buses. A method for overcoming such potential errors and making the model more powerful for normative analysis is to relax the assumptions. After the analysis using the model is concluded, the author discusses how altering the assumptions will tend to alter, or not, the conclusions. Authors in the economics literature increasingly do not relax their assumptions. Although this frustrates the usefulness of the analysis to the lay audience, the practice may be justified by the argument that the analysis did not intend to have a normative application. A complete analysis may be considered to be the object of further study.

Mathematical modeling comes from physics and its goal is to use equations to describe a phenomenon. Whereas in physics the phenomenon is the motion of bodies and particles, in economics (and law) the phenomenon is the reaction of individuals to their environment (including its rules). Although physicists seem to keep finding ever more complex behaviors of ever smaller particles, particles neither employ strategies nor have will. Modeling human interactions is likely the more formidable task.

The ideal of modeling is generality. Models are general if they apply in every occurrence within the family of circumstances that each model analyzes. Models reach generality by being abstract and independent of the scale and range of their parameters. The model must be abstract in the sense that its analysis does not depend on the specific circumstances. The model must also capture every similar situation, independent of size, location, or other parameters. Generality is achieved through simplification, which is an art in itself. Generality, however, runs contrary to the instincts of detailed factual description that the process of the common law develops and rewards.

Abstraction exists when the analysis is freed from specific circumstances. In examining conduct on roads and sidewalks, for example, icy conditions are a circumstance that will strongly influence conduct. A model of road conduct under icy conditions is poor because it fails in every other case. Its lack of generality restricts its application.

Generality is achieved through simplification. Successful simplification strips the studied conduct from every aspect that is specific and reconceives it in general terms, independent of the scale and range of any parameters. Thus, the analysis is general by design.

A superb example of simplification is the analysis of negligence. Conventionally, negligence was seen as a phenomenon full of specificity: did the injurer exercise the care of a "reasonable person" in the circumstances? The simplification that allowed a general analysis of this setting took three generations of scholarship to become established. The first breakthrough was Judge Learned Hand's famous formula that compared the cost of care to the expected accident costs. That was a starting point for textual analysis by now Judge Guido

Calabresi, then Professor. The general model of negligence is offered by Professor Steven Shavell.[3]

The law-and-economics analysis of negligence reaches generality by not specifying conduct. Instead, the metric is the total cost of accidents, which divides into cost of care and expected injury. The result is that as the cost of care increases, expected injury decreases. From a social perspective, the optimal solution is now obvious. Society as a whole suffers both types of costs and it needs to minimize their sum. Thus, the legal system must give its subjects the incentive to take no more than the cost-justified care. Too much care is wasteful because it costs more than the expected injury it prevents. Too little care implies that an incremental increase of care would cost less than the injuries it would prevent.

A crucial simplification is the substitution of "cost of care" and "expected injury" for the particular circumstances of each case. The additional parameters of the possible care of the victim, risk aversion, litigation financing, credit-proof defendants, and possibly several more were swept aside, even though they may be significant in the incentive structure of negligence liability. The extent to which these simplifications are considered excessive depends on the goals of the analysis. To observe the incentives that negligence liability produces on solvent risk-neutral entities who can estimate expected injuries, the model is near perfect. In practical terms, this group may comprise most corporate and commercial activity and, therefore, have extensive application. This model probably can not predict accurately the conduct of individuals. The model also serves as a benchmark against which details of the tort system can be measured, such as whether juries are giving injurers the proper credit for balancing the cost of care with estimates of expected injury, a concept that is severely questioned by empirical and experimental evidence of Professor Kip Viscusi.[4]

C. Modelling Applications

Having discussed the compromises involved in the simplification that is necessary for mathematical modeling, we can now proceed to two techniques that take advantage of the mathematical nature of the model.

---

[3] Steven Shavell, *Economic Analysis of Accident Law* (Cambridge, MA: Harvard University Press, 1987).

[4] W. Kip Viscusi and Reid Hastie, "What Juries Can't Do Well: The Jury's Performance as a Risk Manager," *Arizona Law Review* 40, no. 3 (1998):901 *et seq.*

The first example uses model-of-negligence law to illustrate the use of calculus for optimization. The second studies the effects of a repeal of affirmative action in education and illustrates the use of differential equations.

i. Modeling Negligence Law: Optimization

Let us start with the established model of negligence already discussed. The negligence rule states that if an injurer is negligent, the injurer is liable for the victim's injuries. Because the general concept of the negligence test is evolving toward the idea that a level of care is compared with an undefined function of the surrounding circumstances, we need to form such a comparison. Calling the level of care l, we can state the rule as if $l < g(.)$ then the injurer is liable.

Injurers choose the level of care l. If care is bothersome or costly, then the injurer might skimp. Suddenly, the model is changing shape and its usefulness is increasing. The real issue is not so much the level of care, but how costly it is. Call this cost c and represent the level of care as a function of that cost, making it $l(c)$.

The model can start considering society's concerns. Presumably, society desires that some cost be incurred, but perhaps not every cost is desirable. More care implies fewer injuries or smaller injuries, so that we can construct one more function, the burden of injuries. Using economic terms, again, this means the cost of injuries and the term cost again includes non-monetary cost. The cost of injuries can be represented as a function, call it $j(\ )$. The cost of injuries depends inversely on the level of care, suggesting that the cost of injuries function, $j(\ )$, takes as input the function of the level of care, $l(\ )$, which, in turn takes as input the cost of care c, producing a nesting of two functions: $j(l(c))$.

We are only a step away from a formal modeling of society's concern. To get to it, the modeler could start by formulating two examples, one with a level of care that is desirable from a social perspective and one with an incrementally greater level of care that is excessive. Because these will be examples, we can drop all concerns about generality and deal with specific numbers. Costs can be denominated in currency for convenience, although utility could be argued to suit better. To maintain the model's abstract nature we can leave the units of cost unspecified.

A level of care that costs 100 causes injury costs of 140. A level of care that costs 110 causes injury costs of 129. Compare the additional care of 10 with the reduction of injuries by 11. The additional care is desirable because injury costs drop by more than the increase of the cost of care.

A level of care of 120 causes injury costs of 121. The additional ten units of cost of care reduce injury costs less than ten units. This incremental increase of care is undesirable from a social perspective.

The examples communicate the concern of comparing the cost of additional care with the gain from reduced injuries. The challenge is to convert them to a general model. We can obtain from the examples the concern of society. Society's interest is to induce the least total cost.

The examples identify two sources of costs. Therefore, the interest of society can be stated as a simple sum. Society suffers the cost of care and the cost of injuries, $c + j(c)$. Calling that sum the total cost of accidents, $a(c)$, we have constructed the model $a(c) = c + j(c)$. Because society seeks to bear the lowest possible total cost of accidents, our objective will be to find how the legal regime can induce a cost of care that minimizes this aggregate cost of care. Notice that, once we established that society's interests regard the cost of care and the cost of injury, the level of care, $l(c)$, which was nested and complicated the first steps of the analysis, disappears. The level of care still exists, may influence findings of negligence, and may be related to the cost of care. Because society does not directly obtain any benefit or harm from the level of care, it is irrelevant for the determination of aggregate costs. Although the level of care influences the cost from injury, it can be considered part of that function. From this perspective, when the model states harm from injury as a function of the cost of care, $j(c)$, it is equivalent to the more verbose variation of stating the cost of injury as a function of the level of care, which in turn is a function of the cost of care, which produces a nested function $j(l(c))$. The two concepts of cost-of-injury functions are different, with the former encompassing the level-of-care function into the cost-of-injury function.

The gain from reducing the negligence doctrine into an equation is that the equation can be manipulated to produce an irrefutable conclusion. The conclusion, however, depends on the shape of the cost-of-injury function. Rather than treating that shape as a complete unknown, economic thinking reveals some important limitations. First, let us look at a situation, where no care whatsoever is taken. This is akin to driving a car with no brakes, or crossing the street without looking for cars. Would some care reduce accident costs? Naturally, yes. Second, can accidents be eliminated by a sufficiently elevated

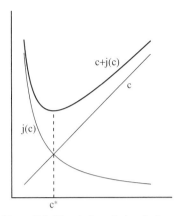

Figure 7.4. The choice of a level of care.

care? Probably not. Although these two answers do not seem particularly revealing, to the economist they indicate three conclusions from which to deduce a likely shape for the cost-of-injury function. Because small levels of care reduce accidents, the function must start with a decreasing slope. Because no level of care eliminates accidents, the cost-of-injury function must never reach as low as zero. Finally, because it is decreasing at small values of care but cannot reach zero when large levels of care are increased, its decreasing slope becomes less so. In other words, $j(c)$ is a decreasingly decreasing function, asymptotic to zero. An equation that exhibits this behavior is $j(c) = 1/c$. Figure 7.4 illustrates $j(c)$, juxtaposed against c and $c + j(c)$. Society minimizes the total costs of care by using care of c^*.

The graphical representation of society's choice in Figure 7.4 may help some jurists grasp the intuition behind optimal care. That is not the main point of producing quantitative models, because others will find the figure obscure or laden with assumptions. The contribution of the quantitative model is that it shows that an optimal care may exist and that this level of care is the point where an incremental increase of care would cost more than the burden of injuries it would prevent. If the "reasonable person" standard of negligence led to care that were greater or less than the optimal, it would be undesirable.

The mathematical nature of the model also allows the precise calculation of the optimal level of care. This is tantamount to finding the value of c at which $c + j(c)$ takes its minimum value. The minimum of $c + j(c)$ is where its derivative with respect to c is zero while its second derivative is positive. Most jurists will not recall how to find the derivative of a function, but mathematics programs, such as *Mathematica* or *Maple*, contain a function that finds derivatives and can solve equations. Most universities have site licenses for those programs and both programs are obtainable from university bookstores and their publishers at academic discounts. The commands for obtaining this result are similar. In *Mathematica*, D[*function, variable*] is the command for finding the derivative and Solve[*equation, variable*] is the function for solving an equation. The commands that would produce the desired result are:

```
Solve[D[c + j[c], c]==0, c]
```

This is a nesting of Solve[ ] and D[ ]. First, D[ ] finds the first derivative of $c + j(c)$ with respect to c. The Solve[ ] function takes that output (the derivative) and solves it for c. If $j(c)$ had previously been defined as $1/c$ (in *Mathematica* j[c_]:= 1/c), then the output would be {{c → −1}, {c → 1}}, which are the two solutions of this equation. Because a negative value of care cannot fit in this analysis, only the second solution is relevant for the model. A check of the second derivative confirms it is a minimum (in *Mathematica* D[c + j[c], {c,2}]/.{c → 1}) produces a positive result. The use of /.{c → 1} after the derivative instructs *Mathematica* to report the outcome using a value of 1 for c. The second derivative was extracted by using the syntax D [*function*, {*variable*, 2}].

ii. Modeling the End of Affirmative Action: Differential Equations

The derivation of an equation by solving differential equations is the second (and last) powerful technique of the calculus that this chapter demonstrates. Differential equations rely on knowledge of the shape of derivatives to ascertain the shape of the underlying equation. Although few applications of differential equations appear in law, one notable exception is an attempt to determine the effect of a sudden repeal of affirmative action in education.[5]

The model assumes that society has an interest in maintaining a proportional composition of the workforce. The analysis begins by supposing that employers hire at a known rate from a pool of educated workers. In other words, employers bring into the workplace new workers and the fraction of the new workers that belong to the minority

---

[5] Nicholas L. Georgakopoulos and C. Reed, "Transitions in Affirmative Action," *International Review of Law & Economics* 19 (1999):23.

is constant. Employers hire the minority, say workers subscripted F (female), with a constant proportion h_F. Workers retire with quit rates q. Correspondingly, all workers have expected career length $1/q$.

From the quit rates and the composition of the workforce we can determine the rate of change of its composition. By combining the overall rate of quits with the employer's minority hiring ratio, h, we find the rate of added minority workers, which is the product, hq. For example, if one tenth of the workers quit each year and half of the new hires are women, an employer with one thousand employees will hire one hundred. Half of those are women, that is, fifty.

From the quit rate we know that the workforce also loses minority workers with a rate qw_F. Continuing the example, if the workforce composition was one fifth female, one fifth of a hundred workers that quit, that is, twenty, were women. Thus, the net rate of change of minority workforce is $hq - qw_F$. The additional women, in other words, are those hired (half of a fifteenth of the workforce) minus those that quit (who are one fifth of the fifteenth of the workforce that quit).

Differential calculus requires treating minority participation as a function of time, which we can write $w_F(t)$. The rate of change of minority participation that we determined in the previous paragraph is its derivative with respect to time. This we write $w_F'(t) = hq - qw$. Although we do not know the composition of the workforce, finding the equation that has $w_F'(t)$ as its derivative reveals how the composition of the workforce changes. The resulting equation is slightly more elegant if we define the initial workforce composition as w_0. Thus, we have a pair of equations, the derivative and the initial state. Solving that system of differential equations seems daunting. Yet, it is only a question of commanding a mathematical software package to do so.

If our software is *Mathematica*, the command for solving differential equations is DSolve [*equations, function, variable*], which takes three parameters, the list of equations, the name of the function, and the variable with respect to which we know the derivative and are solving the system. In our case the function is $w_F(t)$ and the variable is t. We find that minority participation in the workforce is

$$w_F(t) = h + (w_0 - h)\, e^{-tq}.$$

The analysis continues by deriving the minority participation in the pool of candidates and then examining the consequences of ending the policy of trying to bring minorities into the workforce and education. An illustrative scenario indicates the possibility that workforce

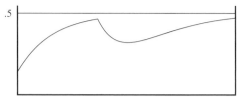

Figure 7.5. An evolution of the composition of the workforce.

participation by the minority may drop.[6] Figure 7.5 shows that the minority's participation was increasing and approaching the horizontal line at 0.5 that indicates proportionality. Then the employer abandons proportional hiring and hires blindly from the pool of candidates. Because the minority happens to be underrepresented in the pool of candidates, the composition of the workforce changes course and moves farther from proportionality before beginning to approach it again.

Differential equations are virtually unknown in legal applications. They are a powerful method with a long and successful record of scientific applications. Modern mathematical software makes them approachable to the legal scholar. Legal analysis that uses differential equations is bound to become more frequent.

D. CONCLUDING EXERCISES

Economic models use terms and idioms that make them unapproachable to many lawyers. Because economics is a science of social welfare, economists should not erect barriers against the use of their product in the applied science of social welfare, law. Hopefully, this chapter explained enough terms and idioms to narrow that gap.

Exercise 7.1: Let us take a simple childhood story as an exercise of modeling. Can you formalize Little Red Riding Hood? What is the story's moral? Which is the conduct that it addresses?

Discussion: Little Red Riding Hood was eaten by the Big Bad Wolf who impersonated her grandmother. When Little Red Riding Hood was on her way to her grandmother, she veered off the path to pick flowers, met the Wolf, and told him where she was going. The usual

---

[6] A *Mathematica* notebook named L&E_DiffEq.nb and containing the analysis of this section is reproduced in Appendix C and is available at the book's Web site, www.fmle-nlg.org. The values used in the example are very close to those used in Figure 1 of the original article.

interpretation of the story stresses that her parents had warned Little Red Riding Hood against deviating from the road and talking to strangers, making those prohibitions the moral. One approach to formalizing the story would be to hypothesize a benefit b from picking the flowers and an expected harm h from the deviation. The story seems to indicate that the harm exceeded the benefit, that is, $h > b$, despite that Little Red Riding Hood thought that was not true. Suppose that Little Red Riding Hood could pick flowers from several locations along the road. One expansion of the model of her choice would assume that the Wolf may hide behind any one of those. A different expansion would explore the possibility that the Wolf knows which location is most appealing to children like Little Red Riding Hood. The modeling choice would change the interpretation of the moral.

Exercise 7.2: What is the maximum of the function $f(x) = 0.3(x-2)^3 - 0.9(x-1)^2 + 3$?

Discussion: We need to find where the slope of the function is zero while at that point the slope is decreasing. The slope of the function is its derivative with respect to x, $f'(x)$. The rate of change of the slope is the derivative of the slope and the second derivative of the original function, $f''(x)$. Find the derivative, equate to zero, and solve for x. Find the second derivative. Calculate its value at the solution.

Using *Mathematica*, first assign the function to a symbol.

```
f[x] = 0.3 (x-2)^3 - 0.9 (x-1)^2 + 3.
```

Take its derivative using the command `D[ ]` and assign it to a symbol:

```
der1 = D[f[x], x].
```

Equate to 0 and solve, assigning the solutions to a symbol:

```
solutions = Solve[der1==0, x].
```

Calculate the second derivative of $f(x)$:

```
der2 = D[f[x], {x, 2}].
```

Evaluate the second derivative at the solutions of the first:

```
der2/.solutions.
```

This is the set of equations used in Figure 7.3.

Exercise 7.3: Star Wars offers a setting to revisit aversion to risk. Risk aversion can be simulated by a particular curvature of the function that illustrates how wealth corresponds to welfare, the utility-of-wealth function (see also discussion in Chapter 4 and Figure 4.1).

Han Solo, a lone intergalactic trader, visits a well-attended casino. Han notices that one species displays a consistent reaction to gambling. The rich and the poor of the species are alike in this regard. The casino offers a rare opportunity to see how this very rational species reacts to gambling. The casino rents its tables but allows those who are gambling not to pay rent. Tables cost 60 credits per hour. One round of the gambling game lasts one minute, so that 60 rounds occur in an hour. From this, Han infers that the rent per round is 1 credit.

Han notices that the poor of the species place even bets (fifty/fifty) of up to 5 credits. If they are pushed to bet more, then they prefer to pay the rent for their table. Han concludes that the calculation the gamblers make is that the gamble makes them suffer anxiety equal to the rental per round. In other words, a 50/50 chance to win or lose five credits is equivalent to having lost one credit. Han also knows that the poor have wealth of about 100 credits. The rich members of the same species have wealth of about 400 credits and gamble up to twenty credits.

Han concludes that the utility-of-wealth function that would describe this species changes slope. If its slope were constant, an incremental change of wealth would have an equal effect on welfare when the change is from 95 to 100 as when it is from 100 to 105. The poor of this species, however, treat the change from 100 to 105 as if it offered them less welfare than to compensate for the chance of a change from 100 to 95.

Han is thinking about the derivatives of the utility-of-wealth function $u(w)$ of this species. He recalls that constant risk aversion has two forms, constant absolute risk aversion and constant relative risk aversion. The disutility of equal gambles is constant, regardless of wealth in the former version. In the latter, disutility is constant as wealth changes for gambles that are a constant proportion of wealth. Han recalls that both are solutions to differential equations that are built on a variable called the coefficient of risk aversion that is symbolized by a.

Constant absolute risk aversion is produced by utility functions that solve the differential equation $u''/u' = -a$. Constant relative risk aversion is exhibited by those that solve $w\,u''/u' = -a$.

Consider the gambles of this species, by the poor and by the rich. Does the species exhibit constant absolute or constant relative risk aversion?

Derive a utility-of-wealth function that matches the conduct of this species.

Discussion: The rich members have four times the wealth of the poor members and they place bets that are quadruple those of the poor members. Because the price of the table is the same, both groups treat those gambles as equivalently onerous. The gambles are not constant in dollars as wealth increases, they are constant as a proportion of (in relation to) wealth. Therefore, the conduct likely corresponds to constant relative risk aversion.

To solve the differential equations in *Mathematica*, use the DSolve[ ] function. In the case of relative risk aversion it becomes:

```
DSolve[w u" [w]/u' [w]==-a, u[w], w].
```

The constants of integration (C[1] and C[2]) can be removed by replacing them with the right constants:

```
% /. {C[1] → 1, C[2] → 0}
```

A special case is that of a coefficient of risk aversion with value 1. Solve that separately.

An attempt to produce the correct coefficient of risk aversion by using the Solve[ ] function likely fails. Consider the numerical alternative FindRoots[ ]. Keep in mind that it takes beginning guesses that will produce different results if the function has several maxima. Verify your result with a Plot[ ].

Exercise 7.4: One of the drollest characters of Star Wars is Jar-Jar Binks, a long-eared worrywart who rarely stops talking. Assume that changes of Jar-Jar's wealth change his welfare by as much as the change of the natural logarithm of Jar-Jar's wealth. The corresponding utility-of-wealth function is $u(w) = c + \ln w$, where c is a constant but its value is irrelevant because we focus on changes of utility (thus, c behaves similarly to a constant of integration) and $\ln w$ is the natural logarithm of wealth. Jar-Jar is confronted with a risk. With equal probability (50/50) Jar-Jar wins fifteen credits or loses fifteen credits. You observe that Jar-Jar is willing to pay twelve credits to avoid this risk. What is the wealth of Jar-Jar before the exposure to this risk?

Discussion: The objective of this exercise is the transformation of the problem into an equation. Once the equation is produced, it can easily be solved by using mathematical software.

The problem gives an equivalence between the welfares that correspond to either one of the outcomes of the risk and the welfare that corresponds to the payment of twelve credits. By using the function for Jar-Jar's utility of wealth, $u(w)$, the equivalence can be restated as that the average of $u(w - 15)$ and $u(w + 15)$ is equivalent to $u(w - 12)$. The average is $[u(w - 15) + u(w + 15)]/2$. The question of the exercise can be restated as asking the value of w for which this is true.

Using *Mathematica*, define the utility function with `u[w_] := c+Log[w]`. Then use the command `Solve` [*equation*, *variable*] to solve `(u[w-15]+u[w+15])/2 == u[w-12]` for the variable w.

This is an application of the risk-aversion analysis of the previous exercise and corresponds to the example discussed in Chapter 6, note 1 and accompanying text.

E. BIBLIOGRAPHICAL NOTE

Truly fun books on math may be an excellent way for approaching this topic again. The many superb choices include all of Maor's books and several code-breaking stories. Eli Maor, *Trigonometric Delights* (Princeton, NJ: Princeton University Press, 1998); Eli Maor, *To Infinity and Beyond: A Cultural History of the Infinite* (Princeton, NJ: Princeton University Press, 1991); Lionel Salem, Frederic Testard, and Coralie Salem, *The Most Beautiful Mathematical Formulas* (New York: John Wiley & Sons, 1992); Michael Sean Mahoney, *The Mathematical Career of Pierre De Fermat: 1601–1665*, (2nd ed. (Princeton, NJ: Princeton University Press, 1994); William Dunham, *Journey through Genius* (New York: Penguin Books, 1991); Simon Singh, *The Code Book* (New York: Random House, 1999).

An advanced but very readable text book of basic economic methods is David M. Kreps, *A Course in Microeconomic Theory* (Princeton, NJ: Princeton University Press, 1990). Readers who are convinced that market forces tend to be desirable – and who may be frustrated over the absence of a chapter on microeconomic equilibrium here – should check the identification of destructive dynamics by Jack Hirshleifer, *The Dark Side of the Force: Economic Foundations of Conflict Theory* (New York: Cambridge University Press, 2001).

The elaboration of the negligence model discussed in this chapter and variations of it are offered by the leaders of the field, Steven Shavell, *Economic Analysis of Accident Law* (Cambridge, MA: Harvard University Press, 1987); William A. Landes and Richard A. Posner, *The Economic Structure of Tort Law* (Cambridge, MA: Harvard University Press, 1987).

An encyclopaedic coverage of differential equations, designed to be used with the *Mathematica* program is Martha L. Abell and James P. Braselton, *Differential Equations with Mathematica*, 2nd ed. (Chestnut Hill, MA: Academic Press, 1997).

8. Confronting Uncertainty: Basic Probability Theory

One of the greatest breakthroughs in the history of mathematics is the development of the ability to quantify uncertainty with probability theory. That is very important for law and economics because individuals and the legal system act under uncertainty. Law-and-economics analysis is only correct if it accounts for uncertainty and for actions in view of uncertainty.

The setting of deciding *Meinhard v. Salmon* illustrates the importance of probability theory.[1] Salmon received a lucrative offer from Gerry, a business acquaintance. The offer could have expanded Salmon's business. Unbeknownst to Gerry, Salmon's business, which was the reason for their acquaintance, had a secret partner, Meinhard. If Gerry knew that Salmon operated in two capacities, as an individual and as a member of a partnership, then Gerry may have specified which of the two he selected as the recipient of his offer. Meinhard, the invisible partner, claimed the offer should be treated as made to the partnership. The litigation that Meinhard started eventually reached the highest court of the jurisdiction and the famous American judge, Benjamin Cardozo, and his colleague Andrews, who is almost equally famous for his vocal dissenting opinions. Previously established law did not answer the question directly. If Cardozo's court attempted the analysis of this setting without being sensitive to uncertainty, they would be missing crucial information. The court established precedent for an uncertain event, the appearance of a lucrative offer or opportunity. It would be clearly wrong to think that parties entering partnerships after the opinion would ignore the possibility that their venture might

---

[1] 249 N.Y. 458 (1928). The text of the opinion is reproduced in Appendix A.

meet lucrative opportunities. Therefore, the analysis must take into account the ways that savvy individuals would adjust their agreements depending on the treatment of uncertain opportunities.

Risk and uncertainty seem to influence a multitude of decisions. Those decisions can only be analyzed with the analytical tools that can address uncertainty and risk, namely, with probability theory. Probability theory describes uncertainty in mathematical terms and allows its analysis. Probability theory developed by attempts to gain an advantage in gambling. Not surprisingly, probability theory is at its most intuitive and works best in the setting of stylized games.

Take the example of a game (and pretend you have never heard of the game roulette). The game involves a disk that spins at the bottom of a shallow bowl and a small metal ball. An attendant spins the disk in one direction and rolls the ball in the opposite direction. Eventually, the ball lands in one of the 37 numbered slots of the disk. Players bet on numbers that correspond to slots. If the ball lands in the slot that a player selects, the player wins and receives 36 times the bet. Consider the decision of a casino on whether to offer this version of roulette. Suppose that the casino expects players to make bets that add up to an amount of about 3,700 each hour. Should the casino offer this game if it pays attendants wages and benefits of about 120 per hour? Does the answer change if the winners still receive 36 times their bet but the disk has 38 slots? Probability theory can answer these questions by calculating the casino's net winnings from the game on average over the long term. If they cover the cost of the attendant, the game will produce a profit in the long run.

In studying human interaction, probability theory is essential because it allows us to take into account the uncertainty of the environment or the future and of individuals' reactions. Probability theory is necessary for any analysis that has the realism of accounting for the unexpected. This unexpected, however, becomes somewhat stylized. The uncertainty is made to somewhat resemble the simplicity of the uncertainty of the roulette wheel.

A. Describing Randomness: Probability and Expectation

The first step in understanding probability theory is to recognize that probability is a number that captures how likely an event is. The concept of probability changes unstructured uncertainty and gives it a specified form. Probability theory takes probability as an input and allows analysis and predictions. The roulette example illustrates how uncertainty changes into probability and how probability theory uses it to draw useful conclusions.

From the perspective of unstructured randomness, the roulette game exposes the casino to the risk of losing almost any amount, repeatedly. From the perspective of probability, however, that is quantifiable. To understand probability, however, we must move away from thinking about a single spin and acquire a larger picture. We must draw analogies.

Probability theory does not eliminate uncertainty. It measures uncertainty and lets us understand uncertainty. That understanding, in turn, has led (and will continue to lead) to discoveries that reduce and control risk, such as the financial teachings about portfolio diversification and the competitive pricing of insurance. Let us not forget the casino example. Probability theory allows casinos to forecast their winnings or losses and to decide what games to offer and with what terms. The film *The Verdict* (1982) with Paul Newman is based on the famous case of the trial about product liability for the placement of the fuel tank in Pinto cars. The manufacturer used probability theory to calculate expected accidents and the related liability and compared it with the cost of repairing the defect. Finance, insurance, and manufacturing are merely examples. Probability theory is necessary for making proper decisions in every field and no less so in law. It was necessary for the lawyers and the courts in Pinto case and it is necessary for the legislators and legal scholars who seek to improve the legal system.

Let us suppose a hypothetical round of roulette with a few scattered bets and try to describe eventualities. Suppose that a bet of 10 is placed on the 7, and a bet of 20 is placed on the 12. Because no other bets are placed, we know that the possible outcomes are three: the number 7 may win, the number 12 may win, or neither. In the first case, the casino, after collecting the 20 bet that was on 12, will give 35 more chips of 10 to the owner of the bet on 7. The casino loses $35 \times 10 - 20 = 330$. By analogy, in the second case, the casino loses $35 \times 20 - 10 = 690$. If neither the 7 nor the 12 win, then the casino wins 30.

The breakthrough of probability theory is that it asks what would happen if this same setting were repeated a vast (infinite) number of times. If, for example, the casino faced exactly that situation, in 100 thousand different spins (games), then how would the casino fare?

We cannot know the exact number of times each slot (number) will win. Yet our intuition allows us to make estimates. Because the disk has 37 numbers and none occurs more often than the others, in about 1/37th of the spins the 7 will win, $100,000/37 = 2,703$ (rounding off decimals). Because the twelve wins equally often, in about 2,703 spins the 12 will win. Neither of the two numbers will win in the remaining spins, that is, $100,000 - 2,703 - 2,703 = 94,594$. We know that the casino loses 330 and 690 in the first two cases and wins 30 in the third. Let us do the corresponding multiplications:

First case (the number 7 wins): lose 330 in 2,703 spins, that is, $-330 \times 2,703 = -891,990$

Second case (the number 12 wins): lose 690 in 2,703 spins, that is, $-690 \times 2,703 = -1,865,070$

Third case (a different number wins): $30 \times 94,594 = 2,837,820$.

The net position of the casino requires that these three results be summed: $-891,990 - 1,865,070 + 2,837,820 = 80,760$. This is the casino's net position after deducting its losses from its gains over 100,000 spins.

How much does the casino win per spin? Divide by the number of spins to find that the casino wins about 0.81 per game.

This is an important conclusion. We calculated that, if the casino faced this exact setting over a large number of games, then it would win about 0.81 per game. Probability theory applies this conclusion to a single game even if it will not be repeated.

What is the probability that in any one spin of the wheel, the number 7 wins? In the analysis above, we proceeded from the assumption that each of the 37 numbers of the disk occur with equal frequency. Therefore, we concluded that a large number of spins would produce about the same number of wins for each number, about 1/37th of the spins. When we return to thinking about a single spin, that 1/37th transformed into a probability. Probability is a fraction that shows the frequency with which an outcome would tend to occur in an infinite number of identical uncertain events. The concept of probability is the foundation of probability theory.

The description of the roulette game, so far, used fractions to express probability. The norm in academic publishing seems to be the opposite. Fractions are reduced to decimals. The 1/37th probability of each number becomes .027. Occasionally, probability appears as a

Table 8.1. *The roulette example expressed in a table*

State	Outcome	Probability	Probability-weighted outcome
The 7 wins	−330	.027	$-330 \times .027 = -8.92$
The 12 wins	−690	.027	$-690 \times .027 = -18.65$
Neither	30	.946	$30 \times .946 = 28.38$
Expectation			$-8.92 - 18.65 + 28.38 = 0.81$

percentage, that is, with the decimal point moved two positions to the right and the sign "%" appended. The 1/37th becomes 2.7%.

Also important is to notice that a shortcut avoids hypothesizing a large number and performing the calculations of multiplying by the large number of events and then dividing by it. The multiplication and the division by the same number cancel out and the direct calculation of the "expectation," also known as "mean," or "average," is possible. This calculation is clarified in Table 8.1. The method does not change. The first column, marked "State," contains the descriptions of each alternative, that is, each way that the uncertainty may be resolved. The column marked "Outcome" contains the corresponding consequences, that is, the amount actually gained or lost. The third column is the probability that this outcome materializes. That sum of the probabilities must always be 1 or 100%. If it is less, the calculation has not accounted for every possible outcome. The last column, called "Probability-weighted Outcome," contains an intermediate calculation, the multiplication of each outcome by its probability. The sum of that column is the expectation.

The exact method used previously to calculate the casino's position after many identical games is used in Table 8.1 to calculate its expectation after a single game. Before, each multiplication included the large number of games and the per-game expectation was the result of the division by that same large number. Because those two operations cancel out, the calculation of expectation bypasses them.

The idea of expectation may seem and may be misleading. To the sceptic, this expectation may seem like a number with no basis in actual experience. None of the actual outcomes matches what is "expected," which seems to indicate that the expectation is impossible. These concerns are correct. Limiting the information about uncertainty to expectation is not relevant for the real world because no actual casino can be certain that it will play a very large number of games. After a losing streak, for example, actual casinos may become insolvent and be unable to continue. That is an analysis of risk that is possible because of probability theory. Before we discuss risk, however, we turn to the use of probability theory in economic modeling.

B. Mathematical Models of Expectation

Mathematical models seek to maintain generality, as we saw in Chapter 7. When a model incorporates probability, generality requires that the model not specify values for the probabilities. If the model were to specify the actual value of any probability, generality would be lost. Therefore, models define probability as a symbol, often p or q.

For probability theory to draw conclusions, it must be used to cover every possibility. This crucial point means that the probabilities of all alternatives must add up to 100% or 1. Thus, if something occurs with probability p, at least one alternative outcome occurs the rest of the time. If that alternative is only one, it occurs with probability $1 - p$.

Economic models define the outcomes that result after the uncertainty is resolved. Instead of laying them out in the form of a table, as in the example of the roulette game, most models form a single equation. The equation performs in a single step the summation used to calculate the expected win of the casino. The summation has several terms; each is the product of the probability multiplied by the outcome.

The example of roulette can easily show this process. Express it using the conventions of economic modeling. All values are replaced with symbols. The example reveals one more modeling habit by numbering equations. A model of the casino might unfold as follows:

Posit a game where players place bets b on N numbers against a casino. In each round, one number wins with probability $p = 1/N$. The casino pays those who bet on the winning number w an amount xb_w, where $x = N - 1$. In a given round bets, $b_i = b_1, b_2, \ldots, b_B$ are placed on B numbers. Players cannot bet on one number, therefore, $B \leq N - 1$. With probability p the jth number wins and the casino has a loss $-xb_j$ on that bet and a gain of all other bets, $\sum_{k \neq j}^{B} b_k$, or

$$p\left(-xb_j + \sum_{k \neq j}^{B} b_k\right). \tag{1}$$

The possibility of a casino loss against any bet is the summation of (1) over all bets:

$$\sum_{j=1}^{B} p \left(-xb_j + \sum_{k \neq j}^{B} b_k \right). \tag{2}$$

The casino may win in the case of the win by a number without a bet with probability $1 - Bp$. When it wins the casino collects all the bets and its corresponding position is

$$(1 - Bp) \sum_{i=1}^{B} b_i. \tag{3}$$

The casino's expected gain Ea is the sum of two terms, (2) and (3):

$$Ea = \left(\sum_{j=1}^{B} p \left(-xb_j + \sum_{k \neq j}^{B} b_k \right) \right) + (1 - Bp) \sum_{i=1}^{B} b_i. \tag{4}$$

This is a hypothetical description of a model that generalizes the roulette game. It uses several of the shortcuts explained in Chapter 7. Although the result is extraordinarily dense, our knowledge of the roulette game and of the vocabulary of modeling from Chapter 7 should allow us to unpack it. The generality of the model, which is a virtue for the economist, stands in the way of the lay reader. The model generalizes in two ways. First, the model abandons the specified bets of the example that began the chapter. The model allows any number of bets to be placed and in any amount rather than two bets of 10 and 20. More remarkable is that the model departs from the specific parameters of the roulette game. Thus, the model allows any number of possible bets and any number of slots in the roulette disc rather than 37. Nevertheless, if we substitute the proper values, the calculation produces the same outcome as in the original example. That two bets are placed implies that $B = 2$. That those bets are for 10 and 20 can be expressed as $b_1 = 10$ and $b_2 = 20$. That the bets are placed in a roulette with 37 slots implies that $N = 37$ and $p = 1/N = .027$. The result is much less intimidating but without the same generality. Preserving the summation signs in (4) while substituting the correct values produces

$$Ea = \left(\sum_{j=1}^{2} .0.27 \left(-35b_j + \sum_{k \neq j}^{2} b_k \right) \right) + (1 - 2 \times .027) \sum_{i=1}^{2} b_i. \tag{5}$$

The formula is composed of two terms, the first containing two summations and the second containing one. The very last summation is the simplest. It sums the two bets for the case that the casino wins. The first summation decomposes into two terms, one where the index j is 1 and a second where it is 2. The summation inside that has a single term, the other bet. The results has three terms. Before substituting the bets it is

$$E a = .027(-35\, b_1 + b_2) + .027(-35\, b_2 + b_1) + (1 - 2 \times .027)(b_1 + b_2).$$

After substituting the bets it is easy to complete the calculation of the example above:

$$\begin{aligned} E a &= .027(-35 \times 10 + 20) + .027(-35 \times 20 + 10) \\ &\quad + (1 - 2 \times .027)(10 + 20) \\ &= 0.84. \end{aligned}$$

The three terms match the three rows of the previous table. Each term is the probability-weighted outcome and the sum of the terms is the casino's expectation.

Mathematical models of probability use conventions that produce a spectacular economy of space at the cost of accessibility. The text that would have been necessary to explain the same analysis to the lay reader would occupy several times the space used by the model. Most readers would tend to find probability models inaccessible. Furthermore, the model does not allow for the immediate verification that it accounts for all possible resolutions of the uncertainty. When the calculation is presented in a table, that is immediately visible, because the column of probabilities has a sum of 1 or 100 percent. In the equation of the probability model, the reader must follow the analysis of the model and track the probabilities of each term.

C. UNCERTAIN UNCERTAINTY: CONDITIONAL PROBABILITY

The preceding discussion of probability involved immediate uncertainty as opposed to uncertainty that could appear as the outcome of one. When probabilities appear only in some outcomes, that is, only with some probability, they are *conditional probabilities*. Examples are games of chance that have two rounds or more, as is the case with craps, a game of dice. If the initial roll of the dice has some values, then the rules require more rolls to determine the winner. The added complexity confuses the calculation of probability. Despite that the probability of the different rolls is known, the probability of winning is not calculated by adding them. Because some first rolls do not determine the outcome but lead to subsequent rolls, the method of adding probability-weighted outcomes seems inadequate.

When the resolution of one (first) uncertainty leads to one or more subsequent uncertainties, the method of calculating and modeling the combined effect involves two types of probability, conditional and unconditional. The conditional probability treats each uncertainty alone, akin to a separate gamble. Unconditional probability takes account of the sequence of uncertainties. Expectations are calculated by summing the products of unconditional probabilities multiplied by outcomes.

Let us use as an example a gamble where four coins are won if the roll of a die produces a 1 but where the player rolls the die only if a coin toss is heads. The die is regular and has six sides, meaning that one sixth of the rolls produce a 1. Yet, the chance of winning the gamble is not one sixth or 16.5 percent. Only half the time is the toss heads. Only then will the roll matter, and a sixth of the time it will be a 1. The "sixth of the time" refers to the roll's conditional probability: conditional on the toss being heads, the probability of rolling a 1 is one sixth. That the gamble is won "a sixth of the time of half the time" refers to the unconditional probability of obtaining 1 in the roll after heads in the toss. Unconditional probabilities are obtained by multiplication of the conditional probability by the probability of the condition. One-sixth of half the time is one-twelfth of the time.

An attempt to express this gamble in a table is confusing. One might expect the table to have two rows, because the coin toss has two outcomes. Yet, one of the two outcomes leads to the second uncertainty, the roll of the die. The relevant outcomes of the die are the roll of a

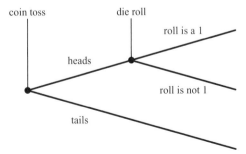

Figure 8.1. The probability tree of rolling a die after tossing a coin.

Table 8.2. *The table corresponding to the example of coin toss and die roll*

State	Outcome	Probability	Probability-weighted outcome
Tails	0	.5	$.5 \times 0 = 0$
Heads, then not 1	0	$.5 \times 0.83$	$.5 \times 0.83 \times 0 = 0$
Heads, then 1	4	$.5 \times 0.17$	$.5 \times 0.17 \times 430 = 0.34$
Expectation			0.34

one or not. As a result, the roll has two outcomes as well. Those two outcomes take the place of the single outcome of the toss that leads to them. Reducing a sequence of uncertainties to a table is not particularly intuitive.

Fortunately, an intuitive expression of a sequence of uncertainties does exist. It is a graphic, rather than a table, and it has the flexibility to display several sources of uncertainty. It is called a "probability tree" and it has a node that branches into the alternatives at each uncertainty (see Figure 8.1).

The example of the coin toss followed by the roll implies a tree with two nodes. The first node is the coin toss. That branches into the alternatives "heads" and "tails." Only "heads" leads to a second node, which corresponds to the roll of the die. That node branches into the alternatives "1" and "not 1."

The probability tree reveals that the outcome of "heads" in the coin toss leads to the roll of the die. That, in turn, leads to two possible outcomes. The tree reveals that the compound gamble has three outcomes. Therefore, a table expressing it should have three rows. Table 8.2 captures this calculation. The first row corresponds to tails, the second to not rolling a 1 after a toss of heads, and the third to rolling a 1 after a toss of heads.

The result is still not as intuitive as it should be because it is not obvious that the sum of the (unconditional) probabilities is 1. It should be obvious, however, that conditional probabilities sum to 1: $.83 + .17 = 1$ and $.5 + .5 = 1$. Let p be the probability of a toss of heads. This implies that tails has probability $1 - p$. Let q be the probability, conditional on a toss of heads, of rolling a 1. This implies that the conditional probability of not rolling a 1 is $1 - q$. The probabilities of the outcomes of the toss sum to 1: $p + (1 - p) = 1$. The (conditional) probabilities of the outcomes of the roll also sum to 1: $q + (1 - q) = 1$. The unconditional probabilities also sum to 1: $(1 - p) + p(1 - q) + pq = 1 - p + p - pq + pq = 1$.

Compound uncertainty leads to complex models. The following example is from an article that discusses differential enforcement against minorities under a possibly biased enforcement authority and an unbiased but imperfectly accurate justice system.[2]

The starting event is the crime, which is committed by a member of either the majority or the minority. Assign q_j to the probability of the crime being committed by a member of the majority, leaving $1 - q_j = q_n$ for the minority. Once a crime occurs, the perpetrator will either be investigated or not. The probability that investigations include perpetrators, depending on their group, is q_{ji} and q_{ni}, for majority and minority, respectively. The unconditional probability of an investigation applying to a crime perpetrated by a majority member and including a majority perpetrator is $q_j q_{ji}$, and $q_j(1 - q_{ji})$ is the probability of an investigation that applies to a crime by a majority perpetrator but that omits the majority perpetrator; $(1 - q_j)q_{ni} = q_n q_{ni}$ gives the probability of an investigation of a crime of a minority perpetrator that includes the minority perpetrator and $(1 - q_j)(1 - q_{ni})$ is the probability of an investigation omitting the minority perpetrator. The article continues by finding that policing and surveillance that disproportionately target the minority (race profiling) will produce disproportionate convictions even if the criminal proclivities of the majority and minority populations are identical. The complex uncertainties take comprehensible shape when presented in a probability tree (Figure 8.2).

The probability tree of Figure 8.2 starts with the uncertainty of the perpetrator, hence its first node is the crime. From this "crime" node originate two branches, corresponding to a majority and a minority perpetrator. Each branch leads to an investigation node, which also has two branches, one for the case where the perpetrator is investigated and one where he is not.

Note that two investigation nodes exist but only one investigation takes place. To calculate probability correctly, we must account separately for investigations that occur after crimes by majority and minority perpetrators because they have different consequences. In this case those are the different probabilities of the perpetrator being investigated, but the nodes might also have involved a different number of alternatives.

2 Nicholas L. Georgakopoulos, "Self-Fulfilling Impressions of Criminality: Unintentional Police Race Profiling," *International Review of Law & Economics*, 24 (2004):169–190.

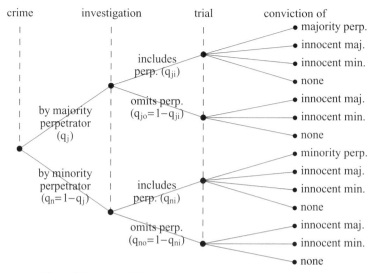

crime   investigation   trial   conviction of

by majority perpetrator (q_j)

includes perp. (q_{ji})
- majority perp.
- innocent maj.
- innocent min.
- none

omits perp. $(q_{jo}=1-q_{ji})$
- innocent maj.
- innocent min.
- none

by minority perpetrator $(q_n=1-q_j)$

includes perp. (q_{ni})
- minority perp.
- innocent maj.
- innocent min.
- none

omits perp. $(q_{no}=1-q_{ni})$
- innocent maj.
- innocent min.
- none

Figure 8.2. A probability tree of crimes, investigations, and trials.

The example of biased investigations ("race profiling") also has a third set of nodes, which correspond to the trial system. Four "trial" nodes exist, one each for majority perpetrator who is investigated, majority who is not, minority who is, and minority who is not. The trial nodes that correspond to investigations including the perpetrator have four branches. Those are the perpetrator's conviction, the conviction of an innocent majority, of an innocent minority, and no conviction. The trial nodes that correspond to investigations that do not include the perpetrator have three branches, since they preclude the conviction of the perpetrator. This probability tree allows us to use the probabilities of the various outcomes to find the composition of the population of the convicted in terms of guilty and innocent by race.

Probabilities begin our understanding of uncertainty. They let us understand simple forms of uncertainty. Using probabilities in probability trees allows us to deal with uncertainty in complex sequences. Probability, however, only applies to categorical outcomes. When the uncertainty regards the value of an outcome, the probability of the outcome is not informative. Rather, relevant information is the probability that the outcome is within some range of values. That is the role of probability distributions, which we will discuss in the next chapter. First we must connect the concepts of this chapter to legal analysis.

D. CONCLUDING EXERCISES

Virtually every court opinion becomes richer when revisited with a focus on uncertainty. Risks that were important to the parties may be absent from the opinion because it comes after the fact and, therefore, after the uncertainties have been resolved. Reviving uncertainties that the opinion does not mention and that the court takes for granted may be difficult but is worthwhile. It gives additional richness to the strategic position of the parties. As a consequence, the normative analysis that leads to a choice of interpretation can change.

At the risk of some repetition, return to the facts of *Meinhard v. Salmon*.[3] Consider the position of the silent partner and investor, Meinhard. Meinhard is a wealthy wool merchant who invests with Salmon in obtaining the 20-year lease of the Bristol Hotel and renovating it. Meinhard remains invisible, while Salmon becomes the manager of the building. During the course of the lease, the owner of the land, Gerry, acquires neighboring properties. At the time the lease is about to expire, Gerry seeks a developer who will tear down the Bristol and erect a larger building on the land that Gerry has assembled. Because he thinks Salmon manages the Bristol alone, when Gerry eventually makes the offer to Salmon he neither excludes nor informs Meinhard. Salmon accepts but Meinhard thinks that he is entitled to participate in the larger project. Cardozo and the majority of the Court holds that the arrangement between Meinhard and Salmon is a partnership and that Salmon's fiduciary obligations require that the larger project be shared with Meinhard.

Exercise 8.1: What uncertainties influence the performance of the investment that Meinhard was making with Salmon in the original lease, that ran from 1902 to 1922? How would those enter Meinhard's calculation of what he would receive from the investment?

Discussion: Examples of the most general versions of such uncertainties may include whether New York would remain the leading port for North America, what economic growth would New York and the United States experience, the direction in which New York City was

---

[3] The case was also discussed in Chapter 6 , exercise 6.5. See Nicholas L. Georgako-poulos, "*Meinhard v. Salmon* and the Economics of Honor," *Columbia Business Law Review* (1999):137.

expanding on Manhattan, and whether Fifth Avenue, on which the Bristol was located, would remain its pre-eminent avenue. More concrete uncertainties may include whether Salmon would prove to be a capable real estate developer and operator, whether the demand for leases of space in the Bristol would be strong, whether the lease would be renewed at the end of its twenty-year term, finally, whether upon its termination Meinhard and Salmon would receive an offer to expand the Bristol. Meinhard likely cannot influence the most general uncertainties that are common for all similar properties. Meinhard can influence others, however, like the selection of his partner or the renovations. Similarly, the quality of the management of the building should influence the owners' desire to renew the lease. The possibility of an expansion seems more of a long shot but it may be extraordinarily valuable.

A confounding uncertainty regards the law. Meinhard chose to remain an invisible participant and should have foreseen that this nature of his participation would lead others to attribute the Bristol's success only to Salmon and, correspondingly, to make offers for development projects to Salmon exclusively. Presumably, this was a consequence Meinhard accepted. Assume that (i) Meinhard expected offers to expand the Bristol itself, however, to be made to both him and Salmon; (ii) Meinhard knew that the law was not settled on this matter; and (iii) Meinhard estimated that the probability that he would prevail in court on this issue was 60 percent. Consider whether Meinhard would want to alert Salmon to his expectation to participate in an expansion. If Salmon did ask Meinhard to join, Meinhard would have to make a decision by 1922, assuming the risk of events after that date. If Salmon failed to offer participation to Meinhard, and litigation would last five years, how would that change Meinhard's risk? Suppose that, despite appearances in 1922, New York entered a recession and Fifth Avenue became a slum by 1926. Would Meinhard continue the litigation to participate in the Bristol's expansion?

It should be apparent that the possibility of protracted litigation gives Meinhard an option. The duration of the litigation allows Meinhard to decide about participating in the expansion after some of its uncertainties are resolved. This option has some value for Meinhard. Compare to that value the legal fees that Meinhard should expect to incur over the course of the litigation.

Suppose that Meinhard had predicted this eventuality in 1902 during the drafting of his agreement with Salmon. Drafting the clause

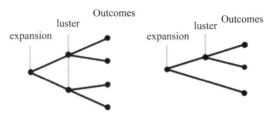

Figure 8.3. Select the appropriate probability tree.

would lead Salmon to always offer Meinhard participation in the expansion, which Meinhard accepts. Did Meinhard have a sufficient incentive to include clauses in that agreement that clarified Salmon's obligation to share an expansion offer with Meinhard? Suppose that Meinhard made the following estimate in 1902 (all dollar amounts are in "1902 U.S. dollars," which means you do not need to worry about discounting and present value). He estimated (1) that an expansion opportunity would have a 5 percent probability to materialize, (2) that Salmon will offer to Meinhard participation with 80 percent probability, (3) that Fifth Avenue will have a 35 percent probability of losing its lustrous image, (4) that his share of the expansion costs would be $200,000, (5) that if Fifth Avenue maintains its lustrous image then his share of the expansion would be worth $350,000 (producing a $150,000 gain), whereas (6) that, if the lustrous image is lost, his share would be worth $100,000 (producing a $100,000 loss), and, finally, (7) that litigation would cost $30,000.

Which of the probability trees in Figure 8.3 represents correctly the uncertainties from Meinhard's perspective about the expansion materializing and the luster of Fifth Avenue being maintained?

It should be possible to determine that the figure on the right is correct and the one on the left is false. The first node corresponds to the uncertainty about the expansion opportunity. The uncertainty can be resolved in two ways: the expansion opportunity will either materialize or not. The uncertainty about the luster of Fifth Avenue should appear in a subsequent node. Should it appear on both branches of the first node? One answer is not universally correct. From the perspective of Meinhard, if the expansion opportunity does not materialize, the luster of Fifth Avenue is irrelevant. By contrast, the lessee of a store in the Bristol may be influenced by whether an expansion occurs as well as by the luster of Fifth Avenue, the latter regardless of the expansion. That is not true for Meinhard. Only if the

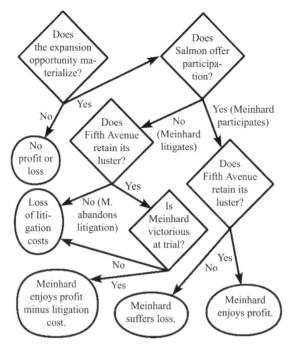

Figure 8.4. A flowchart of Meinhard's decisions.

expansion materializes does the luster of Fifth Avenue have an impact on Meinhard. Thus, the branch that corresponds to the expansion opportunity not materializing does not need a node about the luster of Fifth Avenue to capture Meinhard's perspective.

How should that tree be augmented to account for whether Salmon offers the opportunity to Meinhard? The answer depends on the consequences of the offer. If Meinhard refuses the offer, then Meinhard cannot litigate. The result is that if the offer is made, Meinhard participates and suffers the uncertainty about the luster of Fifth Avenue. If Salmon does not make the offer then Meinhard litigates and decides whether to participate after determining whether Fifth Avenue maintains its luster. It may be easier to develop the probability tree after a logical diagram. The logical diagram in Figure 8.4 starts from the top left with the question whether the expansion opportunity materializes. If it does, the next question is whether Salmon offers participation to Meinhard. If he does, then the next question is whether Fifth Avenue maintains its luster, with Meinhard bearing that risk. If Salmon does not offer participation to Meinhard, Meinhard litigates and the next question is again whether Fifth Avenue maintains its luster. If not, Meinhard abandons the litigation. If yes, then the outcome depends on the result of the litigation. Thus, the question whether Meinhard wins arises, and only if he wins does he participate.

The probability tree would have a node at each question of the logical flowchart, where questions are represented with diamond-shaped boxes. The same number of branches would exit each node as the number of arrows leaving the corresponding diamond in the flowchart. Although in this example this number is invariably two, the number of branches in other settings obviously may vary.

Flowcharts and probability trees are tools to help organize and visualize complex settings. The same setting can be organized in different ways without being incorrect. For example, it is possible to have the second question be whether Fifth Avenue maintains its luster, and then ask whether Salmon offered participation to Meinhard. The result seems less intuitive and somewhat clumsy. Salmon's offer of participation to Meinhard comes at an earlier time than when Fifth Avenue might lose its luster. This grates logic but not probability theory. As long as the different sources of uncertainty and the outcomes are correct, the result is the same.

Consider the following three probability trees. All three illustrate the same sources of uncertainty as the logical flowchart above. Only one is wrong. Which one?

All three trees have nodes that correspond to the uncertainties of whether the expansion materializes, whether Salmon offers participation to Meinhard, whether Fifth Avenue retains its luster, and whether the trial ends in Meinhard's favor. The corresponding nodes are marked "expansion," "offer," "luster," and "trial." The branches of the expansion node are marked by their probabilities, p_e being the probability of the expansion opportunity materializing and $1 - p_e$ being the probability of no expansion opportunity. The branches of the offer node are marked p_o for the probability that Salmon offers participation to Meinhard and $1 - p_o$ for the probability of Salmon not making that offer. Similarly, the branches of the luster node are marked p_m and $1 - p_m$ for the probability that Fifth Avenue maintains its luster and that it does not. The branches of the trial node are marked p_v and $1 - p_v$ for the probability of Meinhard being victorious and not.

Compare this first graph in Figure 8.5 with the logical flowchart. Both have the same structure. The nodes of the tree match the questions of the flowchart.

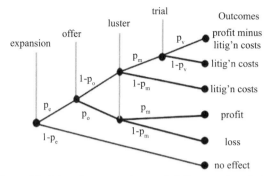

Figure 8.5. Select the appropriate probability tree, first choice.

The second tree (Figure 8.6) may seem identical with the first but a closer look reveals a difference. Notice the order of the nodes. The probability tree in Figure 8.6 has as its second node the luster of Fifth Avenue and as its third node Salmon's offer. This is the reverse order from the first tree (in Figure 8.5). Is this tree wrong? Can you restructure the first tree so that the order of the nodes is expansion, offer, trial, luster?

The third probability tree (Figure 8.7) is similar to the second but has two nodes that correspond to the trial. What events lead to each? Is this tree correct?

Verify the similarity between the first two graphs by calculating the expected value that Meinhard enjoys. This process also lets us review conditional and unconditional probabilities.

What is Meinhard's expectation conditional on the expansion opportunity materializing, if the agreement includes the clause? The answer must assume that the expansion opportunity has materialized

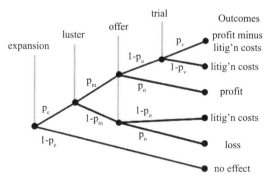

Figure 8.6. Select the appropriate probability tree, second choice.

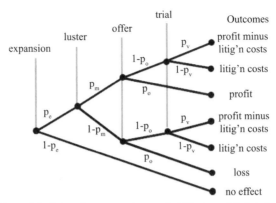

Figure 8.7. Select the appropriate probability tree, third choice.

and that the agreement between Meinhard and Salmon contains a clause stipulating that Salmon must offer to Meinhard participation in expansion opportunities. From this we can conclude that Salmon does make the offer. Because the economics favor participation, we must also assume that Meinhard does participate. If Fifth Avenue fails to maintain its luster, Meinhard suffers a loss; otherwise, he enjoys a gain. Using the corresponding probabilities and values leads to the conditional expectation: $.35 \times (-100,000) + .65 \times 150,000 = 62,500$. What is Meinhard's unconditional expectation of value from the expansion if the agreement includes the clause? ($.05 \times 62,500 = 3,125$ plus the probability-weighted value of the outcomes other than expansion; those we can ignore because they neither influence nor are influenced by the clause.)

What is his expectation conditional on the agreement not containing the clause and Salmon making the offer to Meinhard about participating in the expansion, and on the expansion opportunity materializing? ($.35 \times [-100,000] + .65 \times 150,000 = 62,500$)

None of these uncertainties includes the uncertainty about the outcome of the litigation because no litigation occurs if Salmon makes the offer. If Meinhard accepts Salmon's offer, then he participates in the expansion; if he rejects the offer then he cannot claim that he is entitled to participate. The circumstances necessary for reaching a court decision are (1) that the agreement does not contain a clause about expansion opportunities, (2) that the expansion opportunity materializes, and (3) that Salmon does not offer participation to Meinhard. If all these conditions hold, then Meinhard can pursue the litigation. He finds out whether Fifth Avenue loses its lustrous image before its resolution.

What is his expectation conditional on the expansion opportunity materializing, Salmon not making the offer, Meinhard litigating, and Fifth Avenue keeping its lustrous image? The only remaining uncertainty is the outcome of the litigation, which Meinhard expects to be favorable with 60 percent probability at a cost of 30,000. The value of a loss is 0, the gain in victory is 150,000, minus costs; therefore, the expectation is $.4 \times 0 + .6 \times 150,000 - 30,000 = 60,000$.

Suppose that Meinhard finds that Fifth Avenue lost its luster the day that Cardozo's favorable opinion is announced. Because investing is a losing proposition, he will not exercise his right to participate in the expansion. Remove the condition about Fifth Avenue's image and state his expectation conditional on the expansion opportunity materializing, Salmon not offering it, and Meinhard litigating. $(0.4 \times 0 + .6 \times [.65 \times 150,000 + .35 \times 0] - 30,000 = 28,500)$.

What is Meinhard's unconditional expectation without the clause about expansions? Recall that after accounting for the probability of the expansion opportunity, we need to account for both alternative actions of Salmon, not making the offer to Meinhard for participation and making the offer. $(.05 \times [.2 \times 28,500 + .8 \times 62,500] = 2,785.)$ We had calculated his unconditional expectation with the clause about expansions as 3,125. The difference between those two figures is the impact of the clause on the expected value of Meinhard's arrangement with Salmon $(3,125 - 2,785 = 340)$. Suppose that the negotiation and the drafting of this clause consumes one hour of Meinhard's own time (the cost of which he estimates at 200) and two hours of his lawyer's time, who charges 100 per hour. Will the negotiating and drafting of this clause appear desirable to Meinhard? Hint: The negotiating and drafting cost is 400 and exceeds the expected gain from the clause.

The purpose of the preceding paragraphs was to demonstrate the use of the basic concepts of probability theory in an actual case. The complexity can increase very quickly, but the result may reveal new and important details. We only explored some uncertainties from the perspective of Meinhard. Needless to say, equal and richer images could result from examining the uncertainties perceived by the other actors in the case, Salmon, Cardozo, and Andrews. Each would be a worthy exercise.

Exercise 8.2: Before closing, let us consider the following line of reasoning and ask if it is correct. If not, where does its error lie?

An opinion adopts an interpretation that imposes liability on a given defendant. Regardless whether this interpretation is desirable, probability theory seems to indicate that it had an effect before being adopted. The parties might have formed an expectation based on the probability that the new interpretation would be adopted. If so, then the new interpretation influenced conduct before its adoption. This means that there was a reduced need for its adoption. Therefore, the normative analysis performed by the court seems pointless insofar as these parties may not have needed the interpretation that the court adopted to have the desirable incentives.

Again, *Meinhard v. Salmon* provides an apt example. Suppose that the normative analysis indicates that fiduciary obligations should be interpreted broadly, as the court did, because that fosters investing by passive investors. However, in 1902 Meinhard may have considered that the courts were likely to impose broad fiduciary obligations. Effectively, therefore, Meinhard invested partly because of broad obligations. Hence, the normative analysis that justifies the opinion seems pointless insofar as Meinhard invested anyway.

Discussion: The error of this line of reasoning is fundamental. The normative analysis is performed for the future rather than the past. The facts of the case, in essence, serve as the starting point. That these parties' actions may not have changed is irrelevant. An interpretation is desirable on the basis of the prospective analysis, depending on the incentives that it gives to future parties in similar positions. In other words, Cardozo's interpretation is desirable because it encourages investments by future passive investors. This is not an error that is due to reduced ability to deal with probabilities. It reveals a misunderstanding of what normative analysis is.

E. Bibliographical Notes

The bibliography of basic probability is not rich. A nice example from the legal literature is Steven Shavell, "Suit, Settlement, and Trial: A Theoretical Analysis Under Alternative Methods for Allocation of Legal Costs," *Journal of Legal Studies* 11 (1982):55 *et seq.* The bibliographical note of the next chapter presents advanced texts.

9. Advanced Probability: Distributions as the Shape of Randomness

Complex as the analysis of Chapter 8 may seem, it did contain an extraordinary simplification. Each source of uncertainty had a limited number of possible outcomes; one outcome typically corresponded to each alternative. When revisiting the facts of *Meinhard v. Salmon* with an eye on probable alternatives (see exercise 8.1), we considered the possibility that its Fifth Avenue location would change character. The building was assumed to have a single value if Fifth Avenue maintained its luster. A more realistic outlook would concede that the value of the expansion might take any one of a range of values.

When uncertainty is about amounts or sizes rather than whether an event occurs, the simple concepts of probability that were introduced in Chapter 8 are inadequate. The alternatives may be infinite and cannot fit in tables or probability trees. However, a concept of probability theory manages to impose order. This concept is the distribution function. The contrast with the probabilities of alternative outcomes (on which Chapter 8 focused) reveals that distribution functions are a step toward generality. Rather than identify the alternatives, a model can use a distribution function that allows any outcome from a specified range that may extend to infinity.

Continuous distributions are at the extreme end of the range of sophistication in probability theory discussed here. The previous chapter started with simple tables. The transition from the table to the probability tree continues with discrete distributions and culminates with continuous distributions. The main constant components along this trip are (1) the weighing of every possible outcome by its probability and (2) that the aggregation of all probabilities is 100 percent, that is, 1. The

175

integral performs the same role in the case of a continuous distribution as the summation in the case of a discrete one.

A. The Shape of Randomness: Distribution Functions

To maintain generality, models use continuous distributions and may even avoid specifying what form they take. This is very confusing for the reader who is not versed in probability theory. When a model states that, for example, "driving speed x follows a distribution function $G(x)$," it seems as if there is nothing behind this function G, particularly because speed is its input rather than its output. The function is unspecified, but it exists. Because it is a distribution function, we know quite a bit about it, including what its output is, which is probability.

Two related functions describe probability: the distribution function and the density function. The first is also called cumulative distribution function or CDF. That gives the probability of obtaining an outcome smaller than or equal to a given value that can be considered a moving threshold. This implies that CDFs are increasing throughout their range, so the bell curve is not one of them. Actually, the familiar bell curve is the second type, a probability density function or PDF. The graphical representation of both types of probability functions almost always places the probability along the vertical axis, or y axis, and the threshold along the horizontal axis, or x axis. The two have a mathematical relation in the case of continuous distributions. The probability density function is the derivative of the cumulative distribution function.

For example, in the distribution of speed, the cumulative distribution function gives the probability of a speed equal to or less than the given speed.

Random variables can take any one value either from a countable set of values or from an infinite range of values. If the possible values are countable, the distribution is discrete, such as the distribution of the roulette or the rolls of dice. If the possible values come from a range of infinite values, then the distribution is continuous, such as the speed of sailboats or driving speed. That a distribution is continuous does not necessarily mean that its range extends to infinity. Take the example of sailboat speeds under a 15-knot breeze. Suppose the slowest boat sails with 3 knots and the fastest with 14 knots. Sailboats have a specific range of speeds, from 3 to 14 knots. The distribution of speeds is continuous, however, because sailboats are not restricted to a countable set of

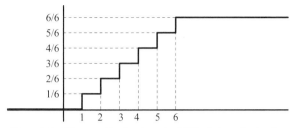

Figure 9.1. Discrete distribution: the CDF of the roll of a die.

speeds within that range. A sailboat that cannot quite reach 10 knots does not need to stay at 9 knots. It might sail at any speed between 9 and 10 knots and those are infinite.

i. Visual Comparison of Discrete and Continuous Distributions

A visual comparison reveals the importance of the difference between discrete and continuous distributions. Using the roll of a die as the example of the discrete distribution, the Figure 9.1 below shows that the probability of a roll smaller than 1 is 0, but at the value of 1 that probability jumps to one sixth. That value remains constant until we reach 2, where it jumps to two sixths. The cumulative distribution function of the discrete distribution looks like steps because it changes values only at those points that are possible outcomes.

The cumulative distribution function of sailboats has a very different appearance. Figure 9.2 assumes that the average sailboat speed is 7 knots and follows the normal distribution. The cumulative distribution function reveals that for each incremental increase of threshold speed, the likelihood of the sailboat going slower than that speed increases. It increases between 5 knots and 5.1 knots as it also does from 5.1 to 5.2

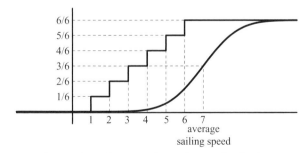

Figure 9.2. A discrete and a continuous distribution.

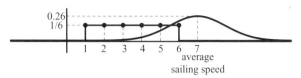

Figure 9.3. Probability densities of a discrete and a continuous distribution.

(but by different amounts). Few sailboats would experience speeds under 5 knots, but a few more if the threshold were 5.1 knots, and yet a few more if it were 5.2.

The resulting shape of the cumulative distribution function is a smooth curve rather than the steps that correspond to the die. The graph in Figure 9.2 juxtaposes both.

Contrasting the cumulative distribution functions with the corresponding probability density functions reveals the difference (Figure 9.3). The sailboat's probability density function is the familiar bell curve. The die's probability density function shows that each side comes up with equal probability.

From the perspective of legal design, the desirable design of rules depends on conduct. When the possible alternatives are not enumerable, then conducts follow a continuous distribution. For example, the proper design of speed limits depends on driving speeds. The speed limit at a turn following a straight road should take into account the speed of approaching cars. The analysis cannot assume that driving speed is known or constant. Driving speed varies and the analysis must take that into account. The distribution of speeds describes that variation. That would be the distribution of speeds. To maintain generality some models avoid any assumptions about the way that speed varies. More approachable are models that do make an assumption about the shape of the distribution.

ii. CDF and PDF: Features and Relations

The most important features of the two types of functions were already mentioned. Cumulative distribution functions (CDFs) are increasing and they range from 0 to 1. For example, if the likelihood of a speed below some number is x, it is impossible that the probability of a speed below a greater number is less than x.

Also, for some low enough number, the probability of a smaller outcome is zero or trivial. For example, under a 15-knot breeze, no sailboat's speed may be less than 3 knots. Similarly, there is some number high enough that all or almost all of the outcomes are lower. The fastest consumer cars cannot presently exceed 200 MPH, although that is just a fraction of the land speed record. It is a value for which we can safely say that driving speed is slower practically 100% of the time.

The reason for the guarded statements "zero or trivial" and "all or almost all" is that the most important distribution never quite reaches 0 or 1. The normal distribution is asymptotic to its bounds in both directions. Freak accidents can happen and outcomes wildly different than the usual may occur. Indeed, gearboxes can get stuck in first gear and new land speed records do occur.

One of the greatest sources of confusion for lay readers is the confusion of cumulative distribution functions and probability density functions. Probability density functions (PDFs) are closer to the intuitions of probability; they resemble the histograms and bell curves that appear in the popular press. Probability density functions do not target 1 and often they hardly approach it. Nor are they increasing throughout their range. In mathematical terms the density is the slope of the cumulative distribution function, its derivative with respect to the threshold value, usually on the x axis. The relation between the PDF and CDF is inescapable. Suppose in a given region, 10 percent of the outcomes materialize. The corresponding column in a histogram would have a height of 10 percent. Necessarily, the cumulative distribution function would increase by 10 percent over the same region. Its slope is determined by probability density at this region.

The relation between distribution and density functions is a very convenient one for mathematical manipulation. By convention cumulative distribution functions are symbolized by capital letters, while the corresponding probability density functions are symbolized by the same letter in lowercase. Because the derivative is symbolized by an apostrophe (which is read as "prime") we know that for a distribution G, $G'(x) = g(x)$. Vice versa, because integration is the inverse of differentiation, we also know that

$$\int g(x)\, \mathrm{d}x = G(x).$$

The integral symbol is part of the contemporary understanding of probability. Integration is analogous to summation, adjusted for continuous distributions.

Summation by its definition applies to the discrete items being added in a sum. Discrete distributions only take specific values. The toss of a coin, the roll of a die, and the spin of a roulette wheel are examples of random processes that have discrete distributions: heads or tails for the coin, the integers 1 through 6 for the die, and 0 through 36 for the roulette. Summation is appropriate. Continuous distributions prevent the application of summation to all their possible values because they are infinite.

The probability density function of a discrete distribution is directly analogous to a histogram. A histogram that depicts the fraction of outcomes that occur at each possible value is essentially a density plot. Take the example of many rolls of a die. Because the die has six sides, each outcome will occur about 1/6th of the rolls. If we plot the fraction of ones, twos, threes, and so forth, each will be about 1/6th. The probability of each discrete outcome is also exactly 1/6th and that is the probability density. Consider the probability of an outcome of 2 or less. The answer is provided by the cumulative distribution function and is the sum of the probability density of an outcome of 1 and the probability density of an outcome of 2. Thus, the summation of the discrete density function $g(x)$ is the discrete cumulative distribution function $G(x)$, which can be written $\sum_{i=-\infty}^{x} g(i) = G(x)$, which is read, "the sum of [the function] g of i [valued] from minus infinity to x is equal to capital gee of x." In the case of the die, the i takes the values 1 and 2, $g(1)$ is 1/6 and $g(2)$ is 1/6, so that $G(2)$ is 1/3.

The density functions of continuous distributions cannot be summed. They must be "integrated," which is analogous to the summation operation on a continuous function. Integration uses calculus to establish the "area under the curve" of the function (see Figure 7.1). A constant of integration, often symbolized by C, is added to indicate that the integration operation does not know where the horizontal axis is. The constant of integration can be conceived as the rectangular area under the function. In probability theory, however, the constant of integration stays mostly away.

The use of integrals, however, is unavoidable in probability models. The average or arithmetic mean of a discrete distribution is obtained by multiplying the probability $p(x)$ of each outcome x by the value of the outcome x. The symbolic representation is

$$\sum_{x=x_{\min}}^{x_{\max}} p(x)\, x,$$

which is read "the sum, with x running from x sub min to x sub max, of the product of p of x multiplied by x." Similarly, the mean of a continuous distribution is the integral of the density function $g(x)$

multiplied by the outcome x:

$$\int_{x_{\min}}^{x_{\max}} g(x)\, x\, dx,$$

which is read "the integral with x running from x sub min to x sub max of the product g of x multiplied by x." If the distribution extends to infinity in the positive direction, then $x_{\max}$ should be replaced by infinity. Vice versa, if the distribution extends to negative infinity, $x_{\min}$ should be replaced by minus infinity. Otherwise, the variables $x_{\min}$ and $x_{\max}$ should hold the boundaries of the distribution. We can similarly write the standard deviation as the square root of the integral of the squared differences from the mean multiplied by the density function.

iii. Truncated and Censored Distributions

One useful application of the integrals is the calculation of truncated means and censored means. The two refer to two different results for outcomes outside some range. A truncated mean corresponds to the dropping of outcomes outside the range. The censored mean corresponds to compressing outcomes from outside the range to its borders. If we ask, for example, what is the average roll of a die if we ignore rolls of 4 and above, the answer is a truncated mean. If we instead assume that all rolls above 3 appear as threes, and ask what is this average, then we seek a censored mean.

Truncated and censored distributions are defined by two attributes in addition to the underlying distribution. The first is the point of the truncation or censoring. The second is its direction, because it influences values above or below that point. When values greater than the point of truncation are dropped, then it is called an "upper" truncation or a distribution "truncated above" that point. The concepts of "lower" truncations or distributions "truncated below" a value are analogous. The same terms apply to censored distributions.

Although truncation appears as the simpler concept, the calculation of the average is easier for censored distributions (see Table 9.1). A usual die produces rolls, but rolls over 2 appear as 2. What is its average roll? This is the average of the distribution of rolls censored above 2. A straightforward application of the methods explained in the previous chapters is effective.

Table 9.1. *A censored distribution of the roll of a die*

State	Outcome	Probability	Probability-weighted outcome
Roll is 1	1	1/6 = .167	.167*1 = .167
Roll is 2	2	1/6 = .167	.167*2 = .333
Roll is over 2	2	4/6 = .667	.667*2 = 1.334
		Expectation	1.834

The additional complexity you will encounter requires that you observe this simple calculation in two other ways by using a more general notation. Becoming familiar with the notation will help you to understand the notation we will use for the continuous distributions. First, substitute the probability density function for the probability values. Let the probability density function of an ordinary die be $p(x)$ and the cumulative distribution function be $P(x)$. This notation departs from the known probability density values of the die, which we know to be one sixth for each number, and the known (cumulative) probability of rolling a number up to a 2, which we know to be one third. Because the censoring conflates to 2 the rolls that are over 2, the cumulative density of 2 does not apply directly. Instead, the (cumulative) probability of 2 is subtracted from 1 to obtain the remaining probability weight. Preparing for one more step of generalization, Table 9.2 also uses symbols for the minimum of the distribution, n, for its maximum, m, and for the censoring point, c.

The calculation of the censored mean can be expressed using a general equation. Whereas the specific one is $p(n)n + p(n + 1)(n + 1) + [1 - P(n + 1)](n + 1)$, the general one uses a summation for all terms except the last.[1] Accordingly, the general equation for the censored mean, $m_{cens,up}$, of a discrete distribution with a domain from n to m, with an upper censoring at c is composed of two terms. One term uses the cumulative distribution function and is the product of the censored probability density, $1 - P(c)$, multiplied by the censoring point c. This is $[1 - P(c)]c$. The other term is a summation of the products of the probability densities of the uncensored outcomes multiplied by their values. The conventional notation would be $p(n)n + \cdots p(c)c$, which is

---

[1]   See, in general, Colin Rose, "Bounded and Unbounded Stochastic Processes," in *Economic and Financial Modeling with Mathematica*, Hal R. Varian ed. (New York: Springer-Verlag, 1993):241–5.

Table 9.2. *The censored die roll, using generalizable notation*

State	Outcome	Probability	Probability-weighted outcome
Roll is n	$n = 1$	$p(1)$	\<same\>
Roll is $n+1 = c$	$n+1 = 2$	$p(2)$	\<same\>
Roll is from $c+1$ to m	$c = 2$	$1 - P(2)$	\<same\>
		Expectation	\<same\>

expressed in a sum as $\sum_{i=n}^{c} p(i)i$:

$$m_{\text{cens,up}} = [1 - P(c)]c + \sum_{i=n}^{c} p(i)i$$

This formula leads immediately to the upper censored mean, $\mu_{\text{cens,up}}$, of a continuous distribution:

$$\mu_{\text{cens,up}} = [1 - P(c)]c + \int_{n}^{c} p(i)i \, \mathrm{d}i$$

A very similar analysis leads to the lower censored mean, $\mu_{\text{cens,low}}$, of a continuous distribution. In a lower censoring, the outcomes smaller than the censoring point, c, are seen as taking the value c, and the remaining outcomes range from c to the maximum, m. Because the lower censoring changes outcomes below c, the equation can use the cumulative distribution function valued at c.

$$\mu_{\text{cens,low}} = P(c)c + \int_{c}^{m} p(i)i \, \mathrm{d}i$$

The additional complexity of the calculation of the truncated mean occurs because the probability density function cannot be applied directly. Because the truncation means that outcomes are ignored, if the probability of the remaining outcomes were not adjusted, the remaining probabilities would not sum to 1. This is easy to see in the tables used above for the censored mean. Omitting the last line of those tables would produce a false calculation. The tables would account for only 2/6ths of the probability.

Realizing the source of the error leads to its correction. Because the truncation reduces the total probability weight, the remaining probability weights must be expressed as parts of the total remaining probability weight rather than as parts of 1 or 100 percent. Returning to the example of the die, if we ignore rolls greater than 2, then the probability of rolling a one is not one sixth but one half. This one half is the ratio of one sixth to the total probability weight that is not ignored, that is,

Table 9.3. *A truncated distribution of a roll of a die*

State	Outcome	Probability	Probability-weighted outcome
Roll is 1	1	$\dfrac{1/6}{2/6} = .5$	$.5*1 = .5$
Roll is 2	2	$\dfrac{1/6}{2/6} = .5$	$.5*2 = 1$
		Expectation:	1.5

the ratio of one sixth to two sixths. Table 9.3 performs this calculation for the example of the die.

Reaching the general formula is again easiest if we pause to substitute symbols. The range of the distribution is from n to m and the upper truncation is at the value of r. Table 9.4 implements this step toward generality by using symbols while restating Table 9.3.

From this point, the general equation becomes apparent. The upper truncated mean, $m_{\text{trunc,up}}$, of a variable subject to a discrete distribution function from n to m is the sum of the probability-weighted outcomes. The equation that the summation produces can be simplified by taking the denominator, which does not change values, outside the sum.

$$m_{\text{trunc,up}} = \sum_{i=n}^{r} \frac{p(i)}{P(r)} i = \frac{\sum_{i=n}^{r} p(i)i}{P(r)}$$

This formula leads immediately to the upper truncated mean, $\mu_{\text{trunc,up}}$, of a continuous distribution:

$$\mu_{\text{trunc,up}} = \int_{n}^{r} \frac{p(i)}{P(r)} i \, di = \frac{\int_{n}^{r} p(i)i \, di}{P(r)}$$

A very similar analysis leads to the lower truncated mean, $\mu_{\text{trunc,low}}$, of a continuous distribution. In a lower truncation, the outcomes smaller than the truncation point, r, are ignored, and the remaining outcomes range from r to the maximum, m. Because the relevant probability is the cumulative one of exceeding the truncation,

Table 9.4. *The truncated die roll, using generalizable notation*

State	Outcome	Probability	Probability-weighted outcome
Roll is n	$n = 1$	$p(1)/P(r)$	\<same\>
Roll is $n + 1 = r$	$n + 1 = 2$	$p(2)/P(r)$	\<same\>
		Expectation	\<same\>

Table 9.5. *Censored and truncated distributions*

The mean of a truncated discrete distribution

	Lower	Upper
Example	The average roll of a die, ignoring rolls smaller than 4.	The average roll of a die, ignoring rolls greater than 2.
Equation	$m_{\text{trunc,low}} = \dfrac{\sum_{i=r}^{m} p(i)i}{1 - P(r)}$	$m_{\text{trunc,up}} = \dfrac{\sum_{i=n}^{r} p(i)i}{P(r)}$
Explanation	The sum of probability-weighted outcomes, from the truncation to the maximum of the distribution, adjusted for the missing probability.	The sum of probability-weighted outcomes, from the minimum of the distribution to the truncation, adjusted for the missing probability.

The mean of a truncated continuous distribution

	Lower	Upper
Example	The average sailing speeds above 5 knots.	Average sailing speeds below 8 knots.
Equation	$\mu_{\text{trunc,low}} = \dfrac{\int_{r}^{m} p(i)i \; \mathrm{d}i}{1 - P(r)}$	$\mu_{\text{trunc,up}} = \dfrac{\int_{n}^{r} p(i)i \; \mathrm{d}i}{P(r)}$
Explanation	The integral of the probability-weighted outcomes, from the truncation to the maximum, adjusted for the missing probability.	The integral of the probability-weighted outcomes, from the minimum to the truncation, adjusted for the missing probability.

The mean of a censored discrete distribution

	Lower	Upper
Example	The average roll of a die, treating every roll smaller than 4 as a 4.	The average roll of a die, treating every roll greater than 2 as a 2.
Equation	$m_{\text{cens,low}} = P(c)c + \sum_{i=c}^{m} p(i)i$	$m_{\text{cens,up}} = [1 - P(c)]c + \sum_{i=n}^{c} p(i)i$
Explanation	The probability-weighted minimum plus the sum from the censoring point to the maximum of the probability-weighted outcomes.	The probability-weighted maximum plus the sum from the minimum to the censoring point of the probability-weighted outcomes.

(continued)

Table 9.5 (*continued*)

| The mean of a censored continuous distribution | |
Lower	Upper
Example	The average driving speed while a minimum speed limit is effectively enforced.	The average driving speed while a maximum speed limit is effectively enforced.
Equation	$\mu_{\text{cens,low}} = P(c)c + \int_c^m p(i)i\,\mathrm{d}i$	$\mu_{\text{cens,up}} = [1 - P(c)]c + \int_n^c p(i)i\,\mathrm{d}i$
Explanation	The probability-weighted maximum plus the integral of the probability-weighted outcomes from the censoring point to the minimum.	The probability-weighted minimum plus the integral of the probability-weighted outcomes from the minimum to the censoring point.

substitute the cumulative distribution function with $1 - P(r)$,

$$\mu_{\text{trunc,low}} = \int_r^m \frac{p(i)}{1 - P(r)} i\,\mathrm{d}i = \frac{\int_r^m p(i)i\,\mathrm{d}i}{1 - P(r)}$$

We can put all these equations in a table that illustrates their use (see Table 9.5).

The use of censored and truncated distributions is still nascent in economic analysis of law, despite their apparent importance. An example of their use is discussed in exercise 9.1.

B. The Normal Distribution

The reader who is familiar with the claim that the normal distribution is practically ubiquitous may wonder why it is not used more. After all, if it is the default distribution of random events, it should serve the purpose of generality. Models could have a general solution for any distribution and continue by reaching more specific results by using the likely distribution of the event, which would often be the normal distribution. This would allow much more powerful results and it has an illustrious precedent, but it is not the practice.

One of the most illustrious precedents of the use of an actual distribution based on its theoretical merits alone is the use of the lognormal distribution in the work of Black, Merton, and Scholes on the pricing of options. Their models sought to derive the value of an option to buy a share of common stock at a specified price and a specified time, what is known in the financial markets as a call option. Because this value

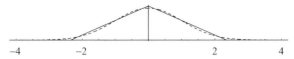

Figure 9.4. The PDFs of the normal distribution and of the triangular distribution.

depends on the distribution of the price of the stock, a distribution had to be specified for the model to produce a solution. The normal distribution was considered inappropriate because it has no minimum (technically, its minimum is minus infinity) while the range of stock prices is limited to positive values. For this reason alone, these authors chose the lognormal distribution. The resulting call option pricing formula revolutionized option markets and led to the authors receiving the Nobel Memorial Prize in Economics. Option valuation is discussed in Chapter 11.

At this stage, it might be useful to give the formulas for the normal distribution. We do not have a formula for its cumulative distribution function and must use the probability density function, which is expressed in terms of the distribution's mean t and standard deviation σ as

$$f(x) = \frac{e^{-(t-x)^2/2\sigma^2}}{\sigma\sqrt{2\pi}}$$

If the analysis must use a cumulative distribution function, the fact that we do not have an expression for the normal distribution leads to a dead end. If an approximation is appropriate, then it might be acceptable to use that of the triangular distribution, which is stated in terms of the minimum and maximum of its range. Figures 9.4 and 9.5 superimpose the graphs of the normal and the triangular distribution. In both figures, the normal distribution is displayed with a dashed line and the triangular distribution with a solid line.

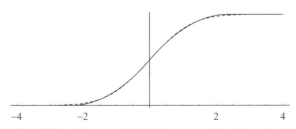

Figure 9.5. The CDFs of the normal distribution and of the triangular distribution.

Table 9.6. *The triangular distribution PDF and CDF*

Range	PDF	CDF
$-\infty < x < \min$	$t(x) = 0$	$T(x) = 0$
$\min \le x < \dfrac{\min + \max}{2}$	$t(x) = \dfrac{4(x - \min)}{(\max - \min)^2}$	$T(x) = \dfrac{2(\min - x)^2}{(\max - \min)^2}$
$\dfrac{\min + \max}{2} \le x < \max$	$t(x) = \dfrac{4(\max - x)}{(\max - \min)^2}$	$T(x) = \dfrac{(\max - \min)^2 - 2(\max - x)^2}{(max - min)^2}$
$\max \le x < \infty$	$t(x) = 0$	$T(x) = 1$

Figure 9.4 displays the probability density functions of the two distributions. The sharp corners of the triangular distribution are in stark contrast with the smooth curves of the normal distribution.

Figure 9.5 displays the cumulative distribution functions of the two distributions. Both distributions have curving cumulative distribution functions. Their differences are barely visible in this form.

Table 9.6 gives the equations of the triangular distribution for the corresponding ranges. The derivation of these formulas is in a *Mathematica* notebook file.[2]

C. CONCLUDING EXERCISE: IMPERFECT ENFORCEMENT

Exercise 9.1: The triangular distribution is a solution to a problem of mathematical intractability. Although the normal distribution is often an appropriate choice for an unspecified distribution, no equation for its CDF exists. The triangular distribution is a potential substitute. This exercise illustrates the problem and the use of the approximation, that is, the triangular distribution.

Explore the consequences of the "$1/p$ adjustment" of penalties when they apply to a conduct that follows a continuous distribution. The $1/p$ adjustment is proposed as the appropriate reaction of the state to imperfect enforcement.[3] When the violators know that they will not be apprehended on every violation, they adjust the nominal

---

[2] A Mathematica notebook named L&E_DeriveNormalDistribution.nb and containing the analysis of this section is reproduced in Appendix C and is available at the book's website, www.pmle–nlg.org. See also Appendix C, Derivation of the Normal Distribution.

[3] See, for example, Gary S. Becker, "Crime and Punishment: An Economic Approach," *Journal of Political Economy* 76 (1968):176–90; see also A. Mitchell Polinsky and Steven Shavell, "Punitive Damages: An Economic Analysis," *Harvard Law Review* 111 (1999):869 (arguing that jury instructions should include directions on adjusting punitive damages for the probability of detection and prosecution).

penalty downward. If the probability of paying the fine f is p, they treat it as a fine of the smaller-size pf. Of course, if the state adjusts the fine by $1/p$, then the expected fine becomes again appropriate (assuming that f is the appropriate fine). This proposal seems intuitive but contradicts the intuitions of equity and the commentary of the Renaissance scholars in favor of increasing the certainty rather than the size of penalties.[4] Is the Renaissance scholar Beccaria correct when he asks for precise enforcement? May the state reduce its expenditures by cutting enforcement and making the $1/p$ adjustment to penalties?

Discussion: The analysis starts by selecting the conduct on which we will apply the analysis. Let us select urban speed under a speed limit of 50 km/h. Experience indicates that the limit is not enforced perfectly because some drivers exceed it without being stopped by the police. Suppose, though, that those who travel at more than 100 km/h do always get apprehended. From this we derive the conclusion that the probability of suffering the penalty increases between 50 and 100 km/h.

To formalize this setting, we must fill in several details such as the size of the penalty and its effect, the distribution of preferences, and the distribution of the uncertainty about precision. The appeal of the normal distribution is that it is likely the most accurate for both. We will soon find that it cannot produce the results that we would like.

Suppose that the penalty $n(s)$ is a function of how speed s exceeds the limit t, so that we can write $n(s) = (t - s)z$, provided $s > t$. This multiplies the difference in speeds by a multiplier z. Table 9.7 lists all the variables used in this model.

We can approximate the effect of the penalty by considering that the preferences of each driver could be expressed in a graph that would look like an inverted U. Its peak corresponds to the driver's ideal speed. If that exceeds the limit, however, the driver reduces speed to the extent the reduction in expected penalty is greater than the impact of the delay. If experience indicates that the drivers who exceed 100 km/h reduce their speed by 10 km/h compared with their ideal, then we can derive the shape of the preferences. The quadratic function, $f(x) = a + bx^2$ takes the shape of an inverted U when the coefficient b is negative. Substituting x by $e - s$ allows us to move its peak to the point e, with s being the speed at which the individual drives and e the preferred speed. Moreover, the variable a is irrelevant because

---

[4]   See, for example, Cesare Beccaria, *On Crimes and Punishments, and Other Writings,* trans. Henry Paolucci (New York: Bobbs-Merrill Co., 1963):93–4.

Table 9.7. *The variables of the model of vague speed limits*

Symbol	Description
s	The actual speed at which an individual chooses to drive.
t	The speed limit. It follows the distribution $R(\ )$.
$n(s)$	The penalty for speeding, which is a function that depends on speed (s).
e	Each individual's preferred (ideal) speed.
$u(s)$	Function that corresponds to the benefit that each individual derives from each possible speed ("utility from speed").
$a, b, x, f(x)$	Used for explanation only, not part of the model.
z	The penalty multiplier, a component of the penalty function, $n(s)$.
r	The reduction of speed that the penalty function induces.
$R(\ )$	The cumulative distribution function of the vague speed limit. The illustrations use the triangular distribution.
$R_L(\ )$	The CDF of the lower half of the triangular distribution.
$R_H(\ )$	The CDF of the higher half of the triangular distribution.
e_L	The preferred speed of each individual that chooses a speed in the lower half of the distribution of the limit.
e_H	The preferred speed of each individual that chooses a speed in the higher half of the distribution of the limit.
m	The maximum of the vague (random) speed limit.

the vertical position (height) of the function is irrelevant because this analysis will not compare individuals' welfare. Thus, an individual's welfare $u(s)$ can be stated as $u(s) = b(e - s)^2$.

An individual who violates the limit chooses a speed such that the marginal reduction of the penalty is equal to the marginal reduction of welfare. Marginal change is the derivative with respect to speed. Accordingly, the s that the individual chooses equalizes $n'(s) = u'(s)$. Solving for s expresses speed as a function of preference e, the coefficient b, and the multiplier z, with the goal of eventually finding b as a function of the induced reduction r of speed by 10 km/h.[5] The solution is $s = e - z/2b$. Substituting s with $e - r$, normalizing b to $b = 1$, and solving for z allows us to state $z = 2r$. When this replaces z in $n(s)$, the result is a penalty function that would induce individuals to reduce speeds by $r = 10$ km/h when they are subject to a certain penalty.[6]

---

[5] Mathematica solves an equation equalizing $f(a)$ to $g(b)$ for a with the command Solve [f[a]==g[b], a], and takes a derivative of a function $f(a)$ with respect to a with D[f[a], a]. Thus, the appropriate command in this case is Solve[D[n[s], s] ==D[u[s], s], s].

[6] A Mathematica notebook named L&E_SpeedingEG1.nb and containing the analysis of this section is reproduced in Appendix C and is available at the book's website, www.pmle-nlg.org. See also Appendix C.

The individuals who drive with speeds above the limit but below the speeds at which penalties become certain, face probabilistic penalties, with that probability reaching 1 at 100 km/h. Because probability always increases, the appropriate function to capture this effect is a CDF; call it $R(x)$. The expected penalty at a speed s would then be $En(s) = R(s)n(s)$. The speed that individual drivers chose would solve $En'(s) = u'(s)$. The distribution that would reflect reality best may arguably be the normal distribution, but its CDF is intractable. Instead we use the triangular distribution. Accordingly we substitute the CDF of the triangular for $R(s)$ in the equation that indicates the speed and find how much drivers reduce speed at the two regions of the distribution. Let us use the subscripts L and H for the functions that correspond to the lower and upper half, respectively, of the triangular distribution.

Some drivers violate the limit but use speeds that exceed the limit by less than half the distance to the speed where apprehension becomes certain. Those speeds fall in the lower half of the range where apprehension is uncertain. The speed of those drivers implies $En'_L(s) = u'(s)$. Solving that for the preference, e, answers the opposite question, giving the preference e that corresponds to each observed speed s in the lower half of the uncertain range. As in this case the minimum of the distribution is equal to the limit, that is, t, the number of variables is reduced. Call the maximum of the range of the speed limit m. Replacing the minimum by t and the maximum by m, and solving, the result is

$$e_L = s + \frac{6r(t - s)^2}{(m - t)^2}.$$

Formulate the equation for the drivers whose speeds are not enough for certain apprehension but are higher than the middle of the range where apprehension is uncertain? Either of the mathematical software packages (*Mathematica* or *Maple*) can solve it and simplify the solution. A convenient simplification is

$$e_H = s + r + \frac{r\left(4(m - s)(s - t) - 2(m - s)^2\right)}{(m - t)^2}.$$

The preferences of individuals who choose speeds inside the range of uncertain apprehension are greater than the speed they choose. The ability of mathematical software to produce graphics allows the illustration of the reaction to limits.

One of the most intuitive displays of the effect of the limit and its uncertainty would place preferences on the horizontal axis and display

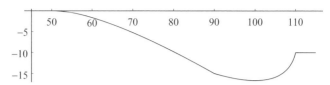

Figure 9.6. The reduction of speed that a vague speed limit induces.

the reduction of speed on the vertical axis. The reduction of speed is the difference between the preference, e, and the actual speed traveled, s. The example already defines the reductions below and above the area of uncertainty. Drivers whose preference is for a speed that complies with the limit have no reason to change their speed. Their reduction of speed is zero. The example also states that drivers who would accept a certain apprehension reduce their speed by $r = 10$ km/h. The reduction of speeds by drivers who choose speeds inside the range of uncertainty is the result of the equations that the analysis produced. Figure 9.6 displays this in negative values, because the difference is always a reduction of speed.

The reductions of speed that Figure 9.6 illustrates exceed within the range of uncertainty the reduction imposed on those who accept certain apprehension. Not only does the maximum deterrence occur within the range of uncertainty but, using the figures of the example, the effect on conduct is more than 50 percent greater there than among those who accept a certain penalty. An additional interesting feature that this figure reveals focuses on the drivers who have preferences so high as to almost accept a certain apprehension. Contrast their deterrence to that of drivers with preferences for speeds ranging from the limit of 50 to about the upper end of the range of uncertainty, about 100. This group is increasingly deterred; drivers with preferences for greater speed are led to reduce their speed more than others.

The opposite phenomenon appears when we examine the drivers with preferences that almost lead them to accept certain apprehension. Those are the drivers with preferences approaching 110. In that narrow range, from about 100 to 110, preferences for greater speed correspond to less deterrence.[7]

---

[7] In this range, the uncertainty of enforcement induces conducts that differ more than the corresponding preferences. This dispersing effect of uncertainty is discussed at length in Nicholas L. Georgakopoulos, "Vagueness of Limits and the Desired Correlation of Conducts," *Connecticut Law Review* 32 (2000):451 (hereinafter "Vagueness").

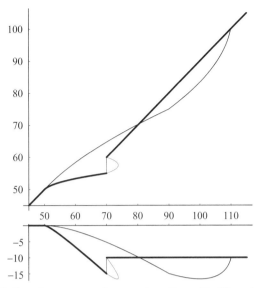

Figure 9.7. Reactions to two enforcement practices with different precision.

This analysis started as an exploration of the preference for precision that we attribute to authors from the Enlightenment, such as Beccaria. That preference is a counterpoint to the apparent appeal of increasing penalties to compensate for the possibility of escaping punishment, the $1/p$ adjustment. The methods we have developed allow us to visualize the consequences of increasing precision.

Increased precision, in this context, corresponds to a narrower range of uncertainty. The result may be that the limit remains unchanged, and apprehension becomes certain much sooner, at much smaller violations. For example, apprehension may become certain at a speed of 60 km/h.

Figure 9.7 illustrates the effect of the increase in the precision of enforcement using two panels. The bottom panel is similar to the previous figure. It displays the reduction of speed that corresponds to each preference. For the comparison, the reactions to the vague limit are also displayed with a line of medium weight. The curve that corresponds to the precise limit reveals a paradox. The curve bends back toward the origin. From the vertical light line at about 70 and for a few units to the right, each preference seems to correspond to three reductions of speed.

The upper panel of Figure 9.7 may produce a clearer illustration of this phenomenon. The horizontal axis again holds preferences, but the vertical axis corresponds to speeds rather than reductions of speeds. Thus, the upper panel connects the conduct that the rule induces, driving speed along the vertical axis, to the preference to which it corresponds along the horizontal. Again the curve of the initial example of uncertain enforcement from 50 to 100 km/h is reproduced to help the comparison.

The range of uncertainty is only visible in the upper panel's vertical axis. In more precise enforcement, the range of uncertainty is from 50 to 60 km/h. The hypothetical defined the effect of the limit on individuals who accept certain apprehension as a reduction of speed by 10. Therefore, the range of speeds from 50 to 60 corresponds to a range of preferences from 50 to 70 km/h. The paradox that appeared in the lower panel reappears. In a narrow range of preferences above 70 km/h, each preference corresponds to three different speeds, one on the heavy line and two on the light segment that curves back toward the origin.

Intuition should reveal that drivers would prefer the greatest of the three speeds. By hypothesis, we know that the driver is willing to accept certain apprehension and chose this speed. Because further reductions of speed are more undesirable, a further reduction of speed cannot improve this driver's situation. Therefore, the areas of the curves that are marked by the light line should be ignored. The practical effect of this corresponds two very different behaviors. A driver who has a preference for a speed slightly under the maximum of the range of uncertainty, such as 69 km/h in this setting, drives with a speed that is well below that maximum, here about 55 km/h. A driver with a preference that is only marginally higher, such as 71 km/h, accepts certain apprehension and exceeds that maximum, here driving at about 61 km/h. No driver chooses a speed between the two.

Exercise 9.2: Compare the consequences of imprecise enforcement using different assumptions about the distribution of preferences in the population. Which enforcement system would be preferable if the distribution of preferences was such that less than 1 percent of drivers had a preference for speeds exceeding 70 km/h? A distribution of preferences that would have this effect would be centered more than three standard deviations lower, as would, for example, one with an average preference for 55 km/h with a standard deviation of 5. What fraction of conducts would exceed 60 km/h? What demands would their apprehension and adjudication place on the justice system?

Exercise 9.3: Compare a distribution of preferences that is much less concentrated. The result is a significant fraction of preferences for speeds exceeding 70 km/h. Analogize to other types of preferences that have great dispersion, such as attitudes toward noise. Should the rules restricting noise be defined and enforced with great precision, over a narrow range of decibels? Individuals also vary significantly with respect to their attitude toward risks. Should the rules imposing personal liability on entrepreneurs for failures of the business be enforced with great precision?

Exercise 9.4: Compare precise rules, such as traffic rules, or accounting rules, with rules that seem more vague, such as constitutional protections or the revocation of limited liability of corporations (veil piercing), or even the negligence rule.[8] How are vague rules different from imprecisely enforced limits that have a precise definition?

Exercise 9.5: Scholars in mathematics, statistics, and physics occasionally display a striking predilection toward using more than three dimensions in their analysis. An example is the application of vector calculus in statistics, where each data point is treated as a dimension. Such multidimensional approaches have been proposed for law.[9] One proposal could be understood as being that each factor or test that contributes to a legal conclusion is a dimension. A rule can then be re-interpreted as imposing consequences for a segment of the space that these dimensions define. What are the dimensions of the rule that intentional killing not in self-defense receives the punishment for murder? How does the analysis change if a jurisdiction distinguishes excessive force from reasonable force for assessing self-defense?

Discussion: The initial rule can be seen as defining a space of three dimensions, the killing, the intent, and the self-defense dimensions. All three must have the appropriate values to trigger the penalty. When a jurisdiction decides to improve the law of self-defense by distinguishing the use of excessive force from reasonable force, the space that the existing model has defined cannot accommodate the new concern. To the extent the model prevents a desirable improvement, it is unhelpful.

---

[8] These issues are discussed in Georgakopoulos, "Vagueness ," 451.
[9] Robert Birmingham and Sharon Jones, "Book Review: A Nice Book," *Connecticut Law Review* 23 (1991): 1043–6.

D. BIBLIOGRAPHICAL NOTE

Advanced texts on probability theory can be extraordinarily inaccessible because the mathematics of probability distributions are unusual. Trying to approach probability theory with the precision and help of mathematical software seems significantly easier. A text that uses *Mathematica* is John J. Kinney, *Probability: An Introduction with Statistical Applications* (New York: John Wiley & Sons, 1997). One that uses *Maple* is Charles M. Grinstead and J Laurie Snell, *Introduction to Probability*, 2nd ed. (Providence, RI: American Mathematical Society, 1997). See also the books listed in the bibliographical note to Chapter 13 on statistics.

10. How to Price Uncertainty: Finance

Much of law is about financial arrangements. This may be an understatement because all of private, and much of public, law rests on the idea that certain wrongs (torts, breaches, etc.) trigger *financial* compensation. Not all payments of a given amount are equal, however, because time and risk matter. This chapter explains how the value of a payment changes with time – what is called *discounting* or the *time value of money* – and how to adjust for the risk of future payments from businesses according to the *Capital Asset Pricing Model*. Legal analysis needs a sound understanding of these topics.

The importance of financial knowledge is starkly visible in *Meinhard v. Salmon* because it involves an overtly financial relation.[1] Salmon received a lucrative offer from Gerry, a business acquaintance. The offer could have expanded Salmon's business. Unbeknownst to Gerry, Salmon's business, which was the reason for their acquaintance, had a secret partner, Meinhard. If Gerry knew that Salmon operated in two capacities, as an individual and as a member of a partnership, then Gerry may have specified which of the two he selected as the recipient of his offer. Meinhard, the invisible partner, claimed the offer should be treated as made to the partnership. The case involved numerous payments at different points in time, illustrating the importance of discounting and valuation. The case is also an excellent example of the practical importance of valuation. The analysis is different if Meinhard's investment was reasonable and, therefore, Salmon's participation and compensation are not clearly gifts, compared with an analysis treating Salmon's participation as a gift. Valuation reveals whether the profits that Meinhard would expect according to the agreement have a

---

[1] 249 N.Y. 458 (1928). The text of the opinion is reproduced in Appendix A.

value consistent with Meinhard's contribution, that is, not significantly smaller than the contribution. The payment by a seasoned merchant of $200 for a stake worth about $100 should trigger doubts, including that the transaction may hide a gift to the other partner of about $100.

Financial theory is misunderstood in law and economics because it uses methods that are largely dissimilar from ordinary economics. A principal difference between finance and economics lies on the focus of economics on incentives. By contrast, finance has the advantage of knowing the incentive, which is profit. This allows financial law-and-economics analysis to focus on actions. Active financial players want to trade profitably, and passive financial players want to invest. From here, it is a relatively simple matter to establish how they behave, then to find the consequences of their actions, and, finally, to proceed with the normative analysis of designing a legal rule that would induce more socially desirable actions.

Although economics knows individuals seek to maximize their welfare, the means by which they do so are unknown. In other words, economic actions do not have a one-to-one correspondence with the immediate reasons for the actions. The same action may be a result of different reasons. Financial actions are closer to a one-to-one correspondence between reasons and actions.

For example, everyone who makes a bank deposit – a financial transaction – has the same immediate reason for that action, to postpone consumption while earning some interest on the deposited funds. Not every buyer of a luxury convertible has the same reason. Some may enjoy the wind in their hair, some may appreciate the sensation of an open top, whereas others may be driven by the image the car conveys to them or to others. All the buyers of the cars maximize their welfare, but in different ways. Furthermore, two individuals who have the same immediate goals may proceed to different actions. Two individuals may enjoy equally the sensation of driving with the top down, but one may buy a luxury convertible and one may not.

Nonfinancial considerations do influence some financial actions and vice versa. The separation of the financial from the nonfinancial world is not absolute. Although these crossover effects may be important, their effect usually is minimal. In any case, a theoretical analysis can justifiably ignore them, preserving a theoretically pure financial reasoning for actors, even if some deviation might be observed in actuality.

Examples of nonfinancial concerns influencing financial actions are easy to find. For instance, depositors may tend to prefer a bank that is conveniently located. The location of the bank is not a financial feature, but it may influence a financial action, the bank deposit. The opposite effect is even more likely. Car buyers will be influenced by the expected resale value of the car, which is a financial feature of a nonfinancial transaction.

This chapter first discusses valuation, then examines its normative implications and closes with the new research area of market microstructure. This chapter visits two methods of valuation, the valuation of certain payments, which is called discounting, and the valuation of risky assets (stocks). Microstructure focuses on the types of players that populate financial markets. Understanding the players reveals how information shapes prices and what the risk of errors is. Chapter 11 will discuss options.

A. Valuation in Perfect Markets

The fundamental principle of valuing financial instruments is indifference between equivalents. The financial markets provide the basic elements of valuation by pricing the market as a whole and riskless credit, that is, setting the interest rate of government obligations (bonds, notes, and bills). Financial theory then explains how every other risky asset can be replicated by combining credit with stocks, the market portfolio.

i. Known Rates: Discounting

Discounting appears in many business and commercial law courses as a necessary tool for the practice of law. The basic premise of discounting is a hypothetical bank that offers terms identical with those used in discounting. If the terms are a rate of 10 percent with annual compounding, the question of discounting a future payment F turns into the question of how much to deposit in the hypothetical bank to find an amount F in the account at the specified future time. Although it is easy to move forward in time, it appears difficult to move backward. Nevertheless, it is a matter of simple manipulation of the equation, using middle school algebra. Consider a deposit of $100 today in a bank that pays interest of 10 percent per year. Into how much money will it grow in one year? Most high school students should easily recognize the answer is $110. That is the level of difficulty of discounting.

What future value F will we find in one year in an account containing an amount P today? If the rate were 10 percent, then F would be

110 percent of P. In symbolic terms, a rate of r leads in one year to $F = P(1 + r)$. If the required period is two years, then the interest that is earned during the first year will be considered to be capital for the second year. The second year's amount, F_2, will be $F(1 + r)$. We can substitute F with $P(1 + r)$, producing $F_2 = P(1 + r)(1 + r) = P(1 + r)^2$. The same process occurs in the third year, so that the annual compounding equation raises to the power of the number of years y the sum of 1 plus the rate, and is $F = P(1 + r)^y$.

Most transactions, however, use monthly compounding. To build that equation we need to move forward one month at a time. In one month, however, the deposit in the hypothetical bank will not have grown by the full percentage of the interest rate, but by the fraction of the year that has elapsed, that is, one twelfth the annual rate. The amount we will find in the bank in one month is $F = P(1 + r/n)$, where n is the number of compounding periods in the year, or, in the case of monthly compounding $n = 12$. In two months we find $F = P(1 + r/n)^2$, and in three months, $F = P(1 + r/n)^3$. In one year the exponent will reach 12, the number of months elapsed. In two years it is 24. This reveals the periodic compounding equation: $F = P(1 + r/n)^{yn}$.

That we are told the future amount F and we want to determine P requires a simple rearrangement to solve the equation for P, which reveals that $P = F/(1 + r/n)^{yn}$.

The power of mathematical software allows us to almost effortlessly move from periodic to continuous compounding. Continuous compounding sounds daunting but requires no more than remembering some early high school math and seeking the limit of the periodic equation as the number of periods tends toward infinity.[2] The software reveals that the solution is $F = Pe^{yr}$, although it does not realize how foreign the symbol for Euler's constant is for most lawyers. Yet, it is on most calculators and in all spreadsheet programs (sometimes called EXP). Its value is about 2.72.

Discounting includes two more important equations. Both are about annual payments, which are called *annuities*. The first regards

---

[2] The corresponding command in *Mathematica* is `Limit[ ]`. Obtaining the simplified version of the equation requires us to apply two more commands, one that expands powers and one that simplifies. The complete command may appear as follows:

`FullSimplify @ Limit[P(1+r/n)`^{yn}`, n→Infinity].`

Use Ctrl-^ to raise to a power and keep the space that denotes multiplication in the exponent, otherwise *Mathematica* treats *yn* as a single symbol.

the value of a constant annual payment with no termination date. The second is the derivation of the value of an annuity with constant growth.

The value of a constant payment is very easy to simulate with a hypothetical bank. If each year, the depositor withdraws all the interest, then the capital remains constant and earns every year the amount indicated by the interest rate. Depositing $100 in a bank that pays 5 percent interest produces a constant annuity that pays $5 annually. Its value is the deposit, that is, $100. Calling the annual payment a and the deposit d, $a = dr$. Dividing both sides by the rate r and simplifying lets us see that the value d of the annuity is $d = a/r$.

The value of a growing payment is much more complex. Each year's payment a_i is the result of growing by the rate g the previous year's payment, a_{i-1}. Thus, their relation follows the discounting equation for a single period, $a_i = a_{i-1}(1 + g)$. Thus, the question becomes what deposit d must be made to allow such withdrawals. Discounting each a can be written

$$d = \frac{a_1}{1+r} + \frac{a_2}{(1+r)^2} + \frac{a_3}{(1+r)^3} + \cdots.$$

This becomes significantly more messy if we substitute the second payment by expressing it as a function of the first payment, which we know to be $a_2 = a_1(1 + g)$. We can just write a instead of a_1, to avoid the repetition of the same subscript. Because we also know that subsequent annual payments follow the compounding formulas we derived, we know that $a_3 = a(1 + g)^2$, that $a_4 = a(1 + g)^3$, and so on. Substituting every annual payment with its expression as a function of the first gives a more complex formula, but one that allows an interesting mathematical manipulation:

$$d = \frac{a}{1+r} + \frac{a(1+g)}{(1+r)^2} + \frac{a(1+g)^2}{(1+r)^3} + \cdots + \frac{a(1+g)^{n-1}}{(1+r)^n} + \cdots.$$

Amazingly enough, this infinite sum can be reduced to a simple form.[3] It simplifies to $d = a/(r - g)$, but it gives correct solutions only if the growth rate is smaller than the interest rate.

Those who have developed a level of comfort with the mathematical software may be ready for an exercise. What is the rate that with

---

[3] The *Mathematica* command is

```
Simplify@Sum[ a(1+g)^(n-1) / (1+r)^n, {n,1,∞}].
```

Table 10.1. *Discounting equations*

Problem	To find future amount	To find present value
Periodic compounding (n periods per year for y years)	$F = P(1 + r/n)^{yn}$	$P = F/(1 + \frac{r}{n})^{yn}$
Continuous compounding	$F = Pe^{yr}$	$P = F/e^{yr}$
Perpetuity of a per year		$P = a/r$
Perpetuity of a growing at the rate of g per year		$P = \dfrac{a}{r-g}$, provided $g < r$.
Finding the continuous rate c equivalent to a given rate r of periodic compounding		$c = n(\ln(n + r) - \ln(n))$
Finding the periodic rate r equivalent to a given continuous rate c		$r = n(e^{c/n} - 1)$

continuous compounding will have the same effect as a given rate under periodic compounding? If the two rates are to have the same effect, they will grow P to the same amount F in y years. Construct the equation and solve for the continuous rate.[4]

Table 10.1 collects the equations that we have produced for discounting.

We have derived the equations for moving value though time, assuming a known rate. When that rate is known, we need no more information to answer valuation questions. The rate is known, however, mostly in cases where the appropriate rate is that of traded government debt, the returns of which can be immediately ascertained from the press. Financial theory has also produced a method for determining the appropriate rate for risky assets, stocks. That method is the Capital Asset Pricing Model.

---

[4] The *Mathematica* command would be

```
Solve[p(1+r/n)^yn == p e^cy, c].
```

Note that the symbol for the continuous rate is c because it cannot be r on both sides of the equation. The double-struck e of the Euler's constant can be produced by the symbols palette or by hitting esc, e, e, esc in *Mathematica*, or else by using the command `Exp[]`. The spaces between symbols are necessary for multiplication. To simplify the result, first apply the command `PowerExpand[]` ant then Simplify []. A single line of code connects the three commands: `Simplify@PowerExpand@Solve[...]`. The result is included in Table 10.1. How should the `Solve[]` command at the first line of this note change to give the periodic rate that is equivalent to a given continuous rate? (Hint: Which is the symbol for the periodic rate?)

ii. Risky Assets

The valuation of risky assets is founded on two premises: first, that diversification eliminates all risk except the uncertainty regarding overall economic performance; and second, that it is possible to capture the tendency of stocks to move with the market as a whole, which, in turn correlates with overall economic performance.

Diversification is the division of invested funds over numerous assets or stocks. The result is that each stock is a minuscule part of the portfolio. Random events that influence the value of a single company will have a trivial effect on the entire portfolio. Moreover, random bad news in some firms will tend to cancel out with random good news in others. Random events that influence a few firms will tend not to influence the performance of diversified portfolios.

The consequence is that diversification reduces risk. As a result, investors will tend to be diversified rather than hold portfolios composed of a few firms. Therefore, random events that influence few firms will tend not to be seen as risk from the perspective of investors. But, despite their diversification, investors cannot avoid the overall risk of economic performance. Surprises about the state of the economy influence even diversified investors because they influence all stocks in the market. Thus, investors do not care about risks that are "idiosyncratic" to specific firms, but they do seek to avoid system-wide or "systematic" risks.

To accept risk, investors who are averse to risk must be compensated. Competition ensures they only demand compensation for risks that they truly bear. Because diversification eliminates idiosyncratic risk, idiosyncratic risk should have no effect on the return that investors require. Since system-wide risk is unavoidable from investors' perspective, they will have to be compensated for bearing it.

An asset does exist that provides the valuation of system-wide risk, that is, the market index, which by definition corresponds to the performance of an investment in every stock.

The final step to the solution to the stock valuation puzzle is that statistical techniques allow us to estimate the degree to which any stock moves together with the market. The question is what change in the stock price does a given change in the market induce, and the answer is given by performing a linear regression, which is discussed in greater length in the chapter on statistics.

The linear regression finds the linear pattern that links changes of the overall level of the market with changes in the price of a single

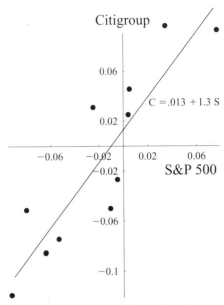

Figure 10.1. The sensitivity of a stock (Citigroup) to changes of the market.

stock. It produces two parameters, known as the alpha and the beta of the stock because of their representations in the regression equation $y = a + bx$, where x is the change of the market and y the change of the stock. The regression mechanics are best illustrated in a graph. Consider a graph where along the horizontal x axis we measure changes in the market and along the vertical y axis we measure changes in the stock. Thus, a month during which the stock declined 5 percent while the market rose 10 percent is represented with a point at co-ordinates $x = .1$, $y = -.05$. After all the data are converted to such points, the regression will determine alpha and beta so as to place a straight line that passes closest to all points.

Figure 10.1 illustrates how the statistical method of linear regression determines the sensitivity of a stock to changes in the market index. The points in the graph are data points. The x coordinate of each point is the change of the market for that period; the market is represented by the Standard and Poors 500 index (the "S&P500"). The y coordinate is the change of the stock in the same period, in this graph the stock is Citigroup and the period is from August 2000 through August 2001. The historical data of monthly price changes of the stock and the market are converted to points. The linear regression calculates the straight

line that lies closest to those points. It defines that line by producing an
a (alpha) and b (beta) coefficient. The line is defined by the equation
$y = a + b\,x$, in this case C = .013 + 1.3 S, where C is the symbol for
Citigroup and S is the symbol for the stock market index S&P500. The
beta coefficient is the slope of that line and it captures the degree to
which the price of the stock tends to change with changes in the market,
that is, the sensitivity of the stock to changes in the market.[5]

Thus, the beta coefficient solves the problem of estimating the systematic risk of the stock. A stock that tends to change half as much
as the market will have a beta of .5. If it is joined with many other
stocks that also have a beta of .5, that diversified portfolio will expose
its holder to half the risk of the market. Where some amount, say 100,
invested in the market might gain or lose 20, the same amount in the
beta one-half portfolio would gain or lose 10. It would be more accurate to say that if the standard deviation of the market portfolio is
20 percent, that of a $b = .5$ portfolio would be 10 percent.

The estimation of betas allows investors to appraise the system-
wide risk to which any stock exposes them. Investors can monitor their
exposure to market risk by calculating the betas of their portfolios and
by screening new investments by their beta or counterbalancing. An
investor who wants, for example, to take no more systematic risk than a
beta of 0.6, can either put 60 percent of his funds in the market portfolio,
or all his funds in stocks with low betas, so that the aggregation produces
an average beta no greater than .6. If a new investment with a .8 beta
is attractive, it can either be included in the portfolio while the overall
size of the portfolio is reduced, or it can be counterbalanced by also
adding an equal amount of .4 beta stocks. The stock's beta is all the
risk information that a diversified investor needs.

The revolution of the Capital Asset Pricing Model is that beta completely describes risk for diversified investors. Diversification eliminates firm-specific risk. Diversified investors are only exposed to
system-wide risk. Betas measure the exposure to system-wide risk carried in each stock. Therefore, betas completely describe risk from the
perspective of diversified investors.

The solution to the problem of valuing risky assets is now available.
The only risk is that of the entire market. If we know how the entire
market is valued, the beta of each stock will allow us to value each

---

[5] This graph is available in the Excel file LawEcMEthods_Finance.xls at the book's
Web site, www.pmle-nlg.org.

stock. This mechanism is known as the Capital Asset Pricing Model (CAPM, pronounced cap-EM) and only requires knowledge of interest rates, the market rate of return, the beta of the security to be valued, and its expected payouts. The CAPM operates on the foundation that functionally identical securities must offer the same returns. If they did not, they would allow traders to take advantage of the difference with no risk, that is, they would give rise to an arbitrage opportunity. Traders would trade the two equivalent goods, buying the cheap and selling the dear. This trading pressure would correct prices.

In the context of valuing stocks, the equivalent assets are the stock to be valued on one side and a synthesized portfolio with equivalent risk on the other. Portfolios of any beta can be synthesized. Betas lower than 1 are synthesized by balancing the investment in the diversified market portfolio with riskless treasury bonds (or bills or notes). Betas greater than 1 are synthesized by borrowing and "over"-investing in the market an amount greater that the available funds.

If the security to be valued has a return different than that of the synthesized equivalent, then traders have an opportunity to profit at no risk. In financial parlance, this is called an arbitrage opportunity. It stands to reason, of course, that obvious arbitrage opportunities cannot persist. They attract trading, which by nature eliminates the discrepancy in prices. The cheap equivalent is bought and its price rises. The costlier equivalent is sold and its price falls. Soon the arbitrage opportunity disappears. The CAPM uses this concept of the impossibility of persistent arbitrage to value securities.

Each security, therefore, must offer the same return as its synthetic equivalent. Each stock is expected to have some earnings or profit per share and some capital appreciation each year. Its price will adjust so that the percentage return investors receive is equal to that expected from a synthetic portfolio having the same beta.

For example, assume that neither the stock nor the market offers any capital appreciation and they pay all profits as dividends. Suppose the market trades at 10 times earnings, offering a 10 percent return to investors, while government bonds offer 4 percent. The stock to be valued has a beta of .5 and expected earnings of 10 per share. The synthetic portfolio with equivalent risk will be half government bonds and half the market, returning 7 percent ($.5 \times .04 + .5 \times .1 = .07$). Therefore the stock's price must be such that the profits of ten per share are a 7 percent return; using the equation for valuing an annuity of \$10 in a 7 percent rate, we find its price must be $10/.07 = 142.85$.

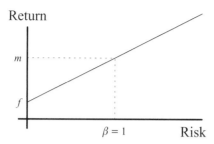

Figure 10.2. The capital market line.

If the price of the stock is higher or lower, the arbitrage opportunity is easy to identify. Suppose that the stock is trading at 135. The annual dividend of 10 now corresponds to a return of 7.4 percent ($135/10 =$ .074). Arbitrageurs will sell portfolios consisting of 50 percent bonds and 50 percent the market and buy this stock. Vice versa, if the stock was priced too high, say at 150, arbitrageurs would sell it and buy the synthetic portfolio.

Thus, the CAPM indicates that any deviation of stocks' prices from the equivalently risky synthetic portfolio will cause massive one-sided trading – buying if the stock is cheaper and selling if it is more expensive. This unsustainable pressure will equalize prices to those of the equivalent synthetic portfolios. As a result, the returns of any stock can be calculated by calculating the returns of the equivalent synthetic portfolio. For a beta of b, that would be $r = (1 - b) f + b\, m = f + b\, (m - f)$, where f is the risk-free rate and m is the rate of return of the market. The result is the "capital market line," the line on which the return of every security lies, given its beta.

Figure 10.2 depicts the capital market line. The x axis measures risk, that is, beta, because that is the only risk that burdens diversified investors. The y axis measures the returns of each asset. The capital market line is defined by two points: the return of risk-free debt (f) and the return of the market (m). All assets lie on the capital market line according to the CAPM because of the possibility of arbitrage with the equally risky synthetic portfolio.

This economic construct rests on numerous abstractions, simplifications, and assumptions. The ones that are mentioned most often regard the cost of transacting, the effects of taxes, the difference between interest rates for lending and borrowing. The question of establishing the expected return of the market and the expected dividends and capital gains from the stock may be even harder. To further complicate things, capital gains and dividends must be differentiated because valuation rests on after-tax returns to individuals.

It is not hard to examine the effect of relaxing these assumptions. Leaving the question of estimating dividends and capital gains for last, the next paragraphs perform this estimation.

By cost of transacting we should understand the cost of trading on the market. This includes explicit and implicit costs. Explicit costs are the brokerage commission and fees levied by the stock exchange or taxes on trading (as opposed to taxes on gains). Examples of implicit transaction costs are the opportunity costs of traders' time or the cost of the exposure to the risks of clearing company solvency or the continued functionality of the payment system. If transaction costs are taken into account, then the arbitrage that the CAPM assumes stops before a complete correction of prices. Arbitrageurs will stop when the difference between prices is less than the transaction costs, because the arbitrageur seeks to profit after payment of the transaction costs. The result is that securities prices do not get corrected up to the capital market line, but only up to a distance from it equal to the transaction costs. This distance transforms the capital market line into a capital market "band."

The difference between interest rates for lending and borrowing changes the capital market line in a different way. Borrowing becomes necessary to synthesize securities with betas higher than 1. Therefore, the interest rate that should be used to draw the capital market line should change at the point that corresponds to a beta of 1. To its right, the higher interest rate of borrowing must be used to "anchor" the capital market line. The result is a line that is less steep to the right of $b = 1$ than to its left. The capital market line now has a "kink". Figure 10.3 illustrates this effect.

Figure 10.3 illustrates the effect of using different interest rates for lending and borrowing. Because synthetic portfolios with betas greater than 1 require borrowing at the "margin" rate, the interest rate of government bonds is less relevant and should not be used. The higher margin rate should be used for such portfolios and securities. The result is that the security market line may have a kink, as indicated in Figure 10.3.

The effect of the borrowing difference should not be overestimated. although borrowing is necessary to synthesize high betas, arbitrage can be performed by using the high-beta securities mixed with government

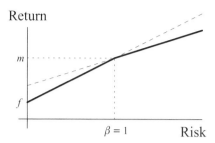

Figure 10.3. The kinked capital market line

bonds to synthesize a $b = 1$ security. Moreover, a large extent of the appeal of the CAPM is that it works by identifying a simple lack of demand for the overpriced stocks and lack of supply for the underpriced ones. This consequence is independent of the kink. Therefore, the kink is not a necessary feature of the capital market but rather a plausible one. It is justified not by an exclusive target for arbitrage, but rather by a disproportionate difficulty for arbitrageurs to reach the orthodox capital market line in those cases in which the security is overvalued (in which case its return is too low and will approach the capital market line from below).

The effects of taxes also complicate forecasting. All entities, individuals as well as corporations, care for after-tax returns rather than for before-tax returns. This would be trivial and irrelevant if the tax rate on interest rates and capital gains was identical. Because they are different, however, all of the CAPM's analysis must be recast in terms of after-tax returns of the market and of the security to be valued. The complexities lie in that this requires the division of total returns into dividends and capital gains as well as the potential of some untaxed capital gains.

A further complication regards forecasting the allocation of earnings between dividends and capital gains. The paradox is that, from a tax perspective, corporations should not distribute dividends, because they are a disadvantaged method. Finance answers this paradox with the suggestion that dividends perform a "signaling" function, communicating to investors the quality of the firm and its management.[6]

---

[6] See, for example, Sasson Bar-Yosef and Lucy Huffman, "The Information Content of dividends: A Signaling Approach," *Journal of Financial. Quantitative Analysis* 21 (1986):47 (the level of dividends reveals the future risk); Kenneth M. Eades, "Empirical Evidence on Dividends as a Signal of Firm Value," *Journal of Financial Quantitative Analysis.* 17 (1982):471. (Contrary to the prediction of the tax explanation,

The conventional way economists have tried to estimate the return of the market is to establish the historical returns. The usual way in which Wall Street tries to estimate market returns is by the price-earnings (P/E) ratio. Both have drawbacks. Historical returns tell little about the future. The price-earnings ratio tells little about what value actually gets paid out to investors. Combined with history and the dividend yield, however, the price-earnings ratio does suggest the possibility of obtaining an after-tax estimate of securities' returns.

The price-earnings ratio is the ratio of the price of the asset to the profits or earnings of the asset. Thus, if a stock trades at a price of 100 and has earnings of 8, its price-earnings ratio is 12.5 ($100/8 = 12.5$). But it is misleading to think of that as equivalent to an 8 percent return. On the one hand, it is more than 8 percent interest because the part that will accrue as capital gains will be taxed at a lower rate and the tax payment is deferred until the time of realization. The same 8 percent is also less than an 8 percent interest, however. Investors only receive a fraction of that 8 percent as dividends. The balance remains in the control of management and exposed to the enterprise's risk. It may be squandered or lost. From a valuation perspective, the price-earnings ratio of 12.5 must be supplemented with the dividend yield. If the dividend yield is 3 percent, the tax effects can be disentangled. The 8 percent return of this P/E ratio may be realized as 3 percent in dividends and 5 percent in capital gains. The dividends may be taxed at over 40 percent, whereas the capital gains may be taxed at less than 30 percent. Suppose, for example, those rates are 50 percent and 28 percent. The result is a 5.1 percent after-tax return ($.5 \times .03 + .72 \times .05 = .051$).

This is deceptively simple, however. The P/E ratios of firms differ, depending on the capital gains that investors expect them to produce, and these often are capital gains through growth and beyond their retained earnings. When we compare two firms that have the same beta, they may have significantly different P/E ratios, suggesting that they may be properly priced but have different expected future capital

according to which dividends expose investors to double taxation, empirical tests confirm that stock price movements are positively correlated with cash dividend changes.) Some recent entries in the voluminous research on dividends include Malcolm Baker and Jeffrey Wurgler, "A Catering Theory of Dividends," *Journal of Finance* 59, no. 3 (2004):1125; Malcolm Baker and Jeffrey Wurgler, "Appearing and Disappearing Dividends: The link to catering incentives," *Journal of Financial Economics* 75, no. 2 (Aug. 2004): 283–317; Shlomo Benartzi, Roni Michaely and Richard Thaler, "Do Changes in Dividends Signal the Future or the Past?," *Journal of Finance* 52 (1997):1007.

gains. To properly determine the after-tax returns that securities offer, one must separate expected capital gains from expected dividends.

Despite these imperfections, the CAPM is a crucial tool for securities valuation. It shows how probability theory and diversification applies in ordinary investment conduct. The development of beta and its measurement allows investors to understand risk. The concept of diversification enables investors to limit their exposure to risk.

B. Normative Implications of the CAPM

The CAPM did influence legal thinking about the regulation of financial markets. It underlined the purpose of disclosure of financial information for the calculation of earnings. It also showed the importance of forecasting future earnings. One of the concluding exercises explores how the CAPM informs the requirement of shareholder approval of mergers.

i. Financial Information

Accounting information serves the purpose, among others, of helping investors value corporations. This is a complex goal that contains a fundamental contradiction.

A conventional approach to valuing an entity would try to appraise its components. When trying to establish the value of an enterprise from this perspective, the most useful information would be about the assets of the firm. Pursuing this line of reasoning suggests that firms should disclose information that allows investors to obtain an accurate picture of the firm's assets and their appraised value.

Of the two principal accounting statements, the balance sheet and the income statement, the assets of the firm are accounted in the former. A focus on assets would argue for improved reporting in the balance sheet and increased reliance on it. For example, instead of showing assets at the historical cost at which they were acquired, assets could be marked-to-market or appraised for their current market value.

The CAPM, however, shows that valuation depends on future earnings and risk. Current assets typically understate the value of a going business. This realization reverses the presumption in favor of the balance sheet and puts the focus on the income statement. The firm's income deserves the fullest accuracy that is possible, even at the expense of accurate representation of assets on the balance sheet.

The tension between an accurate representation of assets and of earnings is palpable in accounting. A third interest that creates further conflicts is the monitoring of expenses. This three-way tension is most clearly exemplified in the treatment of acquisitions in exchange for stock. According to the recently discontinued "purchase accounting" method, these acquisitions were treated as purchases, so that assets were added to the balance sheet. Because the consideration was not cash, it was deceptive to think that the purchase corresponded to an expense. Even more fundamental, however, was the discrepancy between the value of the purchased business and the appraisal of its assets. The purchase of the going business surely values it more than its assets, but that created an accounting discrepancy. The assets brought onto the acquirer's balance sheet were much less than the price paid. The notion of "good will" was created to fill that gap, so that the premium paid for the going business over its assets was carried on the balance sheet as one more asset called good will, even though it did not correspond to any intangible asset or any clients good will. To further complicate matters, this good will was amortized, creating an expense that distorted earnings.

From this example, it appears that accurate representation of assets dominated accuracy of earnings. Taking the CAPM seriously would suggest that earnings must be represented accurately and that assets and cash may be compromised, if necessary. It would be deceiving, however, to conclude that the "purchase accounting" treatment was clearly false. The numerous compromises involved in the choice among alternative treatments may well suggest that "purchase accounting" was desirable despite the misrepresentation of earnings that it produced.

ii. Forecasts

The CAPM leads unambiguously to the conclusion that valuation depends on the estimation of future returns from each firm. Nevertheless, until the seventies, firms could not disclose their forecasts. The announcement of a forecast would invite liability for securities fraud whenever the forecast would not materialize. Buyers of the stock would allege that its prospects were falsely inflated and would have a securities fraud claim.

Securities law should help rather than frustrate the accurate valuation of securities. The CAPM illustrated the error of the effective prohibition of forecasts. In 1981, the Securities and Exchange Commission solved this paradox by enacting rule 175, which insulates forecasts from securities fraud liability.[7]

C. Financial Market Microstructure: The Game-Theoretical Foundation of the CAPM

One of the important developments in financial economics in the past twenty years is a new focus on the details of the interaction between market participants. This approach is known as *market microstructure*. The name conveys the change of the scale. Before market microstructure, the research in financial economics had a timescale measured in years or decades, as it focused on individuals' saving for retirement and firms' raising capital for production. The events at the focus of the research that constitutes market microstructure are the individual trades of shares that make up the daily activity in the stock markets.

The methods of microstructure reveal important details about financial markets. Microstructure understands market interaction by separating the motivations behind trades into four categories. *Informed* are trades made on the basis of superior information. *Life-cycle* or *uninformed* trades are made for saving or consumption. Those are made without the benefit of information and, following the CAPM, they are either random or in index funds. The time horizon of roundtrip life-cycle trades is important even if it is flexible. *Noise* trades are those that are made with the false impression of being informed, usually on public information or fads. *Liquidity-providing* trades are motivated by meeting the trading demand of others and receive some price advantage. Providing liquidity is risky, however, and exposes to losses against informed trades. The *specialists* of the New York Stock Exchange and other exchanges' *market makers* are dedicated liquidity providers because they have an obligation to be ready to trade and publicize the prices at which they are willing to buy or sell. They must

---

[7] SEC Release 33-6291, 46 FR 13988 (February 25, 1981). The rule provides this safety by insulating from liability certain "forward looking statements." The language of section (c) defines those to include management's forecasts: "(c) For the purpose of this rule the term 'forward looking statement' shall mean and shall be limited to: (1) A statement containing a projection of revenues, income (loss), earnings (loss) per share, capital expenditures, dividends, capital structure or other financial items; (2) A statement of management's plans and objectives for future operations; (3) A statement of future economic performance contained in management's discussion and analysis of financial condition and results of operations included pursuant to Item 11 of Regulation S-K."

stay abreast of information. The exchanges and the listed corporations try to reduce the exposure of the market makers to new information by making major announcements after hours or by suspending trading during breaking information.

The classification is obviously one of trades. The same individual may trade under any of these motivations. Nevertheless, the exposition usually assigns these adjectives to traders rather than trades. This is a sleight of hand that facilitates the exposition but confuses readers who take it literally. Talking of traders rather than trades might seem justified if the focus is only on informed and noise trading, because it might be reasonable to assume that the same individuals tend not to be well informed and subject to fads or errors. Even if the separation of noise traders from informed traders is correct, both can also make life-cycle and liquidity-providing trades.

A prominent line of microstructure scholarship studies the *spread*, that is, the difference that market makers maintain between the price at which they are willing to buy (the *bid*) and sell (the *ask*). The streams of uninformed purchases and sales provide income that must cover various costs, including the cost of carrying the inventory and the losses to informed traders.[8] The logical next step was to investigate the evolution of prices under the pressure of informed trading. Because microstructure relies on the classification of trades, the analyzes about the possibility of survival of noise traders can be placed under microstructure despite that it tends to examine long time horizons. Not only is the survival of noise trading possible in theory, but evidence also shows persistent deviations of prices from proper valuations.[9]

D. Normative Application of Microstructure: Insider Trading

An application of microstructure's dichotomy between noise traders and informed traders was examined under the discussion of bounded rationality in Chapter 3. A more quantitative analysis is the justification of insider trading. This is an ideal application for this stage because it combines Coasean irrelevance, algebraic optimization, and probability theory in a financial microstructure analysis.

---

[8]   See Maureen O'Hara, *Market Microstructure Theory* (Oxford: Blackwell Publishers Ltd., 1995):20 *et seq.*
[9]   Chapter 3, notes 14–18 and accompanying text.

The twist that allows the application of microstructure to insider trading is that the definition of informed trades includes the trades that are motivated by inside information. Approached from a normative perspective, the definition of insider trading is fluid and will be the outcome of the analysis. Effectively, this problem is re-cast as one of finding the optimal definition of insider trading. The lessons of microstructure also include the concept that some informed trading is unavoidable and necessary for maintaining some degree of accuracy in prices and the ensuing optimal allocation of capital. The question that does remain, however, is what is to be optimized? What objective could the regulation of informed trading serve? The long-standing position of early economic analysis was that no such objective existed. Therefore, regulation of insider trading was pointless at best and was seen to impede accurate pricing at worst.[10]

The breakthrough that microstructure allows is that it provides the objective for the regulation of insider trading. Practically everyone saves for retirement, directly or indirectly through retirement plans, private or governmental. Regulation of financial markets that renders them more hospitable to life-cycle trading increases the fraction of retirement savings that go to the stock market compared with bank deposits or other investments, such as real estate. Increased life-cycle capital would mean lower cost of capital for firms.

The bid-ask spread reveals that the cost that burdens life-cycle trades is related to the profits of informed trading. The bid-ask spread must compensate market makers for informed profits. Therefore, a policy that minimizes informed profits would minimize the spread and reduce the cost of trading for life-cycle traders.[11]

Thus, microstructure conceptually changes the question of insider-trading regulation. The point of the early law-and-economics analysis that the prohibition reduces the accuracy of stock prices is valid. Microstructure adds a countervailing effect from reduced informed profits. At the cost of some reduction in accuracy, a market becomes more attractive to life-cycle trading, thus reducing the cost of capital and increasing productivity. Society faces an optimization problem in

---

[10]   The analysis of Henry Manne is the classic representation of this position, see Henry G. Manne, *Insider Trading and the Stock Market* (New York: Free Press, 1966).

[11]   The same is true even if market makers are removed from the picture. In that case, life-cycle trading has direct losses equivalent to the profits of informed trading. These losses have a function that is equivalent to transaction costs because they deter trading. Life-cycle trading can avoid the losses by not trading.

designing the regulation of informed trading. By restricting informed trading, society reduces productivity as a consequence of reduced accuracy of prices. Nevertheless, society is in a better position as long as the policy leads to additional life-cycle investing, and the ensuing reduced cost of capital causes a greater increase of productivity.

The problem may seem daunting. Revisiting insider trading as a definition of a subset of informed traders reveals an extraordinary simplicity. Simplified, insider-trading rules prohibit trading on non-public information obtained from privileged access to it through employment (or any subsequent transfer of it that starts from an employee).[12] From the perspective of microstructure, the key word is non-public. The number of informed traders is relevant because it determines how competitively they trade, in other words, how aggressive they and their trading orders are. This, in turn, influences their profits.

The quantitative foundation of the analysis has similarities to the work relating the bid-ask spread to informed profits. The analysis follows closer the basic assumption of studies of price changes that each trade changes price by an amount that depends on the size of the trade. Thus, each trade is assumed to occur at a price p_i equal to that of the previous trade, p_{i-1}, plus an adjustment according to trade size, ds_i. The coefficient d indicates how sensitive is price to size s_i. A small value of d corresponds to small sensitivity, what we tend to associate with *market liquidity* or *depth*. Accordingly, the evolution of prices follows this equation:

$$p_i = p_{i-1} + ds_i.$$

Against this background, an informed trader faces a simple optimization problem. Suppose, first, that the informed trader will only trade once. Then, this trader's profit b is the difference between the price at which he trades, p_i, and the value of the stock, v, times the number of shares he trades, s_i. The profit is $b = s_i(v - p_i)$. The price depends on the previous price, p_{i-1}, over which the trader has no control. It also depends on the size of the informed trade itself, s_i. This dependence becomes clear if we substitute p_i in the profit from its

---

[12] Needless to say, much additional nuance exists. The prohibition is more expansive when the information is about tender offers, as in *United States v. O'Hagan*, 521 U.S. 642. It is narrower otherwise, as in *Chiarella v. United States*, 445 U.S. 222 (1980). It rewards whistle blowing, as in *Dirks v. SEC*, 463 U.S. 646 (1983). The analysis of the text follows Georgakopoulos, "Insider Trading as a Transactional Cost: A Market Microstructure Justification and Optimization of Insider Trading Regulation." *Conn. L. Rev.* 26 (1993): 1–51.

formation based on the previous price. The trader's profit is given by this equation:

$$b = s_i[v - (p_{i-1} + ds_i)].$$

Because his profit depends on the size of his trade, he will select the size that maximizes it. Taking the derivative of profit with respect to trade size and solving for zero gives the optimal trade.[13]

The notion that an informed trader knows that he will never have a chance to trade again is related to a degree of competition. A trader knows that no opportunity to trade again exists if the number of informed traders is very large. When the number of traders who have the information is small, then each one may trade again. If ten traders have the information, each informed trader would have a 10 percent probability of trading again in each subsequent trade until informed trading is no longer profitable. The optimization problem of the informed trader must be adjusted for the possibility of trading again.

The solution requires a recursive approach, starting from the end of trading. During the penultimate trade, only one more trade is possible. Therefore, the trader's expected profits include those that can be had from the final trade, adjusted for the probability q_{i+1} of trading again. The equations simplify easier by restating $q_i = 1/n_i$, where n_i is the number of competing informed traders. The size of the current trade determines not only the profit from the current trade but also that from the next. In the final trade the size is determined by the price that will result from the current trade. The form of the penultimate trade's profits is:

$$b = s_i(v - p_i) + s_{i+1}(v - p_{i+1})/n_{i+1}.$$

Substituting the prices and sizes so that they are expressed as functions of the existing price p_0 and the prospective trade gives the expected profits. The problem is essentially the same, to select the trade size that maximizes profits. Mathematical software easily produces a solution. One more step back in time, however, makes the result very complex.[14] The challenge is to establish the pattern. It turns out that that the optimal size of each trade depends on the number of

---

[13] Using Mathematica and having saved the profit equation as b and using p0 and s1 for p_{i-1} and s_i, the corresponding commands are

```
b=s1(v-(p0+gs1)),D[b, s1];Solve[%==0, s1], Simplify@PowerExpand@%.
```

The result indicates that the optimal trade is $s_1 = (v - p_0)/2d$.

[14] A *Mathematica* notebook named L&E_it.nb and containing the analysis of this section is reproduced in Appendix C and is available at the book's Web site, www.pmle-nlg.org.

subsequent trades. If the informed trader may trade a number of times j, the ith trade has ideal size:

$$s_{ij} = \frac{p_{i-1} - v}{d} z_{ij},$$

where

$$z_{ij} = 1 - \frac{1}{2 + \sum_{n=i+1}^{j} 1 q_n z_{nj}(z_{nj} - 1) \prod_{m=i+1}^{n-1} (z_{mj} - 1)^2}$$

This analysis supports the argument in favor of insider-trading rules by showing that reduced competition produces smaller trades. The intuition underlying this conclusion is that reducing the profits from the current trade is advantageous if the trader has a high probability of profiting from future prices. Essentially, reduced competition means that the trader who does expect to enjoy profit from future prices has an incentive not to correct prices, because leaving the false prices in place leads to greater profits from future trades.

The effects of the prohibition are illustrated by comparing two regimes: the lack of a prohibition and the next narrowest prohibition where informed trading is prohibited only if the informed trader is alone. The formal model allows the comparison of total profits and the evolution of price.

The early law and economics analysis ignored profits by treating them as constant. It focused exclusively on price. The objective was accuracy of prices. In the context of this model, accuracy is the speed of the approach of price to value.

The model allows the comparison of the two alternative price paths. Those are illustrated in Figure 10.4. Time unfolds along the horizontal axis from left to right. The vertical axis holds price, with value (100) at the low end and the price that exists before the new information (110) at the top. The price starts approaching value immediately if the lone informed trader may trade. If the lone informed trader is not allowed to trade, then price stays false until more traders obtain the information. The approach of price to value in this case is faster, which is an important consequence of the microstructure model. Nevertheless, the price under the prohibition is never closer to value than under unregulated informed trading.

The microstructure analysis reveals that a countervailing effect exists in the profits of informed traders. The profit from each trade is the

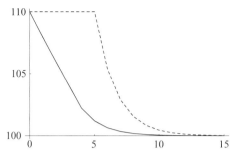

Figure 10.4. Insider trading: impact on prices.

product of the price-to-value difference by the size of the trade. Thus, it cannot be seen in the illustration of the price alone, Figure 10.4. Figure 10.5 illustrates profits by displaying the product of trade size by price-to-value difference as rectangles.

The horizontal dimension of each rectangle is the trade size, making its surface the profit. Each regime corresponds to a different sequence of rectangles. In the illustration, the rectangles that correspond to unregulated informed trading are boxed, whereas the wire frame corresponds to the profits when lone informed trading is prohibited. The critical point is that the prohibition always reduces total profits. If the lone informed trader's temporal advantage consists of few trades then the reduction of profits may be small. Nevertheless, also small is the cost of the prohibition, that is, the delay of the accuracy of prices that it causes. If the lone informed trader has a temporal advantage of many

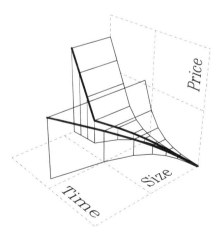

Figure 10.5. Insider trading: prices and profits.

trades, then the prohibition reduces informed profits a lot, compensating for preserving inaccuracy over a slightly longer time.

E. Concluding Exercises

Exercise 10.1: Suppose that the government decides to obtain funds by selling promises to pay 100 coins in one year and promises to pay 100 in two years. The promises will be transferable, like securities and like the "treasury bills" and "treasury bonds" that the U.S. government issues. Suppose that complete agreement exists in the market about interest rates. Any funds borrowed during the first year would need to offer a return of 5 percent (annually discounted). Any funds borrowed during the second year would need to offer a return of 10 percent. In other words, the interest rate will change from 5 to 10 percent in one year. You will repeat more easily the calculations under different hypotheses, as you are eventually asked, if you place them in a spreadsheet column, the first three rows of which contain the inputs, that is, the face amount (100), interest during first year (5%), and interest during second year (10%).

(a) At what price will the one-year promise trade?
(b) At what price do you forecast the two-year promise will trade in one year?
(c) Based on the previous answer, what is the price that the two-year promise will trade now? It may be easier to think about this answer if you imagine that trading in these promises occurs once a year, rather than daily; the interest rate does not change gradually. The rate changes at once. At the strike of midnight, it jumps from 5 to 10 percent.
(d) Suppose Peter Flatter mistakenly assumes interest rates are the same in both years. Given only the price that you calculated for the two-year promise, what would Peter think the interest rate is?
(e) If Peter intends to invest some funds that he knows he will need in one year, which promise will he buy? What return will Peter actually receive?
(f) Answer questions a to e again, in a second column of the spreadsheet, using monthly compounding and with the rate changing from 4.8 percent in the first year to 9.7 percent in the second.

(g) Answer questions a to e again, in a third column, using continuous compounding and with the rate changing from 4.7 percent in the first year to 9.6 percent in the second.

Discussion: The first two questions are a simple application of the discounting formulas. How much must you deposit in the (P)resent with a bank that pays a (r)ate of interest of 5 percent so as to find the (F)uture value of 100 in one (y)ear? The equations are in Table 10.1.

Once you answer the first two questions, the third reveals the phenomenon of the "yield curve." Although almost every investment or loan appears to have a single interest rate or yield, a comparison of their values on the market reveals the additional nuance that the rates applied to different years can be different. The fourth question should reveal the error to which ignoring the yield curve may lead. Peter's assumption of constant rates makes the two-year promise appear attractive. He does not actually enjoy that return, however. At the end of one year his return is equivalent to having bought the one-year bond that has the ostensibly lower return.

Exercise 10.2: Corporate law imposes elevated procedural requirements for the validity of some transactions. Whereas corporate law leaves most decisions about corporate conduct in the hands of the board of directors, decisions about fundamental changes require a shareholder vote. The shareholders must approve transactions such as mergers and sales of substantially all assets. The definition of what proportion of assets constitutes "substantially all" so as to trigger a shareholder vote is a contested issue that some courts relate to a test of whether the sale was a fundamental change of the corporation's business.[15] How may the CAPM inform what transactions constitute fundamental changes?

Discussion: From some perspectives, the CAPM has no bearing on the definition of fundamental changes. The shareholder vote seeks to protect shareholders when the magnitude and the rarity of the transaction are such that delegation of the decision to the directors is pointless or inappropriate. Moreover, any deviation between the interests of directors and shareholders can have devastating effects in this extraordinary setting. By contrast, directors' decisions about the course of business

---

[15]   See, e.g., *Farris v. Glen Alden Corp.*, 393 Pa. 427 (1958).

have smaller consequences and can be controlled by incentive design and monitoring.

The CAPM does suggest, however, that the shareholders' interest in the corporation must be seen from the perspective of the diversified shareholder. Although diversified shareholders are still concerned with loyalty and careful decision making, their diversification changes their stance. Diversification suggests that investors do not want their corporations to diversify to reduce risk and that they may not want their corporations to change their risk.

Corporate managers may seek to have several businesses under one corporation for strategic reasons. They may also seek to have several businesses to reduce their risk by diversification. From the diversified investors' perspective, this diversification is duplicative and wasteful. The interpretation of fundamental changes should be sufficiently broad to require a shareholder vote for nonstrategic diversification transactions. Although this interpretation appears to be a stretch, in regimes that give some respect to defensive tactics, defences may function as a partial substitute in the cases where the diversification would occur through the acquisition of listed companies. Takeover defences have been attacked as undesirable because the management of the targets of the acquisitions, whose careers are at stake, will tend to be biased against the takeover. Thus, this protection of the targets hinders hostile acquisitions, setting a negotiating background that also enhances the ability of targets to refuse friendly overtures. The result, indirect as it may be, is that acquisitions are hindered, as they should be from the perspective of diversified investors.[16] Naturally, this protection is partial because it does not apply to acquisitions of unlisted targets.

Diversified shareholders should also be concerned about any changes of their portfolios' risk. Each investor's holdings are tailored to the amount of market risk (beta) that each investor wants to take. If the risk of the portfolio changes, the investor will want to adjust the portfolio so as to return to the desired risk.

Fundamental corporate changes are major changes of the corporation's business. A firm that until yesterday was in oil retailing may merge with an oil exploration company. The result is that its shareholders may find that the market risk of their portfolios has significantly changed. To return to their desired risk they may need to change either

---

[16] I have also argued that acquisitions should be hindered to maintain dispersed ownership of corporations. See Nicholas L. Georgakopoulos, "Corporate Defence Law for Dispersed Ownership," *Hofstra Law Review* 30 (2001):11.

the composition of their portfolios or their leverage and allocation of assets to or away from stocks.

The investor faces three concurrent problems when exposed to drift of the portfolio's risk. First, the investor must recognize the change of risk. Then, the investor must quantify the change. Finally, the investor must enter into the transactions necessary to revert to the preferred exposure to risk.

When corporate law requires a shareholder vote for fundamental changes, the process that is set in motion does help shareholders in this triple problem. First, by being notified of the vote, they are notified of the impending change in beta. Then, the disclosures that the corporation makes to inform shareholders for the vote may also allow shareholders to extract some estimate of the beta their holdings would have after the transaction. Finally, if the change is such that they cannot revert to their desired risk, shareholders may vote against the transaction and avoid having to incur the transaction costs of adjusting their portfolios. In an economy with developed capital markets the last problem is very unlikely to arise.

The notice and disclosure system that is an indirect consequence of shareholder votes on fundamental changes can be improved easily. This is no surprise, of course, because it was not designed for protecting investors against beta drift. The key is to design for it so that it would give warning and information about changes of beta.

The results flow immediately. On mergers, case law requires a vote by the shareholders of one of the merging corporations (even though by using subsidiaries as both merging corporations the letter of the law could be satisfied by an internal vote by each parent company as its subsidiary's sole shareholder). The concern about beta drift indicates that if only one body of shareholders is to be notified, arguably that body should be the one likely to experience the larger change. If the merging corporations are of significantly different sizes, that body will be the smaller corporation.

When judging the adequacy of the disclosure to the voting shareholders, the analysis above suggests an additional concern. Shareholders will benefit by information that helps them estimate the risk (beta) of the merged firms. The disclosure for the vote should estimate the resulting beta or provide information that would help investors estimate it.

In sum, the CAPM had a profound effect on our understanding of securities' markets. Its impact on legal thinking is significant but not nearly complete. Chapter 11 studies the pricing of derivatives.

F. Bibliographical Note

A time-saving trick that many of my students find effective is to obtain the foundation of an understanding of the financial world through ostensibly extracurricular reading. All of Chernow's books are very enjoyable. His biography of Rockefeller also displays some interesting legal strategies that recommend it to readers of this book.[17] Ron Chernow, *The Titan: The Life of John D. Rockefeller, Sr.* (New York: Random House, 1998); Ron Chernow, *The House of Morgan: An American Banking Dynasty and the Rise of Modern Finance* (New York: Touchstone, 1990); Roger Lowenstein, *When Genius Failed: The Rise and Fall of Long-Term Capital Management* (New York: Random House, 2000).

An excellent lay introduction to both the economic theory (the CAPM) and the institutional details of the financial markets is Robert A. Schwartz, *Equity Markets: Structure, Trading, and Performance* (New York: Harper & Row Publishers, 1988). Slightly technical but still very approachable to the lay reader is the introduction to financial market microstructure, Maureen O'Hara, *Market Microstructure Theory* (Cambridge, MA: Blackwell Publishers, 1995). The specialized statistics for dealing with sequences of securities prices are covered in Andrew Harvey, *The Econometric Analysis of Time Series*, 2nd ed. (Cambridge, MA: MIT Press, 1991).

Important new entries in the bibliography of finance examine errors, a topic discussed briefly in Chapter 3, in Bounded Rationality. These entries include Andrei Shleifer, *Inefficient Markets: An Introduction to Behavioral Finance* (Oxford: Oxford University Press, 2000); Robert P. Flood and Peter M. Garber, *Speculative Bubbles, Speculative Attacks and Policy Switching* (Cambridge, MA: MIT Press, 1994). A lay recounting of market errors throughout history is Charles P. Kindleberger, *Manias, Panics, and Crashes: A History of Financial Crises*, revd. ed. (New York: Harper Bros., 1902).

---

[17] At the time that Rockefeller created Standard Oil each state did not recognize corporations incorporated in other states. As a result, Standard Oil had to exist as a separate corporation in each state. The shares of the several corporations were held in a trust by the management of the "parent" corporation.

11. Finance and Probability: Options and Derivatives

Options are extraordinarily important because they capture the difference between obligation and freedom. Financial economists only recently developed the ability to quantify the effect of some options. This new ability to quantify options obviously has enormous value for legal analysis, because law focuses on obligations and freedoms.

Option theory presents a new aspect of *Meinhard v. Salmon.*[1] Salmon received a lucrative offer from Gerry, a business acquaintance. The offer could have expanded Salmon's business. Unbeknownst to Gerry, Salmon's business, which was the reason for their acquaintance, had a secret partner, Meinhard. If Gerry knew that Salmon operated in two capacities, as an individual and as a member of a partnership, then Gerry may have specified which of the two he selected as the recipient of his offer. Meinhard, the invisible partner, claimed the offer should be treated as made to the partnership. The litigation that Meinhard started eventually reached the highest court of the jurisdiction, judge Benjamin Cardozo, and his dissenting colleague, Andrews. Previously established law did not answer the question directly. If Cardozo and his court had had a better handle on options they might have realized that participation in a subsequent venture was an option. Nowadays, such an option can be valued and similar "derivatives" are traded routinely in exchanges. Compared with the valuation of stocks, the valuation of derivatives is a simple application of probability theory. The premise, however, that simplifies the valuation of derivatives is solidly founded on economic or financial reasoning. The valuation of the simplest derivatives – futures and forwards – is straightforward from there.

---

[1]   249 N.Y. 458 (1928). The text of the opinion is reproduced in Appendix A.

After defining derivatives, this chapter analyzes the premise of their valuation. Then this chapter applies probability theory to the valuation of an option to buy, known as a call option.

A derivative is a contract that depends on the future price of some item. It is a financial contract because a derivative only creates obligations about the payment of money – no service, processing, or delivery of the underlying good is contemplated in derivative contracts. Derivatives further divide into financial and nonfinancial. Financial derivates are based on underlying goods that are financial, such as currencies, stocks, interest rates, or stock indices. When the underlying good is not financial, the derivative is not financial and is often called a commodity derivative. Examples are corn, sugar, coffee, pork bellies, or steers. Precious metals are hybrids, having both financial and nonfinancial features. They are considered commodities.

Options are derivatives with contingent obligations. Derivatives with fixed (i.e., noncontingent) obligations are futures and forwards. Options give one side a right but not an obligation to buy or sell the underlying asset. The other side has the contingent obligation to, respectively, deliver or buy the asset. For example, the option to buy 100 shares of Citigroup for US$40 per share gives to its holder the right but not the obligation to make that purchase. The obligor under the same contract has the obligation to produce the corresponding shares, but only if the option holder decides to exercise the option. Therefore, the obligation is contingent.

Futures and forwards are closely related and much simpler than options, because no contingency is involved. They are fixed contracts about the underlying goods, purchases, or sales without any conditions. The defining difference of futures as opposed to forwards is that they are traded in organized exchanges. As a result, to facilitate trading they are formally defined, and the exchanges subject the parties to continuously show they can meet their obligations by depositing additional amounts if necessary. Both features facilitate trading. The former is necessary for the traded futures to be comparable and fungible, which is necessary for frequent trading and for substitutions of one contract with another. The latter is necessary for ensuring of the ability of the parties to perform.

It is easy to see how one can use futures to eliminate the risk due to holding an underlying good. The archetypical example has farmers hedging the risk of their crop. The farmer, who expects the harvest of wheat, can eliminate the risk of wheat price changes. Even if the particular wheat differs slightly from the one traded as futures, the farmer need only find the difference in price due to the difference of the wheat grade, convert to adjusted units of traded wheat, and sell the appropriate amount with a settlement date near the harvest. For example, the value of the farmer's wheat may be double that of the wheat that has the exchange's grade. If the farmer expects a harvest of about 100 units, the farmer will sell about 200 units on the exchange. If the harvest will be in August, the right futures wheat contract to sell would be the August one, that is, the one with settlement in August. After this trade, if the prices of wheat fall by, say, 50 percent, then the farmer will lose 50 percent from the value of the crop but gain an equivalent amount from the gain in the contract of having sold wheat at a high price.

Similarly, a financial institution that wishes to avoid the risk of 100 million in securities that it holds can sell 100 million in futures of the index that most closely corresponds to its portfolio.

These transactions show the relation between the underlying asset and the value of the futures contract. The two are in a constant relation. For valuing futures, the crucial feature of these hedges is that they eliminate the risk due to price changes. Whether price goes up or down, the hedged portfolio does not change value.

This elimination of price risk opens the way to the valuation of futures. The elimination of the risk is important because it shows that subjective attitudes toward risk, that is, each investor's degree of risk aversion, are irrelevant for the purchasing decision of the future or forward contract.

A. OPTION PRICING

Options are derivatives that, unlike futures, give their buyer a right but not an obligation to trade in the underlying asset. The seller who grants this right has a contingent obligation. The option is a "call" if it grants the right to make a purchase. Perhaps the origin of the name is that the buyer "calls" to the seller to deliver the securities. The option is a "put" if it grants the right to sell. An explanation of the "put" name is that the option holder "puts" the securities in the hands of the grantor (seller) of the option. Thus, call options are options to buy securities, and put options are options to sell securities.

The agreed stock price is called the *strike price*. If the parties to an option have agreed that the underlying trade will take place at US$40,

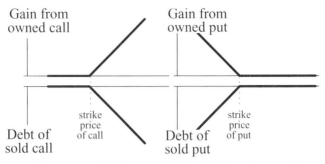

Figure 11.1. The amounts that buyers and sellers of calls and puts receive or owe.

the option has a strike price of $40. A holder of a call option would have the right to buy at $40. A holder of a put would have the right to sell at $40. Across from these would sit the grantor (seller or *writer*) of the call who has the contingent obligation to buy at a $40 price, and the writer of the put who has the contingent obligation to sell the underlying security for $40.

The trigger of the contingency of the option is the price of the underlying security compared with the strike price. If that price indicates an advantageous transaction, the holder will exercise the option. Calls are exercised when the market price is above the strike price. Having the right to buy for $40 a stock that trades at $50 has monetary value; having the right to buy for $40 a stock that trades at $30 is pointless because one can buy it for $30. Conversely, holders of a (put) option to sell the stock, will only exercise it if they cannot sell it more advantageously. When the price is $50 and the strike of the put is $40, the holder will prefer to sell for $50. But when the current price is $30, the holder of the put prefers to exercise the option to sell it for $40. Puts are exercised when the current price is below the strike price.

These payouts of calls and puts can be visualized graphically. Figure 11.1 shows what each party expects to have at expiration depending on the price of the stock, which is along the x axis. The y axis holds the option's payout.

In each panel, the horizontal axis (x axis) holds the price of the underlying stock, and the vertical axis (y axis) holds the payout of the option. The top-left panel is the payout to the buyer of a call. The holder receives no value if the stock price is below the strike price. For every increment that the stock price rises above the strike price, the call holder receives an equal increment of value. The result is a graph with an inflection point at the strike price and which is zero to its left and increases diagonally to its right. The seller of the call has an equal loss; hence, the graph for the seller's position (bottom left) is the same image, reflected upside-down. The buyer of a put enjoys the payouts expressed by the top-right graph. The put has zero value above the strike price, increasing value below it. The seller of the put, bottom right, again experiences the upside-down reflection of the buyer's payouts.

The holders of options usually benefit from postponing the comparison of current price with the strike price until the time that the option expires. An exception exists for puts in the case of large price declines, but both these are results of the analysis of pricing, which we will see in due course.

Options do not seem to allow a risk-eliminating hedge, but if traders knew the relation between the value of the stock and the value of the option, then they would be able to hedge against small price changes of the stock. Suppose that it were known that from $1 below the strike price of $40 to $1 above the strike price, the value of the option changes $0.70 for each $1 change of the stock. Despite that different relations will exist outside this range, when the stock is at $40, a portfolio that has 7 shares of the stock for every 10 options it has granted is hedged. If the stock price rises to $41, the $7 gain will cancel out with a $7 loss from the options. Similarly, if the stock price drops to $39, the $7 loss from the stock will cancel out with a $7 gain from the options. That in either case a new relation of stock-price changes to option-price changes will arise only means that the ratio of the two in the portfolio will have to change for the portfolio to remain hedged. But because this hedge is possible, despite its requirements for adjustments, it means that option ownership does not necessarily entail risk. Because option ownership can be riskless, there is no reason to account for tastes about risk in the valuation of options (unlike the CAPM, which does account for tastes regarding risk by using as input the market return for the portfolio with beta of 1). In other words, no adjustment for risk is made in the valuation of options because their holders can avoid risk. Therefore, the riskless rate should be used to price options.

Although probability theory uses the normal distribution in many settings by default, it is not considered appropriate for option pricing because the normal distribution has no lower bound. Stock prices, by contrast, have a value of zero as their lower boundary. Therefore, finance theory substitutes the lognormal distribution, which has zero as its lower bound. Although this makes sense, the result is functions that are much less intuitive because the lognormal distribution does not take the mean and standard deviation as inputs. The mean and standard deviation of the expected stock price at expiration must be manipulated to produce the coefficients that the lognormal distribution requires. To avoid this confusion, the following exposition uses mean and standard deviation, and the corresponding computer file explains how they are transformed into the coefficients of the lognormal distribution.[2]

The premise of valuing options is the understanding of the relation between the randomness of stock prices and time. Statisticians can readily produce mean price changes and standard deviations for any period, but an option-pricing formula needs to extrapolate the standard deviation as the time to expiration elapses day by day, if not hour by hour. By considering the evolution of price as the accumulation of random price changes, finance scholars were able to import the analysis of such randomness by physicists who studied the motion of liquids. Research on these "diffusions" or "Brownian motions" reveals the relation between standard deviation and time. The standard deviation increases with the square root of time. Thus, if the annual standard deviation of a stock is 30 percent, the standard deviation for a period t is $.3\sqrt{t}$, where t is the time measured in years. This allows the adaptation of historical evidence about the stock's variability to the time defined by the option's expiration.

Thus, if we had the expected mean for the time of expiration, we could calculate the standard deviation. Then constructing the bell curve of stock price probabilities would be easy. It would be the lognormal distribution that would correspond to this mean and standard deviation. Let us assume this mean is known and is m.

Once we have constructed in this way the distribution of stock prices at the time of expiration, we can determine the expected payout of the option at expiration. Restrict the analysis to call options. For every possible price above the strike price, the option is worth the

---

[2] Despite the daunting appearance of the task, the transformation from the normal to the lognormal distribution is fairly simple with mathematical software. Using *Mathematica*, for example, we find that the lognormal distribution is defined in the "package" named ContinuousDistributions (Load with <<Statistics `Continuous-Distributions`). After loading the package, *Mathematica* can create a system of two equations, one equating the mean of the lognormal to one variable and a second equation equating its variance to a second variable, and solve for the two parameters of the lognormal distribution. The corresponding command is:

```
Solve[{ Mean[LogNormalDistribution[ mu, sig]==mn,
Variance[LogNormalDistribution[ mu, sig]==sd^2}, {mu, sig}].
```

difference between the price and the strike. Because the distribution gives the probability of every possible price, we need only multiply this difference by the probability and integrate.

Thus, the desired function would be the integration of the product probability times payout, with price going from the strike price to infinity. The payout is the difference between price and the strike price, and probability follows the lognormal distribution. Calling the strike price k, the mean price m, standard deviation s, and the PDF of the lognormal distribution $g(m, s, x)$, we have

$$f(x) = \int_k^\infty g(m, s\sqrt{t}, x)(x - k)\mathrm{d}x.$$

This is the expected payout of the call.

To find the present value of this we need only discount it to the present. Using continuous compounding, a future amount F is discounted to a present value P by using Euler's constant $e = 2.72\ldots$ in the formula $P = Fe^{-rt}$, where r is the rate and t is the time. Discounting our expected payout, we have

$$e^{-rt} \int_k^\infty g(m, s\sqrt{t}, x)(x - k)\mathrm{d}x.$$

The only variables that we have not specified in this formula are m and r. The variable m is the expected price of the stock. One might think that the appropriate derivation of it would rely on the CAPM, which gives the stock's expected return according to its beta. The market gives that rate of return to the holder of the stock because of its risk. The option can be hedged, making it riskless. Therefore, the holder of the call should not receive compensation for carrying the stock's risk, because some option holders will not be carrying that risk. By the same token discounting should be done assuming no risk; hence, r must be the riskless interest rate. Therefore, the current stock price must be grown at the riskless interest rate to find the appropriate expected stock price at the time of expiration of the call option. With continuous compounding, the expected future mean price m is the current price p multiplied by e^{rt} and the option pricing formula becomes

$$e^{-rt} \int_k^\infty g(pe^{rt}, s\sqrt{t}, x)(x - k)\mathrm{d}x.$$

The famous Black-Scholes-Merton call-pricing formula differs from this formula in that it makes the transformations necessary to

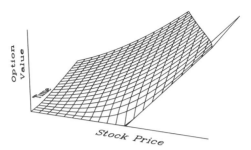

Figure 11.2. The value of a call option as time approaches expiration.

avoid the integration sign. These transformations are possible by using equation-solving software, such as the *Mathematica* program.

Having the symbolic form of the call-pricing formula, it is a simple matter to calculate the reaction of its value to the various parameters of its formula, namely the price of the stock (p), volatility (s), and time (t). Those reactions are given by the derivatives with respect to each variable. The effect of time and price are clearer, however, from a three-dimensional "surface" graph of the value of the call (on the z axis) against the price of the stock (x axis) and time (y axis) (Figure 11.2).

The x axis holds the price of the underlying stock. At expiration the call pays the amount by which the stock price exceeds the strike price, forming the familiar graph that has an angle at the strike price formed by a horizontal line over all lower prices and a line with slope 1 for higher prices. The value of the call before expiration is always greater and only descends to this level at the time of expiration.

The effect of volatility on call prices is more counterintuitive. For years I have shown to my students a visualization of the call-pricing formula, which looks like a wedge. The solid is defined by the graph of the probability distribution of the stock's future prices and by the graph of the payouts of the option.

The price of the stock is on the x axis (the horizontal axis parallel to the page, width), the option's payout is measured along the y axis (horizontal but perpendicular to the page, depth), and the z axis (the vertical axis, height) holds probability density. The graph of the probability distribution of the stock's future prices is similar to a bell curve. The graph of the option's payouts is on the surface defined by the x and y axes, the horizontal surface or floor of the graph. The "bell curve" of the distribution of possible stock prices forms a curved or rippled surface that defines a volume or a solid under it. The payout function makes a vertical slice diagonally, forming a sharp wedge at the

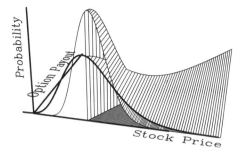

Figure 11.3. The solid that corresponds to the option-valuation formula.

strike price. The option-pricing formula calculates the volume of the solid.

Figure 11.3 displays two bell curves. The taller and more peaked bell curve corresponds to the safer stock that has a lower volatility, whereas the lower peak with the fatter "tails" belongs to the riskier stock. Both have the same mean; the slightly different location of their peaks (modes) is explained by the asymmetrical nature of the lognormal distribution. When dispersion increases, the peak moves toward zero to counter the effect of the "fatter tail" toward infinity.

When volatility is low, the bell curve of future stock prices is narrow and tall. When volatility is high, the bell curve is wider and has a lower peak. The figure shows that greater volatility increases the volume of the solid because it increases the probability of outcomes that have large payouts.

Figure 11.3 helps understand the effect of risk on option prices. The graph displays the value of options on two stocks that differ only in volatility. Which solid's volume is greater? If we only consider the two-dimensional display of the stock's bell curve, two contradictory effects appear. More volatility adds probability weight to the tails but subtracts it from the peak. The third dimension reveals that the loss at the peak corresponds to small payouts. The lower peak produces a small reduction in volume. The fatter tails, however, add much volume because they correspond to large payouts. The call option of the riskier stock is more valuable. This counterintuitive value-increasing effect of risk becomes even more pronounced if we consider a greater strike price, where the riskier surface would be everywhere higher than the safer.

The option-pricing formula is much more than a means for appraising some obscure financial instrument. It is not only an excellent application of risk-sensitive valuation, but it also gives a deep understanding of valuation of contingent claims. Furthermore, the lessons of the option-pricing formula regard changes in the environment that are counterintuitive, such as that increases in risk raise value or the increased sensitivity to time with the approach of expiration.

The pricing method that was applied to calls cannot be applied to puts, because, under some circumstances, the holder of the put will exercise it before expiration. The result is that situations exist where the value of the put does not depend on the distribution of price at the time of expiration but on the "path" that the price follows before expiration. This makes the pricing of puts "path-dependent," precluding the use of a formula that rests on distribution at expiration as does the call-pricing formula.

Instead, puts are valued approximately, by recognizing that they can be part of a hypothetical portfolio that replicates a share of stock at the time of expiration. Selling a put, buying a call with the same strike price, and holding cash equal to the strike price produces a portfolio equivalent to owning a share of the stock. If the stock price rises above the strike price, the call increases in value. If the stock price falls below the strike price, the sold put exposes the portfolio to losses. As a result, the same relationship should hold before expiration, but an adjustment should be made for the interest that the cash would earn.

This method is called the put-call parity. The parity exists under a different construction of equivalent portfolios. A bought call and a sold put are equivalent to holding a share and having debt equal to the strike price. Debt equal to the strike price means a subtraction from the value of the stock of the discounted present value of the strike price at expiration. Thus, if the stock is at US$22, the strike is $20, and if expiration is in six months, that present value may be $19.50, leaving $2.50 for the value of the owned call and sold put. If the call is worth $4, the put should be worth about $1.50.

Appealing as the put-call parity may appear, it is not an accurate valuation method, in part, because of uncertainties regarding interest rates; in part, because of the complex hedge; and in part, because the portfolio does not avoid the path-dependence issue.

B. NORMATIVE IMPLICATIONS OF OPTION PRICING

In legal thinking, the understanding of the effect of risk on contingent claims has changed corporate law's concept of the board's fiduciary obligations, our understanding of bankruptcy law, and the regulation of derivatives markets.

i. Recipients of Fiduciary Obligation

The various securities that a corporation issues can be seen as contingent claims against the value of the corporation. They can be analogized to options by examining the shape of their payout function compared with the value of the firm at the time of their maturity.

The easiest application compares debt claims with equity claims. At the time that the debt matures, the equity holders will retain control of the firm if the firm can pay the debt. Thus, they retain the balance of value remaining after payment of the debt. Provided the value of the firm exceeds its debt, for every additional increment of value in the firm, the equity holders enjoy an equal increment of more value. If the firm cannot pay its debt, its liquidation for the benefit of the creditors implies that equity holders receive nothing. The resulting image is that, as the value of the firm increases, shareholders receive nothing when the value of the firm is small, up to the point where the debt is satisfied; from that point and up, shareholders enjoy the increases of value in full. This, of course, is strongly reminiscent of the payout of calls.

Debt holders enjoy increases of the value of the firm only up to the point where its value is enough for repayment. From that point on, increases in the value of the firm do not benefit the debt holders. The image of increasing payout followed by constant payout is that of the sold put.

Consider the choice of corporate projects in view of the understanding of debt and equity as contingent claims. Consider a corporation that is barely solvent, being worth only a little more than its debt load. The corporation has available to it a low-risk project that produces a value for the entire firm of either 105 percent of its debt or 115 percent. Essentially, this project guarantees a 100 percent payment of debt and leaves equity with an additional 5 or 15 percent of the value of the debt. The alternative is a high-risk project, which will either leave the firm with 50 percent of the debt or 160 percent. This exposes the debtors to a loss of half their claim, whereas shareholders receive either nothing or the 60 percent balance. Suppose that both projects involve 50/50 probabilities. From the perspective of equity holders, the 5-or-15 choice is worth 10 on average, while the 0-or-60 choice averages to 30. Diversified equity holders disregard the additional risk and would prefer the managers of all their corporations to choose the project with the greater expected value for the shareholders. Nevertheless, this is not the best for society, because the average value of the firm is 105 percent as opposed to 110 percent for the lower-risk project. Equity holders benefit from the additional risk just as the holders of calls do. Society, however, is ill served, because projects of inferior value are systematically preferred.

To cure this paradox, corporate law has revived a dormant doctrine. Up to the thirties, corporate boards' fiduciary obligations were considered to run to both equity and debt holders.[3] During the takeover battles of the seventies and eighties, courts increasingly held boards accountable only to equity holders.[4] But in the nineties the old notion of having the board protect bondholders was revived, expressly to deal with the risk-preferring decision making of equity holders regarding projects the outcomes of which produce firm values that straddle the debt claim, as the one we saw immediately above.[5]

ii. Automated Reorganizations via Options

A striking application of option theory appears in the design of bankruptcy reorganization. Scholars have proposed that using options can simplify the reorganization process.[6] The possibility of a reorganization is considered a revolutionary improvement of bankruptcy law. The problem that insolvency poses is that its default outcome was liquidation of the firm's assets and cessation of its activities. Many insolvent firms may be more valuable as going concerns rather than dismembered at liquidation.

Reorganization law, however, is not free of concerns. Once the default in favor of reorganizations is in place, the possibility arises that

---

[3] *Pepper v. Litton*, 308 U.S. 295, 311 (1939) ("a breach of the fiduciary standards of conduct which he owes the corporation, its stockholders and creditors.").

[4] The ultimate example is the refusal to protect bondholders against an increase in risk that halved the value of the bonds at the buyout of RJR Nabisco. See *Metropolitan v. RJR Nabisco*, 906 F.2d 884 (1990).

[5] *Credit Lyonnais Bank Nederland, N.V. v. Pathe Communications Corp.*, No. CIV.A.12150, 1991 Del. Ch. LEXIS 215, at *1 (Del. Ch. Dec. 30, 1991).

[6] See Lucian A. Bebchuk, "A New Approach to Corporate Reorganizations," *Harvard Law Review* 101 (1988):775. A precursor to the proposal of distributing options instead of other claims was the idea to distribute options to a fraction of the firm and use their eventual prices to infer the value of the firm. See Mark J. Roe, "Bankruptcy and Debt: A New Model for Corporate Reorganization," *Columbia Law Review* 83 (1983):527.

firms could be wastefully kept operating too long. Whereas without reorganizations the main error is false liquidations, with reorganization law arrives the concern about false continuations.

The web of incentives that a reorganization produces justifies the concern about false continuations. The owners and the managers of the enterprise have much to gain and little to lose if the reorganization succeeds. The professional creditors may not be eager to bear the burden of administration and management and are sometimes barred from such involvement by banking or insurance regulations. Moreover, the social sensibilities of judges and trustees may well push toward one more attempt to save the jobs and the dislocation that a business shutdown would entail. Therefore, the "negotiated" reorganization that bankruptcy law envisions does offer grounds for fear of false continuations.

Options offer an alternative model of reorganizations. Instead of a court-supervised, negotiated reorganization, the options approach suggests giving claimants a package of options. The options that each claimant receives are designed to give the claimant the exact rights to the enterprise's value that priorities require. Although that is what each claimant would receive in a reorganization, the options have an important advantage. They accomplish the re-allocation of control automatically.

The option solution is to distribute to the various classes of claimants options such that, *contingent on* the value of the reorganized firm, claimants receive exactly the amount to which they are entitled. Each class of claimants holds a call option against the immediately senior class and grants a call option to the immediately junior class. The most senior class receives the equity on a temporary basis. The functionality of the result can be clarified in an example.

Suppose a firm has three classes of claimants: senior debt, junior debt, and equity. Senior creditors receive equity subject to a call option in favor of the junior creditors. Junior creditors have a call option against the seniors and give a call option to the next senior-most class and so on until the old equity holders, who receive a call against the most junior class but do not grant any call because they are entitled to the residual value. The result is that each class is entitled to "buy out" the class that is immediately senior to it, but each class may also be bought out by a more junior class.

The effect of this scheme is that each class will exercise its calls as long as that produces value for it, that is, as long as the value of the firm is greater than the claims of the more senior classes. Thus, all in-the-money senior claimants will see their claims bought out. All out-of-the-money junior claimants will not exercise their options or receive any value. The reorganized firm's ownership will reside in the hands of the class that held the residual claim, the class that was only partly in the money.

Suppose that our reorganized firm had US$100million (100m) debt to secured creditors, 50m debt to unsecured creditors, and equity. The value of the reorganized firm is not known and the option approach allows reorganization without its knowledge. The secured creditors receive the equity of the firm subject to an option to sell it for 100m to the unsecured creditors. As a result, the secured creditors will keep the entire firm if the unsecured creditors decide not to exercise their options, that is, if the value of the firm is up to 100m. The secured creditors' option can be divided into any number of smaller options. If the firm's equity is divided into one million shares, each share given to the secured creditors will be coupled with one granted option to sell that share for 100 to the unsecured creditors. Note, that if they do sell, their claim is satisfied in full.

The unsecured creditors receive the call option against the secured creditors and grant a call option to the old equity holders. That call option allows the old equity holders to buy the equity of the firm from the unsecured creditors for 150m. Thus, the equity holders will buy the firm if they consider it to be worth more than 150m, and the purchase will satisfy the 50m claim of the unsecured as well as the 100m claim of the secured.

If the value of the firm is between 100m and 150m, then the unsecured creditors would exercise their call options and purchase the firm, but the equity holders would not exercise their options. Thus, the unsecured creditors would get control of the firm. The plan is displayed more clearly in Table 11.1.

Each row of Table 11.1 corresponds to a different class of claims in this simple example with three classes of claims. The most senior class in this example is secured creditors with claims that aggregate 100 million. Next in seniority are the unsecured creditors with claims aggregating 50 million, and last and most junior are the equity holders.

After the first column identifies the claimants, the second column contains the assets that they would receive in an options-based reorganization. The third column contains the outcome, that is, the conditions under which this class will own the equity of the reorganized firm.

Table 11.1. *Reorganisation using options*

Claim	Options received and granted	When in control?
100m secured	Receive common stock; grant 100m call to unsecured	If firm value is under 100m
50m unsecured	Receive 100m call against secured; grant 150m call to old equity holders	If firm value is between 100m and 150m
Common stock	Receive 150m call against unsecured	If firm value is over 150m

Thus, the secured creditors receive the equity and grant a call option to sell it for 100 million to the junior creditors. Because the junior creditors will only exercise their call option if the firm is worth more than 100 million, the secured creditors become the equity holders of the reorganized firm if it is worth less than 100 million in the eyes of the unsecured creditors.[7] If the unsecured creditors do decide to exercise their call option, the secured creditors will be satisfied in full, receiving the 100 million of their claim.

The unsecured creditors, in turn, receive the call option granted by the secured creditors to buy the firm for 100 million and grant a call option to the old equity holders to sell the equity of the firm for 150 million. Because the old equity holders will only exercise their call option to buy the firm if they consider the firm worth more than 150 million, the unsecured creditors become the owners of the equity in the reorganized firm in the case that its value is between 100 and 150 million.

Finally, the old equity holders receive the call option granted by the unsecured creditors to buy the firm for 150 million and become the equity holders if they consider exercising this option to be advantageous. If they do exercise their call option, the 150 million they must pay are enough to satisfy the 100-million claim of the secured and the 50-million claim of the unsecured creditors.

If the option-based reorganization operates as it is designed to, it would achieve the goal of distributing the value of the firm according to the bankruptcy code. The reduction or elimination of judicial oversight from the bankruptcy process, however, may raise issues that other objectives of bankruptcy law are not met.

---

[7] But even if the unsecured do not exercise their option, the secured will be forced to sell the firm if the old equity holders decide to exercise, in this example, by deciding that the firm is worth more than 150 million.

iii. The Options Understanding of the New Value Exception

Option theory also led to a new understanding of a facet of reorganization law called the new value exception. Under U.S. reorganization law, the reorganization of the capital structure of the debtor is implemented by means of a plan that is approved by two different majorities of every class, simple majority by count, and two-thirds majority by amount. If such majorities approve the issuance of equity to the old equity holders, such a plan can be approved provided it meets the other requirements of §1129(a), notably including that every creditor receive at least what they would have received in liquidation and that the new capital structure be viable. A plan for a new capital structure can also be approved despite the contrary vote of one class of creditors. In that case, for the court to approve the plan, one of the additional requirements is that the plan must satisfy the absolute priority rule, that is, pay junior claimants only after satisfying their seniors.[8] The need for an inclusion of the absolute priority rule in contested reorganization plans – known as *cramdowns* – is obvious. Without this protection, cramdowns would become vehicles for extracting value from the objecting class of creditors.

Next to absolute priority, however, appears the new value exception.[9] It overcomes the objecting creditors' claim for receipt of the residual value or for full payment when the reorganized firm issues new equity securities for new consideration, which is the new value. Because the consideration is an infusion of new assets into the firm, no principle dictates that it should move out of the firm. Payments to existing security holders would be tantamount to purchases of the securities they held, but the substance of the transaction would be an issuance, not a sale.

The shape of the new value exception would determine the consequences of an objection to a new value plan. For example, the shape of the new value exception would determine whether an objection to a plan would function as a preclusion of the possibility of issuance of new equity to the old equity holders, whether the objection would lead to a forced auction of the enterprise, whether the objection would function as a forced auction of the new equity, or, finally, whether a new value plan could be approved despite the objection with no more

---

[8] See 11 U.S.C §1129(b).
[9] See *Bank of America v. 203 North LaSalle Street Partnership*, 526 U.S. 434 at 446 (1999) (citing Georgakopoulos, "New Value").

requirements. At present, the new value exception functions as a forced auction of the new equity, but whether that is also true in closely held corporations, the reorganization of which involves issues regarding the fresh start of the owner-managers, remains open.

The debate of the new value exception was powerfully influenced by option theory. Before the Supreme Court confined the contours of the new value exception in the way above, Judge Frank Easterbrook of the 7th Circuit observed that a new value plan functioned as an option, held by the old equity holders. Pursuant to the new value exception, the old equity holders had the option to purchase equity in the reorganized firm. Because options are valuable, the new value exception appeared as a violation of absolute priority. Absolute priority requires that classes junior to the objecting creditor receive no value (unless the objecting creditor is paid in full).

The use of concepts from options does clarify the issues surrounding the new value exception. First, the observation of Judge Easterbrook that the exclusive right to buy equity in the reorganized firm is an option may be correct in some reorganization settings. All kinds of rights or opportunities in that setting can be correctly characterized as options. Calling a right an "option" does remind one of its value, but it does not answer the normative question of the desirability of the existence of this right, in particular, when the underlying normative question is as complex and unclear.

The right to purchase the equity of a reorganized firm is valuable if it allows the holder of this right to buy the equity for less than its value. Such a right would be equivalent to a call option to buy stock at a price below the market price. A simplistic view of reorganization law would indeed perceive an exclusive right to purchase the equity pursuant to the new value exception as such a right. It appears that the reorganization has produced a valuable enterprise and that its equity would have a market value greater than the accounting "book value" for which the old equity holders may purchase it. When I studied the practice under the new value exception, the new value exception was never applied in this way but always consisted of an extra payment to the most junior creditors.[10]

An example illustrates this concept. Consider as the baseline case one where the reorganized firm is worth 100 as a going concern. After the old creditors receive 100 in debt claims against the reorganized firm,

---

[10]   Georgakopoulos, "New Value," 125.

the new value plan has the old equity holders contribute 15 as equity; the 15 stay in the firm, and the old equity holders receive the equity at book value. If we think that the old equity holders will exercise their "right" of having a new value plan only if the new equity will be worth more than 15, then it does appear as if they have a valuable option by virtue of their ability to propose a new value plan.

Compare with this a plan according to which creditors still receive 100 of debt claims against the reorganized enterprise but where the new value contribution of the old equity holders went not to the firm but to the creditors. The puzzle, of course, is whether such equity – in essence, bought in exchange for a payment to the creditors – can ever have positive value and why equity holders may acquiesce to pay and obtain such equity. A benign explanation would have the equity holders place a large subjective value on the control of enterprises with which their persona is entwined, such as enterprises that they or their family created. A malign explanation would recognize that the equity in such undercapitalized enterprises is likely to benefit from an amelioration of the circumstances with little downside risk. The risk hurts the creditors, whereas the gains accrue to the equity.

Both the benign and the malign motivations, however, are still compatible with the option approach. The equity holders who buy control that is of great subjective value to them are receiving a bargain.[11] The equity holders who are buying control in undercapitalized enterprises are also receiving a bargain insofar as they will only accept to take this risky endeavor if the price is right, that is, favorable.

That the opportunities offered by the new value applications appear as options should not be understood as answering the question of the desirability of the exception. Every opportunity, whether presented by the market or the law, appears as an option. The merits of the new value exception are not revealed by the options analogies.

The ubiquity of options is also apparent if we examine equity ownership and the reorganization process before the plan. Equity holders of a failing firm can always choose to inject cash into their firm to prevent its failure. This is an option, the option to attempt a resuscitating cash infusion. Like other options, it is valuable because it will only be

---

[11]   Although this is a bargain that would also be available to them outside bankruptcy because they are willing to pay more than others for the control of this enterprise. This weakens the option argument, because, from the perspective of buyers with high subjective value, every seller would be offering a bargain.

exercised if advantageous. A group of financial economists have valued the added value that this "option" gives to ordinary equity ownership.[12]

A look into the bankruptcy process for more options that may contradict the absolute priority rule is an interesting exercise. The equity holders' exclusive right to propose a plan is generally acknowledged to be valuable, as is their right to manage the enterprise during the reorganization process as a debtor-in-possession. These three "options" that the equity holders enjoy – the resuscitation option, the plan-proposal option, and the management option – could easily be considered essential components of equity ownership. This is not to say that bankruptcy law could not choose to eliminate them for the purposes of bankruptcy, but silence cannot be interpreted as their elimination. The text of §1129(b) can be interpreted either way. If its mandate is about the distribution of claims against an insolvent company in violation of strict priority, the purchase of equity with new value cannot be a distribution, and, consequently, it should not violate §1129(b). The Supreme Court in *203 N. LaSalle*, took the opposite view, that the exclusive right to buy equity, although not distributed by virtue of the reorganization plan, does violate §1129(b). The result is that plans proposing the issuance of equity for the contribution of new value cannot give the old equity holders the exclusive right to buy the new equity. The exact contours of this "non-exclusivity" are still unclear. Arguably, excluding creditors from competing for the equity should be acceptable, and the new value exception should be fully available, in cases that pose issues regarding the "fresh start" and the productivity incentives of individuals.[13]

---

[12] B. Cormell, F. A. Longstaff, and E. S. Schwartz, "Throwing Good Money after Bad? Cash Infusions and Distressed Real Estate," *Real Estate Economics* 24 (1996):23.

[13] One or more senior creditors may properly be barred from competing for the new equity. Because their reasons for seeking to acquire the equity are likely to promote their positions as creditors, and because their acquisition may lead to a liquidation of the enterprise that no "true" equity holder, that was not also trying to promote a creditor's interest, would decide, the exclusion of creditors seems amply justified.

Then, reorganizations of family firms may involve the family's fresh start rights. Such a setting must be distinguished from *203 N. LaSalle*, where the insolvency did not jeopardize the capacity of the firm's owners and investors to devote their labor to its most productive use. The family enterprise, the failure of which would prevent its owners from deploying their labor in its most productive use, should lead courts to allow the use of new value plans even if the right to purchase the equity is exclusively in the old equity, the family. After all, we know from the Supreme Court's fresh start jurisprudence that the ability to avoid an encumbrance on future earnings by changing to a presumably less productive job is inapposite; the fresh start protection is a protection of the maximally productive activity, *Local Loan v. Hunt*, 292 U.S. 234 (1934). (Encumbrance on future wages violated the fresh start policy and threatened

C. CONCLUDING EXERCISES

Exercise 11.1: Compare a hand-to-hand, instantaneous exchange of a good for cash to a contract. The contract is a sale executed before production. It obligates the buyer to pay the purchase price and the seller to deliver the good (i.e., the buyer has the remedy of specific performance). Consider the seller's uncertainty about the costs of producing the object of the sale. If the market price is fixed while production costs vary, then by entering into the contract the seller takes some additional risk. Even if the production costs are surprisingly high, nevertheless, the seller will be forced to bear them and produce the item at a loss. Using the background assumptions of a fixed market price and variable production costs, consider the seller's outcome (profit or loss) as a function of production costs. If production costs are nil, the seller's profit is the price. As production costs increase, the profit drops correspondingly. Profit reaches zero when costs are equal to price. Further increases lead to losses, that is, the seller's outcome is a negative number. The seller who is not bound by contract avoids negative outcomes by exercising the option not to produce. Option theory calls this a *real* option to distinguish it from financial options. (a) If financial options on the costs of production were traded, which financial option would place a seller bound by contract in the same position as if the seller was not bound by contract? (b) How does that imply that the contract price differs from the fixed market price?

Discussion: The essence of the question is whether the contract involves a sale of an option or a purchase of an option. Because the contracting seller bears an additional risk, avoiding this risk must be equivalent to the purchase of an option. This means that a seller must receive some additional compensation for being bound by contract for relinquishing that real option.

The seller suffers a loss when the production costs would make the instantaneous exchange unprofitable. As production costs increase, so do the seller's losses. Accordingly, the option that the seller obtains (buys) by not agreeing to be bound in this contract is a call on the seller's production costs. Someone holding a call option on production costs (an amount necessary to produce one unit of the good) would enjoy at expiration an incremental profit for every equal increment that

---

"pauperism," even though the encumbrance could be avoided by the debtor if he changed jobs.)

production costs exceed the strike price (and fixed market price). Buying that call option would mean that for every increase of production
costs, the contract seller earns that much from the option and loses the
same amount due to performing the contract. The seller is insulated
against high production costs.

Suppose that the only uncertainty is labor costs. The contract obligates the seller to hire the necessary labor regardless of its cost. The
option's underlying good (analogous to the stock underlying stock options) is the cost of production. The strike price is the fixed market
price for the object of the sale.

Presumably, for a seller to agree to be bound in contract, the seller
must receive a premium equal to the value of this call option. A difficulty of observing the option is that the salience of the object of the
sale impedes treating that value as fixed, which is what the example
requires.

Exercise 11.2: Continuing the same example, suppose that instead of
specific performance, the seller who chooses to breach has a known
monetary obligation, *liquidated damages*.[14] Allow some uncertainty
about the price at which the seller may obtain an identical item on the
market to satisfy the buyer, what is known as a *cover purchase*. At the
time that the parties write their contract, they know the expected price
of the good. Suppose they specify a price of 22 in the contract and
liquidated damages of 10. Consider the seller's best action if his costs
made performance unappealing and the price of the good is 24. After
spending 24 for a cover purchase, the seller receives the contract price
of 22, for a net cost from the cover purchase of 2. A breach costs 10.
Therefore, the seller will obtain the cover purchase. Compare this with
the seller's choice if the market price of the good goes to 34. A cover
purchase costs 12 whereas breach costs 10. To what financial option do
liquidated damages correspond?

Discussion: Recall from the previous question that the contract functions as the surrender by the seller of a call option on production costs.
In that setting, the seller's profit cannot fall below zero without contracting. With liquidated damages, the seller's profit can be negative but
has an essential similarity to not entering in the contract. The seller's

---

[14] The term "liquidated damages" refers to a contractually specified amount. The source
of the specificity of the damages is not relevant for the example.

downside is again limited; it cannot exceed the liquidated damages. The liquidated damages restore to the seller a call option. The main difference is that it has as its strike price the expected market price plus the liquidated damages.

As in this example, the market price of the object of the sale is allowed to fluctuate; this creates additional complications. From the seller's perspective, the option that the seller surrenders when agreeing to be bound by contract has a strike price that is variable and depends on market value, as the seller's profit or loss depends on the difference between contract price and production costs. The buyer has a similar position when we compare the buyer's benefit with the cost of the item. A buyer who enters into a transaction after precisely ascertaining the benefits would never enter a disadvantageous purchase. If at the time of the contract the buyer's benefits are not precise, then by entering into the contract the buyer takes some risk. The buyer's benefits may not exceed the price.

Exercise 11.3: The identification of contract components as options allows the application of conclusions from option valuation into contract analysis. (a) Option valuation shows that volatility of the underlying good increases the value of the option. (i) What does this imply for the value of contract law for industries with high volatility of production costs compared with its value for industries with low volatility of production costs? (ii) What does the increasing value of options with respect to volatility imply for the value of contract law if we compare the uncertainties faced by buyers and sellers? (b) Option valuation shows that the passage of time reduces the value of the option (Figure 11.2). That reduction is steepest for the *nearest, at-the-money calls. Nearest* means that little time remains until expiration. The relation of strike price to asset price places options in three categories. If the strike price is below the stock price, the option is *in the money*. If the strike price is above the stock price, the option is *out of the money*. The options with strike prices closest to the current stock price are called *at the money*. What does the sensitivity to time imply for the interpretation of contract clauses regarding arbitration? More generally, what does this nature of the time sensitivity of option values imply for the civil procedure of contract disputes?

Discussion: The analysis starts by assuming a constant market price, as above. In that setting, we saw that the seller who enters a contract

relinquishes a valuable call option. Its value is greater for larger volatility of production costs than for smaller. The seller who enters into a
contract relinquishes that option and, presumably, is compensated for
that. As a positive (descriptive) application, a plausible conclusion is
that sellers facing more volatile production costs will demand greater
premiums for being bound contractually. Normative conclusions are
not as clear. A legal system that provides effective enforcement of
contracts would tend to allow those buyers who have a strong demand for the item to reach contracts even with sellers who have production costs with great volatility. This would be less likely in legal
systems with a poor ability to enforce contracts. Sellers in those jurisdictions would either require an additional premium to compensate
for the uncertainty that the contract would not be enforced or refuse
to be bound for any amount. Some contracts would not materialize.
The weakness of the law leads to a loss of the joint gains from some
contracts.

Arbitration is related to time by being potentially faster than a
trial. As a consequence, one possible line of reasoning would consider
the parties' use of arbitration clauses as an indication that they seek
speedy resolution of the dispute at the cost of losing the procedural
protections of a formal trial. The shape of the erosion of the value
of a call option may be taken into account. Consider a court that is
sceptical toward the use of arbitration clauses in a specific type of contract and is faced with a choice of reviewing two arbitration decisions,
one that has been delayed and is clearer and a second that is ambiguous and close in time, meaning that the performance would occur
in the near future. To the extent that "ambiguous and close" corresponds to enforcement of near, at-the-money options, that is a dispute
that delaying its resolution would tend to erode more the value of
the related options. Granted, the close dispute may be more likely to
have received the wrong arbitration decision, which argues in favor of
its review. However, the parties accepted the compromised accuracy
of arbitration with their contract. Moreover, the ambiguity suggests
that its resolution by the court may more likely be wrong. The balance may lean in favor of only reviewing the less timely and clearer
decision.

The options perspective may allow an important distinction in civil
procedure between disputes with active options and disputes with ex-
pired options. Many legal systems have summary or emergency procedures to which the former must be subjected.

D. BIBLIOGRAPHICAL NOTE

Truly extraordinary for its clarity and readability is the introduction to options by John Hull, *Options, Futures and Other Derivative Securities* (Englewood Cliffs, NJ: Prentice-Hall, 1989).

A thorough technical presentation of the methods used in option valuation is John C. Cox and Mark Rubinstein, *Options Markets* (Englewood Cliffs, NJ: Prentice-Hall, 1985).

The deployment of the *Mathematica* program to tackle the issues of finance and option theory is demonstrated in Hal R. Varian (ed.), *Economic and Financial Modeling with Mathematica* (New York: Springer-Verlag, 1993).

12. Using Spreadsheets

This chapter lays the foundation for the introduction of statistics by Chapter 13. Statistical analysis easily becomes concrete with a tool that processes the mathematics. Spreadsheet software is such a tool. Spreadsheets are surprisingly useful. This should come as no surprise, given their popularity. Readers who have a significant level of comfort with spreadsheets or who intend to use different software for statistical analysis can skip this chapter.

Some scholars have questioned the capacity of spreadsheets to perform statistical calculations with the appropriate accuracy. The popularity of spreadsheets suggests the opposite may be true. Programs occasionally have bugs but bugs in popular programs are more likely to be identified and will tend to be identified sooner and be corrected faster. The experience with an error in some Pentium III chips is a good example of how popularity breeds robustness. The error was covered in the popular press, and not only did the manufacturer correct the error but the press reported how users could overcome Excel's tendency to preserve the false calculation in old spreadsheets.[1]

A. THE BASICS

A spreadsheet program is the next step in the evolution of calculating devices. As revolutionary as the electronic calculator might have seemed to the users of the abacus and engineers' rulers, spreadsheet

---

[1] See, for example, Stephen Manes, "Fixing What You Thought Fixed," *New York Times* January 31, 1994, p. c8 col. 4 (discussing how Excel spreadsheets that were created on a computer with a faulty Pentium III, even after its replacement, produce faulty results due to programming shortcuts that prevent "full" recalculation, which is only produced by the undocumented keystroke Ctrl-Shift-F9).

programs are an even greater change. Spreadsheets change the very concept of calculating and the level of complexity to which calculations can be taken. Because of the power of spreadsheets, not being able to use spreadsheets is a major handicap.

A spreadsheet program is a field of "cells." When opening Excel, the principal part of the screen is separated in rows and columns that form the cells. The user can place the cursor in any cell by using the arrow keys or by clicking with the mouse. The user types in the cell, then presses the Enter key for the spreadsheet program to process and display what was entered.

The rows are numbered, and the columns correspond to letters. The result is that cells can be referenced by their letter-number coordinates. The cell A1 is the top left one, first column, first row. Next to A1 is B1, and under A1 is A2. This coordinate system is very important because referring to other cells, is the source of the power of spreadsheets. Cells that make calculations can refer to other cells and use their values. This sheet of cells, which most users understand as the spreadsheet, is called the worksheet by Excel. An Excel file (called a workbook) contains several worksheets. We can navigate between sheets by the tabs at the bottom of the worksheet (Sheet 1, Sheet 2, . . .). Excel opens a staggering 16 worksheets by default. Delete them by right-clicking their tabs and choosing delete; also right-click to insert new ones or rename existing ones. The default can be changed to a more manageable number, such as 3 or 4 in the menu/Tools/Options/General.

Cells can contain text, numbers, or calculations, which can be based on values held in other cells. Their text can be formatted the same way that text can be formatted in word processors. It can take different fonts and colors, it can be bold or italic, and it can be justified left or right. By default, text is left aligned and numbers are right aligned. This difference helps catch some errors. If a number appears at the left edge of a cell, the spreadsheet may be treating it as text. Either delete and re-enter or choose /Format/Cell to change to a number or general format.

Numbers in cells can be integers, decimals, and fractions, but they can also be times and dates. Fractions are entered by separating the integer part with a space from the fractional part, such as 7 3/8. Times and dates are entered in their short form, such as 10:15 A.M. or 7/12/01. The short form corresponds to the choices made in the International Settings of Windows.

The power of spreadsheets is realized when cells perform calculations. Enter a calculation by starting the cell's contents with an equal (=), plus (+), or minus (−) sign. Simple calculations can be entered by using the familiar signs of the calculator: +, −, *, /, ^ for addition, subtraction, multiplication, division, and raising to a power. Parentheses can be used to ensure that the calculations are made in the order that the user specifies, rather than using the built-in defaults. Multiplication, division, and raising to powers are the principal candidates, since $3 + 5/8\char`\^2$ is different than $(3 + 5)/8\char`\^2$, $3 + (5/8)\char`\^2$, and $(3 + 5/8)\char`\^2$.

More complex calculations can be made by entering into the cell functions or formulas, such as =SQRT(4) or @SQRT(4) for calculating the square root; note that, in addition to the other signs, cells containing a function can begin with @. Excel has a surprisingly large number of built-in functions. Moreover, the user has the ability to write "user-defined" functions. Navigating the sea of built-in functions is a key skill in unlocking the power of spreadsheets.

i. Obtaining Built-in Help about Functions

Excel provides two ways to search the universe of functions that it offers. The more thorough and informative way is the use of Excel's help files, which are accessed by pressing the F1 key or the /Help/MicrosoftExcelHelp menu command. By default, the help command in some versions of Excel brings on the screen an animated paper clip "office assistant" nicknamed "Clippy," which tries to lead the user to the right help file. All too often the full-text help file cannot be reached through "Clippy." Such has been the frustration with Clippy that the recent versions of Office have Clippy disabled by default. Clippy should be disabled to be able to access the index of Excel's help files. To disable Clippy, when Clippy appears, click on the Options button that appears immediately above and left of Clippy. In the screen that follows remove the selection mark from "Use Office Assistant" and click the OK button. Clippy will not appear in response to the F1 key or the /Help/MicrosoftExcelHelp menu choice.

Once the office assistant Clippy has been disabled, a user's call for help produces a searchable index to Excel's help files. By typing text in the search box, one is led to an entry in the index, which appears immediately under the search box. Hitting Enter or double-clicking on an index entry brings up the chapters or topics in the help files that contain the selected word. The list of titles of help files appears under the window with the index. Clicking on any of those headings displays the text of this help file in the right-hand side of the help window. As

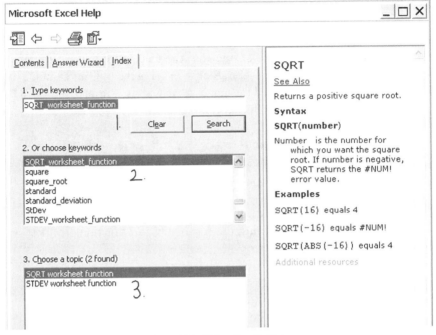

Figure 12.1. Using Excel's Help.

shown in Figure 12.1, the help system uses a search box (marked 1 in the picture), an index window (marked 2), and a window with a list of topics (marked 3), which are all one under the other on the left side of the help window. On the right is a window with the actual text of the help file.

An example is necessary. Suppose we are searching for ways to take the square root of a number. Hitting the F1 key, or selecting the Help menu and Microsoft Excel Help, brings up the help screen, usually on the right side of the screen. Make sure the Index tab is selected and place the cursor at the search window (marked with a handwritten 1 in the illustration) so we can start typing the term for which we will search, "square." As we start typing, the index window (number 2) scrolls, to words starting with s, then to those with sq, and squ. It is worth keeping an eye on the index window. One of the choices that appear when we are only two keystrokes into the search term is SQRT_worksheet_function. Because we are looking for a function to use in a worksheet, this is a good candidate for the searched term. By double-clicking it, a few topics appear in the window with the list of topics (marked 3). One is the SQRT_Worksheet_Function. Clicking on that brings up the help file on the SQRT function, which is the text seen in the illustration. In addition to its text, the help file has several links leading to more information. One link, the underlined *See Also* at the top, leads to related functions. This last path is often invaluable for finding the right function.

The help file defines the parameters that a function may take, because some take several. The help file also defines how the function operates.

ii. Using the Function Wizard

In addition to the help files, Excel assists the user to find the appropriate function by a "function wizard." Wizards are used by Excel to help the user through a complex task, such as setting up a graph or applying a complex function. The function wizard proceeds in two steps, first helping the user identify the function that will be used, then assisting the user to properly insert the appropriate parameters in the function.

The function wizard can be called two ways. The first is a toolbar button. The button for the function wizard looks like "ef of x," fx. The second appears after the user starts typing in a cell. As soon as an equal sign is typed in a cell, a change occurs to the row immediately above the worksheet area and below both the menu items and the buttons. In the far left, a function name appears with a down arrow. Clicking the displayed function name activates the function wizard or clicking the down arrow, whereupon several more functions appear – any of which can be chosen – and below the additional functions a "more functions..." option. The circled areas on Figure 12.2 indicate these two triggers of the function wizard.

The first screen of the function wizard has two windows (Figure 12.3). The left one has categories of functions, such as mathematical, statistical, or financial. In the right window appear the functions that fall within each category. We can search through the functions by scrolling through them. If we highlight a function, its description appears under the two windows at the bottom of the function wizard. For the cases where those descriptions are sufficient, the function wizard is a very effective method of searching for a function.

At this point it is worth going through the list of categories of functions. A good understanding of the categories helps immensely in the search for the right function.

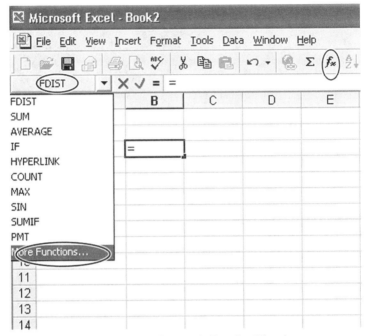

Figure 12.2. Calling Excel's Function Wizard.

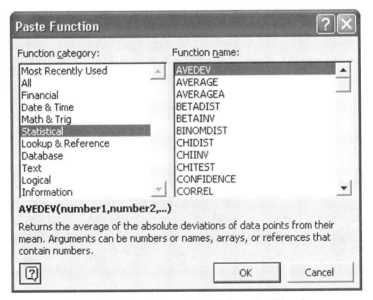

Figure 12.3. The window of Excel's Function Wizard.

The categories of functions that the function wizard offers are: Most Recently Used, All, Financial, Date & Time, Math & Trig, Statistical, Lookup & Reference, Database, Text, Logical, and Information. If user-defined functions exist as well, they form one more last category. Let us explore the categories of built-in functions.

iii. Categories of Built-in Functions

Financial functions make frequently used financial calculations, such as calculating the future value of an investment (the FV function, which is accompanied by a PV function), the internal rate of return of a stream of payments (the IRR function), loan payment and its interest, and principal components (the PMT, IPMT, PPMT functions). Financial functions require special care because most assume periodic payments and treat interest rates as applying to that period. The monthly interest rate must be used, in other words, if the payments provided in the spreadsheet are monthly. Moreover, Excel makes some default assumptions about the timing of the first payment – immediately or at the end of the first period – which are crucial for the accuracy of the outcome. A noticeable omission is that no functions use continuous compounding, whereas continuous compounding is essential from the perspective of financial economics, in general, and options pricing, in particular. Given these drawbacks and the ease of writing discounting functions, I never use the FV and PV functions. It is much safer to make a table of dates and use periodic compounding or continuous compounding functions that use those dates, and then sum their outcomes to obtain present or future values. As an example, I set a series of payments at different arbitrary times in the future and discount them by using continuous compounding to the present in the ContIRR worksheet of the LawEcMethods.xls file which is available from www.pmle-nlg.org. The sheet also uses date calculations, the IF function, and a macro, which are discussed below.

Date & Time functions help calculations of time. Excel converts dates and times into numbers, and these functions help make calculations based on the relation between number and date/time. The function TODAY returns today's date and is useful in keeping time calculations up to date. The function NOW does the same with time. Specific parts of time can be produced by the HOUR, MINUTE, and SECOND functions. Entering =HOUR(NOW()) in a cell returns the current hours and =SECOND(NOW()) the seconds. This is updated only whenever the spreadsheet recalculates, which by default is on the completion of each cell entry. You can force a recalculation by hitting F9. The functions YEAR, MONTH, and DAY do the same for dates. After inserting dates in cells, Excel can perform calculations, typically subtracting the earlier date from the later to find their difference. The difference will be expressed in days, so a division by 30 or 365 is necessary to use months or years. Excel may format the result or operations on dates as a date because it inherits the formatting of the referred cells. In such a case it may be preferable to choose /Format/Cells from the menu and revert to the General format or to a Number format. The ContIRR worksheet that applies the continuous compounding uses the difference between dates to perform the discounting calculation. Because the continuous compounding calculation uses an annual interest rate by convention, time must be measured in years. Consequently, the result of subtracting dates is divided by 365 to convert days into years.

The Math & Trig category, obviously, contains the mathematical and trigonometric functions. The number of functions under this category is large and their use extraordinarily varied. In addition to the various trigonometric functions (SIN, COS, TAN, ASIN, ACOS, ATAN, etc.) we find here the square root, exponential and logarithmic functions (SQRT, EXP, LOG), and pi (PI) a function for converting to roman numerals (ROMAN) rounding down and rounding up (ROUND, ROUNDDOWN, ROUNDUP). Several functions perform various adding operations, from straightforward (SUM) to conditional (SUMIF) and further complications (SUMPRODUCT, SUMSQ, etc.). The example worksheet with the continuous discounting calculation, ContIRR, uses the EXP function, of course, for the continuous compounding.

The Statistical category is very rich in functions. It contains functions that derive the typical descriptive statistics (AVERAGE, AVEDEV, STDEV, STDEVP, MAX, MIN, MEDIAN, MODE, PERCENTILE, QUARTILE) as well as more advanced ones for correlation, covariance, skewness, and kurtosis (CORREL, COVAR, SKEW, KURT). Also, here are functions that perform statistical tests (CHITEST, TTEST, FTEST) and that return values from various distributions (NORMDIST, NORMSDIST, CHIDIST, BINOMDIST, EXPONDIST, FDIST, POISSON, WEIBULL) as well as some inverted distributions.

Under the category Lookup & Reference are functions that return column or row addresses, or that refer to a cell, when the row and column coordinates are specified. Some are useful in producing grading sheets, such as RANK and MATCH. The OFFSET function is useful for extracting data from tables.

The database functions essentially extract descriptive statistics from databases. They are self-explanatory: DAVERAGE, DCOUNT, DMAX, DMIN, DSTDEV, etc. The GET function retrieves data from a database according to specified criteria. For the database functions to operate, we must place our data in a range of cells, each column containing a different category of data, where the first row contains the column titles. The "database functions" help topic gives further details.

The text functions operate on text. They can determine the length of a "string" of characters (LEN), change capitalization (LOWER, UPPER, PROPER), identify the location of a substring (FIND), or obtain part of a string (LEFT, MID, RIGHT).

The most useful logical function is IF, which can be nested and used in array formulas to produce extraordinary results. In the example of the continuous discounting in the ContIRR sheet of the LEconMethods.xls file, the IF function is used to test that the dates are in the right order, that is, that the program is asked to discount to a present value rather than grow to a future value. The logic of the statement is: if the present date is later than the date of the payment, then display an error message, else perform the discounting calculation. The syntax of IF is IF(*condition*, *result if true*, *result if false*). In the continuous compounding example it takes the form IF(targetdate>paymentdate, "Error: dates reversed!", amount*EXP(-rate*(paymentdate-targetdate)/365)). The result is that it shows the text "Error..." if the dates are reversed; otherwise it performs the discounting.[2] Time is calculated by subtracting the present date from the payment date and converting into years by dividing by 365. If the relevant target date should be updated to the current date, then replace target date with the formula NOW( ).

The information functions report on the state of cells. Again, they are mostly self-explanatory, such as ISBLANK, ISERROR, and ISNUMBER.

After choosing a function and clicking the OK button, the function wizard presents its second and final screen. Here, the wizard helps with the syntax of the selected function and the input of its parameters. A separate box appears for each parameter. Parameters that must be provided have descriptions in bold. While the cursor is in one of the boxes, the user can either enter a value or click on worksheet cells, and

---

[2] In continuous compounding, catching this error may not be necessary because the subtraction of a subsequent date from an earlier one results in a positive exponent and grows instead of discounting the amount, as it should.

a reference to those cells will be placed in the box and, eventually, the function. References to multiple cells can be made either by clicking and dragging the mouse pointer over the several cells, or by clicking the cell at one end of the field of cells, holding the shift button, then clicking the other end or selecting it by using the arrow keys. Both these methods can also be used when the function is entered by typing it in the cell.

While we place values or references in the boxes, the wizard displays the values of the referenced cells or the result of the calculation, next to each box. When all the required boxes have values, the function wizard also displays the result of the function under the boxes.

The power of functions is great, but typing them in multiple cells seems overwhelming. With the proper use of relative and absolute references, we only need to enter a function once. Then we can cut and paste it in all the cells of a table with all necessary changes happening automatically.

iv. Relative and Absolute References in Copying

Good use of absolute and relative references is one of the most useful skills in building a spreadsheet. The judicious use of absolute and relative references allows the user to place a calculation in a single cell, copy and paste it, both down and across without any changes, so as to create tables with multiple outcomes. The adjectives "absolute" and "relative" modify references. These references are those included in calculations inside cells, referring to other cells. The calculation in the referring cell uses the values of the referred cells. The use of absolute and relative references allows the user to create a table in only three steps, placing values along its borders, creating a single cell with the calculation, and pasting it onto the cells that will be in the table. Without proper use of absolute and relative references, the user will be forced to enter the calculation in each cell.

Relative references identify the referred cell by its location *relative* to the referring cell. When the referring cell is copied and pasted to new cells, the relative references that the copied cell contains are updated to refer to new cells. These new referred cells are in the same relative position with respect to the new referring cell as were the cells referred by the copied cell with respect to the copied cell. If such a cell would fall outside the spreadsheet, the impossible reference to the nonexistent cell is replaced by the error code #REF.

Relative references are the default type of references, when cells refer by using the already familiar column-row format, such as pointing with B2 to the value contained in the second column, second row cell.

Absolute references are not updated when cells are copied and pasted. The referred cells remain unchanged if the reference to them is absolute. The user specifies absolute references by placing a dollar sign ($) in front of the reference to the column or the row. The references to $B2, B$2, and $B$2 are the three possible uses of absolute referencing to cell B2. Absolute references take three forms. First, the reference may be absolute only with respect to column but not row. In this case, when the referring cell is copied across (i.e., to other columns), the reference does not change because the reference to the column is absolute while the row has not changed. When the copied cell is pasted down (i.e., to other rows), it gets updated. As the cell is pasted to each next row, the reference changes by one row. When the copied cell is pasted diagonally, the expected result occurs: the column is not updated, while the row is. When building spreadsheets, references that are absolute as to column are useful to refer to header columns (i.e., columns to the left or right of the table that hold varying values). The creation of a cell with references that are absolute only as to column allows the pasting of the cell down and across with it still referring to the appropriate cell of the header column.

References that are absolute as to row are not updated when copied down, but change column by column when copied across columns. When building spreadsheets, references that are absolute as to row are useful to refer to header rows (i.e., rows at the top or bottom of the table that hold varying values). The creation of a cell with references that are absolute only as to row allows the pasting of the cell down and across with it still referring to the appropriate cell of the header row.

Finally, a reference can be absolute as to both column and row. In this case, the reference does not change with copying and always points to the same cell. Use references that are absolute both ways to refer to constants, to values that remain the same in every calculating cell of a table.

Let us put absolute references to use in a simple table that will calculate the future value to which a given amount will grow, being deposited at various interest rates and for various lengths of time (Figure 12.4). Because interest rate and time vary they will form the header row and column, while the amount is constant. Type "Future values of" in cell A1, 10 in cell C1, and "Time\Rate" in cell A2. Type 1 in A3 and

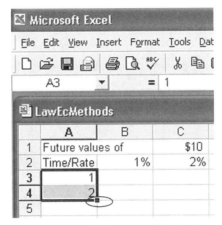

Figure 12.4. Initiating auto-fill in Excel.

2 in A4. Type 1% in B2 and 2% in C2. You could also type .01 and .02 and then hit the % toolbutton to convert their format to percentage. We have set up a 2 × 2 table with a header column of times (1 and 2 years) and a header row of interest rates (1% and 2%).

We can easily expand the header row and column by using Excel's "auto-fill" feature, which expands selected patterns. Select A3 and A4. The bottom-right corner of the frame selecting the cells has a black square, indicated in the first accompanying screen shot with a hand-written circle. Expand the selection down by clicking and dragging this square. The number to which the auto-fill reaches appears next to the expanding selection, the "10" of the second screen shot (Figure 12.5). The new cells receive the values 3, 4, 5, . . . 10, continuing the pattern 1, 2. The same process, performed on the cells B2 and C2, expands the 1 percent and 2 percent rates to 3 percent, 4%, and so on. Our table can be easily expanded at will. Next, enter the formula for a 2-year deposit at 2 percent. This would be $10*(1 + .02)\hat{}2$ and it should be placed in cell C4. Instead of the value 10, use a reference to cell C1, where we have placed the amount. Because this must remain the same in every cell, it must be a reference that is absolute as to both column and row, $C$1. Instead of .02, use a reference to cell C2, which holds the interest rate. Because, as we paste this formula down and across, the interest rate will always be at row 2 but at different columns, the reference must be absolute only as to row, C$2. Finally, instead of 2, use a reference to cell A4, which holds the number of years. Because we paste this formula down and across, the years will always be at column A but at different rows, the reference must be absolute only as to column,

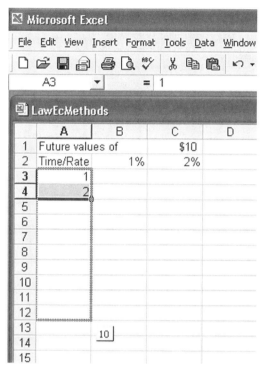

Figure 12.5. Completing auto-fill.

$A4. The result is we should type in cell C4 the formula =$C$1*(1+ C$2)^$A4. Instead of typing the references we can just click on the appropriate cell and hit the F4 key to cycle through the possible reference forms. Copy and paste the cell on the entire table. Row and column references update or not according to the type of reference. The result is numerous cells containing the right formula, copied from the single cell we wrote (seen in the highlighted area of Figure 12.6, partly obstructed by the chart wizard).

Absolute and relative referencing help the construction of spreadsheets immensely. They are easy to use and recognize: the dollar sign precedes the absolute reference. Using absolute and relative references allows us to form a calculation only once and reproduce it by pasting. The next section introduces Excel's graphical abilities.

B. Graphics

Excel has extensive graphic-production abilities. The graphics we can produce in Excel are useful to display data and mathematical functions.

Excel is not the most effective program to produce graphics. Specialized programs designed for mathematics, such as *Mathematica*; for statistics, such as Stata; or for presentations, such as PowerPoint, have some specialized advantages for their topics. *Mathematica* has a greater ability to give graphical representations of mathematical functions and geometric shapes with a greater ability to customize them. Stata can produce unusual visual representations of voluminous data. PowerPoint can produce unusual visual effects, graphics, and movie clips that facilitate presentations. Excel has powerful general graphing abilities with significant latitude for customization. Rarely does the user reach the limits of Excel's graphical abilities.

Excel provides the user with a wizard to assist in the production of graphics. This "chart wizard" is invoked by clicking on a tool button that has a bar graph. It is circled in the screen shot illustrating the first screen of the chart wizard, Figure 12.6.

Before clicking on the button to invoke the graphing wizard, we should select the cells we want to graph, including any descriptive headers. The graphing wizard uses the selected cells as input. It is not necessary to have selected a range of cells, nor is the selection binding. The wizard gives the opportunity to make or change the selection.

The first screen that the wizard produces gives us the choice of a chart type. Chart types are the families or methods of a visual presentation of the data. After the user chooses a type, sub-types appear on the right of the choice, giving a more detailed choice. After choosing a 3D surface graph, as in Figure 12.6, we see that Excel offers four alternative sub-types. The next section covers the various chart types, before the following sections finish the description of the graph wizard and discuss the manipulation of graphs. The button "Press and Hold to View Sample" lets the user see the graph Excel would build according to the current choices.

i. Chart Types

The chart types offered by Excel's chart wizard are column graphs, bar graphs, line graphs, pie charts, X-Y graphs, area graphs, doughnut charts, radar, 3D surface graphs, bubble charts, stock charts, and three types of 3D bar graphs (cylinder, cone, and pyramid). Plain 3D bar graphs appear as choices under column and bar graphs.

Column and bar graphs present sequences of data, each data point represented by a vertical column or horizontal bar. The height or length

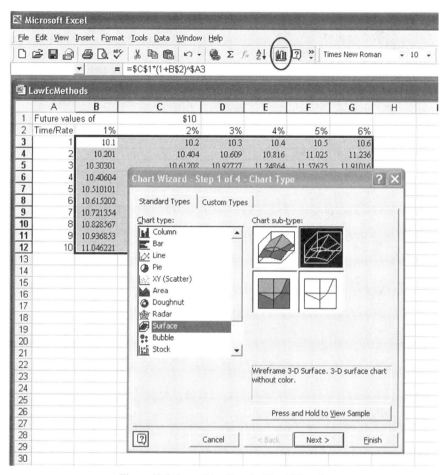

Figure 12.6. Launching Excel's Chart Wizard.

of each bar expresses the value of the underlying cell. Bar graphs give a visual indication of the progression of changes in values. Bar graphs are typically used, for example, to illustrate the progression of profits for investors. Excel offers several choices of bar graphs. The simplest form is a bar graph of a single category of data, such as annual profits. If the data are in several categories, such as annual profits and annual total sales, bars of different color are produced. Excel calls the categories of data "series." The bars of each category of data are then matched and appear together. The graph wizard offers three alternatives for bar graphs with multiple categories of data (series) (clustered, stacked, and 100% stacked). Clustered graphs have the bars of each series extend from the same edge, the floor or left edge. Clustered bar graphs illustrate the evolution and comparison of sizes. Stacked bar graphs add the series to form a single bar, segments of which correspond to each series. Stacked bar graphs illustrate the contribution of each series to a total. In the 100 percent stacked bar graph, the series of data form a constant 100 percent aggregate, which takes the entire height of the graph, and those columns of equal height are divided according to the ratios of the series of data. Where, for example, the first series of data has a 6 and the second a 3, the resulting column will divide at the 2/3 point. The division of the column would look identical if the first series had 20 and the second 10. Percentage bar graphs help illustrate changes in ratios and the composition of a whole into which the various categories aggregate.

Line graphs are, in essence, very similar to bar graphs. Instead of the column or bar, line graphs connect the values with lines. The choices are similar to stacked and 100 percent stacked. Area graphs are the same, but with the areas under the lines filled.

Pie charts and doughnut graphs illustrate the proportion taken by different values within a series of data. Each point is illustrated as a pizza-like slice from a circle. The size of each slice corresponds to the value of the corresponding point. Two series of data can be fit on a single pie chart, which takes the form of two concentric circles, each divided according to each series of data. The chart wizard gives the user the option to choose between placing the underlying cell value next to or on each slice of the pie. Using a further option, the user can also separate a chosen slice from the rest of the pie chart.

An X-Y graph presents twice the amount of information that other graphs do, because instead of being based on a single series of data, each point illustrates two values, an x and a y coordinate. Accordingly, each point reflects the corresponding values from two series of data. The sub-types of X-Y graphs regard the existence of a second series of points and whether they will be connected by straight or smoothened lines. X-Y graphs are among the most useful and most flexible graphs. As unconnected points, X-Y graphs can illustrate complex data. As connected points, they lend themselves to the illustration of mathematical functions or estimated reactions.

Bubble charts add one more piece of information to X-Y graphs. Instead of marks, bubble charts place a circle or bubble at the point indicated by the coordinates. The size of this bubble corresponds to a third piece of data. Bubble charts are an effective way to communicate a 3D relation, as long as the data points are few.

Radar charts are the least frequently used. The data are presented in circular way, as distances from the center of the graph. A polygon is created for each category of data. The data points of each series are connected with a line that, after passing from the representation of each point on each spoke, connects again to the first point. Perhaps we can say that the data are presented as distorted circles.

Stock charts seek to communicate several categories of data. In the simplest of its forms, the series are the high, low, and closing price. Additional possible series are an opening price, and a number of shares traded, which is called volume. The corresponding sub-types are described accordingly in the wizard. Stock charts produce a vertical line from low to high price with a notch to the right at the closing price. The volume is measured by a column that corresponds to a different scale, on the right of the graph.

Most 3D graph types are, in essence, their two-dimensional equivalents graphically enhanced to appear three-dimensional. This is the case in 3D pie charts and, perhaps slightly less so, in the case of 3D bar charts and 3D X-Y graphs. The same applies to the 3D surface chart. It does not use 3D coefficients to locate each point on the surface. If we build a table with evenly spaced header row and column data, we can produce the illusion of a true 3D graph.

The 3D surface chart produces a surface in three dimensions that is similar to a grid formed by lines that run in the direction of the two horizontal axes, the x axis and the y axis. The 3D surface graphs are useful in presenting 3D mathematical equations.

Let us implement a 3D surface graph using the table of future values we created previously when discussing relative and absolute references. Highlight the contents of the table – not the header row or column – and click the chart wizard tool button. Select the surface graph, and as sub-type the unfilled wire graph as in Figure 12.6. A crude preview of the graph we will produce can be seen if we click on the button "Press and Hold to View Sample." Click on the "Next >" button to proceed to the second screen of the chart wizard.

ii. Completing the Chart Wizard

Although we could have pressed the "Finish" button to end the wizard, it offers us three more steps that are meaningful. The second screen has two tabs at the top. The "Data Range" tab lets us select or change the range where the data the chart will use is stored. In our case, we do not have to make or change the selection because we highlighted the data range before calling the chart wizard. The "Data Range" tab, however, lets us make a fundamental choice regarding whether the data are in columns or rows. Excel tries to guess the direction of the data, but we may want to change that guess. In the case of the 3D graph it does not make much of a difference, but we can make this chart look much better by doing so. Notice that at Excel's current defaults, the graph axes would be marked with a sequence of numbers on one side (1, 2, etc.) and series names on the other (S1, etc.). We can designate that Excel will form the labels for the x axis from the values. The other horizontal axis (the y axis) would then display the series names as labels. We can edit those, however, so that the display will be a percentage. For each percentage to be a series, because percentages are in the header row of our table, we must change Excel's choice to "series are in columns."

The "Series" tab lets us rename the series. Select the series to be renamed in the box on the left and type a new name in the "Name" box. Obviously, Series1 should be renamed to 1 percent, Series 2 to 2 percent, and so forth. Below the name box we see where we can select the labels to be used for the x axis (Figure 12.7). Click in the box and select the values for years used in our table, as illustrated in the screen shot. Press "Next >" to pass to the third screen of the chart wizard.

The chart wizard at this stage offers four tabs with further choices. In the "titles" tab we can set the title of the chart as well as the titles or labels of the axes. The "axes" tab lets us choose to hide one or more of the axes. The "gridlines" tab lets us remove the horizontal lines that appear on the back walls of the graph or to add such gridlines along the other dimensions. Finally, the "legend" tab lets us disable the legend box with the names of the series by unchecking the "show legend" mark.

We can now hit the "Finish" button to skip the final screen of the wizard. It would ask whether to place the chart in a separate "chart sheet" rather than in the current worksheet, which is the default. The chart should now appear on the worksheet as we designed it. We can click on it and move it or resize it. Charts bear much more customizing.

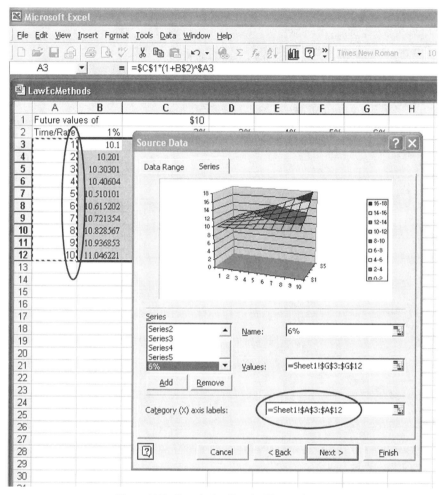

Figure 12.7. Completing Excel's Chart Wizard.

iii. Manipulating Charts

Pressing the "finish" button is not an irreversible action. When the chart is selected, Excel's "Data" menu changes to a "Chart" menu, and each one of its choices corresponds to a step of the chart wizard. Furthermore, the chart can be customized and manipulated to an even greater extent. The most useful changes regard the appearance of the graph – line and point colors and weights, axis scale and appearance, and background color. Even data can be added to tables, either by

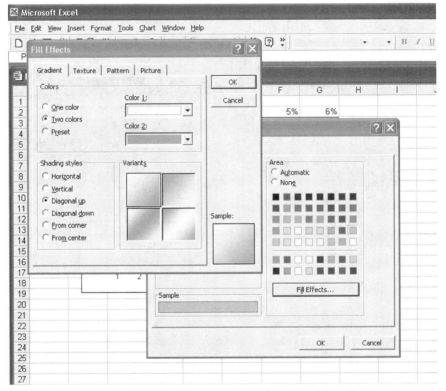

Figure 12.8. Color schemes for improving a chart in Excel.

cutting and pasting or by adding a =SERIES function. Finally, Excel allows us to place any text anywhere inside the chart.

To change the appearance of any element in a chart, we need only select it and right-click. One of the choices is to format the selected item. We can typically change the designated markers and their colors, add or eliminate connecting lines and change their weight, color, and other properties, such as whether they are dashed or dotted lines. We can change the background color and its fill pattern – Figure 12.8 livens up the future values' graph by changing the wall fill to a diagonal fade. This choice appears when we click the "Fill Effects" button on the formatting window. In the case of axes we can also change their default lengths and intervals. By choosing the corners of 3D graphs we can change perspective and viewing angle. Again, several paths lead to the result: dragging to rotate the graph or right-clicking to enter a perspective wizard.

To add data to graphs we can highlight the data to be added, copy, and then select the chart and paste. If the newly pasted data are not visible, perhaps the error can be fixed by selecting the chart and editing the series through the /Chart/SourceData menu. Data can also be added through the /Chart/AddData menu choice. The most controllable way to add data, but also the most complex one, is to highlight a series and copy the line that appears in the function box "=SERIES(...)". Then paste it on the chart and edit it so that it refers to the appropriate data ranges.

By highlighting the chart and clicking on the function input area above the cells of the worksheet, we can also add text to the chart. After we hit Enter we can click and drag the text to locate it appropriately in the chart. This is particularly useful for labeling areas or data points in graphs.

C. Solving Equations

This heading is a misnomer. Excel does not truly solve equations. True solutions that leave symbols unevaluated require mathematical software, such as *Mathematica* or *Maple*. Excel and the other spreadsheets do not have that ambition. Nevertheless, Excel does include two tools for obtaining desired values through an iterative guessing process. The two are the Solver and Goal Seek.

i. The Solver

The more powerful tool is the Solver, but it is not loaded by default. To enable the Solver one must choose /Tools/Add-ins and check the "Solver Add-in." Then, the Solver is enabled, but for the current session only. If the Solver add-in was not installed during Excel's installation, we might need to insert the installation CD and select the Solver add-in. If you do that, do not forget to also select the Visual Basic Help, which is not installed by default and is necessary for writing macros, as we will see below.

After the Solver is enabled, it resides in the Tools menu. The Solver screen is very informative (Figure 12.9). Our primary choices are (1) "Set target cell," which we select; (2) "Equal to" its maximum, minimum, or a value that we specify; (3) "By changing cells" that we specify. These choices are in the upper-left quarter of the Solver window. The buttons that look like miniature spreadsheets minimize the

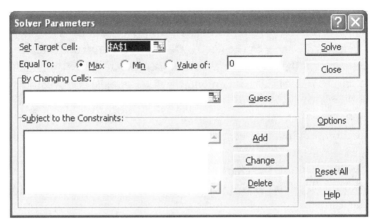

Figure 12.9. The window of Excel's Solver.

window to allow us to select cells from the spreadsheet. We can even add constraints, namely, that some cells must not exceed specified values or fall below the value of other cells and so forth. The "Options" button lets us choose the precision of the result, and the "Solve" button launches the Solver.

The typical use of the Solver is to find what input value produces a certain result in a function. The cell holding the function will be the target cell, which the Solver will seek to maximize, minimize, or make equal to some value. The referred cell will be the one we will designate as the cell that the Solver will change in the "By changing cells" box. If the Solver does not converge to a solution, although we know that a solution exists, we may need to give a realistic guess by pressing the "Guess" button. If trying to find the interest rate that produces a certain value, use .1 as a guess.

ii. Goal Seek

Goal Seek is a rudimentary version of the Solver that is loaded on start-up. Goal Seek also resides in the /Tools menu, but only gives the user three choices: the target cell, the target value, and the cell to be changed. Again, the buttons that look like miniature spreadsheets minimize the window to allow the user to select cells from the spreadsheet.

If we are not seeking a maximum or minimum, we know that we do not need constraints, and we hope that we will not need a guess to obtain an answer, the Goal Seek tool is adequate and avoids the extra time and computer resources required to load the Solver.

D. MACROS AND USER-DEFINED FUNCTIONS

The final skill in extracting value from Excel is writing macros and user-defined functions. The greatest hurdle here is that Excel does not load by default the Help file for the macro editing environment. Thus, the first step is to obtain the installation CD and add the Visual Basic Help Files. While we have the Installation CD out we might as well install the "Digital Signature for VBA Projects" under the "Office Tools" node. That allows one to place a digital "signature" on projects. If the security settings are left at "High," then Excel strips the macros from any spreadsheet it opens that was not created in the same computer. A "Medium" security setting gives the user the option of retaining macros from projects that have digital signatures. Security settings are at the menu /Tools/Macro/Security.

Writing macros does not require an understanding of the arcane Visual Basic for Applications language. As in many other applications, a sequence of actions can be "recorded" into a macro. If the macro is to repeat those actions, we can edit it to add a loop that will apply it repeatedly. A convenient way to use macros is to assign them to a tool button, key combination, or a graphic that will then act as a button that runs the macro. The following sections go over an example of recoding a macro, editing it by adding a loop, and assigning it to a graphic.

i. Recording a Macro

Suppose we find ourselves using the Goal Seek tool often in a particular setting. Perhaps that is the calculation of the internal rate of return to compare two projects that have payouts at different times and which are discounted by using continuous compounding. We set up a spreadsheet that does the discounting using a hypothetical interest rate for each of the two projects, but instead of invoking the Goal Seek tool manually twice, a macro will run it twice automatically, once for each project. Before we run Goal Seek the first time, we select /Tools/Macro/Record New Macro. Name the new macro ContIRR, give it a brief description, choose to place the macro in the current

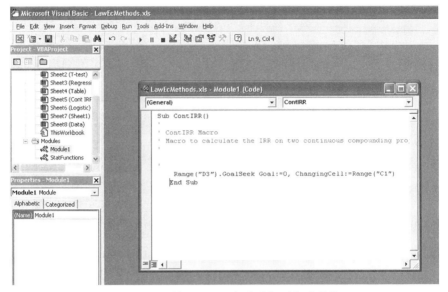

Figure 12.10. Editing a macro in the Visual Basic Editor.

workbook, and click the button OK. A "stop recording" button should appear on the screen. Now all our actions are being recorded, so we invoke from the /Tools menu /Goal Seek. Place in the window the correct references or values and click on its OK button to run Goal Seek. When it produces an answer, we click on the stop recording button. Enter the Visual Basic Editor either by pressing Alt-F11 or /Tools/Macro/Visual Basic Editor and find the macro.

The Visual Basic Editor will probably appear with four sections in its screen. The most important ones are the top left and the top right. The top left, titled "Project-VBAProject" in the screen shot of Figure 12.10 has a list of all the major things that are open in Excel. Those in bold correspond to files, and one of them is the file we have open. It is a VBAProject as far as the Visual Basic Editor is concerned and its name is in the parentheses in the line that is in bold: VBAProject(LawEcMethods.xls). This "project" divides into "Microsoft Excel Objects" which are the worksheets and into "Modules," which hold Visual Basic code. The recorded macro is placed in a new module, Module1. If we double-click that, its code will appear, as it does in the main window in the screen shot of Figure 12.10.

We see that the macro has a single substantive line of code, starting with `Range("D3")`. It has a line that starts the macro and holds its name: `Sub ContIRR()`. It has a line that ends it: `End Sub`. The lines in green text that start with the apostrophes are "comments," rather than instructions to execute. By comparing the line of the macro that would call the Goal Seek tool as we did, we see that the target cell is in the parentheses after `Range`, the target value is set next as the `Goal`, and the cell to be changed is in the parentheses after "`ChangingCell:=Range(`". Essentially, we have deduced the way that the Goal Seek tool is invoked by Visual Basic for Applications. We are now ready to edit the macro so that it calls the Goal Seek tool again for the second project.

ii. Editing a Macro

Editing the macro consists of entering the text of the Visual Basic commands that the macro will execute. We can create counter loops using a For/Next sequence (`For` counter=counter+1, commands, `Next`) or conditional loops using the While/wend loops (`While` condition, commands, `Wend`). As with spreadsheets, the If then/else sequence is very useful (`If` condition `Then`, commands, `Else`, commands, `End if`). The Help files for the visual basic editor explain the numerous commands nicely.

In our macro, however, the task is much simpler. We can highlight the single line of code that calls the Goal Seek tool, copy and paste it immediately below itself. Then, we must change the references so that they correspond to the second project of which we want to calculate the internal rate of return, cells I3 and H1. We can verify that our macro runs properly by changing the interest rate guess or the values in the spreadsheet, returning to the Editor and then pressing the play button to run the macro.

If we installed the Digital Signature tool, we can sign the project while in the Editor by choosing /Tools/Digital Signature. Signing the project will inform those who open the spreadsheet using "Medium" security, who wrote its macros, so they can choose to leave them active.

If we do not like the name of our module (Module1) we can change it from the lower left window of the editor, visible in Figure 12.10. This holds the various "properties" of the current item. In our module, its only property is its name. Just click at its name "property" and type a new name. If we were to create "forms" with buttons and text boxes, those would have numerous properties, such as their location on the screen, their size, their fonts, and text.

An additional window allows us to run commands immediately without running the entire macro. It is called "Immediate" and can be made visible from the menu /View/Immediate window.

iii. Assigning a Macro to a Graphic

Macros can be called by using the menu /Tools/Macro/Macros, but it is much easier to assign them to a graphic. Drag a text box from the graphics tool bar and position it in the sheet. Type in it text such as "Press to Determine the Two Projects' IRR" and format it by centering the text horizontally and vertically, changing the background color to red, the lines to thick yellow, and the text to light green. All these settings are accessible by right-clicking at the frame of the text box and choosing the option "Format Text Box." The same menu that pops up when we right-click the frame of the text box lets us "Assign Macro" to the text box. Choose the name of our macro from the Assign Macro window and click the OK button. When we place the cursor over the text box now, it turns into a hand, ready to press the button. If we want to move or edit the text box, we need to press Ctrl before clicking it, to avoid running the macro.

iv. Entering a Function

Entering a function is very similar to writing a macro. The additional difficulty is that we cannot "record" a function. Thus, we need to open a module and type the commands that will form the function. The LawEconMethods.xls workbook contains the `tstat` function, as it is described in the section on statistical tests of Chapter 13.

A complication of functions and macros is that the built-in functions that can be used on them do not match the functions of the spreadsheet. Thus, a function cannot use the `ttest` built-in function that can be used in a spreadsheet.

E. Downloading and Combining Data

A particular challenge for beginners in empirical work, after finding sources of the data, is the process of importing data into the program that they will use for their analysis, such as Excel.

Increasingly, sources of data enable downloading. The download is typically a text file, with the extension `.txt` after the filename.

Frequently, the downloaded file uses commas to separate columns, in which case it may be called a CSV file, for "comma-separated values." Even easier are "tab-delimited" text files, where columns are separated with tabs. Sometimes, however, columns are not separated at all. Such files are called "fixed-width" because they format each column to take the same number of characters in each line.

Rarely are all the desired data available in a single source. After importation, to reach the ability to analyze the data, the researcher must overcome one more mechanical hurdle, the combining of data from different sources. Therefore, a note on combining data follows the description of importing data, below. Needless to say, frequent and multiple backups prevent embarrassment with surprising regularity.

i. Data Files Separating Columns with Commas or Tabs

The advantage of files that use special characters to separate columns is that spreadsheets can readily import them. Fixed-width files, unless processed, are treated as giving a single long word in each row, which spreadsheet programs put in a single cell. If a fixed-width file is imported incorrectly, it will often only occupy the leftmost column. This will manifest itself by long rows across cells, without being truncated along cell divisions, because Excel prints the text in the full cells over empty cells.

The characters that separate columns are called delimiters. Thus, the type of delimiter can be used to describe the file with the data. When tabs are used, the file can be called a tab-delimited file, whereas a file that uses commas is a comma-delimited file or a file with comma-separated values. The latter name is also used to form the filename extension, `csv`, so that a file named `mydata`, if it is assigned this extension, becomes `mydata.csv`. Such files are text files, encoded identically to files with the "txt" extension, which customarily indicates text files. Since Windows 95, operating systems tend to hide the extensions from the user by default. Change this default choice to reveal extensions. In Windows, this is done through the "Control Panel." Open "Folder Options," choose the "View" tab, and uncheck the option "Hide extensions for known file types." "Folder Options" is also accessible from the "Explorer" where it is in the "Tools" menu.

The convenience of delimited files lies in the ease with which they are imported as spreadsheets. The extreme is opening a

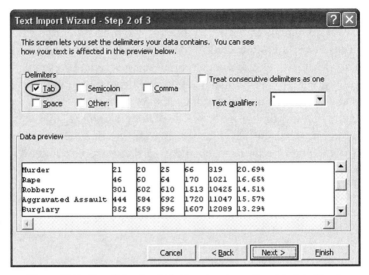

Figure 12.11. Specifying the delimiter when importing data into Excel.

comma-delimited file in Excel. Double clicking a filename with a `csv` extension automatically opens it in Excel. Unfortunately, the comma is too frequent a character for safe use. Commas are often used in text and even in numbers that should occupy a single cell. Other delimiters are more consistent. The tab character is often used as a delimiter and produces more predictable results.

Tab-delimited files are also text files, usually with the conventional `txt` filename extension. Each row of data contains tabs that separate the values of adjacent cells.

When a spreadsheet program opens an unrecognized file, it presents the user with a "wizard" that seeks to establish how the file will be converted into a spreadsheet. In Excel, the first window also displays the current guess about how the file's contents would be converted to a spreadsheet. At the top half, the window asks for a selection between the usual delimiters and offers the option of defining a different delimiter using the "Other" choice. The screen image appears in Figure 12.11; the mark indicates that the delimiter is the tab character.

In some tab-delimited files, the next screen of the wizard may be unnecessary and the "Finish" button skips it. An additional step is necessary, however, when importing numerical data that should not be treated as values, such as phone numbers.

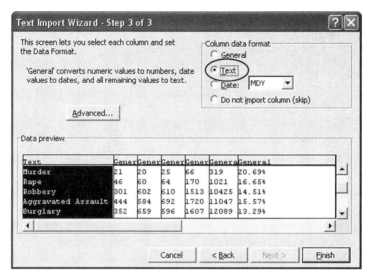

Figure 12.12. Specifying the type of imported data in Excel.

ii. Specifying the Type of Data

The next step in the process of importing data into spreadsheets regards the treatment of the data by the spreadsheet. The wizard calls this a selection of "Data Format," but the selection influences the substantive treatment of the data rather than its presentation. By default, Excel treats columns that contain only digits as numbers. This is usually correct, but its implication is that zero digits at the beginning of numbers or at their ends after decimal points are lost and may lead to errors if the column contains characters such as dashes or periods. Leading zeros may be important, dashes may not indicate subtraction, and periods may not be decimal points. This is often the case with zip codes, postal codes, telephone numbers, or other such numbers that are not truly used as values. In such cases, the spreadsheet must treat the column as text. The next window of Excel's wizard allows the user to determine the "Data Format" of each column (Figure 12.12).

Again, the wizard displays a few rows of the spreadsheet at its bottom half. The choices are at the top right. In the figure, one column is highlighted. Above each column is a heading that indicates the format that Excel will apply. The default is "General" where Excel follows its default algorithm that leads to treating numbers as values. Select each column that should be treated as text and change its format at the top right. Figure 12.12 shows how to specify that the highlighted column will be treated as text.

iii. Fixed-Width Data

If the data file is not a delimited file, then it likely uses the fixed-with format. In that case, the first step of the importation process is different.

In fixed-width files, textual and numerical values are appended together into long lines. When numerical values are joined in such a file they give the forbidding appearance of absurdly long numbers.

Fixed-width data are padded with spaces or zeros so that all the rows of each column have the same width. Unlike delimited data, where each cell can contain a longer or shorter entry, fixed-width data have entries of the same length. For example, a delimited file would use six digits to display the number 123456 in the second column and only three to display the number 123 at the next row in the same column. A fixed-width file may use nine digits for each, displaying 000123456 and 000000123. If the third column has the number 1234 formatted in nine digits, the fixed-width file would not separate them in any way, displaying 000123456000001234.

To decode a file that holds data in fixed-width format, we need to find the information of what locations hold what data. The locations are sometimes called columns, and the information of what is in each column is often called a key, guide, or coding sheet. It may be a separate text file or it may be given in the same file, above or below the data.

Once we have the information about the content of the fixed-width file by columns, importing it into a spreadsheet only requires conveying this information to the spreadsheet program. In the case of Excel's wizard, this means choosing the fixed-width format in the first window, instead of delimited data. The lower half of the screen defines the columns by using a graphical interface. Vertical lines appear with small triangles at their tops. Click and drag the lines to the appropriate places to import the data correctly.

Columns can also be defined by entering the number of characters each takes. In such a case we need to give special attention to the counting practices of the data file and the spreadsheet program. Some start counting at one, others at zero. Verifying outcomes is imperative. This is easiest by choosing a few data points with known values and examining each one of the corresponding imported cells.

iv. Combining Data

Analysis often requires combining data from different sources. In such cases, after importing two or more sets of data, a process for aligning them and verifying that they match is necessary. Each set of data must have a label for each record, such as name, state, city, organization, or postal code (each row holds the data for one "record"). The match is correct when the labels are the same in every row. If, for example, the city population comes from one source and the crime rate from a different one, attributing a large city's crime to a rural village would be quite alarming.

For the analysis to be rigorous, the data must match, not only by label but also in substance. The typical danger here is that the two sources use different geographical definitions. For example, both sources may report the data by city, but one may include greater metropolitan areas in cities whereas the other source uses narrow city borders. Conceivably, the data could be matched by manually combining the suburbs into metropolitan areas.

It is important not to allow the complexity of the mechanics to detract from analysis. For example, suppose that the objective is to calculate the per capita number of classical entertainment venues, symphonies, ballets, and operas. One data source may have city and medium metropolitan area data and a second may list operas, symphonies, and ballets by city. If individuals travel great distances for such entertainment, then arguably the relevant population is neither that of the city nor the medium metropolitan area. Rather, the proper match may require finding the population of the greater metropolitan area of each city. Unless the two data sources can be matched properly, the analysis and its conclusions are suspect. When two sources are combined, the scholar's description of the data must not only sufficiently describe the data but it must also demonstrate that the matching is appropriate.

If the different sources of data are immediately compatible, the mechanical process of aligning the data involves moving the data and verifying the alignment. Moving is a matter of selectively inserting blank cells or deleting them, where one set of data does not include a record that the other set does have.

A function that identifies discrepancies verifies the matching and helps the alignment. That data are combined means that a single spreadsheet holds two or more sets of data. Proper alignment means that each label of each record of one set is identical with the label of the other sets in the same row, because each row holds the data for one record. If the data sets report statistics by city, the city names are repeated. If we have aligned the data correctly, the column that corresponds to city names in the first set of data and the equivalent column in the second set have the same city in every row.

A spreadsheet function that makes a comparison and reacts to its success or failure is the `IF` function. It takes two or three terms. The first term is the test or condition, the second term is the result that the function will produce if the condition is true, and the third term is the result if the condition is not true. The syntax is =`IF`(condition, true result, false result). Because we want to test the equivalence of the labels, the condition will be their equality. If it is true, the function could stay quiet, for example, by resulting in an empty string, "". If not true, the function should draw attention to the discrepancy, for example by returning a string like `"<-ERROR"`. If, for example, the labels are city names that are in columns B and L, the function in the third row could be =`IF(B3=L3, "", "<-ERROR")`. This can be placed in a cell to the right of the two data sets. Copying and pasting it in every cell of the column will make the comparison for every row.

Once we have the column of comparing `IF()` functions, we can easily identify discrepancies. We simply scroll down and easily cover voluminous data. It is important to remember, however, that the insertions and deletions of cells that align the data do have an influence on the functions. The references in the function to cells track the insertions and deletions. The result is that the `IF()` functions in rows below the insertion or deletion no longer compare labels in the same row. For example, the second set of data that has its labels in column L may include in row seven a city that is missing from the first set. Suppose we compensate by inserting cells A7 to K7. The `IF()` functions, from row seven and lower, adjust and compare the next row's city from column B with that in column L. The function in the seventh row, for instance, turns into =`IF(B8=L7, "", "<-ERROR")`. After each insertion or deletion, the `IF()` function from the top row must be copied and pasted in the column again.

F. Concluding Exercises

This chapter explained the principles of spreadsheets, the use of functions, absolute and relative referencing, and the production of graphics.

Dexterous use of all these features of Excel makes it an extraordinarily powerful tool for analysis and argumentation.

Visit the statistical resources clearinghouse of the University of Michigan at http://www.lib.umich.edu/govdocs/stats.html. Find data that may confirm or refute one of your hunches about changes that did or did not occur. Download the data into Excel and use its statistical tools to explore the events.

G. Bibliographical Note

Beginners may find helpful the reference book from the "for Dummies" series, Greg Harvey, *Excel 2000 for Windows for Dummies* (Foster City, CA: IDG Books Worldwide, 1999).

Users with more comfort may prefer *Statistics for Managers Using Microsoft Excel* by David M Levine (Upper Saddle River, NJ: Prentice Hall, 2002).

Macros are an advanced subject that might not tend to make particularly readable books. Most popular seem to be the books by John Walkenbach, *Excel 2002 Power Programming with VBA* (New York: John Wiley & Sons, 2001) and by Rob Bovey, Stephen Bullen, John Green, and Robert Rosenberg, *Excel 2002 VBA: Programmers Reference* (Indianapolis, IN: Wiley, 2003). Also useful may be the CD-ROM by Hans Herber and Bill Jelen, *Holy Macro! It's 1,600 Excel VBA Examples* (Uniontown, OH: Holy Macro! Books, 2002).

Astonishingly enough, scientific articles almost uniformly do not reveal the software and hardware that were used to perform the statistical analysis. Because occasional bugs can be discovered at later times that may influence the results, this practice is questionable. For example, it is likely that some scientific publications relied on statistics performed using the faulty Pentium III chips but it is impossible to know which, if any.[3]

The situation is hardly better in legal publishing. Few articles do acknowledge the software that they use or explain the detail regarding how they calculate their results. Those few include Nicholas L. Georgakopoulos, "Judicial Reaction to Change: The California Supreme Court around 1996 Elections," *Cornell Journal of Legal and Public Policy* 13 (2004):405–430; Gloria Jean Liddell, Pearson Liddell, Jr., and Stephen K. Lacewell, "Charitable Contributions in

---

[3] See note 1.

Bankruptcy: An Empirical Analysis," *American Business Law Journal* 39 (2001):99; Gregg G. Van Ryzin and Marianne Engelman Lado, "Evaluating Systems for Delivering Legal Services to the Poor: Conceptual and Methodological Considerations," *Fordham Law Review* 67 (1999):2553; Steven W. Rhodes, "An Empirical Study of Consumer Bankruptcy Papers," *American Bankruptcy Law Journal* 73 (1999):653; Michael Geist, "Fair.com?: An Examination of the Allegations of Systemic Unfairness in the ICANN UDRP," *Brooklyn Journal of International Law* 27 (2002):903; Kenneth N. Klee, "One Size Fits Some: Single Asset Real Estate Bankruptcy Cases," *Cornell Law Review* 87 (2002):1285.

13. Statistics

Statistical analysis probably conjures nightmares about matrix algebra. This chapter will avoid any reference to math. The goal here is to present statistics as a tool of contemporary reasoning and argument, without which legal thinkers cannot apply their training, vocation, or profession. Statistics is routinely used at trials and is used in a large portion of legal scholarship. A legal thinker – lawyer, legislator, law professor, or judge – cannot function without an understanding of statistics.

A subsidiary goal of this chapter is to show that statistics does not deserve the aura of quantitative inapproachability that it has in the legal community. Ubiquitous user-friendly software and powerful computers have turned statistics into a method of building facts into argument that is easy to deploy and is approachable to everyone, regardless of quantitative background.

Section A discusses how statistical methods are used in legal thinking. The focus is on assisting arguments about interpretation and rule making, rather than on establishing facts for the purpose of fact-finding at trials. Fact-finding uses statistical analysis directly and through experts, so a layman's guide is not necessary. Section C introduces the fundamental ideas of statistics. The concepts of the average and standard deviation enable the formation of expectations about occurrences of the data. The idea of distributions explains in greater detail how the outcomes are dispersed. Section D introduces empirical research by the use of statistical tests. Statistical tests are the tools used to construct arguments from the data. Statistical tests are used to reject hypotheses. They indicate whether the data is consistent with alternative theories about what the data should show.

This chapter assumes some minimal familiarity with spreadsheets. Those who do not have this familiarity can review Chapter 13.

A. THE USE OF STATISTICS IN LEGAL THINKING

For many, the possibility of empirical research is the principal advantage of the economic analysis of law. Such a belief clearly understates the contributions of law-and-economics theory. Yet, clearly, the empirical scholarship that has been produced by scholars related to the law-and-economics school has often been striking.

For statisticians and econometricians, the goal is not application of existing statistical methods, but the development of new ones. The skill that is necessary is the creative use of mathematical and statistical techniques coupled with economic reasoning and inference. In law, however, the innovative nature of statistical methods is irrelevant. The focus is on the normative value of the conclusions, namely, the importance of the lessons that the research can provide about the current shape of the legal system, its implications for social welfare, and the conclusions about legal change. Because the emphasis is not on cutting-edge statistics, and econometricians are effectively deterred from conducting mundane statistics, the field of simple applications of statistical tests is left open to the scholars in economic analysis of law.

Moreover, any difficulties with statistics and the aversion to quantitative methods that lawyers usually have need not be surmounted. The simple statistical tests are so much part of the culture that they are already programmed into commercial spreadsheet programs, such as Excel and QuatroPro. This chapter describes how anyone can use Excel to produce sound elementary statistics. There are vast fields for application of the basic empirical methods, which anyone who can use a spreadsheet can deploy. There is nothing methodologically special about Excel, other than that it is probably already installed on most researchers' computers.

The availability of software, however, does not make empirical research easy. The deployment of statistical methods is very difficult because statistical analysis cannot test for true causation. A statistical study that finds the outcome that a theory predicted does not validate the theory. Any other theory that would predict the same outcome has equal validity. This process of doubt is analogous to criminal defence: an alternative explanation of the evidence reduces the validity of the theory that the prosecution sought to advance with the evidence. Empirical research is inextricably linked with the corresponding theory that explains the outcome. The persuasive weight of empirical work is a joint product of evidence and theory. From the perspective of the sceptic, evidence never proves, it only disproves.

Despite this scepticism, empirical work in economic analysis of law can be fruitful. Some examples of successful empirical research can be seen in the work of Margaret Brinig, John Lott and John Donohue, and they come from opposite ends of the political spectrum.

Professor Brinig's work builds on the economic understanding of the inherent inequality of the bargaining position of man and woman in the marital relationship.[1] Women have a much shorter reproductive life cycle and their marital opportunities are more sensitive to age than those of men. This discrepancy is bound to influence bargaining power in the marriage and, in particular, in its breakdown. If the outside "marriage market" offers consistently inferior opportunities to wives rather than to husbands, wives will tend to compromise more to maintain the marriage. But the law can influence this discrepancy. Divorce law that punishes the spouse that is at "fault" is not perfectly gender neutral, because the party likely to abuse power tends to be the husband. Accordingly, strict divorce law balances the bargaining imbalance in the marriage. This theory would be an interesting curiosity, perhaps even an offensive stretch, if Professor Brinig had not been able to back it up with empirical support. She studied the change in the frequency of spousal abuse in states where divorce law changed. She found that upon the adoption of "no-fault" divorce, spousal abuse rose. Her hypothesis is that this was an expression of the phenomenon that husbands, freed from the penalty for fault, were taking advantage of their superior bargaining position. Granted, competing hypotheses might explain the same phenomenon. Even the competing hypotheses, however, would have to rest on a bargaining imbalance between the sexes. Therefore, this evidence supports Brinig's conception of family law as a legal remediation of bargaining imbalance.

John Lott's work avoids the problem of the persuasiveness of the theory that underlies the statistical evidence by examining directly the

---

[1] Lloyd Cohen, "Marriage, Divorce and QuasiRents; Or, 'I Gave Him the Best Years of My Life'," *Journal of Legal Studies* 16 (1987):267; Margaret F. Brinig and Steven M. Crafton, "Marriage and Opportunism," *Journal of Legal Studies* 23 (1994):869.

consequences of legal change, be it laws that allow civilians to carry handguns or the gaining of voting power by women.[2] In examining the impact of handguns, Lott compares the crime rates before and after the changes that allowed citizens to carry concealed firearms. Before the new laws, the type of license to carry a concealed firearm was issued at the discretion of the police. The legal change consisted of "shall issue" laws, which required the police to issue licenses to individuals who met their requirements. Lott considers carrying a concealed weapon as a powerful deterrent against crime. Part of its benefit is that it is a precaution that is not visible by the prospective criminal. Thus, concealed carrying also deters the crime that would have been directed at individuals who do not carry firearms. The LOJACK stolen vehicle recovery system has a similar property and was analyzed by different authors in a subsequent study.[3] Lott compared crime rates across the adoption of "shall issue" laws and found a strong effect on crime. He also studied drawbacks associated with gun ownership, such as accidents, and found that gun carry laws do not increase accidents.

John Donohue, writing with Steven Levitt, touches an issue even more explosive than handguns and universal suffrage.[4] They show that the universal availability of abortion after *Roe v. Wade* lowered crime 18 years later without reducing birth rates. The hypothesis is that the mandated availability of abortion allowed some women to avoid bearing some children that they did not have the capacity to nurture. The research also implies that the associative effect of badly educated children may be cumulative. The power of this evidence is astonishing, particularly compared with the earlier evidence that the mandated availability of abortion reduced the number of single-parent families. The reduction of single-parent families by the availability of abortion, is intuitive, but not dispositive from a normative perspective. The opponents of abortion can argue that its availability reduced marriages as well as single-parent families, and proceed to argue that the reduced number of two-parent families has socially deleterious effects, in addition to the social harm of abortion to social order. The evidence that

---

[2]   John R. Lott, Jr., and Lawrence W. Kenny, "Did Women's Suffrage Change the Size and Scope of Government?," *Journal of Political Economics* 107 (1999):1163–98.

[3]   Ian Ayres and Steven D. Levitt, "Measuring Positive Externalities from Unobservable Victim Precaution: An Empirical Analysis of Lojack," *Quarterly Journal of Economics* 113 (1998):43–77.

[4]   John J. Donohue, III, and Steven D. Levitt, "The Impact of Legalized Abortion on Crime," *Quarterly Journal of Economics* 116 (2001):379–420.

crime was reduced as an immediate – although temporally remote – consequence of abortion indicates that losses due to fewer marriages either did not exist or were swamped by the effect of the avoidance of undesirable births.

These are important pieces of scholarship that were conducted with simple statistical methods. They are significant contributions to legal thinking that cannot be ignored, definitely not with the excuse that statistical work is unapproachable to the uninitiated. Moreover, the simplicity of these methods, together with the lack of interest that econometricians have in deploying simple statistical methods, show that legal scholars are well positioned to do important statistical work. Legal scholars if they are to carry the burden of being the curators of the legal system, must know statistics.

B. Fundamentals: Descriptive Statistics and Distributions

Statistics is the science of aggregating data and using it to test the truth of hypothetical propositions. By aggregating data, statistical methods allow us to describe the group through figures called *descriptive statistics*. The most familiar of these is the *average* or *arithmetic mean*. The average allows us to form an expectation about the described feature.

A crucially important second descriptive statistic is a measure of dispersion or variability, that is, difference from the average. The intuitive measure of this would tell us how far from the average the outcomes are likely to be on average. This statistical measure exists. It is called *average deviation* or *mean deviation*, but it is used rarely. Instead, statisticians describe variability by using *standard deviation*, which involves squaring and taking square roots, which is not only unsettling to lawyers without a quantitative bent, but also removes any immediate intuitive understanding of either standard deviation or the variability that it implies. The advantage of standard deviation is due to familiarity. We know the likelihood of outcomes occurring within one standard deviation from the average, about 68 percent, and within two standard deviations, 95 percent. The true use of standard deviation is that it is the input to various statistical tests. The square of the standard deviation is called *variance*.

When we are given the mean and standard deviation, we can use the normal distribution to establish the exact probability that we obtain an outcome in any specified range. The mean and standard deviation coupled with the normal distribution form a complete description of the randomness of the outcomes, without need for modes, medians, quartiles, or any other descriptive statistics. Of course, the premise is that the outcomes do follow the normal distribution.

The normal distribution is of fundamental importance because the cumulation of randomness produces aggregates that follow the normal distribution.[5] Therefore, when studying complex outcomes, which are necessarily produced by numerous influences, the normal distribution is often the appropriate description of their random behavior. Departures from the normal distribution can be justified, as they are in the analysis of call options on stocks. Because stocks do not take negative values, the normal distribution is considered inappropriate and the lognormal distribution is used in its place.[6]

In statistical tests, three other distributions are often used, the t distribution or "Student's t" distribution, the χ distribution (pronounced so as to rhyme with pie), and the F distribution.

Other descriptive statistics, that are not used nearly as often, are the mode, median, quartiles, and percentiles. The *mode* is the value that occurs most frequently in the data. The *median* is the central value of the data. If the data were ranked by value, the middle value would be the median. If the median or mode differ significantly from the mean, this may indicate that the underlying distribution of the data is not symmetrical, which would also suggest that the use of normal distribution is likely not appropriate.

Quartiles communicate information about dispersion. Akin to the median, they are the values that occur at the one quarter count and the three quarter count of the data. The second quartile is the median. *Percentiles* function analogously.

C. EMPIRICAL RESEARCH

An empirical study must start with a detailed description of the sources of the data and provide a general statistical description of the data. Often, this may be enough and the researcher deploys no more than the descriptive statistics discussed in the preceding section. A description of the data and a detailed discussion of it may be very informative, even if devoid of statistical tests. If the focus is on the data's normative

---

[5] See Appendix C, describing the derivation by Gauss.
[6] See Chapter 11, discussing the derivation of the formula for valuing call options.

implications, rather than the statistical rigor of the research, such qualitative analysis may often have great contributions to make, perhaps even greater than "rigorous" quantitative research.

The very complex relationships that are likely to arise in the setting of a legal question are well suited to qualitative analysis. The data can be counted and measured, but even exceptionally rare details may be important for the law. To bring to the reader's attention this texture, some authors abandon numbers and discuss the stories behind some of the interesting data points. Chapter 11 discussed this author's study of the new value exception.[7] That work included a statistical analysis of new value opinions. An interesting perspective, however, was revealed by the more detailed examination of a few firms, the owners and employees of which tried to turn them around. Qualitative analysis is similar to the conventional legal method of analysis of judicial opinions. The principal difference is that instead of analyzing and comparing courts' holdings, the researcher analyzes and compares factual settings. Even if statistical analysis will follow, the descriptions of the actual dynamics of some data points may speak volumes.

Spreadsheet programs make quantitative statistical work quite easy. Two basic methods will be explained here: the comparison of averages of different samples, and the regression analysis known as ordinary least squares. The logit and probit regression and the use of *two-step* least squares are mentioned below as potentially useful advanced methods. Comparing averages or frequencies and regression are easy to do in an Excel spreadsheet. Logit, probit, and more advanced methods require specialized software. Their treatment here is not complete, but it illustrates the limits of the regression method, enhances reading comprehension, and points to the next statistical tool rather than directly sanctioning their use.

i. Basics: Comparing Data That Take Values and Data That Fall into Categories

Often, the only conclusion that we need to draw from the data is whether it is different from either a value or a different set of data. Data take values if they are measurable sizes, dimensions, or attributes,

---

[7] This analysis of the new value exception was discussed in Chapter 11. See also, Nicholas L. Georgakopoulos, "New Value, Fresh Start," *Stanford Journal of Law, Business and Finance* 3 (1997):125 *et seq.*; and Nicholas L. Georgakopoulos, "New Value, After *LaSalle*," *Bankruptcy Developments Journal* 20 (2003):1–24.

such as height or weight. Categorical data take one of a specified group of values. Take a historical event, such as the removal by the California electorate of three of the state's Supreme Court Justices in the 1986 elections. Consider the question of whether their careers on the bench were unusually short compared with the careers of previous justices. The duration of careers is measurable and takes a wide variety of values. The statistical answer to the question whether their careers were short is the outcome of a *statistical test*.

Consider alternatively the frequency with which justices voted for the death penalty during the period before the 1986 election. Votes for or against the death penalty are categorical data, where each datum takes a binary form – yes/no, vote for/against, success/failure, true/false. Again, a statistical test provided the answer of whether the frequency of the categories is unusual. A different test is required in such a case. In a way, noncategorical variables are easier to test, so we can cover them first.

The test of whether the average of a data set of values is different than a specified value or whether two subsets of the data have different average values is called a *t* test. Applied to a single sample, the *t* test establishes the probability of getting this sample from a process that produces random numbers that have a specific "target" mean. Statisticians call this (likely counterfactual) target a *null hypothesis*. Statistical tests are applied to reject it. As the probability that the data can arise by chance becomes smaller, the credibility of the existence of a difference increases. If we can say that the odds that a sample could be produced, given the null hypothesis, by chance is no more than 1 percent, this implies a 99 percent chance that the sample was produced by a different generative process.

The *t* test relies on a variation of the normal distribution called the *Student t* distribution because it was published under the pseudonym "Student." This also accounts for the statistical term *t test* for the test comparing means and *t stat[istic]* or *t ratio* for its intermediate product.

It is easy to conduct *t* tests in spreadsheets because most have two functions that help perform *t* tests, TDIST and TTEST. In the case of the single sample, the function that produces the probability that the sample could be due to chance is called the TDIST, and it takes as parameters the *t ratio*, the number of degrees of freedom, and the number of tails in our test. Thus, we would enter in one of the cells in an Excel spreadsheet =TDIST(x, y, z) and press Enter or an arrow key. The x should be the t ratio or, much more effectively, refer to a cell where the t ratio is calculated. The y should be or refer to the number of degrees of freedom. The degrees of freedom in a t test of a single sample are the number of data points minus one. The z should be 1 or 2 according to the number of tails (sides) of the bell curve that we want included in the test. Using a two-tailed test is usually the appropriate figure when seeking to reject a null hypothesis of equality. When the analysis can exclude one direction of the difference then a single-tailed test is appropriate. For example, if the analysis can preclude that more policing can lead to more crime, then the t test of whether increased policing decreased crime can be one-tailed.

To derive the t ratio, we need to establish the mean or average of the data and the estimate of the standard deviation of the random process that generated the data. The mean is calculated in spreadsheets by using the AVERAGE function, and the estimate of the standard deviation is calculated by the STDEV function. The t ratio is the difference of the average of our data from the value of the null hypothesis divided by the estimate of the standard deviation. The spreadsheet cell calculating the t ratio could be `=(AVERAGE(B1:B20)-D1)/STDEV( B1:B20)`, assuming that the data are stored in the cells B1 through B20 and the null hypothesis in cell D1. To avoid negative values, include the function that converts to absolute values, ABS, in which case the cell contents should be `=ABS(AVERAGE(B1:B20)-D1)/STDEV(B1:B20)`. There is no reason to include the STDEV in the ABS because the standard deviation is always positive.

In the comparison of two sub-samples, the t test produces the probability that the same generative process generates both subsets. A t test that produces a small probability that the two sets can be produced by the same "engine" lends credence to an argument that the difference in the data is attributable to a cause other than randomness.

The two sets of data are compared in Excel by placing the data in contiguous cells. Excel ignores empty cells, but the two "ranges" (areas or fields composed of multiple cells in a spreadsheet) of data to be compared must be contiguous. The test is performed by using the TTEST function, which takes as parameters the two ranges of data being compared, the number of "tails" in the test (usually 2) and the type of test being performed, paired, homoskedastic or heteroskedastic. The syntax is `TTEST(basedatarange, comparisondatarange, tails, type)` where the typical heteroskedastic test corresponds to a type of 3. The first two parameters are the ranges of the spreadsheet where

the data have been placed. If the base data are in cells B2 through
B12 and the comparison data are in D2 through D10, that segment
would read B2:B12, D2:D10. The third parameter is set to 2 so as to
specify a "2-tailed" test, and the fourth to 3 to specify a non-paired
comparison of unequal samples having changing dispersions (that are
"heteroskedastic"). Heteroskedasticity is a feature of the data according to which dispersion (standard deviation) of each data point may
be different. When that is acceptable, which is usually the case, a type
of 3 is appropriate. We will not encounter heteroskedasticity again.
A type parameter of 1 specifies a paired test, which we will also not
discuss here.

   A different path to the same outcome would use the TDIST function. The TDIST function produces the probability values that correspond to the *t* distribution. It takes as input the adjusted distance between the means being compared, the number of degrees of freedom
(in the case of the *t* test of two samples, total data points minus 2), and
whether the comparison is one- or two-tailed (usually two-tailed). If a
study reports *t* stats, those can be placed inside the TDIST function to
determine the probability of no difference that they imply. If the data
for the *t* test are not directly available – if, for example, the comparison
is against the mean, standard deviation and count reported by a source,
the TDIST function can be used to perform the *t* test.

   The formula for the distance between means relies on the mean of
the compared populations – the AVERAGE function of Excel – and the
estimate of the standard deviation of their generative process – the
STDEV function – as opposed to the actual standard deviation of
the data, which is STDEVP in Excel. Statistics books offer versions of the
formula for adjusting the distance of the means for *t* tests, depending on
the situation, primarily the number of observations being compared.
If you find yourself using a particular one consistently, consider programming it into an Excel user-defined function.

   Functions are akin to macros, but they take values as input and
return a value as output so that they can be used in spreadsheet
cells. Macros, by contrast, usually manipulate the spreadsheet itself.
The user defines functions in the Visual Basic Editor – enter it from
Tools\Options\Macro\Editor or by hitting Alt-F11. They are defined by entering into a "module" (select your spreadsheet in
the top left window and choose \Insert\Module) the lines Function *functionname* (*functionparameters*) and End Function
(Excel enters this automatically) and between them the calculation

of the function. The result is conveyed to the spreadsheet by being assigned to the name of the function in one of the last lines of the function.

The following example takes six values as input, which are the base data mean (m1), standard deviation (s1), and count (n1), and the same statistics of the comparison data (m2, s2, and n2, respectively) and uses them in a user-defined function called "tstat" which produces the *t* stat that can be used as input in the TDIST function.[8] The first line defines the function – its name and the parameters it receives when it is called, assigns names to those parameters – the next three lines assign values to three new parameters (called param1 to param3), while the fifth line uses those to complete the calculation and assigns the result to the name of the function. The final line concludes the function:

```
Function tstat(m1,s1,n1,m2,s2,n2)
param1=(n1-1)*s1^2+ (n2-1)*s2^2
param2=n1+n2-2
param3=1/n1+1/n2
tstat=Abs(m1-m2)/Sqr((param1/param2)*param3)
End Function
```

The function takes the six parameters, m1, s1, n1, m2, s2, and n2, and uses their values to perform a sequence of calculations. The function computes three intermediate values, param1, param2, and param3. It then uses those three intermediate parameters in an equation to assign a value to the name of the function itself. This way, the result is passed back to the spreadsheet. The user can type =tstat(a,b,c,d,e,f) in a cell and obtain the *t* stat for the six variables passed to the function. Those can be numbers or references to cells that contain the averages, standard deviations, and counts for the two sets of data. Of course, the tstat function is most useful used inside the TDIST function, as in TDIST(tstat(a,b,c,d,e,f), g, 2). At this book's Web site, www.pmle-nlg.org, you can download a spreadsheet named LawEcMethods.xls, which contains the tstat function.

Whether one uses the TTEST function or applies a distance-of-means formula to the TDIST function, both produce the same result. They display the probability that the same process may have produced

---

[8] The formula is from Spence, Cotton, Underwood, and Ducan, *Elementary Statistics* (Englewood Cliffs, NJ: Prentice Hall), 4th ed. (1983) equation 10.6, p. 172.

the two sets of data (or, more accurately, that these samples would be observed if the means of the two processes were equal).[9] In principle, this number under the single-tailed test can range from 50 percent to almost 0. The intuition behind the 50 percent maximum is that if both populations have the same means, then the probability that the comparison data have a higher or lower mean than the base data is 50 percent, even odds). Therefore, to be convincing that the two are truly different, the research should produce a low figure. Traditional hurdles of "confidence levels" are 10 percent, 5 percent, and 1 percent.

Many econometric works do not report probabilities but t stats. These t stats are the input into the t distribution that would produce the appropriate probability that the two samples have the same mean. Reporting t stats instead of probabilities may be useful to readers who are very familiar with t tests, but it does not make sense for a lay audience such as the audience of legal scholarship. To the lay audience the measure that seems most accessible is the probability that there is no difference, what the TTEST and TDIST functions report. Statisticians call this probability the "p value." This short label is convenient for presenting results in tables, where one of the columns or the rows can be labelled "p value" instead of "probability difference is due to chance."

If the data do not take multiple values but are divided into categories, the appropriate test for determining whether their division among those categories is different than the expected is the χ test, pronounced chi-test (where chi rhymes with pie). The idea is to determine whether a given categorical outcome – such as the number of votes for capital punishment, or the number of graduates who chose different legal careers – is different from the expected. In essence the chi-test is a test of difference of frequencies. It returns the probability that the frequency of an outcome in the comparison data can be the result of an expected frequency, the frequency of the base data or an overall frequency, depending on which we will use as a foundation for the expected frequency.

Again, Excel offers a function that performs χ tests and gives the probability of obtaining the observed frequencies. The function is CHITEST. It takes two parameters, the range with the comparison

---

[9] In technical terms, the "null hypothesis" is that both sets were produced by the same mean. Even in this case, in some rare case, the two samples will differ enough to reject the null hypothesis. Then the p-value gives the probability that observed differences in the data would arise if the null hypothesis was true.

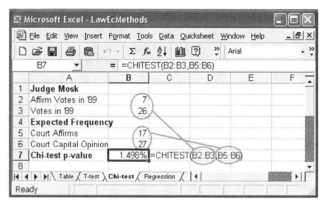

Figure 13.1. A χ test in Excel.

data and the range with the expected data. Both ranges must have the same shape and size. The syntax is CHITEST (*comparison-frequencies, expectedfrequencies*).

A simple example of a χ test can be seen in comparing a binary variable, judges' votes in capital cases. Take the question whether Judge Mosk in 1989 voted in a way different than his court, the California Supreme Court. The court performs appellate review of death penalty opinions, which means that it only reviews the propriety of the reasoning of the lower courts, not the merits of the case independently. The court issued 26 capital punishment opinions, and 17 of those affirmed the imposition of the death penalty, whereas the remaining nine found error with the lower courts' opinions. Judge Mosk only cast 7 affirming votes in 26. We could ask what is the likelihood that the court's standards for what is error are the same with Mosk's by comparing the frequency with which they find error. The comparison data are 7 in 26. Suppose we place those numbers in cells B2 and B3 of a spreadsheet. We consider 17 in 27 the expected outcome and place those values in cells B5 and B6. Those two ranges are passed to the CHITEST function. Figure 13.1 displays the resulting spreadsheet. The probability that Judge Mosk votes were generated by the same mechanism that generated the votes of the court is given by CHITEST (B2 : B3, B5 : B6), which evaluates to 1.5 percent.

The advantage of the χ test is that it can be used on a broader number of categories than binary categorizations such as voting for or against the capital punishment. Again, the CHITEST function is sufficient to produce results, but some attention must be paid to the construction of the expected frequencies. Perhaps it is easiest to visualize the data as a table, where the categories are the different rows, and the alternative subsets that will be compared are in columns. The categories hold the count of occurrences within each subset. The categories may be votes allocated among several alternatives or choices made between several types of careers, and so forth. The subsets may be different elections or different graduating classes. The question answered by the χ test is what is the probability that the proportion of votes or career choices is identical across elections or graduating classes? A small value lends confidence to the idea that the frequencies change over the subsets.

In constructing the expected frequencies, we must construct an expectation for each entry in the table of rows and columns of frequencies, the categories and subsets of the data. The exact way in which expectations should be calculated depends on the hypothesis that the research is trying to reject, the "null hypothesis." If the null hypothesis is equal division across categories, each estimated frequency cell should contain the sum of all categories for this subset divided by the number of categories. In other words each cell in the expected frequency range should contain the sum of the corresponding column of data divided by the number of rows of data.

An example of such a study could be a study of the outcomes of two six-sided dice for fairness. Suppose we observe 600 tosses and record the result of each die. After we count the ones, the twos, through the sixes for the first die, we repeat for the second. The result is a six-row, two-column body of data. The comparison data would have the total outcomes in each column, 600, divided by the six sides of the dice, namely 100. The χ test would give the probability that the dice are similar and fair.

A more likely null hypothesis would be that all subsets are allocated between categories in the same way. In other words that each cell contains the same proportion of that cell's column as that row's overall proportion of the total population. The comparison data has to be the sum of the row divided by the sum of the table – this ratio is the proportion allocated to this category over the entire data – multiplied by the sum of the column. An example is necessary.

Suppose the data consist of the number of law school graduates that enter each of private practice, academia, and government. The subsets consist of three years of data, from 1975, 1985, and 1995. The null hypothesis is that the ratio of each class making each career choice is constant. Each comparison cell will hold the ratio making that choice

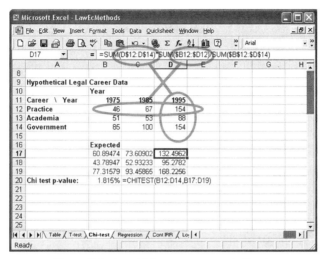

Figure 13.2. A multiple category χ test in Excel.

in the overall data, multiplied by the number of graduates for this year. In the case of graduates entering private practice, the ratio would be the sum of all graduates entering private practice – the sum of the row – divided by the sum of all graduates. The ratio would then be multiplied by each year's number of graduates to determine the number of graduates that would have entered private practice for that year, if they entered private practice with the overall ratio.

Figure 13.2 shows a possible spreadsheet of such a test in Excel. If the data are entered in Excel into rows 12 through 14 and columns B through D, the top-left cell in the expected frequencies range can contain=SUM(B$12:B$14)*SUM($B12:$D12)/SUM($B$12:$D$14). When this formula is copied and pasted across and down to fill a 3×3 range, the references to rows or columns that are preceded by "$" signs do not change, but all others are updated so as to refer to the next row or column. The first term, for example will remain unchanged in the two cells under it, but will refer to columns C and D when pasted to the next two columns. The ability to alternate between references that are fixed and references that are relative (and, therefore, change with copying into other cells) is one of the most convenient features of spreadsheets. As it is, this function operates as follows on the sums of column, row, and all data: column*row/all.

The CHITEST function should then refer to the two sets of data, the actual frequencies and the expected frequencies. The actual frequencies were placed, above, in cells B12:D14. If the expected frequencies are in cells B17 through D19, the function would take the form CHITEST(B12:D14, B17:D19). Its result is the probability that these allocations can be observed if the true allocation of career choices is constant. The example of the California Supreme Court votes on capital sentencing and that on the constancy of career choice are also in the online sample spreadsheet.

In sum, the simplest question that we can ask of data is whether they can be the product of chance. The t test and the χ test provide those probabilities.

ii. Determining Influences: Multiple Outcomes

Regression analysis seems to be everywhere in empirical scholarship, and with good reason. It is an extremely easy tool that is also very powerful. Regression analysis can determine the influence of each explanatory variable to the outcomes. It looks for and imposes a simple structure, that of an influence that changes at a constant rate, that is, a linear relation between the outcome variable and the explanatory variables. The regression essentially places the explanatory variable on the x axis and the outcome variable on the y axis, and it draws a straight line such that the line is the closest possible to all data points. In mathematical terms, regression tries to produce the coefficients a and b to produce the equation $y = a + b * x$ that closest fits the data, which are the several x and y. The a is also called the intercept and the b (or the several b's in the case of multiple regression, which takes the form $y = a + b1 * x1 + b2 * x2 \ldots$) is called the regression coefficient.

The function of regression analysis may become clearer through a graphical demonstration using a simple example. Suppose that the data consist of four observations of the crime rate against the number of police per person. According to the FBI's Uniform Crime Report of 2000, Boston, Wilmington, Hartford, and Philadelphia had estimated crime numbers of 106,761, 13,661, 39,424, and 216,479 crimes, respectively, with metropolitan populations of 3,469 thousand, 217 thousand, 1,046 thousand, and 4,945 thousand residents. According to a contemporary Directory of Law Enforcement Agencies of the Bureau of Justice Statistics, the police departments of these cities employed 2,850, 289.5, 625, and 7,370 full-time-equivalent individuals (counting part-time employees as half) and served populations of 548, 73, 124, and 1,524 thousand, respectively.

Note that the Uniform Crime Report aggregates metropolitan areas, but the directory does not; this discrepancy will have to be addressed in the design of the study. Can these data tell us something about the relationship between police and crime? Because the cities have different sizes, we must convert police and crime into ratios. An intuitive measure would be police per 1,000 residents and crimes per 1,000 residents. It is a simple matter to place the necessary equation, 1,000*police/population in a cell in the row that corresponds to Boston, referring to the cells that hold the values for police and population for Boston. After doing the same for crimes, copy and paste down to the other cities. The relative references automatically update the formulas, saving the effort of typing them again.

This is the stage for harmonizing the metropolitan reporting of the Uniform Crime Report with the reporting by city of the Directory. Compute the police ratio by dividing by the city population as reported by the Directory, while computing the crime rate by dividing the metropolitan number of crimes by the metropolitan population of the Uniform Crime Report.

The results are 5.2 police and 30.7 crimes for Boston, 3.97 police and 62.9 crimes for Wilmington, 5.03 police and 37.7 crimes for Hartford, and 4.84 police and 43.8 crimes for Philadelphia. Spreadsheet software uses the function LINEST to calculate a straight line passing closest to the four points (5.2, 30.7), (3.97, 62.9), (5.03, 37.7), and (4.84, 43.8). LINEST takes as parameters the range of outcome variables, the range of explanatory variables, and two logical parameters. If the first is set to TRUE, then Excel does not impose a crossing at the origin, and if the second is set to TRUE, then Excel produces several additional statistics. Because the intercept must not be forced to be at the origin and the additional statistics are necessary to properly report the statistical conclusions of the regression, it is important not to omit the two "true" parameters.

Because the LINEST function returns several values, Excel requires us to place the function in several cells concurrently to obtain all the statistics it produces. Excel's documentation calls this type of function an "array formula." For Excel to treat a function as an array formula, it must be entered by pressing Ctrl-Shift-Enter instead of a simple Enter or arrow key. Moreover, for the array formula to present all its results, it must occupy several cells. This is done by first selecting the many cells, then typing the formula, and ending with a Ctrl-Shift-Enter.

The number of cells that LINEST occupies depends on the number of explanatory variables. The width of the output range of LINEST is one column wider than the number of explanatory variables. Each column is devoted to one variable and one more column is used for the intercept.

The number of rows that LINEST produces is constant, always five (in the extended output that we have chosen by using "true" as its last parameter). The first row consists of the estimates (called *betas*) of the influence of each explanatory variable and the estimate of the intercept. The second row holds the standard errors of each of these estimates. The other rows are only two cells wide. The third row holds the "R-squared" (R^2) and the standard error of the estimated y. These are important statistics that influence the confidence that one can place in the results of the regression. The fourth row holds the "f stat" and the number of degrees of freedom. Those are necessary for the computation of the probability that the results of the regression are due to chance, the F test. The last row holds the "regression sum of squares" and the "sum of squared errors," which will not occupy us any further. All these are described in the help files of Excel, which are accessible through the F1 key if they are installed and the Office Assistant disabled, as explained in Chapter 12. These statistics are worth a close look.

The betas and the intercept are the principal output of the regression. They state the influence that the explanatory variables have on the outcome variable according to the data. In the example of our four-city crime rate study, we obtained an estimate of the effect of changes in the police per population and an estimate of the intercept. The estimate of the intercept is in the rightmost column and the estimates for the other explanatory variables are in reverse order, the first column reporting the estimate for the variable that was in the last column of explanatory variables. According to the data for the three cities, the intercept is 163.8 crimes and the effect of one additional enforcement officer is −25.2 crimes. In other words, each police officer per 1,000 population prevents 25 crimes annually, and with no police, these cities would have about 164 crimes per 1,000 residents. Even though both these statements correspond to the regression coefficients, they are both naive and false in particular, the latter. The lack of any police would present a vastly different environment of crime than that existing in these cities. Taking the conclusions of a regression and applying them outside the range of values studied by the regression – what is called extrapolation as opposed to interpolation – is highly suspect.

Let us continue analyzing the output of LINEST before we return to the fallacies of this example.

The second row contains the standard errors for the coefficients that were reported in the first row. Because the regression analysis is making an estimate, the error with which this estimate is made is crucial. The standard error is used to reject hypotheses about the coefficients. Most often the hypothesis to be rejected is that the explanatory variable has no effect on the outcome variable. That is a simple t test. Apply the TDIST to the estimate divided by its error using the regression's degrees of freedom to determine its statistical significance. Because the estimate for the influence of the police is negative, take the absolute value by using Excel's ABS function.

The R^2 measures what fraction of the variation in the outcome variable is explained by the variation of the explanatory variables. This is an essential measure of how much the regression explains. In this regression example, the R^2 is more than 98 percent, which is astoundingly high. It suggests that the crime rate is almost deterministically set by the policing rate. We are justified in being suspicious of this, as we will see.

The R^2 should be reported for every regression – and it always is – but if we focus on statistical significance and forget about R^2 the result may be misleading. An example of such a misleading conclusion is that it may be the cause of the fury unleashed against *The Bell Curve*, the book of Herrnstein and Murray that presented voluminous statistical evidence that race and wealth had a significant effect on success. The regressions were statistically significant as far as t tests, χ tests, and F tests were concerned. Therefore, the *Bell Curve*'s thesis was consistent with the evidence. Little attention was placed on the R^2 values, however, and they were telling a very different story. Many of their regressions, despite their statistical significance, had R^2 in the teens or even lower. Their very first regression of poverty against schooling on p. 595–96 is a typical example, with R^2 of 10 percent for the entire sample and 6 percent for the high school sub-sample. This indicates that the effect that the regression found explained only a very small fraction of the difference in individuals' success. A low R^2 should also make the regression results suspect. If these explanatory variables do not explain the behavior of the outcome variable, perhaps other variables or a different theory explain them better. In the example of the *Bell Curve*, perhaps the quality of the schools is the better predictor of success, and race and wealth are simply related to school quality.

The standard error of the y estimate performs a function similar to R^2. This error applies to attempts to calculate the expected result for a hypothetical set of explanatory variables. This, in other words, is the error we will encounter if we deploy the regression to predict an outcome. We can use the normal distribution to determine that about 68 percent of the time the outcome will be within one error from its prediction, and 95 percent of the time within two errors. Although the standard error is so obviously important in practical applications of the regression, it is often not reported in scholarly studies because the R^2 conveys intuitively information that is analogous.

The last two statistics that will occupy us are the F stat and the degrees of freedom. LINEST places both in the fourth row of its output. The F stat is the input to the calculation of the regression's overall likelihood to be due to chance, which is called an F test. In other words, we can use the F stat to establish the level of confidence that the regression's results are due to some cause as opposed to randomness.

As in the case of the t test and the χ test, this confidence is again stated as the probability that the regression's outcome is due to chance. This time the probability is calculated by the Excel function FDIST, which takes three parameters as input, the F stat reported by LINEST and two different counts of degrees of freedom. The second parameter is the number of explanatory variables in the regression plus one, or the number of columns in LINEST's output (provided it is shaped correctly). The last parameter is the degrees of freedom reported by LINEST. For the regression to be a credible account of the influence of the explanatory variables on the outcomes, the output of the FDIST function must be a small percentage. In the case of our four-city crime model, the p-value produced is very reassuring. The FDIST function reports that the odds of these results occurring by chance are 0.69 percent. Again, we will see, the numbers are misleading.

It is time now to return to the fallacy of the regression that we used as an example. Before engaging the technical errors, we should pause on its underlying theory, that the crime rate is correlated to the size of police staff. It turns out that the Bureau of Justice Statistics also reports the number of sworn officers and the number of officers in various categories in significant detail. The data allow a verification of the conclusion that staff deters. Perhaps officers deter and bureaucrats do not. But perhaps officers without administrative support are ineffective.

I am conceding so far the premise that the size of police departments is related to deterrence. We only need to construct a plausible
alternative hypothesis to undermine the support of the evidence for
this theory. An obvious direction to search for a theory explaining both
low crime rates and numerous police is economic prosperity. Because
the data do not contain economic variables, one can easily argue that
what appears as deterrence is in fact driven by economics. An alternative theory explaining the same data can be formed by borrowing a
line from John Lott's research on the effect of laws about firearms and
hypothesizing that perhaps cities with more conservative politics have
both liberal firearm "carry" laws and more police, but the deterrent
effect is due to the firearm carry laws rather than to the number of
police.

We can continue formulating alternative theories. The data validate
equally all the theories that are consistent with the data. For empirical
research to validate one rather than any other of these theories, the
competing ones must be tested and rejected. To reject these two examples, we would need to add economic and cost-of-living data to test
the hypothesis that crime and police are both driven by prosperity, and
to add data about gun carry laws.

This is the greatest weakness of empirical research. Statistical evidence only displays correlations; it cannot prove causation. The persuasiveness of the theory advanced by the empirical research may have
little to do with the evidence and much to do with its other appeal.

That empirical evidence can rarely prove theories does not detract
from its usefulness. Evidence can be fascinating even if it is offered
without a theory, in which case it invites explaining and theorizing
about the paradoxes displayed by the evidence. Just like good theory,
empirical work is at its best when it is paradoxical and counterintuitive.

Let us return to the fallacies of our regression. Let us consider
whether the conclusions of the regression should be applicable to
Miami and to Atlantic City. Both are vastly different from the cities
of the sample. Miami is alleged to be a port city in the trade of illegal
drugs. Moreover, Miami's ratio of police to population is lower than in
the other cities. Applying the regression's model to derive the crime
rate of Miami would be to extrapolate without any justification.

Miami's police force numbers 3.64 per 1,000 residents according
to the Directory. According to our regression, its expected crime rate
should be $163.7 + (-25.2) \times 3.64 = 72.5$. According to the error of our
y estimate, 68 percent of the time the crime rate of such a city should

be between $72.5 - 2 = 70.5$ and $72.5 + 2 = 74.5$ and 95 percent of the time between 68.5 and 76.5. In fact, it is 98.3 crimes per 1,000 residents.

Atlantic City presents an even more different environment. In contrast with the other cities, in which residents engage in various manufacturing and service jobs, Atlantic City is dominated by the provision of a particular entertainment service, gambling. The consumers of the service are primarily non-residents and grounds may exist to suspect that the crime rate in Atlantic City is not related to the number of residents of the city as in other cities, except Las Vegas, perhaps.

The numbers support the theory that Atlantic City is different. With 11.2 police per 1,000 residents, we would expect Atlantic City to have less crime than any city on our sample. The crime rate of Atlantic City, however, is 66 per 1,000 residents. The model would have predicted $163.8 + (-56.1)*11.2 = -118$. Of course, this is extrapolation taken to an extreme. The 11.2 police per thousand residents of Atlantic City are so far out of the range of values that the explanatory variable takes in the regression data, that applying the regression produces the uninformative estimate of a negative crime rate.

Neither Miami nor Atlantic City refutes the model if we can argue them out of the sample, but they also suggest that the model is incomplete. Take the lessons of Atlantic City. Perhaps the model should take into account the city's gambling attraction, either as a variable that takes many values – examples would be number of casinos, game tables, or annual casino hotel room visitors – or as a dummy variable that only takes 0 and 1 values, assigned by the researcher, to study a binary explanatory effect. Casino cities would get a value of 1 in their casino city dummy variable, and all other cities would have a 0. The regression coefficient of the casino city variable would estimate the additional crime rate due to this property of the city. Other examples of explanatory effects that could be dummy variables would be whether the city is a state capital, is a university city, or has a major-league team.

The use of dummy variables should be well justified. Overusing dummy variables also creates the possibility of an impossible model, one where no role is played by the intercept. For example, we cannot use two dummy variables, one for casino city and one for lack of casinos, because they are mutually exclusive and would take over the role of the intercept. Using only the casino city dummy variable lets us predict crime for both types of cities. The casino city beta coefficient explains

Crimes per 1000

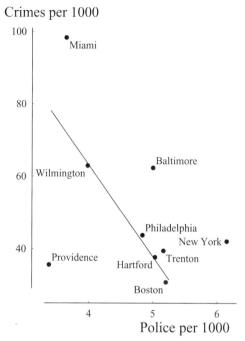

Figure 13.3. Linear regression.

the additional crime, and the intercept is the basis for comparison if the city is not a casino city.

Similar errors are possible with variables that take many values. Having a variable with the number of professional sports teams, for example, would interact with a dummy variable of whether the city has a major-league sports team. Such errors may be identified by LINEST and result in errors being reported by the LINEST function, but not necessarily. The best safeguard is to have a well-reasoned regression model. The role of each variable must be clearly understood and its inclusion in the regression must be justified.

To see a further possible error in this regression of crime on police, let us bring into the sample a few more data points, a few more cities: Providence, Trenton, New York, Miami, and Baltimore (see Figure 13.3). Let us leave Atlantic City out of the sample, conceding that it may be too different.

Running the regression with the new sample is very instructive. The R^2 drops from 98.6 percent to 21.2 percent, the standard error of y increases from 2 to more than 20. The t tests and the F test all indicate the results may well be random. The probability that the police rate has no effect on crime is 21 percent, and the odds that the regression results are due to chance are 22 percent.

We can get a visual grasp of the change by looking at the data points that are the basis for the regression. In Excel we can easily produce a graph by highlighting the two adjacent columns of crime and police and clicking on the chart-wizard tool button, which looks like a bar graph. After clicking the chart-wizard button, the next screen asks about the chart type. We must choose X-Y Graph, so that the two columns are used as x and y coordinates. We can then click on the "Finish" button, leaving the default choices for the other options.

The resulting graph is several points in the x-y plane. Each represents a city. If the police rate was on the left one of the highlighted columns, the horizontal x axis corresponds to the police and the y axis to the crime rate. Clicking and leaving the cursor on a particular point brings up its coordinates. From the coordinates we can determine to which city each point corresponds. Our original cities lie on a single sloping line. The additional cities do not line up as nicely. The model of the original regression fitted a line along Wilmington, Philadelphia, Hartford, and Boston. After deriving this line, the regression statistics showed great confidence in the predictive abilities of that model. Now that more cities have been added, the data no longer lie on a single line. The statistics reported by LINEST show lack of confidence. The reason for the lack of confidence should be apparent in Figure 13.3. The data points do not line up. The conclusions from the simple model were false and misleading because those cities were selected on the basis of this graph, so that they would line up and validate a regression model. The power of handpicking should also show how strongly the biases of the researcher can influence the result. By formulating a reason to leave Miami, Providence, and Baltimore out of the sample, the researcher can turn random dots into powerful statistics.

The graphical representation of the data also shows that a look at the graph may be worth much more than any table calculating statistical figures. A look at the graph also lets the researcher know about the nature of the data, such as whether a certain explanatory variable has a linear, escalating, or decreasing effect, or whether it is more appropriately modeled by a dummy variable.

The possibility of seeing graphical representations of the data does not end when we have more than one explanatory variable. Granted, we can no longer use a straightforward x-y graph. The idea is to graph one of the explanatory variables along the x axis. Along the y axis we must not place the actual outcome data, because part of their variation is explained by the explanatory variables that do not appear in the figure. The y axis must show the deviation of the actual outcome from the prediction ignoring the variable of the x axis. To do this we calculate a predicted value on the basis of the actual explanatory variables that are not displayed and a common constant value of the explanatory variable we want to examine. This common value can be the minimum, or the average value of the variable we are graphing. From the actual value of the outcome variable, we subtract the value we computed according to the regression's other variables, keeping the chosen explanatory variable constant. The result is values of the difference of the outcome variable from the regression's prediction for it, ignoring the variation in one explanatory variable. When this explanatory variable becomes the x-coordinate on the graph, and the differences computed above become the y coordinates, we are forming a graphical representation of the variation in the outcome variables that are not explained by other variables (on the y axis) against the one variable (on the x axis). This way we can see whether a pattern exists with respect to each variable in isolation.

An example is necessary. Suppose we run a regression with two explanatory variables, police authorized to make arrests and the ratio of other staff to officers. The idea behind this model is that perhaps police authorized to arrest do deter crime, but other enforcement staff only deters to the extent it renders the arresting police more effective. Too little support staff may be as incapacitating as too much bureaucracy. It is interesting to note that the effect of this term is expected not to be linear, because the crime rate should be expected to drop as small ratios of staff to officers approach the optimal, but then decline when the ratio exceeds the optimal. Although regression analysis imposes a linear structure on the data, some nonlinear relationships can be explored.

To explore nonlinear relations, the explanatory variables, the x data, must undergo some transformation. More intuitive transformations are to square some of them or to multiply one by a dummy variable, making it disappear when the dummy is zero. A less intuitive transformation is the "taking of logs." This rests on a mathematical relation of logarithms. The sum of logarithms of numbers is equal to the logarithm of their product. This process of "taking logs" converts a multiplicative relation ($y = x1*x2$) to a linear one ($\ln(y) = \ln(x1) + \ln(x2)$) so that the linear regression model can be applied. Special care must be taken in this case because the reported statistics regard the logarithms rather than the variables before their transformation.

Despite these numerical tricks, which somewhat broaden the reach of regression analysis, it remains a tool of limited scope. Regression analysis cannot be applied to complex relations. The idea that the ratio of staff to officers has an optimal, for example, is one such relation, too complex to be explored by using the linear regression. A graphical presentation of the errors might have been able to unveil such a relation. That would require regressing crime against officers, subtracting the actual crime from the estimate, and creating a graph where those errors are on the y axis and the cities staff-to-officer ratio is on the x axis. Although this sounds promising – despite being statistically unapproved – it does not produce the desired results in practice. The resulting graphic can be seen in the sheet "Data" of the LawEcMethods.xls spreadsheet.

iii. Determining Influences: Yes/No Outcomes

Regression analysis is appropriate if the outcomes being studied take many values. If outcomes are binary – yes/no, true/false, success/failure – then regression analysis fails because there is no line to be fitted. If we visualize the binary outcomes on the y axis and the (single) explanatory variable on the x axis, the data take the form of points along two horizontal lines, failures along zero and successes along 1. Using regression analysis for "fitting" a line is wrong. Instead, statisticians have developed a method two variations of which, "logit" or logistic regression and "probit," try to match the distribution of successes and failures to a probability distribution tied to the explanatory variables.

The logit and probit methods can be analogized to a "cumulative" histogram of successes. Take as an example of an outcome variable the question of whether an individual who went through bankruptcy 3 years ago is actively employed depending on pre-bankruptcy salary. The outcome variable is binary: employed or not. The explanatory variable takes many values. Some individuals may remain unemployed at every salary level. The frequency of this, however, may be systematically related (or inversely related) to pre-bankruptcy income.

To determine this relationship, logit and probit analysis checks whether the fraction of successes/trues/ones in the data (as opposed to

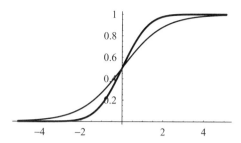

Figure 13.4. The curves that correspond to probit and logit.

failures/falses/zeros) increases or decreases as pre-bankruptcy salaries increase. In essence, the data are parsed into a running tally of the fraction of successes above and below this level of income. Suppose the overall "success" rate is 70 percent. The fraction of successes may range from 50 percent to 85 percent. If the fraction of successes increases as salaries increase, the salary will receive a positive coefficient, indicating that a higher salary increases the probability of being employed. Probit tries to fit the fraction of successes, given the salary level, to a cumulative normal distribution as a function of salaries. Logit fits it to the logistic equation, $e^x/(1 + e^x)$. The probability of success given the explanatory variables is equal to that produced by the normal distribution equation or the logistic if they take as input the results of the regression.[10]

Figure 13.4 illustrates the difference of the two functions. It displays the cumulative distribution functions that correspond to the two regressions. The standard normal distribution, illustrated by the heavier line, is steeper.

In both the cases of logit and of probit, the actual coefficients that are produced by the regression are not particularly intuitive. Usually, the reported results try to convey the underlying effect by stating the change in the probability of the outcome given a unit change in the explanatory variable. An example of such a statement would be that

---

[10] In mathematical notation, probit selects the value of a and b to fit the model $\Pr(y \neq 0|x) = N(a + b^*x)$, where $N(\cdot)$ is the cumulative normal distribution, whereas logit selects them to fit $\Pr(y \neq 0|x) = e^{(a+b^*x)}/(1 + e^{(a+b^*x)})$. This means that logit and probit create a function $a + b^*x$ of the explanatory variables (the various x), such that the probability that each outcome is a success, given its explanatory variable, is equal to either the cumulative normal distribution valued at the result of this function of the explanatory variables, or equal to the logistic equation valued at the result of this function.

the likelihood of being employed after a bankruptcy filing increases by 2 percent for every 1,000 of pre-bankruptcy income.

Unfortunately, neither logit nor probit can be easily performed on Excel. They require the use of dedicated statistical software. The programs SPSS and particularly STATA appear to have become the standards. They include a wealth of available statistical tests, which are documented unusually well in their manuals.

iv. Observations That Are Filtered by a Threshold

Other types of statistical analysis that will not be pursued in depth here are (a) the instrumental variable or two-stage regression and (b) Heckman's two-step regression. Both were developed by Heckman and rely on interactions between the explanatory variables (the x). In the instrumental variable regression, some of the explanatory variables may influence another, which influences the dependent variable (the y). In the second case of the two-step regression, some observations of the dependent variable may be missing, depending on the corresponding explanatory variable (the x). For example, when studying salaries of a group depending on their education, the least educated may be unable or unwilling to obtain employment. Therefore, the observed salaries exist conditional on education.

The use of the two-step regression becomes necessary when the observed data are missing observations that do not meet some necessary criteria. The methods are particularly apt when analyzing what factors contribute to reach a status that not all units achieve. For example, in the context of law students, one would need to use this method to ascertain what attributes contribute to admission in law school. If the data comprise only law students, the data do not reveal the full variation of each attribute in the population. If law school students have high grades from their previous institution, the data do not include all such grades in the population. Systematically, those with low grades do not become law students.

These methods use the ideas of the truncated and censored distributions that we saw in the chapter on probability theory. They extrapolate the shape of the entire distribution given that the data represent only a segment of it. Such analysis cannot be done easily in a spreadsheet. Like logit and probit, these methods require the use of specialized statistical software.

D. Concluding Exercises

Exercise 13.1: Compare statistics with other methods of aggregating evidence. How different is a factual statement made through statistics from a factual statement made by several witnesses? How different is a statement of causation made through statistics from one made by an expert in that field?

Discussion: Statistics aggregate evidence and test hypotheses. Statistical analysis, however, does not assign causation. The hypotheses tested may include causation but the test is limited to the relation (or correlation) between variables rather than the mechanism of cause and effect. The transition from the fact of a correlation to a theory of cause and effect is a major leap. Regardless of how strong the factual statement is, it is not a theory. The justifications of legal rules, however, are theories or beliefs about causes and consequences of conduct. Statistics can be a tool that helps the formulation of normative statements, but it can also be confusing. Statistics can never be, however, a trump card against doubt or a license to not fully articulate and support normative arguments. The next exercise focuses on a surprising confirmation of the importance of explanatory theories.

Exercise 13.2: Assume that you support socioeconomic diversity in the police force, perhaps believing that diversity increases police effectiveness. Using data from 1984 to 1994, a researcher produces statistical evidence that increased minority participation in the police force reduces deterrence and increases crime. Does this evidence persuade you to abandon the goal of having a police force that is representative of the diversity of society?

Discussion: The claim that the evidence is irrelevant cannot be sustained without further argumentation. When the evidence shows that minority participation in the police force increases crime, the only obvious conclusion is that to reduce crime, the police must reduce minority participation. One may despise the conclusion but ignoring evidence may be considered bad faith. The obvious conclusion may be despicable, but for it to be shown to be false, one must make an argument showing its falsity.

Consider the alternative of granting the relation that the evidence reveals but questioning its cause. The increased crime and reduced deterrence may be results of a different cause than the increase in minority police.

This question is based on an actual statistical article.[11] The idea that the evidence has a different cause seems unlikely, but it turns out to be true.

A different cause is unlikely because for a different cause to lead to these results, many of the police departments that decided to hire more minorities must have also changed for the worse when they made that decision. The correlation of the decision to hire minorities with a worsening of police administration seems highly implausible. Minority hiring and promotion by police departments was induced by a change in the standards for hiring and promotion that was indeed common across police departments. Nevertheless, John Lott reports that integration was pursued at the behest of the Justice Department by a lowering of the standards for police hiring and promotions from *all* social groups. The lowered standards allowed increased hiring of traditionally disadvantaged minorities. Simultaneously, the lowered standards eroded the quality of non-minority hires, who did not have the corresponding educational and socioeconomic disadvantages. As a result, the hiring of minority police did correlate with a decrease in quality, but that was mostly a decrease of the quality of the majority hires. The most unlikely objection to the evidence turns out to be accurate!

As soon as the true cause of the decreased deterrence is uncovered, the nature of the evidence and its policy implications change in a dramatic way. Rather than being an argument against affirmative action, the evidence becomes an argument in favor of selective hiring within each socioeconomic group and an argument for race norming, which was avoided by the Justice Department in its drive for police integration.

Exercise 13.3: Select a legal rule. Produce alternative explanations for its adoption. What statistical evidence would support each explanation? How would each piece of evidence interact with the other competing explanations?

---

[11] John R. Lott, Jr., "Does a Helping Hand Put Others at Risk?: Affirmative Action, Police Departments, and Crime," *Economic Inquiry* 38 (2000):239.

Exercise 13.4: Draft a guide to student editors of law reviews about the policies they should follow when publishing articles containing statistical analysis.

Discussion: Statistical analysis presents a challenge to student editors of law reviews. This is a complex and idiosyncratic issue.

The use of statistical analysis clashes with an institution that appears mostly in the United Sates, law reviews that are edited by students. Students bring much to the table as editors of legal texts but also have some drawbacks. The advantages of student editors include that they have not adopted the professional expression and jargon and that students ensure that the sources to which an author refers agree with the proposition the author claims they support. The students' sophistication in this aspect is such that they have extensive guidelines about how to indicate citations to sources that offer direct support, rather than inferential support, and when to allow a citation to the entire text rather than cite to an internal page (a "pinpoint" citation).

Students tend not to be familiar, however, with the use of statistics and the drawing of statistical inference. The contrast is so stark that the guidelines for citation formats (the famous "Blue Book") do not contain guidance for statistical support. Accordingly, an author who publishes a statistical study, for example, of death penalty opinions, may be required to provide citations to each opinion, whereas an author who publishes a statistical study involving interviews may be allowed to draw inferences without providing further proof. This is, at the least, inconsistent and, at best, it indicates that student editors of law reviews can improve their guidelines.

The normative exercise is to devise the goals to which the guidelines of student editors should aim when they publish statistical analyzes. How should the editors verify the data? How should the editors verify the calculations and the propriety of the methods used? How should the editors enable the readers to confirm the authors' data, methods, and analysis?

E. Bibliographical Note

Beginners and those who look for a painless refresher on the basics of statistics may find useful the popular book by Larry Gonick and Wollcott Smith, *The Cartoon Guide to Statistics* (New York:

HarperPerennial, 1993). A readable and simple introduction to statistics is Peter Kennedy, *A Guide to Econometrics* (Cambridge, MA: MIT Press, 1992). More formal introductions to econometrics are Philip Hans Franses, *A Concise Introduction to Econometrics: An Intuitive Guide* (Cambridge: Cambridge University Press, 2002); Robert S. Pindyck, *Econometric Models and Economic Forecasts*, 3rd ed. (New York: McGraw Hill, 1991); Janet T. Spence, John W. Cotton, Benton J. Underwood, and Carl P. Duncan, *Elementary Statistics*, 4th ed. (Englewood Cliffs, NJ: Prentice-Hall, 1983). A detailed explanation of correlation and regression analysis, starting with the underlying concepts in statistics, moving toward complex analysis can be found in the book by Jeremy Miles and Mark Shelvin, *Applying Regression & Correlation: A Guide for Students and Researchers* (Thousand Oaks, CA: Sage Publications, 2001).

Fascinating applications of statistics to social sciences are offered by Ray C. Fair, *Predicting Presidential Elections and Other Things* (Stanford, CA: Stanford University Press, 2002). This book is likely to be particularly able to hold the interest of jurists because it focuses on elections and the consequences of aging.

A vivid history of the battles over importing statistical methods for use in economics and social sciences, with only an occasional equation, is presented by Stephen M. Stigler, *Statistics on the Table: The History of Statistical Concepts and Methods* (Cambridge, MA: Harvard University Press, 1999).

The specialized statistics for dealing with sequences of securities prices are covered in Andrew Harvey, *The Econometric Analysis of Time Series*, 2nd ed. (Cambridge, MA: MIT Press, 1991); John Y. Campbell, Andrew W. Lo, and A. Craig MacKinlay, *The Econometrics of Financial Markets* (Princeton, NJ: Princeton University Press, 1997). Not approachable for the lay reader but a fine advanced textbook that deploys the *Mathematica* program is Colin Rose and Murray D. Smith, *Mathematical Statistics with Mathematica* (New York: Springer-Verlag, 2002).

14. Conclusion: Importing Methodological Innovations

Economic analysis of law is an extraordinarily young discipline. The topics for fruitful research form a vast multitude. The array of the traditional methods of economics and the sciences are an enormous resource for the scholar that would be missed if this book had focused on one or two novel methods. Moreover, novel methods do tend to receive enough attention to be thoroughly covered and explained. The reader should be able easily to supplement the gaps in those directions.

A greater and more systemic concern is the failure of some new methods to gain favor in the legal academy. Law, in general, and economic analysis of law, in particular, could and should take advantage of every rigorous new method that the sciences produce. A few legal scholars have engaged the methods of fractals, evolutionary theory, and cellular automata with some success. The legal academy, however, seems almost indifferent to those methods. Because the discipline's success requires the ability to broaden the palette of tools for analysis, it is important to assimilate new methods even when they do not have wide applicability.

As an exercise of our own ability to adopt new methods, this book will close with a very brief discussion of cellular automata, fractals, and evolutionary theory.

A. Cellular Automata

Some problems in physics proved intractable for the traditional methods without being fundamentally complex. Some have surrendered

315

answers when scholars approached them by using a remarkably simple tool, cellular automata.

The method of cellular automata is the antithesis of the continuity that lies at the foundation of geometry, algebra, and calculus. Whereas those mathematical methods see an infinitude of points related through shapes and functions, the method of cellular automata partitions space into discrete units, the "cells" of the method's name. Each cell changes states automatically according to very simple rules.

For example, a model may posit a line of cells that start with the value 0 and change to 1 if one but not both adjacent cells are 1; two adjacent cells with values of 1 cause a "crowding out" and the cell reverts to 0. The issue may be to observe the introduction of an innovation, a cell becoming a 1, and how this spreads over time. As the rules become more complex, each iteration changes the system of cells and traditional methods are unable to predict the state of the system, even after a small number of iterations. Different rules lead to patterns with different features and interest.

Cellular automata produce interesting graphic displays. Because traditional graphics are pointless, the scholars who work on cellular automata developed new ways to display their findings. The states of cells are routinely color coded, and the transformation of a line of cells is often displayed by laying its successive stages adjacent to each previous one, creating a patterned grid. When the analysis applies to a two-dimensional array of cells, some scholars may use their computers during presentations to display the evolution of the array.

One of the leading scholars who use cellular automata is physicist Steven Wolfram who made a splash in physics circles with articles that are among the most frequently cited. The leading mathematical software package, *Mathematica*, is his creation, which he claims to have built in his search for tools that would further research about cellular automata (CA). His recent book, *A New Kind of Science*, displays many CA graphics while advancing the thesis that physics can only decode the last secrets of the natural world by using CA methods, which are not amenable to analytical shortcuts. Rather than deriving a function that can be used to predict events such as planets' positions, the CA method needs to track the interactions of components as cells. As the components become smaller – in physics they may become molecules or atoms, in the social sciences they may become firms or individuals – making a prediction cumbersome.

The legal applications of cellular automata build on bounded rationality. The few available models study individuals (the cells) who react only to their neighbors rather than to wider society. The questions address, for example, whether innovations spread,[1] or whether resources are allocated efficiently by actors who have only local information.[2] They tend to indicate that efficient action and innovations spread fast even in conditions of very limited communication and knowledge.

B. FRACTALS

As mathematicians, with the increase of computing power, became increasingly able to explore iterative equations, they produced radically new views of equations and new efforts to find order in the results. One phenomenon that kept appearing was self-similarity. One of the most famous self-similar iterative graphics is the Mandelbrot set, a shape that seems initially like an irregular drawing of a Venn diagram of two intersecting sets. A magnification of its apparently irregular boundaries reveals that they hide small-scale copies of the larger image. Greater magnification reveals ever more copies. Figure 14.1 illustrates three magnifications of the Mandelbrot set. The largest panel is the full Mandelbrot set and the characteristic double circle dominates its center. Along its border, numerous replicas of the double circle appear. One of the fjords of the large panel is magnified. In this magnification appear more shapes similar to the full Mandelbrot. A further magnification of one of its fjords reveals even more similar shapes.

Objects that display self-similarity are called fractals. The name is derived from a feature of the geometry of self-similarity that the proper number of dimensions of space that a fractal object occupies is fractional. An ordinary line has one dimension, but a line with self-similarity may tend to vanish to a collection of points or may tend to spread in two dimensions and occupy the entire surface. Although the main distinguishing feature of fractals is self-similarity, their name is due to their being misfits in traditional geometry.

---

[1] See Randal C. Picker, "Simple Games in a Complex World: A Generative Approach to the Adoption of Norms," *University of Chicago Law Review* 64 (1997):1225 *et seq.*

[2] See Seth J. Chandler and Christian J. Jacob, "Behavior and Learning Under the Law: Automata Containing Evolutionary Algorithms," *The Mathematica Journal* 8 (2001):301–25.

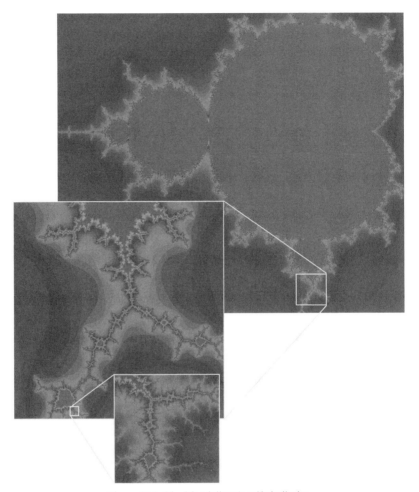

Figure 14.1. The Mandelbrot's self-similarity.

As mathematicians looked closer at self-similarity it became increasingly obvious that the real world fit the new mathematical construct much better than it fit the traditional Euclidian geometry of solids. A tree is a sphere on a cylinder mostly in the eyes of small children; more apt seems to be the description of a tree as a pattern of branches that split into several smaller branches until it about occupies the space of the sphere that the younger eyes see. Trees, leaves, rocks, rivers, ferns, clouds, snowflakes, cities, blood vessels,... the list of natural objects that are fractals seems endless.

This book has discussed a type of self-similarity that is at the foundation of one of the applications of fractals in law. When Chapter 9 and Appendix C discuss the derivation of the normal distribution by Gauss, it is revealed to be the result of the sum of other distributions. Those, in turn, may themselves be sums of others, and so on.

Consider the modeling of randomly moving elements by the "Brownian motion," which adds normal variables for each unit of time. Although the process of simulating this type of motion seems discrete, the chosen interval of time can be infinitely divided without changing the character of the motion. If one normal variable represented change in a week's time, it could be the sum of seven daily normal variables, each of which could be the sum of hourly variables, and so on with minutes, seconds, and so on. The fractal nature of the Brownian motion is part of what makes the call option pricing formula that we saw in Chapter 11 so effective. The nature of the model makes the unit of time irrelevant.

Social change was treated as a Brownian motion in a comparative analysis of legal change.[3] That analysis treats society as changing randomly with a drift toward progress. The task of the legal system is to update the law to keep it current. The conclusion indicates that individuals prefer the gradual change of common law to the more rare but also more pronounced change of civil law because they are risk averse.

A more overt application of fractals in the law attempts to estimate the fractal dimension that citation patterns reveal.[4]

Applications of fractals in law will be successful if they can demonstrate the fractal nature of the object or take it as given as in the case of an exogenous phenomenon such as social change. The challenge of treating legal phenomena as fractals is that they are not subject to the precise measurement of geometrical bodies. The proof of the self-similar nature of a tree is the comparison of the branching of a bough and a twig. The jurisprudence of civil rights or of the first amendment may also display some self-similarity. The strength of reasoning by analogy – unique, perhaps, in law – may argue strongly in favor of finding and reproducing self-similarity. Yet, legal doctrines may be abandoned and novel arguments and interpretations may be followed,

---

[3] Nicholas L. Georgakopoulos, "A Comparison of Civil and Common Law as Evolutionary Systems," *International Review of Law and Economics* 17 (1997):475–89.

[4] David G. Post and Michael B. Eisen, "How Long is the Coastline of the Law? Thoughts on the Fractal Nature of Legal Systems," *Journal of Legal Studies* 29 (2000):545 *et seq.*

brushing self-similarity aside. When does the law stop expanding the old way and adopt a new method? What are the consequences of either method of expansion?

C. EVOLUTIONARY THEORY

Last in this trio of nascent legal methods is the one with the longest and strongest pedigree, evolutionary theory. Evolutionary theory is deceptively simple and surprisingly universal. The *survival of the fittest* seems trite and even socially insensitive; yet, every facet of everything that has survived the evolutionary process is fit by virtue of its survival.

A new challenge that evolutionary theory poses is the shifting definition of the competitors for survival. In the natural sciences, the focus may shift from species to clans and genes. Yet, ideas are equally subject to selection. One of the legal applications of evolutionary theory argues that some ideas, like neo-Nazi or racist ideas, may be such powerful competitors that they may threaten institutions that are essential for society, science, or progress.[5] Constitutional protections of free speech, therefore, should not extend to such ideas. Evolutionary neural science looks to economics to explain the evolutionary fitness of cognitive strategies.[6]

In view of evolutionary theory, legal analysis approaches hubris. If what has survived is fit, changing it may have devastating consequences that we cannot foresee. Consider the hate that is the seed of the destructive social and political ideas that seem so obnoxious. The same hate may be instrumental in creating the unity necessary for a successful response to an attack. If what exists is fit, how can law dare make any changes without destroying the source of the fitness?

D. TO END

When a long tour comes to an end, its individual segments may seem blurred. The methods that this book surveyed should indeed be blurred, as each one is worthy of its own book or even library. Economic analysis of law started a revolution by bringing rigorous, scientific analysis to law. The change is radical. The prospective gains

---

[5] Jeffrey E. Stake, "Are We Buyers or Hosts? A Memetic Approach to the First Amendment," *Alabama Law Review* 52 (2001):1213 *et seq.*

[6] Paul W. Glimcher, *Decisions Uncertainty, and the Brain: The Science of Neuroeconomics* (Cambridge, MA: MIT Press, 2003).

are enormous. Hopefully, this book gives enough of an introduction to the many rigorous methods discussed here so that interested scholars, having a feel for the breadth of their toolset, can either increase our tools or further perfect the use of existing ones.

E. BIBLIOGRAPHICAL NOTE

Lay introductions to fractals can offer spectacular graphics, as Heinz-Otto Peitgen and P. H. Richter, *The Beauty of Fractals: Images of Complex Dynamical Systems* (New York: Springer-Verlag, 1986); Heinz-Otto Peitgen, Hartmut Jurgens, and Dietmar Saupe, *Fractals for the Classroom: Part One – Introduction to Fractals and Chaos* (New York: Springer-Verlag, 1992). More formal but very approachable alternatives are Michael Barnsley, *Fractals Everywhere* (San Diego, CA: Academic Press, 1988) and Kenneth Falconer, *Fractal Geometry: Mathematical Foundations and Applications* (New York: John Wiley and Sons, 1990).

A splendid combination of fractals and evolution is demonstrated by Christian Jacob, *Illustrating Evolutionary Computation with Mathematica* (San Diego, CA: Academic Press, 2001).

A fascinating first account of incorporating evolutionary fitness in economic theory is Richard R. Nelson and Sidney G. Winter, *An Evolutionary Theory of Economic Change* (Cambridge, MA: Belknap Press of Harvard University Press, 1982).

Cellular automata are presented with graphics that rival those of fractals by Steven Wolfram, *A New Kind of Science* (Champaign, IL; Wolfram Media, 2002).

Appendix A: *Meinhard v. Salmon* 249 N.Y. 458 (1928)

Cardozo, Chief Judge

On April 10, 1902, Louisa M. Gerry leased to the defendant Walter J. Salmon the premises known as the Hotel Bristol at the northwest corner of Forty-second Street and Fifth Avenue in the city of New York. The lease was for a term of 20 years, commencing May 1, 1902, and ending April 30, 1922. The lessee undertook to change the hotel building for use as shops and offices at a cost of $200,000. Alterations and additions were to be accretions to the land.

Salmon, while in course of treaty with the lessor as to the execution of the lease, was in course of treaty with Meinhard, the plaintiff, for the necessary funds. The result was a joint venture with terms embodied in a writing. Meinhard was to pay to Salmon half of the moneys requisite to reconstruct, alter, manage, and operate the property. Salmon was to pay to Meinhard 40 per cent. of the net profits for the first five years of the lease and 50 per cent. for the years thereafter. If there were losses, each party was to bear them equally. Salmon, however, was to have sole power to "manage, lease, underlet and operate" the building. There were to be certain pre-emptive rights for each in the contingency of death.

They were coadventurers, subject to fiduciary duties akin to those of partners. *King v. Barnes*, 16 N. E. 332. As to this we are all agreed. The heavier weight of duty rested, however, upon Salmon. He was a coadventurer with Meinhard, but he was manager as well. During the early years of the enterprise, the building, reconstructed, was operated at a loss. If the relation had then ended, Meinhard as well as Salmon would have carried a heavy burden. Later the profits became large with the result that for each of the investors there came a rich return. For each the venture had its phases of fair weather and of foul. The two were in it jointly, for better or for worse.

When the lease was near its end, Elbridge T. Gerry had become the owner of the reversion [i.e., the land subject to the lease. Ed.]. He owned much other property in the neighborhood, one lot adjoining the Bristol building on Fifth Avenue and four lots on Forty-Second Street. He had a plan to lease the entire tract for a long term to someone who would destroy the buildings then existing and put up another in their place. In the latter part of 1921, he submitted such a project to several capitalists and dealers. He was unable to carry it through with any of them. Then, in January 1922, with less than four months of the lease to run, he approached the defendant Salmon. The result was a new lease to the Midpoint Realty Company, which is owned and controlled by Salmon, a lease covering the whole tract and involving a huge outlay. The term is to be 20 years, but successive covenants for renewal will extend it to a maximum of 80 years at the will of either party. The existing buildings may remain unchanged for seven years. They are then to be torn down, and a new building to cost $3,000,000 is to be placed upon the site. The rental, which under the Bristol lease was only $55,000, is to be from $350,000 to $475,000 for the properties so combined. Salmon personally guaranteed the performance by the lessee of the covenants of the new lease until such time as the new building had been completed and fully paid for.

The lease between Gerry and the Midpoint Realty Company was signed and delivered on January 25, 1922. Salmon had not told Meinhard anything about it. Whatever his motive may have been, he had kept the negotiations to himself. Meinhard was not informed even of the bare existence of a project. The first that he knew of it was in February, when the lease was an accomplished fact. He then made demand on the defendants that the lease be held in trust as an asset of the venture, making offer upon the trial to share the personal obligations incidental to the guaranty. The demand was followed by refusal and later by this suit. A referee gave judgment for the plaintiff, limiting the plaintiff's interest in the lease, however, to 25 per cent. The limitation was on the theory that the plaintiff's equity was to be restricted to one-half of so much of the value of the lease as was contributed or represented by the occupation of the Bristol site. Upon cross-appeals to the Appellate Division, the judgment was modified so as to enlarge the equitable interest to one-half of the whole lease. With this enlargement of plaintiff's interest, there went, of course, a corresponding enlargement of his attendant obligations. The case is now here on an appeal by the defendants.

Joint adventurers, like co-partners, owe to one another, while the enterprise continues, *the duty of the finest loyalty. Many forms of conduct*

permissible in a workaday world for those acting at arm's length, are for-
bidden to those bound by fiduciary ties. A trustee is held to something stricter
than the morals of the market place. Not honesty alone, but the punctilio
of an honor the most sensitive, is then the standard of behavior. As to this
there has developed a tradition that is unbending and inveterate. Uncom-
promising rigidity has been the attitude of courts of equity when petitioned
to undermine the rule of undivided loyalty by the "disintegrating erosion"
of particular exceptions. *Wendt v. Fischer*, 243 N.Y. 439, 444, 154 N. E. 303.
Only thus has the level of conduct for fiduciaries been kept at a level higher
than that trodden by the crowd. It will not consciously be lowered by any
judgment of this court. [Emphasis added. Ed.]

The owner of the reversion, Mr. Gerry, had vainly striven to find a tenant who would favor his ambitious scheme of demolition and construction.
Baffled in the search, he turned to the defendant Salmon in possession of
the Bristol, the keystone of the project. He figured to himself beyond a
doubt that the man in possession would prove a likely customer. To the
eye of an observer, Salmon held the lease as owner in his own right, for
himself and no one else. In fact he held it as a fiduciary, for himself and
another, sharers in a common venture. If this fact had been proclaimed,
if the lease by its terms had run in favor of a partnership, Mr. Gerry, we
may fairly assume, would have laid before the partners, and not merely
before one of them, his plan of reconstruction. The pre-emptive privilege,
or, better, the pre-emptive opportunity, that was thus an incident of the enterprise, Salmon appropriated to himself in secrecy and silence. He might
have warned Meinhard that the plan had been submitted and that either
would be free to compete for the award. If he had done this, we do not
need to say whether he would have been under a duty, if successful in
the competition, to hold the lease so acquired for the benefit of a venture
then about to end, and thus prolong by indirection its responsibilities and
duties. The trouble about his conduct is that he excluded his coadventurer
from any chance to compete, from any chance to enjoy the opportunity for
benefit that had come to him alone by virtue of his agency. This chance, if
nothing more, he was under a duty to concede. The price of its denial is an
extension of the trust at the option and for the benefit of the one whom
he excluded.

No answer is it to say that the chance would have been of little value
even if seasonably offered. Such a calculus of probabilities is beyond the
science of the chancery. Salmon, the real estate operator, might have
been preferred to Meinhard, the woolen merchant. On the other hand,
Meinhard might have offered better terms, or reinforced his offer by

alliance with the wealth of others. Perhaps he might even have persuaded the lessor to renew the Bristol lease alone, postponing for a time, in return for higher rentals, the improvement of adjoining lots. We know that even under the lease as made the time for the enlargement of the building was delayed for seven years. All these opportunities were cut away from him through another's intervention. He knew that Salmon was the manager. As the time drew near for the expiration of the lease, he would naturally assume from silence, if from nothing else, that the lessor was willing to extend it for a term of years, or at least to let it stand as a lease from year to year. Not impossibly, the lessor would have done so, whatever his protestations of unwillingness, if Salmon had not given assent to a project more attractive. At all events, notice of termination, even if not necessary, might seem, not unreasonably, to be something to be looked for, if the business was over the another tenant was to enter. In the absence of such notice, the matter of an extension was one that would naturally be attended to by the manager of the enterprise, and not neglected altogether. At least, there was nothing in the situation to give warning to any one that while the lease was still in being, there had come to the manager an offer of extension which he had locked within his breast to be utilized by himself alone. The very fact that Salmon was in control with exclusive powers of direction charged him the more obviously with the duty of disclosure, since only through disclosure could opportunity be equalized. If he might cut off renewal by a purchase for his own benefit when four months were to pass before the lease would have an end, he might do so with equal right while there remained as many years. Compare *Mitchell v. Read*, 19 Am. Rep. 252. He might steal a march on his comrade under cover of the darkness, and then hold the captured ground. Loyalty and comradeship are not so easily abjured.

Little profit will come from a dissection of the precedents. None precisely similar is cited in the briefs of counsel. What is similar in many, or so it seems to us, is the animating principle. Authority is, of course, abundant that one partner may not appropriate to his own use a renewal of a lease, though its term is to begin at the expiration of the partnership. *Mitchell v. Read*, 61 N.Y. 123, 19 Am. Rep. 252; Id., 84 N.Y. 556. The lease at hand with its many changes is not strictly a renewal. Even so, the standard of loyalty for those in trust relations is without the fixed divisions of a graduated scale. There is indeed a dictum in one of our decisions that a partner, though he may not renew a lease, may purchase the reversion if he acts openly and fairly (citations omitted). It is a dictum, and no more, for on the ground that he had acted slyly he was charged as a trustee. The holding is thus in favor of the conclusion that a purchase as well as a lease will succumb to the infection of secrecy and silence. Against the dictum in that case, moreover, may be set the opinion of Dwight, C., in *Mitchell v. Read*, where there is a dictum to the contrary. 61 N.Y. 123, at page 143, 19 Am. Rep. 252. To say that a partner is free without restriction to buy in the reversion of the property where the business is conducted is to say in effect that he may strip the good will of its chief element of value, since good will is largely dependent on continuity of possession. *Matter of Brown's Will*, 242 N.Y. 1, 7. Equity refuses to confine within the bounds of classified transactions its precept of a loyalty that is undivided and unselfish. Certain at least it is that a "man obtaining his *locus standi*, and his opportunity for making such arrangements, by the position he occupies as a partner, is bound by his obligation to his copartners in such dealings not to separate his interest from theirs, but, if he acquires any benefit, to communicate it to them." *Cassels v. Stewart*, 6 App. Cas. 64, 73. Certain it is also that there may be no abuse of special opportunities growing out of a special trust as manager or agent. *Matter of Biss*, [1903] 2 Ch. 40; *Clegg v. Edmondson*, 8 D. M. & G. 787, 807. . . .

We have no thought to hold that Salmon was guilty of a conscious purpose to defraud. Very likely he assumed in all good faith that with the approaching end of the venture he might ignore his coadventurer and take the extension for himself. He had given to the enterprise time and labor as well as money. He had made it a success. Meinhard, who had given money, but neither time nor labor, had already been richly paid. There might seem to be something grasping in his insistence upon more. Such recriminations are not unusual when coadventurers fall out. They are not without their force if conduct is to be judged by the common standards of competitors. That is not to say that they have pertinency here. Salmon had put himself in a position in which thought of self was to be renounced, however hard the abnegation. He was much more than a coadventurer. He was a managing coadventurer. *Clegg v. Edmondson*, 8 D. M. & G. 787, 807. For him and for those like him the rule of undivided loyalty is relentless and supreme. *Wendt v. Fischer*, supra, *Munson v. Syracuse, etc., R. R. Co.*, 8 N. E. 355. A different question would be here if there were lacking any nexus of relation between the business conducted by the manager and the opportunity brought to him as an incident of management. *Dean v. MacDowell*, 8 Ch. Div. 345, 354; *Aas v. Benham*, [1891] 2 Ch. 244, 258; *Latta v. Kilbourn*, 150 U.S. 524. For this problem, as for most, there are distinctions of degree. If Salmon had received from Gerry a proposition to lease a building at a location far removed, he might have held for himself the privilege thus acquired, or so we shall assume. Here the subject-matter of the new lease was an extension and enlargement of the subject-matter of the old one. A managing coadventurer appropriating the benefit of such a lease without warning to his partner might fairly expect to be reproached with conduct that was underhand, or lacking, to say the least, in reasonable candor, if the partner were to surprise him in the act of signing the new instrument. Conduct subject to that reproach does not receive from equity a healing benediction.

A question remains as to the form and extent of the equitable interest to be allotted to the plaintiff. The trust as declared has been held to attach to the lease which was in the name of the defendant corporation. We think it ought to attach at the option of the defendant Salmon to the shares of stock which were owned by him or were under his control. The difference may be important if the lessee shall wish to execute an assignment of the lease, as it ought to be free to do with the consent of the lessor. On the other hand, an equal division of the shares might lead to other hardships. It might take away from Salmon the power of control and management which under the plan of the joint venture he was to have from first to last. The number of shares to be allotted to the plaintiff should, therefore, be reduced to such an extent as may be necessary to preserve to the defendant Salmon the expected measure of dominion. To that end an extra share should be added to his half.

Subject to this adjustment, we agree with the Appellate Division that the plaintiff's equitable interest is to be measured by the value of half of the entire lease, and not merely by half of some undivided part....

The judgment should be modified by providing that at the option of the defendant Salmon there may be substituted for a trust attaching to the lease a trust attaching to the shares of stock, with the result that one-half of such shares together with one additional share will in that event be allotted to the defendant Salmon and the other shares to the plaintiff, and as so modified the judgment should be affirmed with costs.

ANDREWS, J. (dissenting).

A tenant's expectancy of the renewal of a lease is a thing, tenuous, yet often having a real value. It represents the probability that a landlord will prefer to relet his premises to one already in possession rather than to strangers. Less tangible than 'good will,' it is never included in the tenant's assets, yet equity will not permit one standing in a relation of trust and confidence toward the tenant unfairly to take the benefit to himself. At times the principle is rigidly enforced. Given the relation between the parties, a certain result follows. No question as to good faith, or injury, or as to other circumstances is material. Such is the rule as between trustee and *cestui* (citations omitted); as between executor and estate (citations omitted): as between guardian and ward (citations omitted).

At other times some inquiry is allowed as to the facts involved. Fair dealing and a scrupulous regard for honesty is required. But nothing more. It may be stated generally that a partner may not for his own benefit secretly take a renewal of a firm lease to himself (citations omitted). In the case of tenants in common there is still greater liberty. There is said to be a distinction between those holding under a will or through descent and those holding under independent conveyance. But even in the former situation the bare relationship is not conclusive. *Matter of Biss* [1903] 2 Ch. 40. In *Burrell v. Bull*, 5 N.Y. Super. Ct. 15, there was actual fraud. In short, as we once said, "the elements of actual fraud – of the betrayal by secret action of confidence reposed, or assumed to be reposed, grows in importance as the relation between the parties falls from an express to an implied or a quasi trust, and on to those cases where good faith alone is involved." *Thayer v. Leggett*, 229 N.Y. 152, 128 N. E. 133.

Where the trustee, or the partner or the tenant in common, takes no new lease but buys the reversion in good faith a somewhat different question arises. Here is no direct appropriation of the expectancy of renewal. Here is no offshoot of the original lease. We so held in *Anderson v. Lemon*, 8 N.Y. 236, and although Judge Dwight casts some doubt on the rule in *Mitchell v. Reed*, it seems to have the support of authority. . . . The issue, then, is whether actual fraud, dishonesty, or unfairness is present in the transaction. If so, the purchaser may well be held as a trustee. . . .

With this view of the law I am of the opinion that the issue here is simple. Was the transaction, in view of all the circumstances surrounding it, unfair and inequitable? I reach this conclusion for two reasons. There was no general partnership, merely a joint venture for a limited object, to end at a fixed time. The new lease, covering additional property, containing many new and unusual terms and conditions, with a possible duration of 80 years, was more nearly the purchase of the reversion than the ordinary renewal with which the authorities are concerned.

. . .

In many respects, besides the increase in the land demised, the new lease differs from the old. Instead of an annual rent of $55,000 it is now from $350,000 to $475,000. Instead of a fixed term of twenty years it may now be, at the lessee's option, eighty. Instead of alterations in an existing structure costing about $200,000 a new building is contemplated costing $3,000,000. Of this sum $1,500,000 is to be advanced by the lessor to the lessee, 'but not to its successors or assigns,' and is to be repaid in installments. Again no assignment or sale of the lease may be made without the consent of the lessor.

This lease is valuable. In making it Mr. Gerry acted in good faith without any collusion with Mr. Salmon and with no purpose to deprive Mr. Meinhard of any equities he might have. But as to the negotiations leading to it or as to the execution of the lease itself Mr. Meinhard knew nothing. Mr. Salmon acted for himself to acquire the lease for his own benefit.

Under these circumstances the referee has found, and the Appellate Division agrees with him, that Mr. Meinhard is entitled to an interest in the second lease, he having promptly elected to assume his share of the liabilities imposed thereby. This conclusion is based upon the proposition that under the original contract between the two men "the enterprise was a joint venture, the relation between the parties was fiduciary and governed by principles applicable to partnerships," therefore, as the new lease is a graft upon the old, Mr. Salmon might not acquire its benefits for himself alone.

Were this a general partnership between Mr. Salmon and Mr. Meinhard, I should have little doubt as to the correctness of this result, assuming the new lease to be an offshoot of the old. Such a situation involves questions of trust and confidence to a high degree; it involves questions of good will; many other considerations. As has been said, rarely if ever may one partner without the knowledge of the other acquire for himself the renewal of a lease held by the firm, even if the new lease is to begin after the firm is dissolved. Warning of such an intent, if he is managing partner, may not be sufficient to prevent the application of this rule.

We have here a different situation governed by less drastic principles. I assume that where parties engage in a joint enterprise each owes to the other the duty of the utmost good faith in all that relates to their common venture. Within its scope they stand in a fiduciary relationship. I assume prima facie that even as between joint adventurers one may not secretly obtain a renewal of the lease of property actually used in the joint adventure where the possibility of renewal is expressly or impliedly involved in the enterprise. I assume also that Mr. Meinhard had an equitable interest in the Bristol Hotel lease. Further, that an expectancy of renewal inhered in that lease. Two questions then arise. Under his contract did he share in that expectancy? And if so, did that expectancy mature into a graft of the original lease? To both questions my answer is 'No.'

The one complaint made is that Mr. Salmon obtained the new lease without informing Mr. Meinhard of his intention. Nothing else. There is no claim of actual fraud. No claim of misrepresentation to any one. Here was no movable property to be acquired by a new tenant at a sacrifice to its owners. No good will, largely dependent on location, built up by the joint efforts of two men. Here was a refusal of the landlord to renew the Bristol lease on any terms; a proposal made by him, not sought by Mr. Salmon, and a choice by him and by the original lessor of the person with whom they wished to deal shown by the covenants against assignment or under-letting, and by their ignorance of the arrangement with Mr. Meinhard.

No fraud, no deceit, no calculated secrecy is found. Simply that the arrangement was made without the knowledge of Mr. Meinhard. I think this not enough.

The judgment of the courts below should be reversed and a new trial ordered, with costs in all courts to abide the event.

Appendix B: Glossary

Agency costs: The economic term for the discrepancy between the performance of a task by the interested party (the principal in economic terms) compared with its performance by an appointee (an agent in economic terms).

Agent: A term that may cause much misunderstanding between lawyers and economists. As a legal term it means a representative with authority to transact in the name of the principal. As an economic term it most often means someone who administers another's interests even if without representing the principal. Occasionally, economists use the term agent as individual when describing a model, for example, "a society consists of N agents, who ... "

At the money: A colloquial expression that is applied to a right, usually an option or a claim in bankruptcy. It means that the right is near its nominal value. In the case of an option it means that the market price of the underlying security is near the strike price. In the case of a claim in bankruptcy it means that the value of the estate is sufficient to repay other claims with greater seniority but not to repay more junior claims. Compare *in the money, out of the money*.

Average deviation: A measure of the dispersion of a distribution that consists of the average difference from the distribution's average.

Average: The center of a symmetric distribution or a measure of centrality of a distribution that is not symmetric. See also *mean*.

axis: See *x axis, y axis, z axis*.

CAPM, Capital asset pricing model: A method of valuing stocks, depending on their systematic risk. See Chapter 10, section A, part ii. It takes three inputs, the stock's systematic risk measured in beta b, the return of risk-free debt R_f, and the return of the market R_m and produces as its output the return of the stock R_s, given by $R_s = R_f + b(R_m - R_f)$.

Censored distribution: A probability distribution where outcomes greater or smaller than the censoring value appear as equal to the censoring value. See Chapter 9, section A, part iii.

Borda-count or voting: An alternative to majority for selecting the winning alternative in elections. See Chapter 3.

Contract: The legal term for an agreement that is enforceable by a right to mobilize the state's police powers.

Cooperation game: See *prisoner's dilemma*.

Coordination game: See *driving side game*.

Credible commitment: A term of *game theory* that indicates a mechanism by which a player convinces others that the player will act in a specified way (make a move) despite that a more appealing action (move) may exist. For example, in the *prisoner's dilemma* each player cannot credibly commit not to confess. From a legal perspective, an enforceable contract may be a credible commitment, depending on its terms and enforcement costs. The mechanisms for credible commitment may be extralegal, a classic example being the exchange of relatives as hostages practiced by local rulers in medieval Europe and Japan. Because each ruler had the other's children, whom he would execute in reaction to a violation of the treaty by the other, both were confident the treaty would be upheld. See *prisoner's dilemma*.

Cumulative distribution function: A function that produces the probability that a realization of a random variable that follows the given distribution will be smaller or equal to a given value. In symbolic terms, if the function $f(x)$ is a cumulative distribution function, then it produces the probability $p(\ )$ that a realization r is smaller or equal to x, that is, $f(x) = p(r \leq x)$.

Data: The plural of the Latin datum, meaning given. Data are the object of *statistical analysis* that produces *descriptive statistics* or *statistical tests*. The Web sites of statistics departments of most major universities contain links to sources of data.

Dating game: One of the archetypal games of *game theory*. Two friends seek to meet for a date at one of two locations. Both prefer getting together but each prefers a different location. A communication needs some additional power of *credible commitment* to induce action because the other player could attempt to *credibly commit* going to his favored location. Because this commitment does not need the strength necessary in *cooperation games* but should be stronger than that of *coordination games*, this is also called a mixed-motive game.

Derivative: A mathematical concept that relates the change of the value of a function to a change of the value of its inputs. In the graphic representation of a function, the derivative is the slope of the function.

Derivative contract: A financial contract, the value of which depends on that of other assets. Options, futures, forwards, and swaps are derivatives.

Descriptive statistic: A number that is calculated by applying a *statistical method* to data and that describes a feature of the aggregated data, such as *standard deviation* or *mean*.

Discounting: A calculation that produces the present value that is equal to a future payment. See Chapter 10, section A, part i.

Distribution function: A function that expresses the probabilities of different outcomes of uncertainty. The two main forms are the *cumulative distribution function* and the *probability density function*, see also Chapter 9.

Driving-side game: One of the archetypal strategic settings (games) studied by *game theory*, see Chapter 3. Drivers do not prefer one side of the street to drive but they have a strong interest in choosing the same side as others to avoid head-on collisions. This, like the *stag hunt game* are considered examples of *coordination games* because the players need only to coordinate to overcome their predicament. Because of the indifference about driving side and the benefit from coordinating, any communication is credible with no need for *credible commitment*.

e: Euler's constant, the basis of the natural logarithm, about 2.72.

Efficiency, efficient: Economic theory has various definitions of efficiency. In law and economics those that appear most are Pareto efficiency and Kaldor-Hicks efficiency. Neither is a test of *optimality*, in the sense of determining that the proposed legal change is the best. Rather, they are tests of the consents of a society's members to changes from a *status quo* and can be considered tests of whether the proposal constitutes an improvement. Pareto efficiency requires actual unanimous consent for the change, whereas Kaldor-Hicks efficiency is satisfied if the gains from the new regime could compensate the dissenters.

Expectation: See *mean*.

F statistic: An intermediate output of statistical analysis that compares ratios. It is the input for the *f distribution* (along with *degrees of freedom*) that states the probability of obtaining that ratio by chance.

Formal: Mathematical, technical; the opposite of casual, informal, intuitive.

Formal logic: The discipline of the systematic study of the drawing of conclusions from premises. [Formal] logic or syllogistic reasoning or the science of logic is considered a branch of philosophy. The use of symbols has given it such a technical or formal nature that it is also called mathematical logic and considered a mathematical discipline. See Chapter 1.

Game theory: A quantitative method of analysis that studies decisions in greatly simplified settings, see Chapter 3.

In the money: A colloquial expression that is applied to a right, usually an option or a claim in bankruptcy. It means that the right corresponds to a safe claim. In the case of a call option (the right to buy at the strike price) it means that the market value of the underlying security is well above the strike price. In the case of a claim in bankruptcy, it means that the value of the estate is sufficient to satisfy in full claims of this seniority.

Informal logic: See *informal reasoning*.

Informal reasoning: Reasoning that produces conclusions that are weak in the sense that they do not have the rigorous support of *[formal] logic*.

Listed corporation: A corporation with shares that are listed for trading in a stock exchange, also known as a public corporation.

Logic: See *formal logic*.

Mathematical logic: See *formal logic*.

Mean: A measure of centrality of a distribution. The arithmetic mean is the average. Also called expectation or the expected outcome.

Mixed-motive games: See *dating game*.

Normative logic: A branch of the discipline of *[formal] logic* that produces conclusions that include obligation, permission, or prohibition. See Chapter 1.

Normative reasoning: The drawing of conclusions about the desirability of interpretations and rules. Normative reasoning is the subject of this book. Normative reasoning is necessarily *informal reasoning* rather than part of *[formal] logic*.

Optimal, optimality: The best possible outcome.

Out of the money: A colloquial expression that is applied to a right, usually an option or a claim in bankruptcy. It means that the right is not likely to realize any value. In the case of a call option (the right to buy at the strike price) it means that the current market price is below the strike price.

Premise: A simple statement that, combined with a second one in a *syllogism*, leads to a conclusion, that is, a new statement that combines them. The study of *syllogisms* is the object of the discipline of *[formal]* *logic*. See Chapter 1.

Principal: In the agency relationship or contract, the principal allows an agent to have authority to transact in the principal's name. Such an agent has the power to bind the principal in contract, for example. In economics and finance, a principal seems to be defined as one who has entrusted value to administration by an agent even if the law does not consider the relationship one of agency. For example, corporate officers are not by law agents of the shareholders but only of the corporation; most economists would call them agents of the shareholders because the officers administer the assets that the shareholders have contributed to the corporation.

Prisoner's dilemma: One of the archetypal strategic settings (games) studied by *game theory*, see Chapter 3. A prosecutor offers each prisoner an incentive to confess; whereas the two prisoners jointly prefer that neither confesses, each prisoner has an incentive to confess to avoid being the only nonconfessing prisoner. The prisoner's dilemma is also called a *cooperation game* because the prisoners can overcome their predicament if they can *credibly commit* to cooperate, Compare the other archetypal settings, the *hawk-dove game, the dating game*, the *stag hunt game*, and the *driving side game*; see also *coordination games* and *mixed-motive games*.

Probability distribution: See distribution function.

Public corporation: A corporation with shares that are listed for trading in a stock exchange, also known as a listed corporation.

p-value: See *statistical test*.

Sample: The statistical term for a set of *data*.

Science of logic: See *formal logic*.

Slope [of function]: The slope of a function expresses its change per unit of change of its inputs. Slope is expressed not in an angle of degrees but in terms of rise-to-length, in other words, how much the function increases for each unit increase of the input. A line with slope of 1 is at an angle of 45 degrees with the horizontal (measuring counterclockwise). See also *derivative* and text accompanying Figure 7.3.

Stag hunt game: One of the archetypal games of *game theory*. Each hunter is indifferent between preys but wants to hunt the same prey as the other; a *coordination game*.

Standard deviation: A measure of the dispersion of a probability distribution that consists of the square root of *variance*, which is the average of the squared distances to the average.

Statistical analysis: The derivation of quantitative conclusions about data, often *descriptive statistics* or *statistical tests*. See Chapter 13.

Statistical test: The application of statistical methods to calculate the probability that the data could have been observed if the *null hypothesis* were true. That probability is often reported in published tables as *p-value*. A low probability indicates that the data are unlikely and suggests that the null hypothesis is also unlikely to be true (although the probability that it is true is not calculated).

Syllogism: A term of *formal logic* that means the sequence of two *premises* that lead to a conclusion.

Syllogistic reasoning: See *formal logic*.

Synthetic portfolio or beta: A mix of securities and borrowing or lending that produces risk of a given beta, i.e., that exposes the holder of the portfolio to systematic risk that corresponds to the fraction beta compared to the risk of the market as a whole. See Chapter 10, section A, part ii.

t distribution: A distribution function that expresses the probability of obtaining given *t statistics* in a specified number of observations. See *t test, statistical test*.

Truncated distribution: A probability distribution where outcomes greater or smaller than the truncating value are not observed. See Chapter 9, section A, part iii.

Truth-valued [syllogism]: A *syllogism* that is either true or false, according to *[formal] logic*. When a truth-valued syllogism is analyzed according to the rules of logic, its conclusion is either true or false. This is not true for some probabilistic conclusions (e.g., tomorrow it may rain) and some normative conclusions (e.g., the Constitution should be interpreted as hindering liability against the press for slander toward politicians; the U.S. approach is to hinder such liability in favor of free speech, whereas the U.K. approach does not; compare *New York Times v. Sullivan*, 376 U.S. 254 (1964) with *Reynolds v. Times Newspapers Ltd.*, 2 A.C. 127, 2001).

t statistic: An intermediate output of the *t test* that consists of the normalized distance of means, adjusting for dispersion. In conjunction with the number of observations, it allows the calculation of the *p-value* from the *t distribution*.

t test: A *statistical test* or method for comparing the mean of one set of data (sample) with a given value or with the mean of a second set. A third form is the paired *t* test in which each data point of one set is linked to a specific one of the other. An example is the test of scores of students in two tests, in which each student's score in one test is linked to (paired with) the same student's score in a second test.

Variance: A measure of the *dispersion* of a *probability distribution*. Variance consists of the average of the squared distances to the average.

x axis: The horizontal axis in a graph with two coordinates, i.e. a 2D graph. The width dimension in a 3D graph.

y axis: The vertical axis in a graph with two coordinates, i.e. a 2D graph. The depth dimension in a 3D graph.

z axis: The vertical axis in a 3D graph.

Appendix C: *Mathematica* Notebooks

The following text is from *notebook* files of the program *Mathematica*. Notebooks are the files that the user of the program creates by typing text. The typed text forms *cells* that perform different functions, depending on their attributes. Notably, only *input cells* can be evaluated, which means that only input cells trigger the mathematical manipulation powers of the program. The result of the program's computations are presented in *output cells*. By default, new text becomes an input cell and the default output is an output cell that is placed below the input cell. The remaining cell styles function akin to the styles of word-processing programs, specifying the typeface and size of the text.[1] In all cell styles, *Mathematica* has the capacity to produce the atypical symbols and text placement of mathematical expressions.

Users can also create *packages* that are files with resources that notebooks can invoke. Because this is an advanced feature that obscures the computational steps from the reader, the notebooks of this appendix do not invoke packages with two exceptions. They do invoke built-in packages, such as `ContinuousDistributions.m`, the package that gives *Mathematica* the functionality to handle some specific probability distributions that are continuous, such as the normal distribution (discussed in Chapter 9) or the lognormal distribution (mentioned when discussing option valuation in Chapter 11). Also, some of the notebooks that do produce three-dimensional graphics invoke the package `Text3D.m`, which I have authored and is available from the Web site of *Mathematica*'s publisher, www.wolfram.com. This package allows the user to place text

---

[1] An additional functionality of some cell styles, like the section cells or subsection cells, is that they automatically partition the notebook and allow the user to minimize only the corresponding segments. That is a feature that is only visible on screen and does not apply to a printed reproduction.

in three-dimensional graphics with the effect of perspective, that is, as if the text was written on a surface inside the graphic (see, e.g., Figures 10.5, 11.2, 11.3). *Mathematica* can place text in three-dimensional graphs even without this package, but then the text is placed on the screen or page without perspective.

The cells of the notebooks reproduced below take three forms: the form corresponding to text cells, the form corresponding to input cells, and the form corresponding to output cells. To illustrate, the following three paragraphs use the corresponding formatting:

Text cells use the normal typeface of the Times-Roman font, in a small size.

`Input cells use the fixed or monospaced typeface of the Courier font, in the same size but in bold.`

`Output cells follow the pattern of input cells, but they are not bold.`

This formatting is important for the reader because it distinguishes commands to the program and the program's responses. **The formatting of input cells means commands given to the program.** `The responses of the program are in the output cell style.` This formatting also corresponds to the defaults of *Mathematica*.

These notebooks do not introduce *Mathematica* and its language. The instruction manual of the program, *The Mathematica Book*, performs this function very well. To help the reader follow the text, some basic notation is explained here.

Built-in commands are distinguished from user-defined functions by starting with a capital. Moreover, commands tend to be complete words rather than abbreviations, such as **`Limit[]`**, **`Integrate[]`**, or **`Solve[]`**. Notable exceptions are the commands for taking a derivative, **`D[]`**, for solving differential equations, **`DSolve[]`**, and for limited, numerical precision, **`N[]`**. Commands take coefficients as their input. Three ways exist for passing coefficients to commands. Usually, the coefficients follow the command in square brackets. For example, the command **`D[]`** taking the coefficient x is written **`D[x]`**. A command may take several coefficients, in which case they are separated by commas. Commands may also take lists and rules as coefficients. An example of a list is a matrix that is a list of lists (a column of rows). The inverse of the matrix ((a, b), (c, d)) is obtained by the command **`Inverse[{{a,b},{c,d}}]`**. A rule is specified by the arrow shape (or "->"). The command for calculating limits takes a rule as its second coefficient, so that the limit of $1/x$ as x approaches infinity is `Limit[1/x,x→Infinity]`. A command that takes a single coefficient can be written as a prefix or postfix. The prefix notation uses the at sign (@). The postfix notation uses a double slash. Thus, passing the coefficient x to the command D can be done by writing `x//D` and `D@x`. The graphics commands below routinely display graphics by using `Show@Graphics[...]` and simplify by using `...//FullSimplify`.

The equal sign assigns an expression to a variable. The variable is on the left of the equal sign and the expression is on the right. The convention of using lowercase variables helps distinguish them from built-in constants like `Pi`, `E`, or `I` (that correspond to π, e, and i). Recall the similar convention of defining functions with lowercase names that helps distinguish them from built-in commands.

Functions are defined using the notation with square brackets, preceding the equal sign with a colon, and following the coefficients with one underscore. Thus, to set the function f to apply to any coefficient and square it, it can be defined with `f[x_]:=x^2` (omitting the underscore and writing `f[x]:=x^2` limits the function to only square the variable x). Otherwise, functions are akin to commands, can take a sequence of coefficients or lists as coefficients, and are subject to the prefix and postfix notation. Thus, after the definition above that squares its coefficient, one can find the square of five by typing `f[5]`, `5//f` and `f@5`. The equation $x^2 + 3y^2$ can be assigned to the function g with `g[x_,y_]:=x^2+3 y^2`. A function (or command) that takes two coefficients can be written using the infix notation, which uses tildes (∼). In this example, typing `5∼g∼3` is equivalent to typing `g[5,3]`.

Despite the flexibility of functions, their definition is more complex than that of variables. Often it is more convenient to assign equations to variables while it is also necessary to retain long equations. If values were assigned to the equation's variables, the model would lose generality. Yet, it is also important to assign values to the variables temporarily only, so as to produce a numerical example. This can be done by using replacement rules. The replacement operator is a postfix and consists of a slash followed by a period (`/.`). For example, if a model produces the equation $x^2 + 3y^4$, it is possible to find this equation's value for the case that x is five and y is two by typing `x^2+3 y^4/.{x→5,y→2}`. The replacement operator can be read as "replacing" so that this example reads "... replacing x with five and y with two."

Rules are also used to deviate from the default values in many of the details of the presentation of graphics. Those are called options. Options must be separated by commas, as they are several coefficients of one command. For example, axes can be hidden by using the rule `Axes→False` in `Plot[...,Axes→False]`.

The notebooks below cannot be read independently from the text to which they refer. Their opening paragraphs state the name of the file and the page to which the notebooks refer.

A. DIFFERENTIAL EQUATIONS IN LAW: THE EFFECT OF TERMINATING AFFIRMATIVE ACTION

Notebook filename: L&E_DiffEq.nb

Refers to page: 148

Much of the output of *Mathematica* is lists and the user is often called to select an item from the list. This is often the case when obtaining solutions by using `Solve[]` and `DSolve[]` as they produce their results in the form of lists even when the solution is only one. The syntax for taking an element from a list is to place the element number in double-square brackets after the list. The first command below illustrates this by taking the first and only element of the solutions produced by `DSolve[]` with `DSolve[...][[1]]`.

This first line combines several of the syntactical abbreviations in sequence. The heart of the line is the command that solves the differential equation, `DSolve[]`. That produces a list of rules as a solution. Therefore, it is followed by the sequence necessary to extract its first element, `[[1]]`. The extracted element is a rule, which means that we want to apply the rule to obtain the transformation that the rule indicates. Accordingly, because the rule is w[t]→ ..., we must write `w[t]/.DSolve[...][[1]]`. We assign the result to a variable by using the equal sign.

By assigning the result to a variable, the result acquires staying power. It stays in the variable.

i. Determine the Participation in the Workforce

For simplicity, omit the subscripts from w_F and h_F. An apostrophe indicates a derivative and the differential equation becomes w'[t]. The command for solving a system of differential equations is `Dsolve[dif==expression,function,variable]`, where dif is the symbol of the differential equation, expression is the equation to be solved, function is the function for which the equation is solved, and variable is the variable with respect to which the differentiation takes place (usually, time). Thus, the analysis of the text suggests solving $w'(t) = hq - qw(t)$:

```
sol1 = w[t]/.DSolve[w'[t]==h q-q w[t],w[t],t][[1]]
h + e^(-q t) C[1]
```

Parsing the line above may be quite difficult for those who are unfamiliar with the *Mathematica* software. The cell below goes through the same steps, one at each line, using the symbol % to invoke the result of the previous line. The lines are spaced to match the locations of the commands in the line above. To see each result, execute the cell after removing the semicolons at the end of each line, which suppress output:

```
        DSolve[w'[t]==h q-q w[t],w[t],t];
                    %                    [[1]];
  w[t] /.            %;
sol1 =               %
h + e^(-q t) C[1]
```

ii. Add the Initial Condition

We can solve this as a system of equations, by including w[0]==w0 as an initial condition. The first output line is the result before the simplification:

```
sol2 = w[t] /. DSolve[ {
          w'[t] == h q - q w[t],
          w[0] == w0
          }, w[t], t][[1]]
sol1 = sol2 // FullSimplify
e^(-q t) (-h + e^(q t) h + w0)
h + e^(-q t) (-h + w0)
```

This is much harder to handle, however, so let us postpone the elimination of the constant of integration C[1].

iii. Manipulate the Exponent to See It Disappear

The sign of the exponent of e is important. If it is negative, then the expression will tend toward zero at infinity. The **Limit[]** function does not evaluate it because *Mathematica* does not know that the symbol q only takes positive values.

```
Limit[ e⁻ᵠ ᵗ,{t→∞}]
Limit[ e⁻ᵠ ᵗ,{t→∞}]
```

After we define the sign of q to be positive, then *Mathematica* finds this limit:

```
Sign[q]^=1;Limit[e⁻ᵠ ᵗ,{t→∞}]
0
```

iv. The Long-Run Participation

Therefore, in the long run, the fraction of the minority in the workforce will tend to approach the rate with which it is hired.

```
Limit[sol1, t→∞]
h
```

v. The Composition of the Candidates

Educators' minority admission ratio a determines the composition c of the pool of educated candidates for jobs, which has constant total size $1/r$ of the size of the workforce (r is the workforce-to-student ratio). The employer experiences quits that are a fraction of the workforce equal to q. Multiply by r to obtain the quit rate as a fraction of the candidate pool. The educator trains the number of candidates necessary to replace the hires in the pool of candidates. The rate with which those removed due to hiring are replaced with minority members in the pool of candidates is a. However, the minority participation in the candidate pool does not increase by that amount because of the minority removed by the hiring. When the employer hires with a rate h, the resulting c' is $(a - h)qr$.

```
sol3 = c[t] /. DSolve[{
        c[0] == c0,
        c'[t] == (a - h)q r
              }, c[t], t][[1]]
sol3 = FullSimplify@sol3
c0 + a q r t - h q r t
c0 + (a - h) q r t
```

When the employer hires blindly, the minority hiring ratio becomes the composition of the candidate pool, $c[t]$. The rate of change of the candidate-pool composition is then $c' = (a - c)qr$.

```
sol4 = c[t] /. DSolve[{
    c[0] == c0,
    c´[t] == (a - c[t])q r
          }, c[t], t][[1]]
sol4 = FullSimplify@sol4
```

$e^{-q\,r\,t}\;(-a+c0+a\,e^{q\,r\,t})$

$a+(-a+c0)\;e^{-q\,r\,t}$

... and a very messy equation gives the minority's participation in the workforce w':

```
sol5 = w[t]/.DSolve[{
    w[0] ==w0,
    w´[t] == sol4 q - q w[t]
          },w[t],t][[1]];
sol5=FullSimplify@sol5
```

$\frac{1}{-1+r}(e^{-q\,r\,t}\;(-c0+a\;(1+e^{q\,r\,t}\;(-1+r)-e^{q(-1+r)t}\;r)+$

$\quad e^{q(-1+r)t}\;(c0+(-1+r)w0)))$

```
sol1/.h→sol4;
Collect[%,{e⁻ᵠ ʳ ᵗ, e⁻ᵠ ᵗ}]
```

$a+e^{-q\,r\,t}(-a+c0+(a-c0)\;e^{-q\,t}\;(-a+w0)$

vi. Graphics

First we set values to boundaries and other repetitive items. Also, we establish a list of graphics options that will be common to all graphics.

```
tsw = 40; tmax = 100; step = 2; tmin = 5;
commgraphopts = {Axes → True,
    Ticks → {None, {{0, "0"}, {.5, ".5"}}},
    PlotRange → {{tmin, tmax}, {0, 1}},
    AspectRatio →.4,
    AxesOrigin → {tmin, 0}};
tmaxs = tmax - tsw;
```

Next is a list of commands for graphics that will appear in the middle of each list of lines. They draw a horizontal line in the middle and switch from solid to dashing lines. All the subsequent lines will be dashing. We must also adjust one of the boundary variables, tmax. It was used as the maximum of the time, but when we go into the next calculations it changes into the time from the switch to no quotas (tsw) to the maximum of the graphics.

```
middlegraphics = {
    Line[{{tmin,.5}, {tmax,.5}}],
    AbsoluteDashing[{3, 2}]};
```

We have four regimes to plot, with under- and overzealous educator quotas and before and after the end of quotas. The next cell creates four sets of rules, that is, temporary assignments of values to variables, one for each setting:

Underzealous, before: eg1a
Underzealous after: eg1b
Overzealous, before: eg2a
Overzealous, after: eg2b

```
eg1a={w0→0,c0→0,q→1/15,r→1.1,h→.5,a→.51};
eg1b={q→1/15,r→1.1,a→.5,
      w0→(sol1/.eg1a/.t→tsw),
      c0→(sol3/.eg1a/.t→tsw)};
eg2a={w0→0,c0→0,q→1/15,r→1.1,h→.5,a→.83};
eg2b={q→1/15,r→1.1,a→.5,
      w0→(sol1/.eg2a/.t→tsw),
      c0→(sol3/.eg2a/.t→tsw)};
```

We can now find the coordinates of a sequence of points on each line. Workforce lines start with wline and candidate lines start with cline.

In the underzealous case, next comes a 1.
In the overzealous case, next comes a 2.
If the line is before the switch of regimes, next comes an a.
If the line is after the switch of regimes, next comes a b.

```
wline1a=Table[{t,sol1}/.eg1a,{t,0,tsw,step}];
cline1a=Table[{t,sol3}/.eg1a,{t,0,tsw,step}];
wline1b=Table[{t+tsw,sol5}/.eg1b,{t,0,tmaxs, step}];
cline1b=Table[{t+tsw,sol4}/.eg1b,{t,0,tmaxs, step}];
wline2a=Table[{t,sol1}/.eg2a,{t,0,tsw, step}];
cline2a=Table[{t,sol3}/.eg2a,{t,0,tsw, step}];
wline2b=Table[{t+tsw,sol5}/.eg2b,{t,0,tmaxs, step}];
cline2b=Table[{t+tsw,sol4}/.eg2b,{t,0,tmaxs, step}];
```

We can finally, lay all this inside the **Graphics[]** command that will construct them and the **Show[]** command that will show them. One more graphic combines these two in one panel.

```
gunder=Show@Graphics[Flatten@{
            Line[wline1a],Line[wline1b],
            middlegraphics,
            Line[cline1a],Line[cline1b]
            },commgraphopts
    ];
gover=Show@Graphics[Flatten@{
        Line[wline2a],Line[wline2b],
        middlegraphics,
        Line[cline2a],Line[cline2b]
        },commgraphopts
        ];
rec1x=0;rec1y=0;rec1xm=1;rec1ym=.6;
rec2x=rec1xm;rec2y=rec1y;
rec2xm=rec2x+rec1xm;rec2ym=rec1ym;
garr=Show@Graphics[{
        Rectangle[{rec1x,rec1y},{rec1xm,rec1ym},gunder],
        Rectangle[{rec2x,rec2y},{rec2xm,rec2ym},gover]
        },AspectRatio→.3];
```

B. Derivation of the Normal Distribution

Notebook filename: L&E_DeriveNormalDistribution.nb
Refers to page: 188

i. Derive the Normal Distribution as Gauss Did

The derivation below relies on mathematical manipulation and has no intuitive appeal. It shows that the sum x of random numbers x_i follows the normal distribution despite that the distribution functions of its components are not known!

The proof assumes we have an estimate t of the likely average of x, so that t is the expected x. The proof also explains that t has its own density function that has its peak at t. Our observed x is composed of $n+1$ components and it follows a probability density function $f(\ )$. So $x = x_0 + x_1 + \cdots + x_n$. Each component follows the (subscripted) probability density function $f_i(\ )$, and the composed function is the product of the components: $f(x) = \prod f_i(x_i)$. Suppose that the average of the $n + 1$ outcomes is z but all are zero, except one, x_0. The sum of the observations, therefore, is $n\,0 + x_0$. Since the average is z, therefore $z = (\Sigma x_i)/(n + 1) = (n\,0 + x_0) => x_0 = (n + 1)z$.

Next, the proof relies on some features of natural logarithms. The sum of the natural logarithms of several numbers is equal to the natural logarithm of their product. Therefore, we can use this feature of logarithms to move from the product of the component distributions to a sum of their logarithms: $\ln'\, f_i(x_i) = \ln f_i(x_i) = \ln f(x)$. Also, the logarithm function is the derivative of itself, so that $\ln'\, f_i(x_i) = f_i'(x_i)$.

Functions $g_i(\ )$ are related to the component distributions, such that adjusted for the estimate t, they have their maxima at the expected zero: $g_i(t - x_i) = \ln f_i(x_i)$. Because we know that t is located at the peak of its density function and that is also the product of the components, we know that the sum of the logarithms of the matching functions is also zero, $g_i'(t - x_i) = 0$.

Return to the case where all the observations are zero except x_0. Because x_0 is equal to $(n + 1)z$, we know that $z - x_0 = -nz$. Therefore, the sum $\Sigma g_i'(t - x_i)$ is equal to $g'(-nz) + ng'(z)$, and the previous paragraph concluded that is equal to zero: $g'(-nz) + ng'(z) = 0$. This is true regardless of the number of distributions from which observations are drawn. Consider the case where only two component distributions exist, so that $n = 1$. The previous equation becomes $g'(-z) + g'(z) = 0$, that is, $g'(-z) + g'(z)$. The same becomes true for all n and we can write $g'(nz) = ng'(z)$. From this, Gauss indicates we can infer that the term z in $g'(z)$ is not raised to a power, that is, $g'(z)$ is linear and can be written $g'(z) = bz$. The methods of calculus can solve the system of two differential equations: $g'(z) = bz$, $g'(0) = 0$. The solution is $(gz) = \frac{bz^2}{2} + C$, where C is a constant of integration:

```
g_s1=g[z]/.Simplify[
    DSolve[{g'[0] == 0,g'[z] == b z},g[z],z]][[1,1]]/.C[1]→C;
TraditionalForm[g s1]
```
$$\frac{b z^2}{2} + C$$

From the definition $g(\ ) = \ln f(\ )$, we need to extract the function that has $g(u)$ as its logarithm, that is, solve for x the equality $\ln x = C + \frac{bz^2}{2}$. The solution is $e^{(bz^2)/2+C}$:

```
f_xs1=x/.Solve[Log[x]==g_s1,x][[1]]// FullSimplify
```
$$e^{C + \frac{b z^2}{2}}$$

For this to behave as a probability density function, then the area under the curve, its integral from minus infinity to plus infinity, must equal one.

The integral can be calculated by restricting b to be negative:

```
fxs2=FullSimplify[Integrate[fxs1,{z,-∞,∞}],{b<0}]
```

$$\frac{e^c \sqrt{2\pi}}{\sqrt{-b}}$$

Equate this to 1 and solve for C to eliminate the constant of integration, and replace b with $-a$ to follow convention:

```
fxs3 = FullSimplify[fxs1/.Solve[fxs2==1,C][[1,1]]]/.b→-a
```

$$\frac{\sqrt{a}\,e^{-\frac{a z^2}{2}}}{\sqrt{2\pi}}$$

Substitute z with $t - x$, from the definition of $g(u) = \ln f(t - x)$. The result is the normal distribution stated using a as its scaling factor. The definition of the dispersion measure will determine how to substitute a. We will use standard deviation and average deviation.

```
fxs4=fxs3/.z→t-x
```

$$\frac{\sqrt{a}\,e^{-\frac{1}{2}a(t-x)^2}}{\sqrt{2\pi}}$$

ii. The Standard Normal Distribution

The standard normal eliminates a and t by positing $a = 1$ and $t = 0$:

```
FullSimplify[fxs4/.{a→1,t→0}]
```

$$\frac{e^{-\frac{x^2}{2}}}{\sqrt{2\pi}}$$

iii. Restating with Standard Deviation

Start by calculating the standard deviation in terms of the integral as it was derived above, that is, including a:

```
ss1=Simplify[√(∫-∞∞ (x-t)² fxs4 dix ,a>0]
```

$$\frac{1}{\sqrt{a}}$$

This solution is the standard deviation. Solve for a to determine how to substitute a:

```
da=Solve[σ== ss1,a]
```

$$\left\{\left\{a \to \frac{1}{\sigma^2}\right\}\right\}$$

Using this rule makes the substitution and gives the normal distribution as a function of a given standard deviation:

```
FullSimplify[PowerExpand[f_xs4/.d_d[[1,1]]
```

$$\frac{e^{-\frac{(t-x)^2}{2\sigma^2}}}{\sqrt{2\pi}\,\sigma}$$

iv. Restating with Average Deviation

To obtain the average deviation calculate the mean truncated above at the middle of the distribution. Adjust by multiplying by 2 instead of dividing by .5:

```
s_s2=Simplify[2 ∫_{-∞}^{t} (t-x)f_xs4 dix, {a>0,t>x}]
```

$$\frac{\sqrt{\frac{2}{\pi}}}{\sqrt{a}}$$

The simplification is imperfect, leaving this compound fraction. Squaring it reveals how it would simplify inside a single radical.

$$\left(\frac{\sqrt{\frac{2}{\pi}}}{\sqrt{a}}\right)^2$$

$$\frac{2}{a\pi}$$

The square root of this would be the average deviation; call it *v*. Solve to determine how to substitute *a*:

```
v_s1=Solve[v == s_s2,a]
```

$$\{\{a\to \frac{2}{\pi v^2}\}\}$$

Making this substitution gives the normal distribution in terms of average deviation:

```
n_v=FullSimplify[PowerExpand[f_xs4.,v_s1[[1,1]] ] ]
```

$$\frac{e^{-\frac{(t-x)^2}{\pi v^2}}}{\pi v}$$

Law students who are averse to square roots and radicals should find this form of the normal distribution much more appealing. We need a way to convert the unfamiliar unit (standard deviation) into the favored one (average deviation). We already have the equivalence from the two integrals above. Solve for average deviation (*v*) or for standard deviation

(σ) to get the equivalences. The numerical values that avoid the π are the result of applying the command **N[]** to each result

```
es1=Solve[(a/.dd)==(a/.vs1),v]//PowerExpand//Simplify
N[%]
es2=Solve[(a/.dd)==(a/.vs1),σ]//PowerExpand//Simplify
N[%]
```

$$\left\{ v->-\sqrt{\tfrac{2}{\pi}}\sigma \right\} , \left\{ v->\sqrt{\tfrac{2}{\pi}}\sigma \right\}$$
`{{v→-0.797885 σ},{v→0.797885 σ}}`

$$\left\{ \sigma->-\sqrt{\tfrac{\pi}{2}}v \right\} , \left\{ \sigma->\sqrt{\tfrac{\pi}{2}}v \right\}$$
`{{σ→-1.25331 v},{σ→1.25331 v}}`

Average deviation is a little less than 80 percent of the standard deviation.

v. The Triangular Distribution

To derive the triangular distribution we start with two goals. The PDF must be symmetrical and integrating it over its entire range must give 1. The user should give min and max and the equation should do the rest.

From min to the midpoint, (min + max)/2, the area must be 1/2. What should the height be? The area of the triangle with width a and height b is $ab/2$. The width is (min + max)/2 − min. We must find the height.

```
Off[General::spell1]
bsol=Simplify[b/.Solve[ ((min+max)/2 -min) b/2 == 1/2, b][[1,1]]]
```
$$\frac{2}{\text{max-min}}$$

The PDF starts at 0 at min and reaches 2/(max − min) at the midpoint.

```
fbelow[x_, min_, max_] :=
Together[a+b x/.Solve[{
a+b min == 0, a+b (max+min)/2 == 2/(max-min)}, {a,b}][[1]]]
FullSimplify@ExpandAll@fbelow[x,min,max]
```
$$-\frac{4(\text{min-x})}{(\text{max-min})^2}$$

The integral to the midpoint is one half:

$$\int_2^3 f_{below}[x, 2,4]\ dx$$
$$\tfrac{1}{2}$$

We do the opposite from the midpoint to the end:

```
f_above[x_, min_, max_] :=
Together@(a+bx/.Simplify@Solve[{a+bmax == 0,
     max+min        2
a+b--------- == ---------}, {a,b}][[1]] )
       2       max-min
f_above[x, min, max]
 4(max-x)
-----------
(max-min)²
```

The CDF is the corresponding integral. Unfortunately, *Mathematica* does not simplify the CDF of the second half perfectly. The second line, below, simplifies the integral (imperfectly). The next cell expands and then simplifies a simpler form of it.

The CDF is the integral:

```
F_blw = Simplify@ ∫ˣ_min f_below [x, min, max] dix
                          4(max-t)
Simplify[½ + ∫ˣ_{min+max/2} ----------dit , {x < max,min < max}]
                          (max-min)²
                     (max-min)²-2(max-x)²
Simplify@Expand@     --------------------
                         (min-max)²
 2(min-x)²
-----------
(max-min)²
-max²-2maxmin+min²+4maxx-2x²
----------------------------
        (max-min)²
-max²-2maxmin+min²+4maxx-2x²
----------------------------
        (max-min)²
```

The preceding are the CDFs. The second one that corresponds to the range above the average, simplifies further to $[(max-min)^2 - 2(max-x)^2]/(max-min)^2$. We can use the **Which[]** command to get general definitions of the CDF and PDF:

```
F_tri[x_, min_,max_] := Which[
    x < min, 0,
         min+max     2(min-x)²
    x < ---------, -----------,
           2        (max-min)²
                  (max-min)²-2(max-x)²
    x <= max,     --------------------,
                      (min-max)²
    x > max, 1]
f_tri[x_, min_,max_] := Which[
    x < min, 0,
         min+max      4(x-min)
    x < ---------, -----------,
           2         (max-min)²
                  4(max-x)
    x <= max,     ----------,
                  (max-min)²
    x > max, 0]
```

If we compare the squared distances of the normal and the triangular, we can find how to superimpose them. The first line creates the sum of the squared distances, as a function of the maximum of the triangular. The maximum is z and the minimum is, symmetrically, $-z$. Then, the command **FindMinimum[]** is applied to the sum to obtain the z that minimizes the sum of the squared differences which turns out to be about 2.35.

```
ssCUM = Sum[(CDF[NormalDistribution[0,1],x]-Ftri[x,
-z,z])^2, {x, -5, 5,.01}];
FindMinimum[ssCUM, {z, 2.5}]
{0.0229306, {z → 2.3498}}
twocdfs = Plot[{CDF[NormalDistribution [0,1],x],
    Ftri{x, -2.35, 2.35]
    }, {x, -4,4},
    PlotStyle → {AbsoluteDashing[{2,2}],
    AbsoluteDashing[{3,0}]},
    AspectRatio → 1/3];
```

To see the difference we must magnify small parts of the graphic:

```
Plot[{CDF[NormalDistribution[0,1],x],
    Ftri[x, -2.35, 2.35]
    }, {x, -3, -1},
    PlotStyle → {AbsoluteDashing[{2,2}],
    AbsoluteDashing[{3,0}]}.
    AspectRatio → 1/2, AxesOrigin → {-1, 0},
    Ticks → {True, False}];
Plot[{CDF[NormalDistribution[0,1],x],
    Ftri[x, -2.35, 2.35]
    }, {x, 1.6, 2.5},
    PlotStyle → {AbsoluteDashing[{2,2}],
    AbsoluteDashing[{3,0}]}.
    AspectRatio → 1/3, AxesOrigin → {1.5,.94}];
```

The differences are more visible if we display the PDFs, in part, because the display expands the y axis:

```
Plot[{PDF[NormalDistribution[0,1],x],
    ftri[x, -2.35, 2.35]
    }, {x, -4, 4},
    PlotStyle → {AbsoluteDashing[{2,2}],
```

```
AbsoluteDashing[{3,0}]}.
    AspectRatio → 1/3, PlotRange → {0,.5}];
```

If we seek to restate the triangular in terms of mean and standard deviation, and accept that the triangular's span will be 4.7 times the standard deviation, then we can restate the minimum and maximum:

$$\frac{2(\text{min-x})^2}{(\text{max-min})^2} /.\{\text{min} \to \text{m} - 2.35\ \sigma, \text{max} \to \text{m} + 2.35\ \sigma\}$$

$$\frac{(\text{max-min})^2 - 2(\text{max-x})^2}{(\text{min-max})^2} /.\{\text{min} \to \text{m} -2.35\ \sigma, \text{max} \to \text{m} + 2.35\ \sigma\}$$

$$\frac{4(\text{x-min})}{(\text{max-min})^2} /.\{\text{min} \to \text{m} - 2.35\ \sigma, \text{max} \to \text{m} + 2.35\ \sigma\}$$

$$\frac{4(\text{max-x})}{(\text{max-min})^2} /.\{\text{min} \to \text{m} - 2.35\ \sigma, \text{max} \to \text{m} + 2.35\ \sigma\}$$

$$\frac{0.0905387(\text{m-x}-2.35\ \sigma)^2}{\sigma^2}$$

$$\frac{0.0452694(22.09\sigma^2-2(\text{m-x}+2.35\ \sigma)^2)}{\sigma^2}$$

$$\frac{0.181077(-\text{m}+\text{x}+2.35\ \sigma)}{\sigma^2}$$

$$\frac{0.181077(\text{m-x}+2.35\ \sigma)}{\sigma^2}$$

Now that we have all forms of the triangular, we return to the question of optimizing speeds. The penalty function is $n(s) = (s - t)2r$, with r being the reduction of speed by the drivers who accept the certain violation, and t the limit. The expected penalty is $\text{En}(s) = R(s)n(s)$ and it will take two forms, one in each side of the distribution. At the lower half, it and its derivative with respect to speed s will be

$$\text{Together@D}[\frac{2(\text{t-s})^2}{(\text{max-t})^2} (\text{s-t})2\ r, s]$$

```
Factor[rs² - 2 r s t + r t²]
```

$$\frac{12(r s^2 - 2r s t + r t^2)}{(\text{max} - t)^2}$$

$$r(\text{s-t})^2$$

```
D[(e - s)², s]
```

$$-2(e-s)$$

Accordingly we can write:

$$\text{Solve}[\frac{12\ r(\text{s-t})^2}{(\text{max-t})^2} == D[(e-s)^2, s], s]$$

```
Factor[max² - 24 e r - 2 max t + 24 r t + t²]
```

$$\{\{s \rightarrow \frac{1}{12r} \ (\text{max}^2 - 2 \ \text{max} \ t + 12 \ r \ t + t^2 - (\text{max-t})$$

$$\sqrt{\text{max}^2 - 24 \ e \ r \ - \ 2 \ \text{max} \ t + \ 24 \ r \ t \ + \ t^2})\},$$

$$\{s \rightarrow \frac{1}{12 \ r} \ (\text{max}^2 - 2 \ \text{max} \ t + 12 \ r \ t + t^2 + (\text{max-t})$$

$$\sqrt{\text{max}^2 - 24 \ e \ r - 2 \ \text{max} \ t \ + \ 24 \ rt \ + \ t^2})\}$$

$$-24 \ e \ \text{max}^2 \ r \ - \ 2 \ \text{max} \ t \ + \ 24 \ r \ t \ + \ t^2$$

C. APPLICATION OF TRIANGULAR DISTRIBUTION: THE UNCERTAIN APPREHENSION OF SPEED LIMIT VIOLATIONS

Notebook filename: L&E_SpeedingEG1.nb

Refers to page: 190

We start with the equations for the expected penalty En, using the CDF of the triangular distribution. The expected penalty En_L corresponds to speeds in the lower half of the range of uncertainty and En_H corresponds to conduct in its upper half. The equations are slightly simpler than they might be because the symbol t serves as both the limit and the minimum of the distribution. The maximum of the distribution is m. In both versions of En, the fraction that is the first term corresponds to the probability of apprehension and punishment, for which we use the CDF of the triangular distribution. The third function, u, is a utility function for speed. Each driver prefers a speed of e, but the expected penalty induces some drivers to reduce speeds. The nominal penalty is $n(s) = 2r(t - s)$. The relative shape of u and n is determined by the assumption that drivers who accept certain apprehension reduce their speed by r. This is the source of the coefficient $2r$ in the penalty function. The maximum of the range of the vague limit is m. The following cell defines those three functions.

$$En_L[s\_] : = \frac{2(t-s)^2}{(m-t)^2} \ (t-s)2 \ r$$

$$En_H[s\_] : = \frac{(m-t)^2 - 2(m-s)^2}{(m-t)^2}(t-s)2 \ r$$

$$u[s\_, \ e\_] := (e-s)^2$$

From the problem, we know that the expected penalty and utlity are related. The speed s that a driver chooses is such that any further reduction would reduce welfare more than the reduction of expected penalty. This means that the reduction of speed stops where the slopes are equal, that is, the derivatives with respect to speed are equal. *Mathematica* calculates a derivative of a function `u[s,e]` with respect to the variable s with the command `D[u[s,e],s]`, or ∂_s`u[s,e]`. As the text explains, we solve for e to find the corresponding preference. The `Solve[]` command produces a "rule" in the form `{e→...}`. To obtain the corresponding equation we preface the `Solve[]` command with `e/.` to temporarily place its result in the variable e by applying the rule to it. This we simplify and the lower and higher halves of the distrubution, respectively, are assigned to the variables e_L and e_H. The first solution below is amenable to the command `Simplify[f]` (also written `Simplify@f` or `f//Simplify`). That is not true of the second one. In that case more effective is the command `Collect[]` that takes two parameters, the first is the equation, the terms of which will be collected, and the second parameter holds the terms that will be collected.

```
eₗ = Simplify[e/.
     Solve[∂ₛEnₗ[s] == ∂ₛu[s,e]
           ,e][[1]]
     ]
eₕ = Collect[e/.
     Solve[∂ₛEnₕ[s] == ∂ₛu[s,e],e][[1]],{(m-t)²,2,r, m-s}]
```

$$s + \frac{6r(s-t)^2}{(m-t)^2}$$

$$r + s + \frac{r(-2(m-s)^2 - 4(m-s)(-s+t))}{(m-t)^2}$$

The next two invocations of `Solve[]` are much simpler. We place in r_L and r_H the equations that correspond to the reduction of speed when the driver chooses a speed inside the range of uncertain enforcement.

```
rₗ = d/. Solve[eₗ - s == d,d][[1]]
rₕ = d/. Solve[eₕ - s == d,d][[1]]
```

$$\frac{6r(s-t)^2}{(m-t)^2}$$

$$r + \frac{r(-2(m-s)^2 - 4(m-s)(-s+t))}{(m-t)^2}$$

We are now ready to produce graphics. The list eg_g holds rules about the values that the example assigns to variables. The `Table[]` command functions as a loop. It produces pairs $\{e, -r\}$ and uses as an iterator the variable s. The rules of the examples are applied to all. Those are later used inside a `Show@Graphics[]` command, inside the `Line[]` command, to draw the corresponding lines in the graphics.

Because the objective is comparison, we will display graphs for two values of the maximum. We build them up gradually, however, first setting $m \to 90$.

The rules that come after the **Line[]** command control how *Mathematica* will display the graphics.

The default is scaling of the axes, with the result that each has a different unit length. Here, both axes use units that have the same length because of the option **AspectRatio** $\to$ **Automatic**.

The option **Ticks** $\to$ ... avoids the default tickmarks. The axes are displayed and their intersection is defined with the options **Axes** $\to$ **True** and **AxesOrigin** $\to$ ...;

```
eg_g = {t → 50, m → 100, r → 10};
r_{L,e} = Table[{e_L /. eg_g, -r_L /. eg_g}, {s, t /.eg_g, (t+m)/2 /.eg_g,
(  (t+m)/2 -t ) / 80 /. eg_g}];
r_{H,e}= Table[{e_H /. eg_g, -r_H /. eg_g}, {s, (t+m)/2 /.eg_g, m/. eg_g,
(  (t+m)/2 -t ) / 80 /. eg_g}];
r_{g1}= Show@Graphics[{
Line[{{t-5, 0}, {t,0}} /. eg_g],
(*line at 0: no deterrence for those who'd comply*)
    Line[r_{L,e}],
    Line[r_{H,e}],
    Line[{{m + r, -r}, {m + r + 5, -r}} /. eg_g]
    (*line at r: the deterrence of those who accept
    certain violation*)
    }, AspectRatio → Automatic,
    AxesOrigin → {t - 5, 0}/. eg_g,
    Axes → True, Ticks → {Table[i, {i, 50, 110, 10}],
            {-5, -10, -15}}];
```

We can also plot the actual speed against the preference (along the horizontal axis):

```
s_{L,g} = Table[{e_L /. eg_g, s}, {s,t/. eg_g, (t+m)/2 /.eg_g,
(  (t+m)/2 -t ) / 80 /. eg_g}];
s_{H,g} = Table[{e_H /. eg_g, s}, {s, (t+m)/2 /.eg_g, m /. eg_g,
(  (t+m)/2 -t ) / 80 /. eg_g}];
e_{g1} = Show@Graphics[{
    Line[{{t-5, t-5}, {t,t}}/.eg_g],
```

```
(*voluntarily complying*)
Line[sL,g] (*violations in low range*),
Line[sH,g] (*viol'ns in high range*),
Line[{{m+r, m}, {m+r+5, m+5}}/.egg]
(*viol'ns of those who accept certain penalty*)
}, Axes → True,
Ticks → {Table[i, 50, 110, 10}], Table[i, {i,
50, 110, 10}]},
AspectRatio → Automatic,
AxesOrigin → {t-5, t-5}/.egg];
```

Let us superimpose a narrower range of uncertain apprehension on the graph of the reactions to a limit.

```
egN = {t → 50, m → 60, r →10};
rL,N = Table[{s, -rL/.egN}, {s, t /.egN, (t+m)/2 /.egN,
((t+m)/2-t) /80 /.egN}];

rH,N= Table[{s, -rH /.egN}, {s, (t+m)/2 /.egN, m /.egN,
((t+m)/2-t) /80 /.egN}];

rL,Ne = Table[{eL /.egN, -rL/.egN}, {s, t /. egN, (t+m)/2 /.egN,
((t+m)/2-t) /80 /.egN}];

rH,Ne= Table[{eH /.egN, -rH /.egN}, {s, (t+m)/2 /.egN, m /. egN,
((t+m)/2-t) /80 /.egN}];

rg,combo = ShowGraphics[{
    Line[{{t-5,0}, {t,0}}/.egg],
    (*line at 0: no deterrence for those who'd comply*)
    Line[rL,e], Line[rL,Ne],
    Line[rH,e], Line[rH,Ne],
    Line[{{m+r /.egN,-r}, {m+r+5, -r}}/.egg]
    (*line at r:the deterrence of those who accept
    the certain violation*),
    AbsoluteDashing[{2,2}],
    Line[{{m+r, -rH/.s → smx1}, {m+r, -r}}/.egN]
    (*dashing line at unused reductions*)
    }, AspectRatio → Automatic, AxesOrigin → {t-5,
    0}/.egg,
    Axes → True, Ticks → {Table[{i, ""},
```

```
{i,50,110,10}], {0,-5,-10,-15}}
(*, PlotLabel → "Speed Reduction"*)];
```

$s_{L,N}$= Table[{e_L/.eg$_N$, s}, {s,t/.eg$_N$, $\frac{t+m}{2}$ /.eg$_N$,

$\left(\frac{t+m}{2}-t\right)$ /80/.eg$_N$}];

$s_{H,N}$= Table[{e_H/.eg$_N$, s}, {s, $\frac{t+m}{2}$ /.eg$_N$, m/.eg$_N$,

$\left(\frac{t+m}{2}-t\right)$ /80/.eg$_N$}];

```
eg,combo = Show@Graphics[{
    Line[{{t-5, t-5}, {t,t}}/.eg_g],
    (*voluntarily complying*)
    Line[s_{L,g}], Line[s_{L,N}],
    Line[s_{H,g}], Line[s_{H,N}],
    Line[{{m+r, m}/.eg_N, {m+r+5, m+5}/.eg_g}]
    (*viol'ns of those who accept certain penalty*),
    AbsoluteDashing[{2,2}],
    Line[{m+r, s_{mx1}}, {m+r, m}}/.eg_N]
    (*dashing line at unused reductions*)
    }, Axes → True, AspectRatio → Automatic
    AxesOrigin → {t-5, t-5}/.eg_g,
    Ticks → {Table[i,{i,50,110,10}],
    Table[i{i,50,110,10}]}];
```

The preceding commands produce an error ("Coordinate s_{mx1} in.... is not a...number") because that variable has not been defined and it is used in the last line in each graph, the one following the command **AbsoluteDashing[]**. The next cell makes that definition so that the dashing lines will be drawn.

To get the dashing lines, we need to obtain the speed that would be chosen by the first driver who might also choose a speed that would lead to certain apprehension. The driver who has those preferences is the one who may choose a speed equal to the maximum m of the limit for a certain violation. Because we know the preferences of those who choose certain violations exceed their speeds by r, we know his preference is $m+r$. The issue is to determine what speed he would choose inside the range of uncertainty, that is, to solve $e_H = m+r$ for s.

Due to the alpahabetical ordering of variables, the result simplifies much better if m is replaced by a symbol later in the alphabet than t. We make a replacement with z, simplify, and then again replace z with m to return to our notation.

Then, we must return to the previous cell and execute it again. The graphs it produces have both distributions. This time, they include the dashing line that separates the regions with duplication.

```
Solve[e_H == m+r, s]
s_mx1 = Simplify@(s /.Solve[e_H == m+r, s][[2]]/.m→ z)
s_mx1 = s_mx1 /.z→ m
{{s→ m}, {s→ (m² + 2mr - 2mt + 4rt + t²)/6r}}
(t - z)² + 2r(2t + z)/6r
(-m + t)² + 2r(m + 2t)/6r
```

The two graphs can be aligned with some precision by placing them inside **Rectangle[]** commands. This is Figure 9.7.

```
x₁ = 20; x₂ =.8x₁; x₃ = 3.4x₁;
gr_dual = Show@Graphics[{
        Rectangle[{0,0},{60,x₁},r_g,combo],
        Rectangle[{0,x₂},{60,x₃}, e_g,combo]},
        AspectRatio → Automatic];
```

D. A Comparison of Insider Trading Regimes

Notebook filename: L&E_IT.nb
Refers to page: 217
A trader approaches the market maker to trade a security. The market maker will adjust price in reaction to the trader's order. If the trader has information about the accurate value of the security, then the trader faces an optimization problem. Placing an order that is too large induces a price correction that erodes profit. Placing an order that is too small leaves money on the table, in the form of a profitable trading opportunity for the next trader. What then is the number of shares that maximizes the trader's profit?

i. Foundation

The essential foundation of the analysis is the process that the market maker uses to adjust prices in the face of large orders. As is standard in this area, the new price is equal to the previous price plus the effect of the current order, depending on a liquidity coefficient, λ. Prices (p) and orders (s) are indexed to indicate their sequence in time. The market maker offers the price:

$$p_{i+1} = p_i + \lambda\, s_{i+1}$$

The trader knows the true value of the stock (v). The trader's profit for each share is the difference between the price of the trade and its value, $v - p$ for purchases and $p - v$ for sales. The trader's total profits (r) depend on the number of shares bought, that is, the size of the order, s. In other words, the trader's total profits are:

```
r = (v - p_{i+1}) s_{i+1}
```

The maximum of profits is where their derivative equals zero:

```
sol1 = s_{i+1} /.Solve[∂_{s_{i+1}} r == 0, s_{i+1}][[1]];
TraditionalForm @ sol1
```

$$-\frac{p_i - v}{2\lambda}$$

Suppose, for example, that Obi-Wan Kenobi knows that the value of the stock of the Intergalactic Bank Corp is 100 credits and the last trade occurred at 110 credits. For every 100 shares that Obi-Wan sells, the price will fall 1 credit ($\lambda = .01$). Obi-Wan reaches the maximum profit if he trades $-\frac{110 - 100}{0.02} = -500$ shares, that is, sells 500 shares.

```
eg1 = { p_i→110, v→100, λ→.01};
sol1/.eg1
-500
```

ii. Problem

The problem is quite different if the informed trader (in the example, Obi-Wan) knows that he may enter subsequent trades. Suppose that Obi-Wan knows that, in addition to the current order, he may also trade with some probability q_i in the next five trades. Then, Obi-Wan's profit is composed of the profit from each of the five trades.

iii. Solution: Statement

The optimal size of the ith trade when the number of possible trades is j, is

$$s_{i,j} = \frac{p_{i-1} - v}{\lambda} z_{i,j}$$

The last term is given by:

$$z_{i,j} = 1 - 1/(2 + \sum_{n=i+1}^{j} 2q_n z_{n,j} (z_{n,j} - 1) \prod_{m=i+1}^{n-1} (z_{m,j} - 1)^2$$

In the text below, the difference of price from value is represented by d_i, which can be used instead of $p_i - v$, for simplicity:

$$s_{i,j} = \frac{d_{i-1}}{\lambda} z_{i,j}.$$

Creating the definition:

$$z_{i,j} := z_{i,j} = 1 - \cfrac{1}{2 + \sum\limits_{n=i+1}^{j} 2q_n z_{n,j}(z_{n,j} - 1) \prod\limits_{m=i+1}^{n-1} (z_{m,j} - 1)^2}$$

iv. Solution: Proof

The proof is recursive. The ideal trade at the penultimate trade requires the calculation of the optimal final trade. Suppose that Obi-Wan knows he might make five trades, at most. The fifth trade will occur at the price after the fourth, p_4.

Substitute $v - p_4$ with d_4. Obi-Wan's trades follow the pattern below:

```
Remove[s, d, r]
d₅ = d₄ - λs₅;
r₅ = d₅ s₅;
s₅ = s₅/. (Solve[∂ₛ₅ r₅ == 0, s₅][[1]]);
z₅,₅
Print["The ideal last trade covers half the price
difference: S₅=", s₅]
Print["This matches d₄/λ z₅,₅, because z₅,₅=", z₅,₅]
d₄ = d₃ - λs₄;
r₄ = d₄s₄ + q₅d₅s₅;
s₄ = s₄ /.(Solve[∂ₛ₄r₄ == 0, s₄][[1]]);
z₄,₅
Print["The ideal penultimate trade, simplified, is
s₄ =", Simplify@s₄]
Print["This matches d_{i-1}/λ z_{i,j}, simplified, because
z₄,₅ = ", Simplify@z₄,₅]
d₃ = d₂ - λs₃;
r₃ = d₃s₃ + q₄d₄s₄ + q₅d₅s₅ //Simplify;
s₃ = s₃ /.(Solve[∂ₛ₃r₃ == 0, s₃][[1]]// Simplify);
Print["The ideal 2ⁿᵈ-to-last trade, simplified,
is s₃ =", Simplify@s₃]
Print["This matches d_{i-1}/λ z_{i,j}, simplified, because
z₃,₅ =", Simplify@z₃,₅]
```

```
d₂ = d₁ - λs₂;
r₂ = d₂s₂ + q₃d₃s₃ + q₄d₄s₄ + q₅d₅s₅ //Simplify;
s₂ = s₂ /.(Solve[∂ₛ₂r₂ == 0, s₂] [[1]]// Simplify);
Print["The ideal 3ʳᵈ-to-last trade, simplified,
is s₂ =", Simplify@s₂]
Print["This matches  dᵢ₋₁/λ  zᵢ,ⱼ, simplified, because
z₂,₅ =",Simplify@z₂,₅]
(*Omitting first trade, too cumbersome:
    d₁ = d₀ - λs₁;
r₁ = d₁s₁ + q₂d₂s₂ + q₃d₃s₃ + q₄d₄s₄+ q₅d₅s₅ //Simplify;
s₁ = s₁ /.(Solve[∂ₛ₁ r₁ == 0, s₁] [[1]] // Simplify);
Print["The ideal 4ᵗʰ-from-last trade, simplified, is
s₁ =", Simplify@s₁]
Print["This matches  dᵢ₋₁/λ  zᵢ,ⱼ, simplified, because
z₁,₅ =", Simplify@z₁,₅]*)
```

The ideal last trade covers half the price difference:

$$s_5 = \frac{d_4}{2\lambda}$$

This matches $\frac{d_4}{\lambda}$ $z_{5,5}$, because $z_{5,5} = \frac{1}{2}$
The ideal penultimate trade, simplified, is:

$$s_4 = \frac{d_3\,(-2+q_5)}{\lambda\,(-4+q_5)}$$

This matches $\frac{d_{i-1}}{\lambda}$ $z_{i,j}$, simplified, because

$$z_{4,5} = \frac{-2+q_5}{-4+q_5}.$$

The ideal 2nd-to-last trade, simplified, is

$$s_3 = \frac{d_2\,(-2+q_5)\,(-8+4q_4+q_5)}{2\lambda\,(16+2q_4\,(-2+q_5)-9q_5+q_5{}^2)}$$

This matches $\frac{d_{i-1}}{\lambda}$ $z_{i,j}$, simplified, because

$$z_{3,5} = \frac{(-2+q_5)\,(-8+4q_4+q_5)}{2\,(16+2q_4\,(-2+q_5)-9q_5+q_5{}^2)}.$$

The ideal 3rd-to-last trade, simplified, is

$$
\begin{aligned}
s_2 = {} & (d_1\,(-2+q_5)\,(-8+4q_4+q_5)\,(-32+q_3\,(-4+q_5)^2 \\
& -2q_4\,(-2+q_5)+17q_5-2q_5{}^2))\,/\,(\lambda\,(-1024-16q_4{}^2\,(-2+q_5)^2 \\
& +1168q_5-460q_5{}^2+73q_5{}^3-4q_5{}^4+q_3\,(-4+q_5)^2\,(-2+q_5) \\
& (-8+4q_4+q_5)-2q_4\,(-288+304q_5-98q_5{}^2+9q_5{}^3)))
\end{aligned}
$$

This matches $\frac{d_{i-1}}{\lambda} z_{i,j}$, simplified, because

$$z_{2,5} = (\,(-2+q_5)\,(-8+4q_4+q_5)\,(-32+q_3\,(-4+q_5)^2$$
$$-2q_4\,(-2+q_5)+17q_5-2q_5^2)\,)\,/$$
$$(-1024-16q_4^2\,(-2+q_5)^2+1168q_5-460q_5^2+73q_5^3-4q_5^4$$
$$+q_3\,(-4+q_5)^2\,(-2+q_5)\,(-8+4q_4+q_5)$$
$$-2q_4\,(-288+304q_5-98q_5^2+9q_5^3)\,)$$

The pattern might be visible in the following illustration:

```
zees = {{"z5,5 =", "z4,5 =", "z3,5 " , "z2,5 ="},
{z5,5, z4,5, z3,5, z2,5}};
back2 = {2 - 1/2 q5 → StyleForm[2 - 1/2 q5,
Background → RGBColor [.9,.8,.2]]};
```

$$back_3 = \{2 - \frac{2q_4\left(1 - \dfrac{1}{2 - \dfrac{q_5}{2}}\right)}{2 - \dfrac{q_5}{2}} - \frac{q_5}{2\left(2 - \dfrac{q_5}{2}\right)^2} \rightarrow$$

$$StyleForm\,[2 - \frac{2q_4\left(1 - \dfrac{1}{2 - \dfrac{q_5}{2}}\right)}{2 - \dfrac{q_5}{2}} - \frac{q_5}{2\left(2 - \dfrac{q_5}{2}\right)^2},$$

```
Background → RGBColor [.9,.6, 1]]};
back4 = {zees[[2,4,2,2,1]] → StyleForm[zees[[2,4,2,2,1]],
        Background → RGBColor[.3, 1, 1]]};
TableForm[Transpose@zees /.back4/.back3/.back2,
TableAlignments → Automatic]
```

$$z_{5,5} = \frac{1}{2}$$

$$z_{4,5} = 1 - \frac{1}{2 - \dfrac{q_5}{2}}$$

$$z_{3,5} = 1 - \cfrac{1}{2 - \cfrac{2\left(1 - \dfrac{1}{2 - \dfrac{q_5}{2}}\right)q_4}{2 - \dfrac{q_5}{2}} - \dfrac{q_5}{2\left(2 - \dfrac{q_5}{2}\right)2}}$$

v. Illustration of Price Path

Establishing default font sizes and other details for the graphics.

```
vadjust =.3;
$TextStyle = {FontFamily → "Times", FontSize → 8};
```

The speed of calculation increases dramatically if we accept finite precision by wrapping the fraction into N[]:

```
x[n_, t_]: = x[n, t]
```

$$= N\left[1 - 1 \left/ \left(2 + \sum_{i=t+1}^{n} 2q[i]x[n,i](x[n,i] - 1) \prod_{j=t+1}^{i-1} (x)\right)\right]\right.$$

Using tables to define groups of variables:

```
itn = 15; (*master number of trades*)
compstarts = 5; (*when competition starts*)
Table[q[j]] = 1, {j, compstarts - 1}];
Table[q[j]] =.2, {j, compstarts, itn}];
pm[0,itn] = 110;
Table[pc[i, itn] = 110, {i, 0, compstarts}];
i = compstarts;
v = 100;
g =.01;
as2 = AbsoluteDashing [{2,2}];
nf[x]: = {x, as2}
tf[x]: = Thread[nf[x]]
```

Storing the prices and sizes for monopolistic and competitive trading:

```
Table[{
    pm[z, itn] = N[pm[z-1, itn] + x[itn, z]
    (v-pm[z-1, itn])]
    , sm[z, itn] = N[x[itn, z] (v-pm[z-1, itn])/ g]},
    {z, 1, itn}];
Table[{
    pc[z, itn] = N[pc[z-1, itn] + x[itn, z]
    (v-pc[z-1, itn])]
    , sc[z, itn] = N[x[itn, z] (v-pc[z-1, itn])/ g]},
    {z, i+1, itn}];
```

Creating the price path line in two dimensions:

The line monoline2d corresponds to monopolistic trading; compline2d to competitive.

```
monoline2d = Line[
            Table[{x, pm[x, itn]}, {x, 0, itn}]];
compline2d = Line[
            Table[{x, pc[x, itn]}, {x, 0, itn}]];
```

Displaying the price path, Figure 10.4:

```
it2d = Show@Graphics[{
    monoline2d, as2,
    compline2d
    }, Axes → True];
```

Creating the numerous components for the three-dimensional graphics, Figure 10.5:

```
monoline = Line[
        Table[{-sm[x, itn], (x-1)/ itn, pm[x, itn]},
{x, 1, itn}]];
compline = Line[
        Table[{-sc[x, itn], (x-1)/ itn, pc[x, itn]},
{x, i+1, itn}]];
sizegridmax = 420;
pricegridmax = 100;
pricegridmax =110;
        pricegridmax + pricegridmin
prgrm = ─────────────────────────────── ;
                     2
innerceiling = Table[
    Polygon[{{-sm[x, itn], (x-1)/ itn, pm[x, itn]},
                    {-sm[x+1, itn], (x)/ itn, pm[x+1,
                    itn]},
            {0, x/itn, pm[x+1, itn]}, {0, (x-1)/ itn,
    pm[x, itn]}}], {x, 1, itn -1}];
innerwall = Table[Polygon[
            {{-sm[x, itn], (x-1)/ itn, pm[x, itn]},
    {-sm[x+1, itn], (x)/ itn, pm[x+1, itn]},
            {-sm[x+1, itn], x/ itn, 5}, {-sm[x, itn], (x-1)/
            itn, 5}}]
compfloor = Table[
    Line[{{-sc[x, itn], (x-1)/ itn, pc[x, itn]},
            {-sc[x, itn], (x-1)/ itn, pricegridmin}}]
            , {x, i+1, itn}];
```

```
compfloortrace = Line[
    Table[{-sc[x, itn], (x-1)/ itn, pricegridmin}, {x,
    i+1, itn}]];
compwall = Table[
    Line[{{-sc[x, itn], (x-1)/ itn, pc[x, itn]},
            {0, (x-1)/ itn, pc[x, itn]}}]
        ,{x, i+1, itn}];
compwalltrace = Line[
    Table[{0, (x-1)/ itn, pc[x, itn]}, {x, i+1, itn}]];
itdiscr = Show[Graphics3D[{
            AbsoluteThickness[3],
            monoline,
            compline,
            AbsoluteThickness[1],
            innerceiling, innerwall, compfloor,compwall,
            compfloortrace, compwalltrace,
            Text["Time", {sizegridmax + 40,.5,
            pricegridmin}],
            Text["Price", {0,.9, prgrm}],
            Text["Trade Size", {180m.9,pricegridmin}]
            }], Axes → {{1, -1}, {1, -1}, {-1,1}},
            Boxed → False,
FaceGrids → {
            {{0,0,-1}, {tf[{0, sizegridmax/2,
            sizegridmax}], tf[{0,.4,.8}]}},
            {{-1,0,0}, {tf[{0,.4,.8}], tf[{
            pricegridmin, prgrm, pricegridmax}]}}
            }, SphericalRegion → True,
Ticks → None,
BoxRatios → {1,1,1},
ViewPoint → {1.958, 2.293, 1.536},
PlotRange → {{0, sizegridmax}, {0,.8}, {pricegridmin,
pricegridmax}}
];
```

Index